"In this highly readable book, Madere and Coy fill the gaps in the literature and EMDR training courses on the use of EMDR in dissociation with chapters such as 'Stumbling into Dissociation with EMDR Therapy,' 'Present and Future Prongs in the Three-Stage Model,' and 'Not All Flashbacks Are Created Equal.' They integrate wisdom from older literature, recent findings, and their extensive experience to create a treatment framework that is nuanced and flexible. The crown jewel is the detailed chapter on perpetrator introjects. This text is required reading for any therapist who would like to be guided safely on the often-treacherous path that is EMDR therapy in dissociative clients."

Marilyn Korzekwa, *MD, FRCPC, EMDRIA-approved consultant and ISSTD fellow; McMaster University, Ontario, Canada*

"*EMDR, Dissociation, and Beyond* truly mirrors the lived complexity of dissociative systems. Madere and Coy write with rare attunement and without pathologizing or oversimplifying. Their reframes, like seeing 'resistance' as boundary setting, or assuming all self-states are listening, show deep respect for inner worlds and responsiveness to lived experience voice and community. The 'Id Protocol' stands out as a model of dignity and collaboration, asking not 'how do we get rid of this part?' but 'do they still want this job?' From mapping to memory networks to trance logic, this book honors every layer of the healing journey. For systems and therapists alike, it offers both precision and compassion... and, most of all, possibility."

Emma Sunshaw, *PhD*, System Speak *podcast*

"Madere and Coy have meticulously adapted Shapiro's EMDR protocols to accommodate the treatment of complex trauma and dissociative disorders. What this approach has given EMDR is a more thoughtful psychotherapy that takes into account the dynamic mind of the client. As therapeutic toolboxes have proliferated, the art of psychotherapy has tended to become more marginalized. This book teaches technique as a measured response to the exigencies of complex minds and thus allows for the integration of technique within a thoughtfully constructed psychotherapy. This is a project whose time is long past due!"

Richard Hohfeler, *PsyD, private practice, Wisconsin, USA; ISSTD fellow*

"When I initially trained in EMDR therapy, I did not believe I worked with clients who struggled with dissociation or met the criteria for a dissociative disorder, so I was not invested in pursuing training in this area. Integrating EMDR therapy into my clinical work rapidly changed that belief and this was the book I desperately needed. This is not a simple 'float on the surface of the topic' type of book—it is a deep dive into an important and complex issue that offers a life raft of explanation, instruction, and hope to those of us doing this work."

Hope Payson, *LCSW, LADC, EMDRIA-approved basic and advanced trainer*

"*EMDR, Dissociation, and Beyond* is a masterful piece of work that is an essential addition to the bookshelves of all levels of EMDR trained therapists. This text offers a conceptual expansion that exquisitely weaves in case examples, bringing to life a nuanced, intentional approach that can be extended to other trauma-specific treatment modalities and approaches. Inviting readers to deepen their thinking beyond simply 'doing' EMDR, this text expertly bridges the fields of complex trauma, dissociation, and EMDR therapy, honoring the learned experience of past and present and the wisdom of lived experience, to offer a more dissociation-attuned EMDR therapy."

Jill Hosey, *LICSW, trauma therapist, author, EMDR trainer, and ISSTD fellow*

"Madere and Coy offer a solid, research-informed guide to treating dissociative disorders, grounded in theory and clinical practice. Their perspective draws from what seems like the entirety of the existing, related literature and distills it into a practical, insightful, and clinically relevant teaching manual."

Dorinna S. Ruh, *LCSW, Advanced EMDR Education, Colorado, USA*

"This text is a goldmine for EMDR practitioners who want to take their clinical work to the next level. The authors synthesize years of clinical experience, professional training, and advanced learning to offer expert treatment approaches and in-depth knowledge and insights about dissociation from multiple related disciplines, all in this one unparalleled resource. I was thrilled to see ego state therapy take a prominent place in this work of integration as I believe it is a game-changer when appropriately combined with EMDR."

Gerry Ken Crete, *PhD, EMDRIA-approved consultant, author, Litanies of the Heart, Advanced EMDR Education, Colorado, USA*

"The authors have diligently worked on research, exploratory thinking, innovation, and engaging communication in this very valuable book, integrating knowledge and wisdom from the fields of dissociation and psychotherapy to find answers for the quest of EMDR therapists for working with dissociation."

Adithy, *PhD, counseling psychologist, Pune, India; ISSTD fellow and founder, ISSTD EMDR Special Interest Group*

EMDR, Dissociation, and Beyond

EMDR, Dissociation, and Beyond delves more deeply into the dissociative disorders' literature than any previous text on this topic, providing much-needed connectivity between two fields that are often at odds. This book expands the possibilities for case conceptualization by more comprehensively integrating wisdom from the study and treatment of dissociative disorders with the practice of EMDR therapy.

Readers will be invited to deepen their knowledge of working with pathological dissociation, reexamine familiar protocols and widely held beliefs, and consider new ways to approach enduring treatment challenges. The chapters lead readers through dimensions of theory and practice applicable to the treatment of dissociation and dissociative disorders, both within and beyond the practice of EMDR therapy. Weaving together strands from many schools of thought and infused with the authors' decades of experience, this book brings together EMDR therapy and the treatment of dissociation in a way that invites the past into the present and opens doors to the future.

Jennifer A. Madere, MA, LPC-S, CSAT, is a psychotherapist, EMDR consultant, trainer, and fellow of the International Society for the Study of Trauma and Dissociation (ISSTD). She is the co-founder of Intuitus Group, a trauma-focused practice in Cedar Park, Texas, USA.

D. Michael Coy, MA, LCSW, LICSW, is a clinical social worker, EMDR consultant, and trainer working in private practice in Bremerton, Washington, USA. He/they are a past president and fellow of ISSTD.

EMDR, Dissociation, and Beyond

Reexamining and Expanding the Frame for Impactful Trauma Treatment

Jennifer A. Madere and
D. Michael Coy

NEW YORK AND LONDON

Designed cover image: Getty Images

First published 2026
by Routledge
605 Third Avenue, New York, NY 10158

and by Routledge
4 Park Square, Milton Park, Abingdon, Oxon, OX14 4RN

Routledge is an imprint of the Taylor & Francis Group, an informa business

ISBN: 9781032712369 (hbk)
ISBN: 9781032712352 (pbk)
ISBN: 9781003410201 (ebk)

DOI: 10.4324/9781003410201

Typeset in Sabon
by Newgen Publishing UK

To my husband Greg, for your patience, support, and care. To my colleagues, for your dedication to helping people reach healing and recovery. To my clients, for sharing your experience and your trust with me.
~ Jennifer

To my husband Anthony and our boys Milo and Frankie, for tolerating me working seven days a week for months on end. To my mentors, colleagues, and clients, for everything I've learned from you. And to my sister Lisa, who eons ago predicted a book was on the horizon. ~ Michael

Contents

Preface

This is an advanced clinical text, not a starter book or a primer. It is intended for practitioners who have been swimming in the water for some time and are ready to explore the deep end of the pool. While we will briefly define and introduce most concepts, we will also assume that the reader has a robust understanding of Eye Movement Desensitization and Reprocessing (EMDR) therapy (Shapiro, 2018), and at least a cursory understanding of the prominent theories of dissociation and the basic tenets of treating pathological dissociation (ISSTD, 2011), including relationally informed psychodynamic psychotherapy and hypnotic phenomena. If any of these topics are new to you, we hope you will feel inspired to seek further training and consultation to expand your basic clinical understanding and skills. From our experience, one cannot 'dabble' in treating dissociative disorders – it's a real investment – if anyone is to benefit in the end. Ongoing learning and development are hallmarks of an effective and resilient practitioner, and we hope that this book will be a useful component of your learning journey.

We come to you with each of us having 20+ years of full-time clinical experience, and, in our respective journeys, finding a shared passion for the assessment and treatment of clients for whom disruptive (or intrusive) dissociative experiences are part of daily life. We each came to discover the necessity of recognizing, understanding, and treating dissociation after training in EMDR therapy. Our prior collaborations have focused on developing connective tissue between the worlds of EMDR and dissociation – this book is both a fruit of those labors and builds upon them. Please allow us to share a bit of our background with you to provide context for our approach to this book.

Jennifer was persuaded to enter a graduate program in counseling psychology at the University of Denver – instead of law school – following an internship in which she worked with at-risk youth. That experience showed her that (a) she could do it and (b) perhaps greater good could be done in working with people directly. Her journey as a clinician commenced in shelter, hotline, and outpatient settings serving victims of intimate partner violence and low-income populations. While trauma and posttraumatic symptoms were ubiquitous there, most treatment was focused on crisis intervention and stabilization. Upon moving across state lines a few years after graduate school, Jennifer found herself building a private practice, and learning more about what treatment looks like *after* the crisis has abated. This led her to seek training in EMDR therapy in 2009. Jennifer's mentors had mentioned how effective and powerful EMDR was in resolving trauma, so it was the natural next step for her. At the time, utilizing the Dissociative Experiences Scale (DES-II, Carlson & Putnam, 1993) to screen for dissociation prior to engaging in reprocessing was not strongly emphasized, so, finding it to feel 'cold,' she didn't use it. She noticed that a few of her clients were not responding as expected to bilateral dual attention stimulation (BL-DAS). Eventually, she realized, through clients' feedback and her EMDR consultant, Rick Levinson, that 'dissociation' was the reason that EMDR was going differently for them. She was curious, and Rick suggested that she find training to support her in helping these clients through the International Society for the Study of Trauma and Dissociation (ISSTD). At the time, there was no one in Jennifer's geographical area who specialized in assessing or treating dissociation; she wondered if she might become able to support other practitioners who encountered similar challenges with their clients. Thus began the journey that led Jennifer to meet Michael, and the development of what you will read in this book.

Michael did not enter graduate-level social work studies with the intention of becoming a clinical practitioner. Instead, he believed that studying clinical social work would make him a more effective social activist. However, he became increasingly interested in this path while working with individuals and groups, first with those in need of case management services to secure housing and employment, and subsequently with those who were diagnosed with HIV/AIDS with co-occurring mental health and substance use challenges. Michael's interest in the impacts of complex attachment wounding – including his own – was fostered by working in residential treatment with severely abused and neglected, adolescent wards of the state and in a locked, inpatient psychiatric facility. Notably, it was during his time working in a residential setting, in late 2007, that Michael was introduced to EMDR therapy. He learned about it as a client, after beginning work with a therapist to help him following a panic attack triggered by working in a setting where violence was the norm, which paralleled the environment in which Michael grew up. And treatment with EMDR helped – so much so that Michael decided he needed to save up to train in the approach, which he did during 2011. Michael's exposure to information about screening for dissociation during EMDR therapy basic training mirrored Jennifer's. However, after completing the course, it did not take long for Michael to begin attracting clients who were much more complex. On the same day in February 2012, he joined both the EMDR International Association (EMDRIA) and ISSTD, the latter specifically to gain access to the Multidimensional Inventory of Dissociation (MID; Dell, 2006). Although Michael began to read more intently about and access EMDR-based training on dissociation, it was only in 2013, when he made a serious error with a client, that he stepped back and began to take dissociation seriously. He had not adequately screened for dissociation, missed and/or did not heed clear contraindications for moving into trauma processing, then breached a client's dissociative amnesia during reprocessing a supposedly single-episode trauma. He decided soon thereafter that he would, in his words, "never allow this to happen again." Michael began to study more intently and obtained ongoing consultation with a foundational thinker/practitioner in the use of EMDR therapy to treat dissociation. In the early years of this journey of learning and discovery, Michael crossed paths with Jennifer. The enduring collaboration that resulted from that meeting has resulted in many shared interests, several of which are documented for you in this book.

We have gained so much from those who traveled on similar roads before us in the fields of trauma, dissociation, and EMDR therapy. This book synthesizes our learning and experience, which is unique in its sum total if not in its parts. We recognize there is nothing new under the sun – nothing that has not been explored or written about before. (Well, almost.) Instead of something brand new, we offer our perspectives on several concepts to help you deepen your understanding and foster your continued growth. We cite our forebears extensively, with the intent of both integrating (and most definitely honoring) the past and offering new avenues of learning beyond this volume.

> *Every intervention is risky if you don't know your client.*
>
> (Kinsler, 2018)

Although it is possible to read chapters *à la carte*, we designed the book to be read sequentially, across four distinct yet overlapping parts. Part I lays out the foundations for the treatment of dissociation from psychological theory, neuroscientific research, and standards of care as we understand them. Knowing and learning from the collective wisdom in both the EMDR therapy and dissociative disorders fields can ground and inform our clinical practice. We discuss the limitations we see in the adaptive information processing (AIP) model for guiding the treatment of people with dissociative disorders (DDs). We then offer our ideas for enhancing the AIP model, based on both historical and contemporary science and theory, to guide treatment. This also informs our proposed, multilayered conceptual framework, which encompasses a three-stage, relational model of trauma treatment, Ego State Theory and Therapy (EST; Watkins & Watkins, 1997), and EMDR therapy. These elements provide connective tissue throughout every chapter in this book.

Part II explores ways that practitioners, consultants, and trainers can apply and promote tenets of ethical and competent practice when employing EMDR therapy with this population. Although the often complex and long-term healing process is usually focused on the client's experience, we must also consider the impact of the therapist's personal history, training, and professional way(s) of being. As such, in Chapter 5, Jennifer specifically discusses the development of the practitioner and some ways in which EMDR therapy consultants and trainers can recognize and address the knowledge and skills gaps that new learners, supervisees, and consultees frequently carry with them into this work.

> *You can close your eyes to reality but not to memories.*
>
> (Lec, 1967, p. 129)

Part III delves into the dissociation-informed practice of EMDR therapy. Jennifer is the lead author for this section, walking through the standard eight phases and three prongs of EMDR therapy within the larger framework proposed in Chapter 3. Employing EMDR in the treatment of clients with DDs demands a nuanced approach. These chapters do not offer a 'recipe' or protocol directing practitioners on what to do. Neither do they serve as a comprehensive literature review of adapted protocols purported to treat dissociation. Instead, practitioners are invited to think critically about what they're doing – and why and how they're doing it – to more nimbly navigate the moment-to-moment challenges of treating dissociation. When EMDR therapy is framed in this way, simple adjustments to the standard procedures that are attuned to the person and present-moment context can be quite effective. Experiences of dissociation often create confusion – for client and therapist alike – about what belongs to past, present, and future realities. Jennifer helpfully situates the three prongs of EMDR therapy within the three-stage model, intentionally incorporating present and future prongs to make them applicable for dissociation-informed treatment.

In Part IV, Michael integrates multiple layers of the treatment frame introduced in Part I to expand the realm of possibility when navigating the most complex dissociative processes. Over the past number of years, Michael has explored in some depth the wisdom contained in older literatures concerned with the study and treatment of dissociation. He has very intentionally integrated Ego State Therapy and clinical hypnosis into his work, both in acknowledgement of the importance of informed clinical practice and expanding conceptualization and treatment in an EMDR therapy frame. He first reexamines the dominant paradigm for 'parts' work, comparing and contrasting Internal Family Systems therapy (Schwartz, 1995) and Ego State Therapy (Watkins & Watkins, 1997). His in-depth explorations of self-system mapping and more complex manifestations of flashbacks consolidate and expand upon ideas drawn from the dissociative disorders literature to enhance the application of EMDR therapy methods. Finally, Michael introduces a protocol he developed in his practice: The *Introject Decathexis (Id) Protocol*. Both we and other practitioners have found this approach to be invaluable when working with perpetrator introjects throughout every stage of treatment.

As you embark on your journey through this book, we urge you to be an informed consumer: Do not simply take it at face value. Carefully examine this, and any other publication (and training) you digest, with a critical eye. No therapy approach or protocol is a replacement for (or short-cut to) the solid knowledge, understanding, and skills needed to treat persons with complex trauma and dissociation – and it unavoidably takes time and dedicated effort to cultivate all of those.

References

Carlson, E., & Putnam, F. (1993). An update on the dissociative experiences scale. *Dissociation, 6*(1), 16–27. hdl.handle.net/1794/1539

Dell, P. F. (2006). The multidimensional inventory of dissociation (MID): A comprehensive measure of pathological dissociation. *Journal of Trauma & Dissociation, 7*(2), 77–106. https://doi.org/10.1300/J229v07n02_06

International Society for the Study of Trauma and Dissociation. (2011). Guidelines for treating dissociative identity disorder in adults, third revision. *Journal of Trauma & Dissociation, 12*(2), 115–187. https://doi.org/10.1080/15299732.2011.537247

Kinsler, P. (2018, June 8). *Relational aspects of therapy* [Webinar]. International Society for the Study of Trauma and Dissociation. cfas.isst-d.org/content/relational-aspects-therapy-0

Lec, S. J. (1967). *Unkempt thoughts*. Minerva Press.

Schwartz, R. (1995). *Internal family systems therapy*. The Guilford Press.

Shapiro, F. (2018). *Eye movement desensitization and reprocessing (EMDR) therapy: Basic principles, protocols and procedures* (3rd ed.). The Guilford Press.

Watkins, J. G., & Watkins, H. H. (1997). *Ego states: Theory and therapy*. W. W. Norton & Company.

Part I

Foundations

Chapter 1

The Complexities of Dissociation

Jennifer A. Madere and D. Michael Coy

Introduction

Foundations are critical for ensuring a solid, sturdy, and enduring structure. The carefully laid foundation of a house supports the frame, the floors, and everything with which we furnish its rooms. Most importantly, when the ground into which that foundation is set is relatively firm, that prevents the structure from sinking or becoming otherwise unstable. Similarly, there are many theories, concepts, and empirical data that support or confound the application of eye movement desensitization and reprocessing (EMDR) therapy and the adaptive information processing (AIP) model in the treatment of persons with dissociative disorders (DDs). Our understanding of each – EMDR, AIP, and DDs – builds on efforts and mis-takes of those who have come before us (yes, mis-takes is intentional).

Francine Shapiro (2001) stated, "I have continued to claim that treating a trauma is like 'removing a quilt from a mattress'; only then are you able to observe the other problems that must be addressed" (p. 420). Based upon our learning, observation, and experience, we are not sure that this is universally true. Instead, we read it as one example of problematic truisms that have become embedded in the foundation and worked their way into the carpentry that forms the overall structure of EMDR therapy training, consultation, and practice. Other EMDR therapy truisms relevant to discussions throughout this book include 'memory networks and self-states are the same thing' and 'the AIP model explains dissociation.' We will address some of these truisms in this chapter, which explores the nature of dissociation, and explicate factors that have negatively impacted mental health practitioners' ability to recognize, diagnose, and learn to treat dissociation, both more broadly and with EMDR therapy specifically.

After establishing that context, three different domains of explanation for dissociation will organize our discussion of the extant literature: Neuroanatomical/neurophysiological, psychological, and subjective/phenomenological. A wealth of historical and recent literature is introduced

DOI: 10.4324/9781003410201-2

here, which provides a foundation for our understanding of dissociation throughout this book.

What Is Dissociation?

How we conceptualize dissociative symptoms and disorders depends heavily upon the way(s) in which we define the term itself. Is dissociation a discrete, spontaneous, but easily recognized experience of detachment, like 'zoning out' or 'going away' that can be managed during reprocessing using special techniques (e.g., Knipe, 2010a, 2010b)? Is dissociation the same as having different, compartmentalized self-states that can be treated with a combination of EMDR therapy and 'parts' work (e.g., Forgash & Copeley, 2008)? Or, does dissociation encompass a complex matrix of overlapping and at times conflictual phenomena that often elude detection, recognition, and/or treatment, requiring significant modifications of standard EMDR therapy procedures to treat (e.g., Paulsen, 1995; Lazrove & Fine, 1996; Shapiro, 2018)? It's complicated.

A long-standing debate exists about whether some or all experiences of dissociation are fundamentally pathological, or whether the frequency/ severity of dissociative experiences exists along a continuum from 'normal' to 'pathological' (Holmes et al., 2005; Loewenstein, 2018; Waller et al., 1996). The Diagnostic and Statistical Manual of Mental Disorders (DSM-5-TR; American Psychiatric Association [APA, 2022]) seems to subscribe to the former stance. It defines dissociation as the "disruption of and/ or discontinuity in the normal integration of consciousness, memory, identity, emotion, perception, body representation, motor control, and behavior" (p. 330). This phrasing suggests that dissociation is inherently pathological.

Dalenberg and Paulson (2009) more pragmatically suggest "it is possible that the difference between normal and pathological dissociation depends upon *how* the dissociative mechanisms are used" (p. 151; emphasis in original). This invites us to consider the form, frequency, and function of different kinds of dissociative experiences, as well as the context(s) in which they occur.

On the question of *form*, research offers evidence for two distinct categories or types of dissociation: detachment and compartmentalization (Butler et al., 2019; Holmes et al., 2005). Butler et al. (2019) found that *detachment* is characterized by experiences of depersonalization, derealization, and (trance-like) absorption, while compartmentalization is marked by ego-alien ('not me') experiences such as feeling split or divided inside; having a subjective sense of other parts (of self) that have different memories, feelings, motivations, and behaviors; somatoform dissociation; amnesia, etc.

The question of *function* invites us first to examine *peritraumatic* dissociation, which Dell (2009a, p. 760) describes as an "evolution-prepared biological defense against immediate danger." In the face of inescapable overwhelm, we may experience peritraumatic dissociation, a "complex array of reactions [...] that include depersonalization, derealization, dissociative amnesia, out-of-body experiences, emotional numbness, and altered time perception" (Thompson-Hollands et al, 2017, p. 19). Frank Corrigan and colleagues highlight that depersonalization and derealization may arise from high-impact shock at the moment of overwhelm, with the latter four of these symptoms resulting from the near-simultaneous release of anesthetic neurochemicals associated with tonic and/or collapsed immobility (Corrigan et al., 2025).

Peritraumatic dissociation, while helpful for reflexive distancing in the face of inescapable pain, has been identified as the single best predictor for the development of posttraumatic stress disorder (PTSD; American Psychiatric Association, 2022). In fact, all of the symptoms of peritraumatic dissociation cited above are recognized by DSM-5(-TR) as symptoms of PTSD and its dissociative subtype. When passive defenses, and the anesthetic neurochemicals associated with them, become a person's primary means for avoiding perceived threat, the brain's processing of information may become chronically disrupted. This, in combination with other factors, can result in the development of a DD (Lanius et al., 2014; Kluft 1985a).

The (De)realization of Dissociation

There is a long history of un(der)awareness of and confusion about dissociation among mental health professionals. We see this as a consequence of a combination of factors – some historical, some enduring – all of which are important to acknowledge. These include (1) a continuing lack of clarity in the diagnostic criteria for DDs; (2) active retaliation against trauma survivors and therapists by those who deny the impacts of abuse and the existence of traumagenic dissociation; and (3) the endurance of myths, misconceptions, and distortions related to dissociation and dissociative identity disorder (DID) specifically. Together, these factors have resulted in limited awareness of and/or access to education and training about the complexities of diagnosing and treating dissociation, and inadequate use of formal evaluative measures of dissociation in clinical practice (Madere & Coy, 2022).

Lack of Clarity in the Diagnostic Criteria

Even today, with a comparatively more nuanced set of diagnostic criteria in both the DSM-5-TR and ICD-11 (International Classification of Diseases, 11th edition; World Health Organization [WHO], 2018), barriers to accurately diagnosing DID remain significant except in perhaps the most florid of client presentations. Why is this? It may come down to a combination of factors: The DSM criteria themselves, clinician's lack of awareness (or avoidance) of diagnostic criteria, and the relative hiddenness of dissociative features (Dell, 2009a, 2009d; Kluft, 1985b, 1991).

The earliest iterations of the DSM categorized dissociation as a form of neurosis (i.e., anxiety), the description of which included a mixture of psychoanalytic conceptualizations and behavioral features. With the advent of DSM-III (American Psychiatric Association [APA], 1980), the standalone diagnosis of multiple personality ['disorder' was added later] came into existence. This third edition of the diagnostic manual marked a major turning point, toward what was considered a more objective, scientifically grounded, consistent, and reliable means for diagnosing in general (Dell, 2001). Those initial criteria, in concert with media depictions of multiplicity, probably helped cement the enduring diagnostic stereotype of DID. Recognition of problems with the criteria focusing heavily upon the observable existence of 'personalities,' and an oversimplification of the complexities of MPD/DID (Dell, 2009d; Kluft et al., 1988), and later revisions of the criteria for MPD/DID, have not been able to remedy this. Table 1.1 depicts the evolution of these criteria comprehensively.

Consultees have expressed to us the belief that one must still see an actual dissociative switch to accurately diagnose DID. Out of necessity, this *was* the case earlier on, owing both to the focus on observable traits in the diagnostic criteria and to the absence of standardized measures of dissociation. It was only in DSM-5 (APA, 2013) that the diagnostic criteria for DID explicitly stated that, "These signs and symptoms may be observed by others *or reported by the individual*" (p. 330; emphasis added). You might wonder why this distinction matters. Kluft (1985b, citing a personal communication with Robert Gurtheil, MD) described MPD/DID as a "pathology of hiddenness" (p. 206) and subsequently reported that, in a sample of 210 patients, only 6.2 percent of these demonstrated obvious dissociative switching. That amounts to 13 patients – and Kluft specializes in treating this population. We are of the opinion that even the current diagnostic criteria for DID and other specified dissociative disorder are inadequate in helping the average clinician definitively diagnose. (For an in-depth discussion of factors that may contribute to this inadequacy, see Dell, 2009d.)

If a therapist is looking for obvious indicators of dissociation as a means for determining whether to proceed with EMDR therapy treatment as usual, the covert nature of dissociative symptoms and a lack of clarity in the diagnostic manual – especially for clinicians new to dissociation – pose significant barriers to ethical practice. Moreover, additional challenges are inherent in identifying and acknowledging the suffering that fostered the dissociation.

Active Retaliation Against Trauma Survivors and Therapists

One need only look at the news to see how denial of the impacts of inescapable pain and human atrocity is alive and well. The same is the case for dissociation, a concomitant result of chronic exposure to physically inescapable pain, at least for some people (someone with dissociative capacities can escape inside rather than via an active defense). Although this denialism has assumed many shapes over hundreds of years (Van der Kolk et al., 1996; Middleton & Dorahy, 2024), since the late 1980s it has surfaced as accusations that trauma survivors suffer from 'false memory syndrome' and therefore cannot be trusted to offer an accurate account of their experience. Therapists have been targeted as active agents in the development of false memories, the argument being that they would suggest to their highly suggestible (female) clients that they had been sexually abused. The False Memory Syndrome Foundation (FMSF), which existed from 1992 to 2019, was the primary organizational proponent of this viewpoint. The FMSF was founded "[t]o seek the reasons for the spread of FMS that is so devastating for families, to work for ways to prevent it, [and] to aid those who were affected by it and to bring their families into reconciliation" (False Memory Syndrome Foundation, 2013). The resulting controversies were collectively referred to as the 'memory wars' (Crook, 2022).

Francine Shapiro (1995, p. 292) was contemporaneously aware of this:

> Currently there is a great deal of controversy regarding the possibility that false allegations of sexual abuse are being made as a result of inappropriate therapy. Although some of these claims may well be coming from perpetrators in denial, it is clear that there is a need for quality control in the mental health profession. There is no question that some therapists are using psychological tools, such as hypnosis, with little or no training and are therefore ignorant of the limitations of these tools and of their potential for contaminating memories or creating false impressions.
>
> Consequently, it is not surprising to learn that some clients have been led to accept images that have surfaced under hypnosis, guided

Table 1.1 Evolution of the DSM Criteria for Multiple Personality Disorder/Dissociative Identity Disorder, 1952–2022[1]

DSM-I (APA, 1952, p. 32)	**DSM-II (APA, 1968, pp. 39-40)**
Dissociative Reaction (000-x02)	Hysterical Neurosis, Dissociative Type (300.14)
Psychoneurotic Disorders, Dissociative Reaction This reaction represents a type of gross personality disorganization, the basis of which is a neurotic disturbance, although the diffuse dissociation seen in some cases may occasionally appear psychotic. The personality disorganization may result in aimless running or "freezing." The repressed impulse giving rise to the anxiety may be discharged by, or deflected into, various symptomatic expressions, such as depersonalization, dissociated personality, stupor, fugue, amnesia, dream state, somnambulism, etc. The diagnosis will specify symptomatic manifestations. These reactions must be differentiated from schizoid personality, from schizophrenic reaction, and from analogous symptoms in some other types of neurotic reactions. Formerly, this reaction has been classified as a type of "conversion hysteria."	300.1 Hysterical neurosis is characterized by an involuntary psychogenic loss or disorder of function. **Symptoms characteristically begin and end suddenly in emotionally charged situations and are symbolic of the underlying conflicts.** **Often they can be modified by suggestion alone.** **This is a new diagnosis that encompasses the former diagnoses "Conversion reaction" and "Dissociative reaction" in DSM-I.** **This distinction between conversion and dissociative reactions should be preserved by using one of the following diagnoses whenever possible.** 300.14 Hysterical neurosis, dissociative type In the dissociative type, **alterations may occur in the patient's state of consciousness or in his identity**, to produce such symptoms as amnesia, somnambulism, fugue, and **multiple** personality.

1 The criteria in Table 1.1 are arranged in the chart according to their alignment with the preceding and subsequent DSM editions' corresponding criteria, when possible. Text in **bold type** indicates language added/changed, and [ ] indicates that language (usually a single word) was removed, in the transition from the previous iteration of the diagnostic manual.

Table 1.1 (Continued)

DSM-III[2] (APA, 1980, p. 259)	DSM-III-R (APA, 1987, p. 272)
MP(D) (300.14)	MPD (300.14)
A. The existence within the individual of two or more distinct personalities, each of which is dominant at a particular time.	A. The existence within the **person** of two or more distinct personalities **or personality states (each with its own relatively enduring pattern of perceiving, relating to, and thinking about the environment and self).**
B. The personality that is dominant at any particular time determines the individual's behavior.	B. **At least two of these personalities or personality states recurrently take <u>full</u> control of the person's** behavior.
C. Each individual personality is complex and integrated with its own unique behavior patterns and social relationships.	

2 Amnesia as a symptom is discussed in the section that precedes the delineation of the diagnoses in DSM-III/-R, but it is not actually included in the criteria for MP(D)/DID until DSM-IV.

Table 1.1 (Continued)

DSM-IV (APA, 1994, p. 487)	**DSM-IV-TR (APA, 2000, p. 529)**
DID (300.14)	DID (300.14)
A. The **presence** of two or more distinct **identities** or personality states (each with its own relatively enduring pattern of perceiving, relating to, and thinking about the environment and self).	A. The presence of two or more distinct identities or personality states (each with its own relatively enduring pattern of perceiving, relating to, and thinking about the environment and self).
B. At least two of these **identities** or personality states recurrently take [ ] control of the person's behavior.	B. At least two of these identities or personality states recurrently take [ ] control of the person's behavior.
C. Inability to recall important personal information that is too extensive to be explained by ordinary forgetfulness.	C. Inability to recall important personal information that is too extensive to be explained by ordinary forgetfulness.
D. The disturbance is not due to the direct physiological effects of a substance (e.g., blackouts or chaotic behavior during Alcohol Intoxication) or a general medical condition (e.g., complex partial seizures).	D. The disturbance is not due to the direct physiological effects of a substance (e.g., blackouts or chaotic behavior during Alcohol Intoxication) or a general medical condition (e.g., complex partial seizures).
Note: In children, the symptoms are not attributable to imaginary playmates or other fantasy play.	Note: In children, the symptoms are not attributable to imaginary playmates or other fantasy play.

Table 1.1 (Continued)

DSM-5 (APA, 2013, p. 292)	DSM-5-TR* (APA, 2022, p. 330)

DID (300.14/F44.81)
** DSM-II diagnosis codes fully retired in favor of ICD F-codes*

A. Disruption of identity characterized by two or more distinct personality states, **which may be described in some cultures as an experience of possession. The disruption in identity involves marked discontinuity** in sense of self and sense of agency, accompanied by related alterations in **affect,** behavior, consciousness, **memory,** perception, cognition, **and/or sensory-motor functioning. These signs and symptoms may be observed by others or reported by the individual.**

B. **Recurrent gaps in the recall of everyday events,** important personal information, **and/or traumatic events that are inconsistent with** ordinary forgetting.

C. The symptoms cause clinically significant distress or impairment in social, occupational, or other important areas of functioning.

D. The disturbance is not a normal part of a broadly accepted cultural or religious practice.

Note: In children, the symptoms are not better explained by imaginary playmates or other fantasy play.

E. The symptoms are not attributable to the [ ] physiological effects of a substance (e.g., blackouts or chaotic behavior during alcohol intoxication) or **another** medical condition (e.g., complex partial seizures).

visualization, or dream analysis as definitive evidence of actual memories, even when corroboration is often impossible. *Clinicians should be aware of their boundaries of competence and of the limitations of their methods before utilizing them in clinical practice. This is why it is vital that the use of EMDR be restricted to trained, licensed clinicians who have been supervised in its practice. Simply reading the cautions offered in the following pages is not a substitute for adequate training.* (Emphasis added)

While Shapiro expresses concern about the risks posed by clinicians' lack of recognition of the "boundaries of [their] competence" and "limitations of their methods," she fails to mention the risk posed by a lack of awareness of the limitations of one's knowledge. *What if a therapist believes they know more than they do?* Implicit bias takes many forms, and our clinical decision-making is sometimes shaped by influences just as invisible as dissociation.

Myths, Misconceptions, and Distortions

It is difficult to grasp what we do not (yet) know. Myths, misconceptions, and distortions easily fill the vacuum, even without our being aware that this has happened. For many of the clinicians we have trained and consulted with over the years, the process began in graduate school, with little to no attention given to trauma in general and dissociation more specifically. Sometimes, distortion can be an intentional act driven by hidden agendas.

Sorting myth from fact can sometimes be a bit like trying to grab smoke. Across two articles, Piper and Merskey (2004a, 2004b) offered several questionable 'facts' about DID. It is beyond the scope of this book to discuss these points in depth; however, it seems important to highlight their pervasive impact and currency.

In their first article, Piper and Merskey (2004a, p. 592) summarize:

1. The literature on Dissociative Identity Disorder (DID) contains "logical inconsistencies" "internal contradictions" and "conflict[s] with known facts and settled scientific principles."
2. "DID cannot be reliably diagnosed."
3. "The diagnosis of DID often leads to clinical deterioration in patients."

In their second article, Piper and Merskey (2004b, p. 678) highlight:

1. "The arguments offered to support the concept of dissociative identity disorder (DID) are illogical."

2. "DID proponents' diagnostic and treatment methods iatrogenically encourage patients to behave as if they have multiple selves."
3. "The unsatisfactory, vague, and elastic definition of 'alter personality' makes a reliable diagnosis of DID impossible."

We are not certain how "known facts and settled scientific principles" (Piper & Merskey, 2004b, p. 678) refute the realities of what many EMDR therapists have seen in practice (e.g., *Dissociative Disorders Task Force Recommended Guidelines* [Shapiro, 1995, 2001, 2018]). Both of us discovered DDs in our practice rather accidentally and sought the necessary training to be able to treat clients with dissociative experience who do, indeed, spontaneously switch from one self-state to another (see Kluft, 2013, for his take on the role of EMDR in proving the existence of DID). As such, we are intrigued that a 'concept' that allegedly does not really exist could make its way into two different diagnostic manuals (the DSM and the ICD) and merit an entire section in each devoted to its phenomenology and symptoms. Experts in the diagnosis and treatment of dissociation have concluded that DID *can* be reliably diagnosed using research-validated measures (e.g., Brand et al., 2016). It seems evident to us that Paul Dell developed the Multidimensional Inventory of Dissociation (MID; Dell, 2006b), at least in part, to challenge the dominant paradigm of DID as 'an alter disorder' (Dell, 2001). This translates to defining DID according to "a person having alters as opposed to identification of a broader range of dissociative symptoms" (Coy & Madere, 2023, p. 668).

Kluft (1989, pp. 83–84) responded to the myth of iatrogenically creating DID in a client (iatrogenesis is the development of unintended, undesirable effects due to the treatment itself), pointing out that

> To prove the iatrogenesis of MPD [DID], it would be necessary to begin with a normal individual and demonstrate that as a result of specified [therapist-driven] interventions, that individual demonstrated the phenomena of MPD on an ongoing basis, with the phenomena manifesting themselves spontaneously and repetitively in a classical manner over time. This has not been done; furthermore, a strong case could be made that it would be ethically reprehensible to do so.

The risk of decompensation is context-specific and by no means universal. As Shapiro (1995) was aware, there can be unanticipated or unwanted treatment effects when working with persons with trauma-laden histories. And what about the risk of a client deteriorating simply by being diagnosed? There is some substance to this claim, particularly if someone is not prepared for that information (Brand et al., 2016). We propose that the *meaning* or implications of a diagnosis often seem to be more jarring than the diagnosis itself. This is a nuanced issue that is not exclusive to diagnosing DDs (Benito-Lozano et al., 2023; Sims et al., 2021). We have encountered plenty of situations when clients responded with relief and hope to someone finally validating that their symptoms mean something. It can be empowering for people to learn that their symptoms are not just 'in their head,' and that, ultimately, both they and their experience matter.

Limited Awareness of and/or Access to Education and Training

How many of us actually have read Francine Shapiro's EMDR therapy text from cover to cover? How many of our basic training programs directed our attention to the *Dissociative Disorders Task Force Recommended Guidelines*, which are nestled in the appendicized section on *Client Safety* in each of the three editions *of* that text? You read that right – these recommendations have existed and remain largely unchanged since their first publication in 1995. The 1995 version stated that "The therapist should screen every patient for the presence of an underlying dissociative disorder regardless of the complaint" (Shapiro, 1995, p. 366). These guidelines offer important information about the use of EMDR therapy to treat persons diagnosed with DDs.

Although the visibility of dissociation – and attention given to assessing it – has changed a lot since we each participated in EMDR therapy basic training, a lot of gaps remain. Unfortunately, some of those gaps are likely influenced by Francine Shapiro's own words.

Shapiro (2018, p. 96) writes that

> While the dissociative disorders constitute a separate section in DSM-5, EMDR specialists regard DID as a complex form of PTSD (Spiegel, 1993) in which the victimization was so great that, for survival, the global memory was compartmentalized to hold different aspects of the pain and disturbance and becomes divided into more dissociative personality states. Thus, *the personality states can be conceptualized as neural network configurations that serve as memory compartments* (Braun, 1988; Lanius & Bergmann, 2014).

We recall Shapiro's (2001) likening of treating a trauma to "removing a quilt from a mattress," and suggesting that "only then are you able to observe the other problems that must be addressed" (p. 420). We see these viewpoints as being in direct contradiction to what the *Task Force* stated as two important therapist-dependent factors (Shapiro, 2018, p. 500):

a. It should be determined whether the therapist is sufficiently trained in the dissociative disorders, as evidenced by the therapist's (1) having taken formal courses in the area and (2) having been supervised in the psychotherapy of dissociative patients.
b. It should be determined whether the therapist is sufficiently skilled in the treatment of dissociative disorders, as evidenced by such abilities as (1) troubleshooting with hostile alters, child alters, and perpetrator alters; (2) anticipating and accommodating transferences; (3) recognizing and working with hypnotic and dissociative phenomena; (4) managing crises; and (5) determining the need for medical and/or inpatient backup.

Unfortunately, we have both encountered therapists who learned that EMDR therapy is the method by which one removes the quilt, only to discover too late that the mattress was not at all what they expected it to be. Further on in the guidelines, the *Task Force* offered guidance on where to obtain training in the DDs, stating that, "Clinicians who seek additional training in the diagnosis and treatment of dissociative disorders should contact the International Society for the Study of Trauma and Dissociation (ISSTD)" (Shapiro, 2018, p. 502).

Chapter 5 will give more in-depth attention to the issue of training and education. Presently, let's revisit a statement drawn from the *Task Force* guidelines (Shapiro, 2018, p. 499) that we frequently quote in presentations: "[T]here is a high cost to patient, therapist, and the therapeutic alliance in failing to adequately consider the possibility of dissociative disorders before first using EMDR in a patient's treatment." How many of us learned specifics about "consider[ing] the possibility of dissociative disorders" in our basic training? We did not learn about that in basic training either.

Inadequate Use of Measures of Dissociation

At a minimum, screening for DDs is critical to avoid prematurely ripping that quilt off the bed. Shapiro finally stated this in the main body of the 2018 text (pp. 96–97). However, significant variance regarding whether, when, and how EMDR therapy basic training courses address dissociation persists – both in North America and worldwide (Leeds et al., 2022). That variance leaves room for significant risk.

EMDR therapy basic training in the USA and Canada consists of 20 hours of didactic learning, at a minimum. Think about how much is crammed into those 20 hours. In 2017, the EMDRIA's training standards required that "Dissociation should be mentioned; learners are encouraged to pursue advanced training to treat dissociative clients" (EMDR

International Association, 2017, p. 8). Updated standards were published in December 2022 and most recently revised again in March 2025. These stated that "Assessment tools and procedures for screening for dissociation" must be taught (EMDR International Association, 2022/2025, p. 17). Though significant, this change occurred only after being made explicit in the main body of Shapiro's text in 2018 and in response to significant lobbying. Even then, for so long, the guardrails in place for using EMDR therapy with dissociation have been dictated by what we don't know and the risks of finding out in ways that are uncontrolled (and potentially uncontrollable).

Frameworks for conceptualizing what we are doing can be quite helpful, not only for avoiding a collision with the unknown but also for making informed decisions based on what we *do* know. Born out of extensive observation, Francine Shapiro (2018) conceptualized three domains of experience that help us track the progression of clients' healing, thematically, via negative and positive cognitions. EMDR trained practitioners will be familiar with those. Now, let us present a different set of three domains. Based on his own observations and study, Dell (2006a) proposed that there are at least three domains of explanation for dissociation. These are (1) the neuroanatomical/neurophysiological, (2) the psychological, and (3) the subjective/phenomenological.

The Neuroanatomical/Neurophysiological Domain

Consideration of the impact of trauma on the human nervous system dates at least as far back as 1900 B.C. (Figley et al., 2017). Our attention is particularly drawn to writings dating to the late-19th and early-20th centuries. The work of Boris Sidis has stood out as having particular, previously unrecognized salience for AIP and EMDR therapy. Sidis was a student of William James and a contemporary of Pierre Janet, Sigmund Freud, and Morton Prince. Among other things, Sidis was interested in association and dissociation at the *cellular* level. He studied how neurons coalesce, or fail to coalesce, into clusters – and networks/systems of clusters. He also examined how established neuronal connections may be *severed* or simply *not connect* in reaction to 'toxins' (Sidis, 1898; Sidis & Goodhart, 1904/1968). This course of study was not mere scientific noodling. Sidis began to more fully explicate his understanding of how pathological dissociation develops. We will revisit this in greater detail in Chapter 2.

Much more recently, significant strides have been made toward revealing the neurobiological correlates of posttraumatic and dissociative symptoms as well as data to support their distinct presence and resolution. Here, we will focus on scientific models and studies that explain and substantiate the observable reality of dissociative symptoms in the brain.

Mapping the Dissociative Subtype of PTSD (DSM) and Complex PTSD (ICD)

The work of Ruth Lanius et al. (2010, 2012) and colleagues in Ontario, Canada, represented a tipping point in neurobiological research related to PTSD. A mound of scientific evidence, including fMRI scans and script-driven imagery, contributed to their argument for a dissociative of PTSD (PTSD+DS) as distinct from non-dissociative or 'simple' PTSD. Distinguishing clinical and neurobiological features was identified. "The dissociative subtype is characterized by overmodulation of affect, while the more common under-modulated type involves the predominance of reexperiencing and hyperarousal symptoms" (Lanius et al., 2010, p. 640). In PTSD+DS they noted patterns of overmodulation of the limbic regions by the areas of the prefrontal cortex involved in arousal modulation and emotion regulation.

For example, in response to reminders of the traumatic memory, subjects with PTSD+DS experienced emotional disengagement via depersonalization or derealization that appeared to be mediated by the prefrontal cortex (specifically, the dorsal anterior cingulate and medial prefrontal cortices). Clinically speaking, this sounds quite like what theorists call non-realization – acting and even feeling as though something isn't happening, that it isn't real – which is a cornerstone of many models of dissociation. The authors went on to highlight how "[t]hese findings have important implications for treatment of PTSD, including the need to assess patients with PTSD for dissociative symptoms and to incorporate the treatment of dissociative symptoms into stage-oriented trauma treatment" (Lanius et al., 2010, p. 641).

A few years later, PTSD was moved from the *Anxiety Disorders* section of the DSM-IV to a section titled *Trauma- and Stressor-Related Disorders* in DSM-5 and the dissociative subtype of PTSD was added as a specifier (APA, 2013, p. 272). The *Dissociative Disorders* section immediately followed, representing an acknowledgement of relatedness between them, while keeping DDs distinct. Following the inclusion of PTSD+DS in the DSM-5 in 2013, and Complex PTSD (C-PTSD) in the ICD-11 (WHO, 2018) in 2018, a flurry of research has begun to produce measures, report on prevalence, and offer considerations for treatment. Considerable overlap was found between PTSD+DS and DDs by Swart et al. (2020), in their investigation of a clinical sample. A combination of clinical interview and psychometric tools indicated that more than 50% of clients who met criteria for PTSD+DS also met criteria for a DD.

Philip Hyland et al. (2020, 2024) examined the relationship of dissociative experiences to the ICD-11 criteria for PTSD and C-PTSD. In a clinical sample, "those meeting the diagnostic criteria for C-PTSD had significantly higher levels of dissociative experiences than those with PTSD" (Hyland et al., 2020, p. 67). Because of how the C-PTSD criteria are organized, dissociative experiences are part of the overall symptom profile rather than a distinct symptom cluster; therefore, dissociation is *not* an essential requirement in making a diagnosis of C-PTSD. A general population sample found that 10% of respondents reported statistically significant dissociative experiences above and beyond meeting the criteria for C-PTSD. The same respondents were also more likely to report more severe physical and mental health issues, as well as a history of emotional neglect and a household member who was mentally ill or had attempted suicide (Hyland et al., 2024). Taken together, these findings imply that making a diagnosis of C-PTSD or PTSD+DS can occur without assessing for dissociative symptoms, *and* that relevant dissociative symptoms and other clinical features may be missed if they are not explored intentionally via a structured clinical assessment.

Researchers also began to explore whether and how EMDR therapy works in treating people who meet these new sets of diagnostic criteria. A series of Dutch studies beginning with Zoet et al. (2018) measured the effects of an intensive treatment program that included EMDR therapy. They argued that a stabilization phase is not needed and that individuals with C-PTSD benefit from unmodified EMDR therapy. Voorendonk et al. (2020) claimed that over 85% of participants diagnosed with C-PTSD no longer met the criteria after eight days of intensive trauma-focused treatment. Posttreatment follow-up was conducted just nine days after discharge from the program, however, and no information was given about what may have influenced participants to decline consent, drop out of the study, or not complete the follow-up measures – all of which were stated to occur. In this study, the CAPS-5 (Clinician-Administered PTSD Scale for DSM-5, Weathers et al., 2018) was employed to identify C-PTSD. No measure was used to screen for or rule out a DD; in fact, the term 'dissociat…' is found *nowhere* in the article. Screening for dissociation *is* an element of practicing EMDR therapy with fidelity; therefore, we think that is a serious oversight and demonstrates either bias or ignorance with regard to dissociation. Further investigation with a more comprehensive diagnostic evaluation is needed in order to consider their argument in a reasonable, ethical practice.

The Realization of DID

Long before the invention of neuroimaging, public and professionals alike have questioned whether DID is real, made up in the mind of the experiencer (fantasy-based), iatrogenic, or altogether factitious by clients and believing clinicians. Fortunately, a number of studies have tested a variety of angles to show that *DID seems to be an observable reality*. It has been observed physiologically, functionally, and anatomically.

Boris Sidis was one of the first to study and substantiate how "the influence of hurtful stimuli...may give rise to functional dissociations" both at the cellular level and in the development of "different individualities" (Sidis & Goodhart, 1904/1968, p. 53). He consistently emphasized that the connections between nerve cells are *functional* rather than organic (Sidis, 1898; 1909; Sidis & Goodhart, 1904/1968). According to Sidis, disruptions in functional connectivity – caused by the contraction of nerve cells and the severing of existing connections in favor of new ones shaped by the reflexive avoidance of hurtful stimuli – could ultimately result in the formation of dissociated personalities, which he understood as sophisticated neural networks operating independently. Recent neuroimaging studies have increasingly highlighted differences in brain connectivity and structure among individuals with PTSD, PTSD with dissociative symptoms (PTSD+DS), and DID. Numerous laboratories and researchers worldwide have contributed to identifying neuroanatomical biomarkers that strongly support the validity of dissociative symptoms, especially in relation to DID.

Building on PTSD-related research, Simone Reinders et al. (2014) launched a series of studies based in the Netherlands. They replicated the script-driven imagery and neuroimaging studies that distinguished between PTSD and PTSD+DS, using PET scan imagery, and added a group: persons with DID. Clinical observation had indicated that persons with DID experience *both* hyper-aroused states *and* hypo-aroused states. Reinders et al. proposed a neurobiological model for DID, based on the PTSD/PTSD+DS model described above, as follows: "the hypo-aroused identity state activates the prefrontal cortex, cingulate, posterior association areas and parahippocampal gyri, thereby overmodulating emotion regulation; the hyper-aroused identity state activates the amygdala and insula as well as the dorsal striatum, thereby under-modulating emotion regulation" (p. 236). Further analysis showed that hyper-arousal in the amygdala and activity in the dorsal striatum appeared *even more* highly inhibited by the prefrontal cortex in the DID group (compared to PTSD+DS). This research substantiated two phenomena that are familiar to clinicians who treat dissociation: (1) dissociative symptoms/self-states manifest patterns of hyper- *and* hypo-activation and (2) internal conflict is a frequent complaint and subject of treatment.

In collaboration with Reinders's lab, Yolanda Schlumpf et al. (2014), based at the University of Zurich, Switzerland, used fMRI data to examine whether: (a) actors could be distinguished from individuals who had been previously diagnosed with DID, and (b) whether any difference in activation could be observed between ANPs (apparently normal parts) and EPs (emotional parts), according to the language of the theory of structural dissociation of the personality (TSDP; Van der Hart et al., 2006). The results of this study showed clear differences between people with DID and actors. Moreover, distinctions were also observed when ANPs were thought to be activated versus when EPs (designated as the subtype of active defense) were activated. These observations indicate that "DID involves dissociative part-dependent resting-state differences" (Schlumpf et al., 2014, p. 1).

Utilizing neuroimaging data from preceding studies, Reinders et al. (2019) found that researchers using pattern classifiers of brain structure/morphology were able to accurately identify the MRI data from individuals with DID as distinct from the images from 'healthy controls.' Impressively, this machine-based system was able to classify true positives (DID) 72% of the time (sensitivity), and true negatives (healthy controls) were correctly identified 74% of the time (specificity). The results of this study indicate that the map of known brain structures and variations associated with DID was starting to fill in quite nicely.

Stepping toward building a functional connectivity 'fingerprint' of trauma-related dissociation, Lauren Lebois et al. (2021), out of McLean Hospital near Boston, Massachusetts (USA), tested whether "brain-based measures of dissociation are sufficiently sensitive and robust to enable individual-level estimation of dissociation severity based on brain function" (p. 166). Findings indicated, yes; fMRI data predicted the severity of trauma-related dissociative symptoms rated on self-report measures of dissociation (they used the 168-item severe dissociation scale from the MID). Intrinsic connectivity analysis of functional brain networks indicated patterns of *uniquely* aberrant network connectivity (differing from the normal course or pattern), with preliminary evidence pointing toward *dissociative experiences as dependent on connections* between regions in the default mode and frontoparietal control networks. "Because [this] model controlled for childhood trauma and PTSD symptom severity, this suggests that trauma-related dissociation has neurobiological substrates that are distinct from PTSD and childhood trauma load." (Lebois et al., 2021, p. 170). When this model is replicated and confirmed in future studies, it could be utilized to establish or objectively corroborate the diagnosis of a DD (e.g., for psychopharmacologic or forensic purposes).

The study of functional connectivity in PTSD+DS is relevant here. In another paper from Ruth Lanius' lab, Shaw et al. (2023) illustrated widespread functional *hyper*connectivity as a characteristic of PTSD+DS in relation to the default mode network (DMN). They hypothesized this to be a compensatory function to preserve global brain function when knowing or feeling would otherwise be too much for the person to tolerate. Several earlier publications from the same lab (Kearney & Lanius,

2022; Terpou et al., 2019) identified increased DMN activity to interfere with self-related processing of traumatic experiences. Terpou et al. (2019) stated that "[f]ragmentation of traumatic memories may result from the overwhelming affect that occurs during original encoding, thus interfering with the consolidation of the memory to long-term storage" (p. 9). As humans, we need sensory integration in order to have a sense of self and a continuous personal history (Lanius & Bergmann, 2014; Sidis & Goodhart, 1904/1968). When sensory information is unconsolidated, reliving of trauma-related sensory information can occur *without* episodic memory or autobiographical recall – as has been experienced by people with DDs. There is no episodic memory, or journey, without a traveler – or in this case, a self (Kearney & Lanius, 2022).

A Biomarker for Dissociative Amnesia

Dissociative amnesia – actions that are fully dissociated from one's conscious awareness – is one of the most specific symptoms that distinguishes DID from other diagnoses. Working with Reinders, Dimitrova et al. (2023) sought to identify a neurostructural biomarker for dissociative amnesia, specifically examining the hippocampus due to its known and vital role in memory. This study built upon previous findings, which pointed to a significant relationship between lower hippocampal volume, higher severity of childhood traumatization, and dissociative symptoms (Chalavi et al., 2015). Dimitrova et al. found *dissociative amnesia* (as measured by the DES) to be *significantly and negatively correlated with hippocampal volume*, while other items on the DES were not found to be significantly related. This relationship with dissociative amnesia was isolated to the CA1 hippocampal subfield of the hippocampus. Similar negative correlations were found between *emotional neglect* and bilateral global hippocampal volume. Thus, Dimitrova et al. proposed that dissociative amnesia and emotional neglect appear to be interlinked.

How else might the CA1 subfield functioning relate to psychotherapy for individuals with severe dissociation? Dimitrova et al. (2023) discussed their findings alongside earlier research observing the CA1 to be associated with memory impairment (*autobiographical* or self-referencing memory in particular [Bartsch et al., 2011]), and the misattribution of self-generated representations (memory) *as external* ('not me') (Chiu et al., 2019; Forrest, 2001). When people register their experiences as 'not me,' we argue that there are bigger considerations for EMDR therapy beyond mere 'processing of traumatic memories.' Can you imagine the dual-attention awareness deemed essential for reprocessing in EMDR therapy co-existing with these phenomena? Our conceptualization must expand to accommodate greater functional and psychological complexity.

The Psychological Domain

Psychological theories of dissociation are explanatory (positing how dissociation develops), descriptive (representing what dissociative experiences are like), or both. Owing to the wealth of resources available about different psychological models, we will not go into great depth here. However, we will touch very briefly upon the predominant theories that will inform later discussions in this book.

The *trauma model* explains that, when humans are unable to integrate ongoing stressors and traumas, they may develop dissociative coping, or DDs (Putnam, 1985; Ross, 2007). Kluft's (1985a) *four-factor theory* attempts to explain the context for the development of DDs by identifying specific conditions, in combination, that underlie them: (1) innate dissociative capacity; (2) exposure to overwhelming experiences (e.g., abuse); (3) underlying individual qualities and characteristics that would support the development of dissociative self-states; and (4) a lack of support from adults who can help the child transcend the overwhelming experience and protect them from future harm.

The TSDP (Van der Hart et al., 2006; Van der Hart & Steele, 2023), or the *structural model*, posits an explanation for and elaborates the features of DDs. According to TDSP, a child who has not yet developed an integrated sense of self is exposed to overwhelming experience, which is essentially traumatic; in response, the personality tends to divide along 'fault-lines,' which results in a 'structural dissociation' of the personality, in which dissociative structures lack integration. However, neither the trauma model nor TSDP adequately explains why some persons who are abused or neglected as children develop DDs, while others do not.

The *autohypnotic model* has a long lineage (Bliss, 1986; Ellenberger, 1970), but was sidelined by the trauma model and TSDP for some years. Dell (2017, 2019) dusted it off and, expanding upon Kluft's four-factor theory, proposed that only a subset of highly hypnotizable individuals (i.e., so-called *virtuosos*; Kihlstrom, 2004), under particular conditions, have the ability to develop a DD, specifically when they are subject to chronic, inescapable pain – regardless of whether it might be considered a 'big-T' trauma. (For a comprehensive discussion of this model, please see Coy, 2025.)

The Subjective/Phenomenological Domain

We have separated this model from the others discussed above because it is Paul Dell's third explanatory domain of dissociation, and also because it is especially relevant to the challenge of recognizing and conceptualizing the treatment of dissociative symptoms. According to Dell (2006a, p. 8), "the phenomena of pathological dissociation are recurrent, jarring intrusions into executive functioning and sense of self by self-states or alter personalities. Such dissociative phenomena are startling, alien invasions of one's mind, functioning, and experience." Based on this proposition, Dell (2006a, pp. 8–9) drew the following conclusions:

1. Pathological dissociation can affect every aspect of human experience;
2. Most phenomena of pathological dissociation are subjective and invisible;
3. There are two major kinds of pathological dissociation: intrusions and amnesias; and
4. Most dissociative symptoms are not fully dissociated from consciousness.

Arguably, Dell's third conclusion is not entirely true, particularly concerning depersonalization and derealization, which are also considered forms of pathological dissociation, both as a discrete disorder in the DSM and within the dissociative subtype of PTSD. Elsewhere, Dell (2019, p. 2) has suggested that "*the dissociation of the dissociative disorders* [emphasis added] has only one generative mechanism: autohypnotic maneuvers that distance the person from circumstances that cause pain, distress, and suffering." Because experiences of pathological dissociation are "overwhelmingly internal and subjective, not external and observable" (Dell, 2009c, p. 226), we find this model particularly relevant with respect to diagnostic assessment, to be addressed in Chapter 6.

Conclusion

Challenges abound for practitioners to recognize, acknowledge, understand, and treat dissociation. These challenges can be magnified when EMDR meets – and sometimes collides with – dissociation. Despite what practitioners may have been taught or assume, severe dissociation is a critical treatment consideration. Dissociative features may not be – and often are not – obvious to the casual observer, but this does not render them irrelevant. Contemporary neurobiological evidence validates the existence of DID and allied disorders, and diagnostic instruments have been developed to illuminate what *is* so often hidden. The literature demonstrating and explicating (disruptions in) functional connectivity in DDs is particularly relevant to EMDR therapy and will inform later chapters. A number of theoretical models offer us means to understand etiology and conceptualize treatment. Having laid this ground, what lies ahead in Chapter 2 is a closer examination of two important components of EMDR therapy in relation to dissociation: The hypothesized mechanisms of action of bilateral dual attention stimulation and the AIP model.

References

American Psychiatric Association. (1952). *Diagnostic and statistical manual of mental disorders*. Author.

American Psychiatric Association. (1968). *Diagnostic and statistical manual of mental disorders* (2nd ed.). Author.

American Psychiatric Association (1980). *DSM-III – Diagnostic and statistical manual of mental disorders* (3rd ed.). Author.

American Psychiatric Association (1987). *DSM-III-R – Diagnostic and statistical manual of mental disorders* (3rd ed., revised). Author.

American Psychiatric Association (1994). *DSM-IV – Diagnostic and statistical manual of mental disorders* (4th ed.). Author.

American Psychiatric Association (2000). *DSM-IV-R – Diagnostic and statistical manual of mental disorders* (4th ed., revised). Author.

American Psychiatric Association (2013). *DSM-5 – Diagnostic and statistical manual of mental disorders* (5th ed.). American Psychiatric Publishing.

American Psychiatric Association. (2022). *DSM-5-TR – Diagnostic and statistical manual of mental disorders* (5th ed., text revision). American Psychiatric Publishing.

Bartsch, T., Döhring, J., Rohr, A., Jansen, O., & Deuschl, G. (2011). CA1 neurons in the human hippocampus are critical for autobiographical memory, mental time travel, and autonoetic consciousness. *Proceedings of the National Academy of Sciences of the United States of America, 108*(42), 17562–17567. https://doi.org/10.1073/pnas.1110266108

Benito-Lozano, J., Arias-Merino, G., Gómez-Martínez, M., Arconada-López, B., Ruiz-García, B., Posada de la Paz, M., & Alonso-Ferreira, V. (2023). Psychosocial impact at the time of a rare disease diagnosis. *PloS One, 18*(7), e0288875. https://doi.org/10.1371/journal.pone.0288875

Bliss, E. L. (1986). *Multiple personality, allied disorders and hypnosis*. Oxford University Press.

Brand, B. L., Sar, V., Stavropoulos, P., Krüger, C., Korzekwa, M., Martínez-Taboas, A., & Middleton, W. (2016). Separating fact from fiction: An empirical examination of six myths about dissociative identity disorder. *Harvard Review of Psychiatry, 24*(4), 257–270. https://doi.org/10.1097/hrp.0000000000000100

Braun, B. G. (1988). The BASK model of dissociation. *Dissociation, 1*(1), 4–23. https://hdl.handle.net/1794/1276

Butler, C., Dorahy, M. J., & Middleton, W. (2019). The detachment and compartmentalization inventory (DCI): An assessment tool for two potentially distinct forms of dissociation. *Journal of Trauma & Dissociation, 20*(5), 526–547. https://doi.org/10.1080/15299732.2019.1597809

Chalavi, S., Vissia, E. M., Giesen, M. E., Nijenhuis, E. R., Draijer, N., Cole, J. H., Dazzan, P., Pariante, C. M., Madsen, S. K., Rajagopalan, P., Thompson, P. M., Toga, A. W., Veltman, D. J., & Reinders, A. A. T. S. (2015). Abnormal hippocampal morphology in dissociative identity disorder and post-traumatic stress disorder correlates with childhood trauma and dissociative symptoms. *Human Brain Mapping, 36*(5), 1692–1704. https://doi.org/10.1002/hbm.22730

Chiu, C.-D., Tollenaar, M. S., Yang, C.-T., Elzinga, B. M., Zhang, T.-Y., & Ho, H. L. (2019). The loss of the self in memory: Self-referential memory, childhood relational trauma, and dissociation. *Clinical Psychological Science, 7*(2), 265–282. https://doi.org/10.1177/2167702618804794

Corrigan, F. M., Young, H., & Christie-Sands, J. (2025). *Deep brain reorienting: Understanding the neuroscience of trauma, attachment wounding, and DBR psychotherapy*. Routledge. https://doi.org/10.4324/9781003431695

Coy, D. M. (2025). The autohypnotic model of dissociation. In A. M. Gómez & J. Hosey (Eds.), *The handbook of complex trauma and dissociation in children: Theory, research, and clinical applications* (pp. 89–106). Routledge. https://doi.org/10.4324/9781003350156-8

Coy, D. M., & Madere, J. A. (2023). Diagnosing the dissociative disorders: conceptual, theoretical, and practical considerations. In M. Dorahy & S. Gold (Eds), *Dissociation and the dissociative disorders: Past, present, future* (pp. 661–672). Routledge. https://doi.org/10.4324/9781003057314

Crook, L. (2022). *False memories: The deception that silenced millions*. Self-published.

Dalenberg, C. J., & Paulson, K. (2009). The case for the study of "normal" dissociative processes. In P. F. Dell & J. A. O'Neil (Eds.), *Dissociation and the dissociative disorders: DSM-V and beyond* (pp. 145–154). Routledge/Taylor & Francis Group. https://doi.org/10.4324/9780203893920

Dell, P. F. (2001). Why the diagnostic criteria for dissociative identity disorder should be changed. *Journal of Trauma & Dissociation, 2*(1), 7–37. https://doi.org/10.1300/J229v02n01_02

Dell, P. F. (2006a). A new model of dissociative identity disorder. *Psychiatric Clinics of North America, 29*(1), 1–26. https://doi.org/10.1016/j.psc.2005.10.013

Dell, P. F. (2006b). The multidimensional inventory of dissociation (MID): A comprehensive measure of pathological dissociation. *Journal of Trauma & Dissociation, 7*(2), 77–106. https://doi.org/10.1300/J229v07n02_06

Dell, P. F. (2009a). Understanding dissociation. In P. F. Dell & J. A. O'Neil (Eds.), *Dissociation and the dissociative disorders: DSM-V and beyond* (pp. 709–825). Routledge/Taylor & Francis Group. https://doi.org/10.4324/9780203893920

Dell, P. F. (2009b). The long struggle to diagnose multiple personality disorder (MPD): Partial MPD. In P. F. Dell & J. A. O'Neil (Eds.), *Dissociation and the dissociative disorders: DSM-V and beyond* (pp. 403–428). Routledge. https://doi.org/10.4324/9780203893920

Dell, P. F. (2009c). The phenomena of pathological dissociation. In P. F. Dell & J. A. O'Neil (Eds.), *Dissociation and the dissociative disorders: DSM-V and beyond* (pp. 225–237). Routledge. https://doi.org/10.4324/9780203893920

Dell, P. F. (2009d). The long struggle to diagnose multiple personality disorder (MPD): MPD. In P F. Dell & J. A. O'Neil (Eds.), *Dissociation and the dissociative disorders: DSM-V and beyond* (pp. 383–402). Routledge. https://doi.org/10.4324/9780203893920

Dell, P. F. (2017). Is high hypnotizability a necessary diathesis for pathological dissociation? *Journal of Trauma & Dissociation, 18*(1), 58–87. https://doi.org/10.1080/15299732.2016.1191579

Dell, P. F. (2019). Reconsidering the autohypnotic model of the dissociative disorders. *Journal of Trauma & Dissociation, 20*(1), 48–78. https://doi.org/10.1080/15299732.2018.1451806

Dimitrova, L. I., Dean, Schi L., Schlumpf, Y. R., Vissia, E. M., Nijenhuis, E., Chatzi, V., Jäncke, L., Veltman, D. J., Chalavi, S., & Reinders, A. (2023). A neurostructural biomarker of dissociative amnesia: A hippocampal study in dissociative identity disorder. *Psychological Medicine, 53*(3), 805–813. https://doi.org/10.1017/S0033291721002154

Ellenberger, H. F. (1970). *The discovery of the unconscious: The history and evolution of dynamic psychiatry*. Basic Books.

EMDR International Association (2017). *Basic training curriculum requirements.* www.emdria.org/emdr-training-education/emdr-training/emdr-training-provider-policies-guidelines/

EMDR International Association (2022). *Standards for EMDR basic training.* www.emdria.org/standards-for-emdr-basic-training-2/

EMDR International Association (2025). *Policies.* Retrieved May 26, 2025, from www.emdria.org/about-emdria/emdr-international-association-policies/

False Memory Syndrome Foundation (2013). *About FMSF – introduction.* www.fmsfonline.org/index.php?about=Intro

Figley, C. R., Ellis, A. E., Reuther, B. T., & Gold, S. N. (2017). The study of trauma: A historical overview. In S. N. Gold (Ed.), *APA handbook of trauma psychology: Foundations in knowledge* (pp. 1–11). American Psychological Association. https://doi.org/10.1037/0000019-001

Forgash, C., & Copeley, M. (Eds.) (2008). *Healing the heart of trauma and dissociation with EMDR and ego state therapy.* Springer Publishing Company.

Forrest, K. A. (2001). Toward an etiology of dissociative identity disorder: A neurodevelopmental approach. *Consciousness and Cognition, 10*(3), 259–293. https://doi.org/10.1006/ccog.2001.0493

Holmes, E. A., Brown, R. J., Mansell, W., Fearon, R. P., Hunter, E. C., Frasquilho, F., & Oakley, D. A. (2005). Are there two qualitatively distinct forms of dissociation? A review and some clinical implications. *Clinical Psychology Review, 25*(1), 1–23. https://doi.org/10.1016/j.cpr.2004.08.006

Hyland, P., Hamer, R., Fox, R., Vallières, F., Karatzias, T., Shevlin, M., & Cloitre, M. (2024). Is dissociation a fundamental component of ICD-11 complex post-traumatic stress disorder? *Journal of Trauma & Dissociation*, *25*(1), 45–61. https://doi.org/10.1080/15299732.2023.2231928

Hyland, P., Shevlin, M., Fyvie, C., Cloitre, M., & Karatzias, T. (2020). The relationship between ICD-11 PTSD, complex PTSD and dissociative experiences. *Journal of Trauma & Dissociation*, *21*(1), 62–72. https://doi.org/10.1080/15299732.2019.1675113

Kearney, B. E., & Lanius, R. A. (2022). The brain-body disconnect: A somatic sensory basis for trauma-related disorders. *Frontiers in Neuroscience, 16,* 1015749. https://doi.org/10.3389/fnins.2022.1015749

Kihlstrom, J. F. (2004). Hypnosis. In C. Spielberger (Ed.), *Encyclopedia of applied psychology* (pp. 243–248). Elsevier/Academic Press.

Kluft, R. P. (1985a). Childhood multiple personality disorder: predictors, clinical findings, and treatment results. In R. P. Kluft (Ed.), *Childhood antecedents of multiple personality* (pp. 167–196). American Psychiatric Press.

Kluft, R. P. (1985b). The natural history of multiple personality disorder. In R. P. Kluft (Ed.), *Childhood antecedents of multiple personality* (pp. 197–238). American Psychiatric Press.

Kluft, R. P. (1989). Iatrogenic creation of new alter personalities. *Dissociation, 2*(2), 83–91. https://hdl.handle.net/1794/1428

Kluft R. P. (1991). Clinical presentations of multiple personality disorder. *The Psychiatric Clinics of North America, 14*(3), 605–629. https://doi.org/10.1016/S0193-953X(18)30291-0

Kluft, R. P. (2013). *Shelter from the storm: Processing the traumatic memories of DID/DDNOS patients with the fractionated abreaction technique.* CreateSpace.

Kluft, R. P., Steinberg, M., & Spitzer, R. L. (1988). DSM-III-R revisions in the dissociative disorders: An exploration of their derivation and rationale. *Dissociation, 1*(1), 39–46. hdl.handle.net/1794/1329

Knipe, J. (2010a). Back of the head scale (BHS). In M. Luber (Ed.), *EMDR scripted protocols: Special populations* (pp. 233–234). Springer Publishing Company.

Knipe, J. (2010b). The method of constant installation of present orientation and safety (CIPOS). In M. Luber (Ed.), *EMDR scripted protocols: Special populations* (pp. 235–241). Springer Publishing Company.

Lanius, R. A., Brand, B., Vermetten, E., Frewen, P. A., & Spiegel, D. (2012). The dissociative subtype of posttraumatic stress disorder: rationale, clinical and neurobiological evidence, and implications. *Depression and Anxiety, 29*(8), 701–708. https://doi.org/10.1002/da.21889

Lanius, R. A., Vermetten, E., Loewenstein, R. J., Brand, B., Schmahl, C., Bremner, J. D., & Spiegel, D. (2010). Emotion modulation in PTSD: Clinical and neurobiological evidence for a dissociative subtype. *American Journal of Psychiatry, 167*(6), 640–647. https://doi.org/10.1176/appi.ajp.2009.09081168

Lanius, U. F., & Bergmann, U. (2014). Dissociation, EMDR, and adaptive information processing: The role of sensory stimulation and sensory awareness. In U. F. Lanius, S. L. Paulsen, & F. M. Corrigan (Eds.), *Neurobiology and treatment of traumatic dissociation: Towards an embodied self* (pp. 213–242). Springer Publishing Company.

Lanius, U. F., Paulsen, S. L., & Corrigan, F. M. (2014). Dissociation: Cortical deafferentation and the loss of self. In U. F. Lanius, S. L. Paulsen, & F. M. Corrigan (Eds.), *Neurobiology and treatment of traumatic dissociation: Towards an embodied self* (pp. 5–28). Springer Publishing Company.

Lazrove, S., & Fine, C. G. (1996). The use of EMDR in patients with dissociative identity disorder. *Dissociation, 9*(4), 289–299. hdl.handle.net/1794/1778

Lebois, L. A. M., Li., M., Baker, J. T., Wolf, J. D., Wang, D., Lambros, A. M., Grinspoon, E., Winternitz, S., Ren, J., Gonenc, A., Gruber, S. A., Ressler, K. J., Liu, H., & Kaufman, M. L. (2021). Large-scale functional brain network architecture changes associated with trauma-related dissociation. *American Journal of Psychiatry, 178*(2), 165–173. https://doi.org/10.1176/appi.ajp.2020.19060647

Leeds, A., Madere, J., & Coy, D. M. (2022). Beyond the DES-II: Screening for dissociative disorders in EMDR therapy. *Journal of EMDR Practice and Research, 16*(1), 25–38. https://doi.org/10.1891/EMDR-D-21-2021-00019

Loewenstein R. J. (2018). Dissociation debates: Everything you know is wrong. *Dialogues in Clinical Neuroscience, 20*(3), 229–242. https://doi.org/10.31887/DCNS.2018.20.3/rloewenstein

Madere, J. A., & Coy, D. M. (2022, April 2-4). *EMDR and dissociation: Learning from the past, looking to the future* [Conference presentation]. 39th Annual Conference of the International Society for the Study of Trauma and Dissociation: Post-traumatic growth in a dissociative world. Seattle, Washington, United States. cfas.isst-d.org/content/emdr-dissociation-learning-past-looking-future-2 – group-tabs-node-course-default4

Middleton, W., & Dorahy, M. J. (2024). *Contemporary perspectives on freud's seduction theory and psychotherapy: Revisiting masson's 'the assault on truth'*. Routledge. https://doi.org/10.4324/9781003431466

Paulsen, S. (1995). Eye movement desensitization and reprocessing: Its cautious use in the dissociative disorders. *Dissociation, 8*(1), 32–44. hdl.handle.net/1794/1592

Piper, A., & Merskey A., (2004a). The persistence of folly: a critical examination of dissociative identity disorder. Part I. The excesses of an improbable concept. *Canadian Journal of Psychiatry, 49*(9), 592–600. https://doi.org/10.1177/070674370404900904

Piper, A., & Merskey A., (2004b). The persistence of folly: Critical examination of dissociative identity disorder. Part II. The defense and decline of multiple personality or dissociative identity disorder. *Canadian Journal of Psychiatry, 49*(10), 678–683. https://doi.org/10.1177/070674370404901005

Putnam, F. W. (1985). Dissociation as a response to extreme trauma. In R. P. Kluft (Ed.), *Childhood antecedents of multiple personality* (pp. 65–97). American Psychiatric Press.

Reinders, A. A. T. S., Marquand, A. F., Schlumpf, Y. R., Chalavi, S., Vissia, E. M., Nijenhuis, E. R. S., & Veltman, D. J. (2019). Aiding the diagnosis of dissociative identity disorder: Pattern recognition study of brain biomarkers. *British Journal of Psychiatry, 215*(3), 536–544. https://doi.org/10.1192/bjp.2018.255

Reinders, A. A., Willemsen, A. T., den Boer, J. A., Vos, H. P., Veltman, D. J., & Loewenstein, R. J. (2014). Opposite brain emotion-regulation patterns in identity states of dissociative identity disorder: A PET study and neurobiological model. *Psychiatry Research, 223*(3), 236–243. https://doi.org/10.1016/j.pscychresns.2014.05.005

Ross, C. A. (2007). *The trauma model: A solution to the problem of comorbidity in psychiatry.* (2nd ed.). Manitou Communications.

Schlumpf, Y. R., Reinders, A. A., Nijenhuis, E. R., Luechinger, R., van Osch, M. J., & Jäncke, L. (2014). Dissociative part-dependent resting-state activity in dissociative identity disorder: A controlled FMRI perfusion study. *PLoS One, 9*(6), e98795. https://doi.org/10.1371/journal.pone.0098795

Shapiro, F. (1995). *Eye movement desensitization and reprocessing: Basic principles, protocols, and procedures*. The Guilford Press.

Shapiro, F. (2001). *Eye movement desensitization and reprocessing: Basic principles, protocols, and procedures* (2nd ed.). The Guilford Press.

Shapiro, F. (2018). *Eye Movement Desensitization and Reprocessing (EMDR) therapy: Basic principles, protocols and procedures* (3rd ed.). The Guilford Press.

Shaw, S. B., Terpou, B. A., Densmore, M. et al. (2023). Large-scale functional hyperconnectivity patterns in trauma-related dissociation: An rs-fMRI study of PTSD and its dissociative subtype. *Nature Mental Health 1*, 711–721. https://doi.org/10.1038/s44220-023-00115-y

Sidis, B. (1898). *The psychology of suggestion: A research into the subconscious nature of man and society*. D. Appleton and Company.

Sidis, B. (1909). Studies in psychopathology: The psychotherapeutic value of the hypnoidal state. *Boston Medical and Surgical Journal, 161*(8), 242–247.

Sidis, B., & Goodhart, S. P. (1968). *Multiple personality: An experimental investigation into the nature of human individuality*. Greenwood Press. (Original work published 1904)

Sims, R., Michaleff, Z. A., Glasziou, P., & Thomas, R. (2021). Consequences of a diagnostic label: A systematic scoping review and thematic framework. *Frontiers in Public Health, 9*, 725877. https://doi.org/10.3389/fpubh.2021.725877

Spiegel, D. (1993). Multiple posttraumatic personality disorder. In R. P. Kluft & C. G. Fine (Eds.), *Clinical perspectives on multiple personality disorder* (pp. 87–100). American Psychiatric Press.

Swart, S., Wildschut, M., Draijer, N., Langeland, W., & Smit, J. H. (2020). Dissociative subtype of posttraumatic stress disorder or PTSD with comorbid dissociative disorders: Comparative evaluation of clinical profiles. *Psychological Trauma: Theory, Research, Practice and Policy, 12*(1), 38–45. https://doi.org/10.1037/tra0000474

Terpou, B. A., Densmore, M., Théberge, J., Thome, J., Frewen, P., McKinnon, M. C., & Lanius, R. A. (2019). The threatful self: Midbrain functional connectivity to cortical midline and parietal regions during subliminal trauma-related processing in PTSD. *Chronic Stress, 3,* 2470547019871369 https://doi.org/10.1177/2470547019871369

Thompson-Hollands, J., Jun, J. J., & Sloan, D. L. (2017). The association between peritraumatic dissociation and PTSD symptoms: The mediating role of negative beliefs about the self. *Journal of Traumatic Stress, 30*(2), 190–194. https://doi.org/10.1002/jts.22179

Van der Hart, O., Nijenhuis, E. R. S., & Steele, K. (2006). *The haunted self: Structural dissociation and the treatment of chronic traumatization*. W. W. Norton & Company.

Van der Hart, O., & Steele, K. (2023). *The theory of trauma-related structural dissociation of the personality*. In M. J. Dorahy, S. N. Gold, & J. A. O'Neil (Eds.), *Dissociation and the dissociative disorders: Past, present, future* (2nd ed.) (pp. 263–280). Routledge. https://doi.org/10.4324/9781003057314

Van der Kolk, B. A., Weisaeth, L., & Van der Hart, O. (1996). History of trauma in psychiatry. In B. A. van der Kolk, A. C. MacFarlane, & Weisaeth, L. (Eds.),

Traumatic stress: The effects of overwhelming experience on mind, body, and society (pp. 47–74). The Guilford Press.

Voorendonk, E. M., De Jongh, A., Rozendaal, L., & Van Minnen, A. (2020). Trauma-focused treatment outcome for complex PTSD patients: Results of an intensive treatment programme. *European Journal of Psychotraumatology, 11*(1), 1783955. https://doi.org/10.1080/20008198.2020.1783955

Waller, N., Putnam, F. W., & Carlson, E. B. (1996). Types of dissociation and dissociative types: A taxometric analysis of dissociative experiences. *Psychological Methods, 1*(3), 300–321. https://doi.org/10.1037/1082-989X.1.3.300

Weathers, F. W., Bovin, M. J., Lee, D. J., Sloan, D. M., Schnurr, P. P., Kaloupek, D. G., Keane, T. M., & Marx, B. P. (2018). The clinician-administered PTSD scale for DSM–5 (CAPS-5): Development and initial psychometric evaluation in military veterans. *Psychological Assessment, 30*(3), 383–395. https://doi.org/10.1037/pas0000486

World Health Organization. (2018). *ICD-11: International classification of diseases*. 11th Revision.icd.who.int/

Zoet, H. A., Wagenmans, A., Van Minnen, A., & De Jongh, A. (2018). Presence of the dissociative subtype of PTSD does not moderate the outcome of intensive trauma-focused treatment for PTSD. *European Journal of Psychotraumatology, 9*(1), 1468707. https://doi.org/10.1080/20008198.2018.1468707

Chapter 2

The AIP Model and EMDR Therapy Meet Dissociation

D. Michael Coy and Jennifer A. Madere

Introduction

Since the 1990s, several practitioners have developed adaptations of eye movement desensitization and reprocessing (EMDR) therapy methods to *treat* dissociation. However, the adaptive information processing (AIP) model has remained intact and unmodified. Considering that Shapiro (2018, p. 26) described AIP as a "working hypothesis only" and "subject to modification based on further laboratory and clinical observation," it seems surprising that the model has not changed or even been debated much since its introduction in the 1990s (see Rydberg et al., 2024). The EMDR International Association's *EMDR Therapy Basic Training Standards* (2025, p. 15) state that "The AIP model guides history taking, case conceptualization, treatment planning, intervention, and predicts treatment outcome."

Is this true for dissociation? Early on, Lazrove and Fine (1996, p. 297) critiqued the AIP model (as explicated by Paulsen [1995]), for both the vagueness of the term 'neural network' and the lack of distinction between a "failure to integrate experience during trauma (integration failure)" and structural dissociation. We share their concern, as we have repeatedly encountered challenges in applying the AIP model to conceptualize treating persons with structural dissociation.

The AIP model was developed through Shapiro's use of EMD and its evolutionary successor, the 'standard protocol' of EMDR, treating people with posttraumatic stress disorder (PTSD) and complex trauma *without* severe dissociative symptoms (i.e., distinct self-states and/or pervasive retrograde or contemporaneous amnesia). For this reason, the model unavoidably relies upon the assumption that all people possess both (1) an adequately integrated sense of self *before* overwhelmingly painful experience intrudes and (2) some degree of explicit awareness of their wounding experience. People who experience structural dissociation and meet

DOI: 10.4324/9781003410201-3

criteria for dissociative disorders (DDs) often possess neither of these (American Psychiatric Association, 2022). Additionally, therapists have for decades observed how bilateral dual-attention stimulation (BL-DAS) may be either unpredictably and rapidly dysregulating or ineffectual as a catalyst for change in individuals with complex trauma and dissociation. The neurobiological correlates for dissociation that we began to explore in Chapter 1 point the way to understanding why EMDR sometimes does not work so well in the treatment of dissociation.

In this chapter, we will first discuss the hypothesized mechanisms of action in EMDR therapy as they pertain to the interaction of BL-DAS and dissociative features. With that in mind, we will turn attention to the development and basic tenets of the AIP model. We will then revisit the AIP model to delve more deeply into its intricacies, illuminate its dissociative 'gaps' and propose a means for bridging these to accommodate dissociation and conceptualize the treatment of DDs.

Mechanisms of Action: EMDR Therapy, BL-DAS, and Dissociation

Questions regarding *how* exactly EMDR works, as well as for whom and under what circumstances, arose early on in the development of the approach and remain an active topic of investigation. According to Francine Shapiro (2018), it is both the procedural elements of EMDR and the AIP model that set EMDR therapy apart from other approaches.

Practically speaking, beyond the procedural elements of the eight phases and three temporal prongs, what sets EMDR therapy apart in our eyes is the use of alternating BL-DAS. BL-DAS takes the form of eye movements, as well as tactile and auditory stimulation. Several hypotheses have been proposed and tested to clarify the mechanisms of action spurred by BL-DAS. The impact of BL-DAS is of particular salience for its use in the face of more severe dissociation. Given how neural models have demonstrated disruptions in functional connectivity in subjects with the dissociative subtype of PTSD (PTSD+DS) and the DDs (Chapter 1), you may be curious about how those findings and differences overlap with the mechanisms of action in EMDR.

How BL-DAS Works

How BL-DAS works is particularly relevant to the use of EMDR therapy in treating DDs because it appears that there is something happening that can be very effective for some people – and very destabilizing for others. Shapiro (2018, p. 357) wrote that

> the addition of the eye movements may cause another configuration of physiological *states* [emphasis added] and responses to *intrude* [emphasis added] on earlier associations. This may, in turn, cause a *disruption* [emphasis added] of the complex of habitual physiological responses elicited by the traumatic memory. The disruption engendered by the simultaneous dual configurations may allow further processing to occur.

That kind of disruption – of maladaptive patterns – is seemingly positive, but it can also have a detrimental effect when dissociative gaps are bridged prematurely via the use of BL-DAS. The associations that BL-DAS facilitates can be destabilizing when the person is not prepared to live with the results of the new or restored knowledge of their past and present experiences. The following sections will focus on the hypothesized mechanisms, what the research says about these, and most specifically, where these mechanisms bump into and overlap with how the literature has found dissociation to impact brain functioning.

Current Hypotheses and Supporting Evidence

At least seven distinct hypotheses have garnered recent scientific attention and found some empirical support (Leeds, 2016; Landin-Romero et al., 2018). First, we will focus on the three most researched hypotheses, which are based upon: (1) working memory taxation, (2) slow wave sleep/memory consolidation, and (3) the orienting reflex. Later discussion will touch upon newer models rooted in a more contemporary, brain-based view of psychopathology.

A prevalent hypothesis focuses on the dual-attention component – the distraction – that eye movements or a combination of stimuli provides to *compete with* the traumatic memory material. The emphasis here is on the taxation of working memory and the decrease in the vividness of intense affect experienced while recalling the traumatic experience. Recent publications by Rameckers et al. (2024) and De Jongh et al. (2024) offer summaries of the evidence supporting the working memory taxation hypothesis. Evidence supporting this hypothesis explains how the 'DAS' aspect of BL-DAS works; however, endorsing this explanation in isolation is problematic for two reasons. First, the bilateral component of the stimulation applied is not always investigated within these studies – in some cases, it is considered irrelevant. Second, those who ascribe to this viewpoint do not consider dissociation or PTSD+DS at all; the term "dissociat…" is entirely absent from both the Ramekers et al. and De Jongh et al. articles. This is particularly notable given that they claim to address all eight phases of EMDR therapy, which ought to include *at least screening* for dissociation. Nonetheless, the De Jongh article mentions the utility of EMDR for Complex PTSD, and Ramekers et al. purportedly measures severity of symptoms using the CAPS-5 (Clinician-Administered PTSD Scale for DSM-5; Weathers et al., 2018), which screens for PTSD+DS but not complex dissociative symptoms.

Sleep-related hypotheses have circulated since the origination of EMDR therapy due to the nature of Francine Shapiro's initial discovery and investigation of the role of eye movements. The initial rapid eye movement sleep hypothesis did not hold up to scientific inquiry, possibly because eye movements during EMDR are not saccadic but rather what is termed 'smooth pursuit' movements. Marco Pagani and colleagues in Italy studied and wrote about this hypothesis most specifically (Pagani & Carletto, 2017). Brain activity measured via qEEG during sets of BL-DAS has been found to strongly resemble slow wave sleep (e.g., Harper et al., 2009). Slow wave sleep is characterized by delta waves and is known to play a role in memory (re)consolidation. This model "proposes that bilateral stimulation during EMDR might reproduce the neurophysiological conditions favorable for memory integration in associative neocortex, weakening the perception of the traumatic memory, reducing its vividness and inducing a sense of relaxation and safety" (Pagani et al., 2017, p. 5). Although other researchers have not taken interest in this hypothesis for EMDR directly, the role of slow wave sleep in PTSD has been further investigated (Richards et al., 2020), as well as its relation to dissociation as an altered state of consciousness (Sodré et al., 2023). We think that the slow-wave sleep explanation better addresses the question of how the 'BL' of BL-DAS works.

A third hypothesis posits that the BL-DAS elicits a recurrent orienting reflex and subsequent parasympathetic or relaxation response. Many clients report finding BL-DAS, especially the tactile variety, to be soothing or calming (reviewed in Pagani et al., 2017). The idea is that the person orients to the external and changing (alternating bilateral) stimulation as a neutral stimulus, which interrupts the overfocus on or avoidance of the traumatic material. This hypothesis is complementary to the working memory taxation viewpoint in how the BL-DAS *interrupts* a hypervigilant or fixed attention on the disturbing material.

More recently, the orienting hypothesis has been knitted into other frameworks such as the network balance model (Chamberlin, 2019), in which psychopathology is suggested to result from aberrant functioning of the brain's three large-scale neural networks (citing Menon, 2011):

1. the default mode network, which manages functions related to autobiographical memory, self-oriented and social cognition, and imagining the future;

2. the central executive network (CEN) facilitates engagement with the external world, goal-directed attention, and execution of actions; and
3. the salience network (SN), which mediates interoception, emotional processing, and network switching.

"The SN facilitates 'bottom-up' stimulus-driven attention that drives orientation to what is most emotionally charged. The CEN facilitates 'top-down' goal-directed attention to what is most relevant" (Chamberlin, 2019, p. 133). This model proposes that voluntary engagement with BL-DAS and distressing memory material assists in rebalancing these networks by restoring more emphasis to the CEN. You may recognize some of these terms from our discussion of the neurobiological correlates of dissociation, as discussed in Chapter 1.

The orienting response and triple-network hypotheses are compelling; however, we wonder about their limitations, especially when it comes to PTSD+DS and more severe dissociation. For instance, the orienting reflex and orienting tension have been proposed as a protective and stabilizing anchor in another trauma-processing modality, Deep Brain Reorienting (DBR; Corrigan et al., 2025). In our experience, EMDR often speeds things up such that this benefit is missed, along with the shock that is held in the body. Shapiro presumed that "since this orienting response occurs during an EMDR session in the absence of actual danger, the reflex is followed by the relaxation associated with parasympathetic activity" (2018, p. 357). That is an assumption, especially when it comes to dissociation, because there may be actual or perceived danger within the person's self-system and how they are perceiving the therapist and the immediate environment at that moment. We also wonder about the parasympathetic response that is observed in response to BL-DAS – could this be conflated with overmodulation, which has been observed as a common function of PTSD+DS? Or, could a collapsed immobility response be mistaken for calm? The potential for a dissociative response of hypo-arousal to be missed by both the practitioner and client seems quite plausible.

Neurobiological mechanisms associated with the effects of BL-DAS overlap with the neural structures and processes associated with dissociative symptoms. For instance, an animal model study by Baek et al. (2019) published in the prestigious scientific journal, *Nature*, identified a pathway associated with fear extinction via bilateral eye movements. They traced the neural pathways activated by bilateral eye movements as starting from:

1. the superior colliculus (SC; portion of midbrain involved in visual-attentional processing and multisensory integration); to

2. the mediodorsal thalamus (MD; relay station to the prefrontal cortex and amygdala); and finally, to
3. the basolateral complex of the amygdala (involved in encoding fear and fear extinction).

The SC-MD circuit was necessary to prevent the return of fear and extinguish the fear response. This is the closest model yet to explain exactly what happens during reprocessing. Szeska et al. (2023) followed up on these findings to investigate whether a similar effect could be observed in humans. Their hypothesis was supported, but did not exactly replicate Baek et al. (2019). Because "increased SC activation" (Szeska et al., 2023, p. 65) was simply presumed and no direct neural measures were used, the generalizability of this study to the human population has yet to be fully verified. But we wondered, *what if this circuit is inhibited – or overmodulated?*

Olivé et al. (2018), in a study involving human subjects, zoomed in on how the SC functions in the role of detecting and initiating a response to a perceived threat (the orienting response), within the innate alarm system (IAS). They compared participants who met criteria for PTSD versus those with PTSD+DS. In fMRI data, resting-state data for persons with PTSD+DS did *not* indicate functional connectivity between the SC and the frontal lobe, indicating that the superior colliculi and IASs are *inhibited* when dissociative symptoms are present. These findings demonstrated that "the SC is involved in the IAS frontal limbic pathway for modulation of emotional responses among the PTSD group only" (p. 569). Responses such as overmodulation, depersonalization, and thwarted or passive responses to threat are likely when the IAS is inhibited. They also observed *increased* functional connection between the SC and the temporoparietal junction in the PTSD +DS group – which is likely to result in emotional blunting and somatic abnormalities such as out-of-body experiences.

This and other research illuminating the neural models of dissociation (see Chapter 1) validate and begin to explain why trauma processing therapies such as EMDR *can* be useful for individuals who experience dissociative symptoms, *and* why they often work differently. 'Differently' can be problematic when EMDR does not work as it's 'supposed to.' Based on our reading of the research, this could be because the pathways upon which EMDR's mechanisms of action rely are inhibited. Since dissociation poses challenges for EMDR therapy in practice, what implications does this have for applicability of the AIP model? We wondered that, too.

The AIP Model

Shapiro (1995) notes that the development of the AIP model followed her discovery of and subsequent experimentation with the effect of bilateral eye movements upon traumatic memories. Although she initially recognized only the desensitization effect of bilateral eye movements, her understanding of their impact evolved over time. Shapiro soon realized that the original 'Eye Movement Desensitization' (Shapiro, 1989) was much more than a simple behavioral technique (Beckman, 2001). The result was a model positing EMDR as a means for processing information through interconnected memory networks composed of both adaptive information and dysfunctionally stored memory material, with bilateral dual-attention stimulus employed systematically via a standardized, phased approach (Luber & Shapiro, 2009).

Shapiro's initial explanatory model, dubbed Accelerated Information Processing, was published in the first edition of the EMDR therapy text (Shapiro, 1995). Even then, she observed that, "When the disturbing events have been processed, they resolve *adaptively* into a more neutral form [...] [emphasis added]" (Shapiro, 1995, p. 49). In 2009, Shapiro described the transition from Accelerated to Adaptive Information Processing:

> When I wrote the first text, in 1995, I called the model the accelerated information processing model and then changed its name for the publication of the [second edition] in 2001 to the adaptive information processing model. Because, whereas in 1995, I was concentrating on the speed and efficiency of EMDR effects, what became clear was that the term "accelerated" was limiting the model. The concept of "adaptive" was really the issue because the information processing system itself would be moving the dysfunction toward adaptive resolution. And it also became apparent that the model's principles were able to explain the phenomena that we see in any form of psychotherapy whether it is progressing rapidly or not. So, the name adaptive information processing seemed to be more on the mark.
>
> (Luber & Shapiro, 2009, p. 220)

As the thinking of Francine Shapiro and other early EMDR therapists evolved, the AIP model came to be described as both *integrative* – including elements of and working alongside or within other models – and *distinct*, owing to its emphasis on adaptive resolution of disturbing memories and the use of specific procedures (Shapiro, 2018). In a review marking 30 years since the initial EMD study, Louise Maxfield (2019) stated that "EMDR therapy differs from other trauma-focused treatments that seek to decrease fear, reduce avoidant behaviors, or change problematic cognitions. Instead, EMDR therapy works on changing the memory" (pp. 239–240).

Shapiro believed that the brain is oriented towards health and has the natural ability to heal – given favorable circumstances. Similarly, the AIP model postulates that there is an innate, adaptive, physiological information processing system in the brain that metabolizes new experiences. Incoming sensory information is integrated and connected to related information that is already stored in memory networks, allowing us to make sense of our experiences. Memories are stored in associated, state-dependent neural networks and are the basis of perception, attitude, and behavior – thus contributing to pathology and health (Shapiro, 2018).

Traumatization occurs when the normal functioning of the AIP system is disrupted due to emotional overwhelm, which inhibits the normal processing and integration of experience. Instead, the overwhelming experience is 'frozen' as a memory in a state-specific form in isolated neural networks, thus disconnected from networks in which adaptive information is encoded. The AIP model postulates that these unprocessed or dysfunctionally stored memories lead to symptoms such as persistent intrusive thoughts, waking flashbacks, nightmares, negative emotions, negative beliefs about self, unpleasant body sensations, and maladaptive responses. New experiences are incorporated into an expanding network that may reinforce rather than disconfirm the previous experiences.

In EMDR therapy practice, an established protocol guides the therapist to first access and assess the cognitive, emotional, and somatosensory aspects of a dysfunctionally stored memory. Then, the unprocessed material that comprises this memory is systematically desensitized (metabolized, reprocessed). Concurrently, these (now less isolated) neural networks begin to spontaneously connect with networks that hold adaptive and/or positively valenced material. The processes of association and generalization allow the previously frozen or isolated material to be linked with positive, disconfirming, and/or adaptive material, leading to the adaptive resolution and (re)consolidation of the memory.

Expanding AIP

The limitations of the AIP model as it currently exists have become increasingly evident in light of newer insights offered by scientific study of the mechanisms of action in EMDR therapy, and continuing research on the application of EMDR therapy to issues beyond PTSD (e.g., Maxfield, 2019). In a comparative analysis and narrative review of proposals to bolster the AIP model, Rydberg et al. (2024) asked whether AIP holds up to scientific inquiry and debate and what may be needed to deepen and update AIP to reflect emerging understandings. This review examined frameworks that consider the brain (and symptoms) only from the amygdala up, with no mention of dissociation. However, two of the models they identified *do* seem to connect with what we know about PTSD+DS and DDs.

Rydberg et al. (2024) argue that Khalfa and Touzet's (2017) theory of neural cognition explains why *alternating* BL-DAS is more efficient than *non-alternating* (i.e., simultaneous constant or intermittent, but no left-right alternation). According to Khalfa and Touzet (2017), "Alternation and intermittency are discontinuities that do not favor predictions. Since predictions authorize inhibition, less predictable [BL-DAS] are more efficient" (p. 5) than stimulation that is not alternating or not intermittent. They also note that alternating BL-DAS leads to more widespread neuronal activation across different areas of the brain than does non-alternating BL-DAS. In our view, these findings align with what we have observed in treating dissociative clients in clinical practice. First, some clients find BL-DAS to be disconcerting from the outset, in part due to the unpredictability of the associations that may arise. Second, more neuronal activation across different, connected brain areas, particularly in the face of more severe dissociation, may pose an increased risk either of under-accessing (resulting in chronic 'looping' or no reprocessing at all), over-accessing ('flooding'), or both. We will elaborate upon this further in Chapters 3 and 4.

The biopsychosocial AIP model (Cotraccia, 2012, 2022) is also suggested by Rydberg et al. (2024) as complementary. This broadening of AIP emphasizes how the therapeutic relationship offers adaptive information that is often missing via a self-modeling system. Many authors have commented on how AIP de-emphasizes the relational process that is ubiquitous in trauma-focused psychotherapy (we do not think this is an issue inherent to AIP).

Minding the Gaps Between AIP and Dissociation

None of the new 'angles' on AIP address its conceptual gaps in the face of severe dissociation. Although the AIP model (implicitly) considers the potential impact of adverse experience in the formation of explicit memory, it does not speak to the impact of adversity upon *identity* formation. Because of this, we find AIP insufficient for conceptualizing the treatment of DDs. We have attempted to supplement the AIP model to accommodate severe dissociation, drawing upon scholarship that significantly predates Francine Shapiro's discoveries. Psychoanalyst Sándor Ferenczi (1929/1994) wrote that "even a retrograde movement, if it be in the direction of an earlier tradition, undeservedly abandoned, may advance the truth...." It was in this spirit that we decided to look back in time to the work of Boris Sidis. We were intrigued by his ideas about the functional association and dissociation of neural connections and the roots of psychopathology.

Information Processing, Memory, and the Self

Sidis's conceptualization of healthy development and the impacts and treatment of trauma not only aligns with Francine Shapiro's but also prefigures central elements of the AIP model by over 90 years. Here, we will set Shapiro's and Sidis's respective thinking side-by-side, with the intent to more definitively bridge the gaps between AIP/EMDR and dissociation. Describing AIP, Shapiro (2006, p. 8) states:

- the "information processing system is intrinsic, physical, [and] adaptive,"
- "this physical system is geared to integrate external and internal experiences,"
- "these experiences are translated into physically stored memories,"
- "the memories are stored in associative memory networks," and suggests that "new experiences link into these [associative] memory networks"

Beyond this level of organization of experience, AIP offers only that memories held in associative networks are the "basis of perception, response, attitudes, self-concept, personality traits, [and] symptoms" (Shapiro, 2006, p. 7). We read this as an essentially cognitive-behavioral conceptualization.

Sidis (1898) offers a bit more granularity to the concept of memory. He refers to a physiological process that facilitates the "association and aggregation of psychic contents [experiential material]" (Sidis, p. 208), which he refers to as *moment-contents*, via functional neuronal connectivity. These experiential materials are visual, auditory, tactile, gustatory, olfactory, and inner-body sensations. (An example might be all the sensory elements to which you are exposed in your environment as you sit reading this book – including the words, the typeface of the text, even qualities of the medium by which you are reading it – as well as how your physiology reacts to all that.) Upon being registered by the brain in a single moment of experience, these are synthesized into what Sidis describes as *moment-consciousness*, or what we would call *memories*. In Sidis's (1898) conceptualization, the different elements of which memories are composed are organized around focal points that represent their most salient aspect(s). This salience is influenced by one's focus of attention, whether voluntary or involuntary. Sidis characterizes this as the stage of *primary* synthesis, noting that "[m]ental synthesis of psychic content in the unity of a *moment-consciousness* [i.e., a memory] is a fundamental principle of psychology" (Sidis, 1914, p. 117). At this primary stage of synthesis, any entity with a nervous system is capable of a degree of *desultory consciousness*, meaning that it possesses a basic awareness of its surroundings and can respond to stimuli.

From the aggregation of experience in the form of memories arises a consciousness composed of increasingly sophisticated networks of experience, with new, similar experiences and the re-enlivening of elements of past experience (both intentional and spontaneous) commingling and reinforcing the functional connectivity that was first established at the deeper, more elementary levels of neuronal development (e.g., for a human, in utero and during infancy and early childhood). At this *reproductive* level of consciousness, there is a synthesis and awareness of lived experience but a lack of capacity for recognition or reflection upon one's experience. Owing to this absence of recognition, Sidis describes this as *desultory self-consciousness*. According to Sidis, this basic level of self-consciousness lacks its own self-directed purpose, aims, motivation, or capacity for either discernment between the past and present or self-reflection. It can know, and thus report, experience, but because it cannot self-motivate, it can only follow directives. This is the *secondary* stage of synthesis (Sidis, 1898). Under non-traumagenic conditions, this would be the level of self-consciousness at which healthy ego states[1] would exist (Federn, 1952; see also Part IV of this book).

It is only at a yet-higher level of neural network sophistication, beyond *reproductive consciousness*, that planning, goal-directed behavior, time-awareness, and self-reflection are possible. Although Sidis does not label this stage of synthesis, we can extend his thinking and dub it *tertiary*, the 'home' of the central executive self, which he referred to as *recognitive consciousness* (Sidis, 1898). He offers that,

> This form of self-consciousness has a series of [memories], and all the moments in the series can be included in and owned by each present moment of self-consciousness. The [memories] are intimately linked and intertwined. [...] This type of consciousness possesses synthesis [at the level of memories], reproduction [at the level of reproductive consciousness], recognition [at the level of recognitive consciousness], *personality*, *personal identity*, and is represented by man's mental activity.
> (Sidis, 1898, p. 200)

This is the level of *synthetic self-consciousness*, at which a non-dissociative individual would *recognize* a coherent, unified sense of self – hence the descriptor 'recognitive.'[2] That coherent sense of self results from both adequate vertical and horizontal integration of neural networks (Lanius et al., 2014) at all three of Sidis's (1898) stages of synthesis. Sidis observed that the "characteristic trait" of the highest level of self-consciousness, specifically in the context of "the ordinary stimuli of the environment," is "a continuous process of association and dissociation of constellations" (Sidis, 1898, p. 211). He uses the term 'dissociation' to refer broadly to the process of learning, and perhaps even the malleability of normal (non-traumatic) memory (Bridge & Paller, 2012), rather than a pathological phenomenon. Sidis (1898) describes the development of a coherent sense of self as a continuous process of association and dissociation within and among different groupings and systems of neurons of increasing sophistication. Sidis's framework for conceptualizing self-organization, with some adaptation, is illustrated in Figure 2.1.

In Figure 2.1, the concentric circles at the level of *reproductive consciousness* reflect "successive beats of [...] consciousness" (Sidis, 1898, p. 206), with each 'beat,' or moment, containing all the previous ones. This would afford a person a relatively continuous sense of their lived experience. Another way of illustrating those successive beats would be a timeline, such as we might create through detailed history taking. The level of 'Un-amassed Moments-Content' was derived and adapted from Janet (1889/2022a) to illustrate the material being aggregated at the level of primary synthesis. Representations of neural networks and the connections to them at the stages of primary, secondary, and tertiary synthesis (shown in grey above) were not included in Sidis's original illustration but do align with his conceptualization. The additions at the secondary stage of synthesis represent different ego states. Although these were extrapolated from Sidis's writings (see Sidis, 1914; Sidis & Goodhart, 1904/1968), he does not use the term 'ego states,' as it had not yet been coined (Federn, 1952).

The Traumatized Self

On Traumatic Experience

In a basic sense, Shapiro and Sidis appear to agree that traumatic experience is endemic to the roots of psychopathology. Shapiro (2018) offers that "As indicated by the AIP model, complaints not organically based [i.e, not due to brain-based cellular damage or anatomical anomaly] or caused by inadequate information are rooted in insufficiently processed memories inappropriately stored in the brain" (p. 38). Sidis (1898) notes that "One psycho-pathological process [...] underlies all the various forms of functional diseases, and that is the process of cell-disaggregation, with its concomitant *dissociation of moments-consciousness* [memories; emphasis added]" (p. 215).

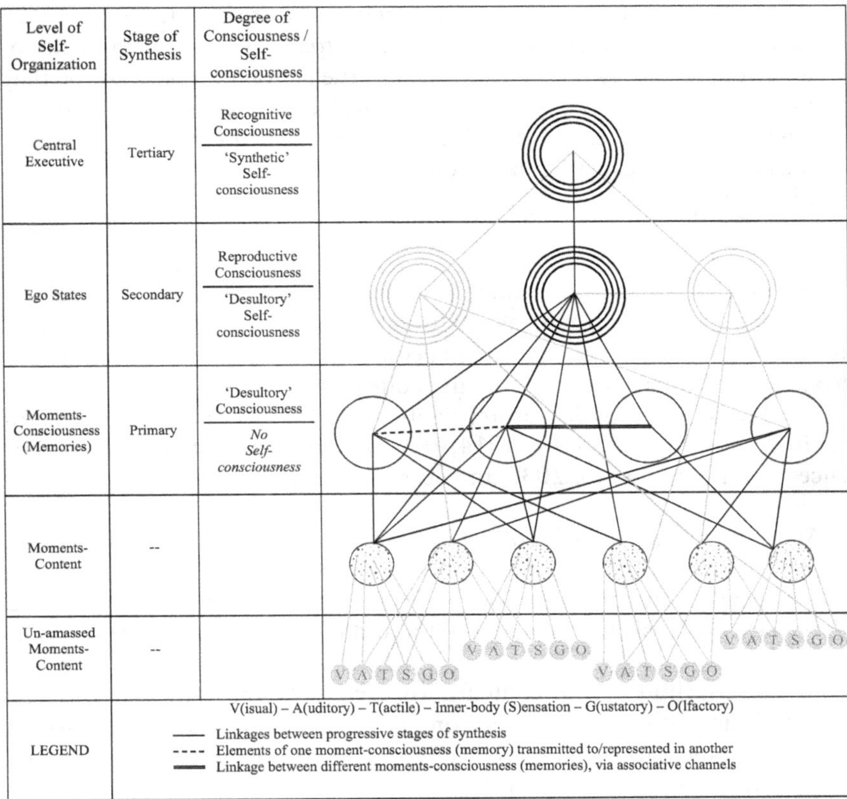

Figure 2.1 Sidis's Organization of the Self.

Source: Adapted by D. M. Coy, from Sidis (1898, p. 206).

Of the adverse experience that leads to insufficient processing, Shapiro (2006) hypothesizes that "high levels of disturbance can cause memories to be stored in the 'wrong' form of memory (inferred by some researchers to be the implicit/nondeclarative memory system)" and that, consequently, "the experiences are stored in a way that do not allow them to connect with any other adaptive information" (p. 8). She continues that the negative aspects of these [past] experiences "color the perceptions of the present," are "stored as memories in the dysfunctional network," and that "this expanding network reinforces the previous experiences" (p. 9). Sidis (1898) complementarily but more specifically observes that

> As the [negatively-valenced] stimuli increase in their intensity, be they of an external or internal nature—be they *toxic*, such as the influence of a poison, or purely mechanical, such as the action of a blow, or be they of a purely internal psycho-physiological character, such as a strong emotion— a process of dissolution sets in, and the highest, the most unstable, the least organized constellations of clusters are the first to dissolve.
>
> (p. 212)

Sidis's idea of 'toxins' infiltrating the nervous system is helpful, particularly if we think of these toxins as the isolated, pain-infused, unmetabolized remnants of overwhelming experiences. Part of what makes something toxic to the human body and brain is our inability to process it. Notably, in the EMDR therapy literature, Paulsen (2009) has also used the word toxin in this context. Sidis (1914) observes that "Pain hammers experiences into the mind" (p. 203), and elsewhere elaborates that

> With the further increase of the intensity of the stimulus the dissolution goes deeper and extends further – the simpler, the more stable, the more organized systems [those which, when aggregated via secondary and tertiary synthesis result in ego states and the central executive] become dissolved.
>
> The psycho-physical content, however, does not disappear with the dissolution of the system; the content exists in the less complex forms of cell-associations, and psychically in the simpler forms of mental [i.e., primary and secondary] synthesis.
>
> (Sidis, 1898, p. 212)

Thus, memory (moment content) does not disappear even when its connection to and access via conscious awareness is disrupted by trauma/toxin. Elsewhere, Sidis (1909) states that "In case of an emotional trauma there is often a breach in the continuity of association. The affected system becomes dissociated from the rest of the personality and is like a splinter in the flesh of the individuality" (p. 356). To contextualize this further, Sidis observed that a neuron exposed to literal toxins will contract, and as a result, its connections with other, neighboring cells will be functionally severed. Conversely, Sidis (1898) also notes that "the organization of a system or constellation of cells is in proportion to the duration and frequency of their associative activity" (p. 210), regardless of the emotional valence of the experience. Readers may be familiar with this same concept via Hebb's Law and the phrase 'neurons that fire together wire together' (Hebb, 1949).

Sidis (1898, p. 211) considered that "a durable, hurtful stimulus is by far" more harmful to the process of cell aggregation than is an isolated stimulus of greater intensity. Early, chronic neglect is a profound, and potentially durable, hurtful stimulus. Bruce Perry (2002) observed that "[t]he earlier and more pervasive the neglect is, the more devastating the developmental problems for the child" (p. 89). Notably, excessive exposure to both noradrenaline (released primarily by the locus coeruleus to facilitate fight-or-flight) and cortisol (released by the adrenal glands) appears to have deleterious effects on brain development and mental health, both at the functional connectivity and cellular levels (Van Ast et al., 2013; Jeong et al., 2025).

On Amnesia

In Shapiro's (2006) view of amnesia, "memory lapses and absence of positive recall are signs of blocked memory networks" (p. 9). Sidis (1898) observes that experiences of "mental shock" are "accompanied by all shades and forms of mental dissociation or amnesia" (p. 215). However, instead of 'blocks,' Sidis refers to memory gaps:

> The breaks and gaps in the continuity of personal consciousness are gauged by loss of memory. *Mental systems not bridged over by memory are so many independent individualities, and if started on their career with a good supply of mental material, they form so many independent personalities.* For, after all, where memory is gone the dissociation is complete. [emphasis added]
>
> (Sidis & Goodhart, 1904/1968, p. 44)

Sidis (1898) illustrates his understanding of the progression of disaggregation of memory as shown in Figure 2.2.

Indicated on the left in Figure 2.2 is the 'normal' association and dissociation, which is reflected in the typical learning process. Note that Sidis uses the term *dissociation* rather broadly, i.e., the opposite of association. Sidis uses the Janetian term *disaggregation* (Janet, 1889/2022a,

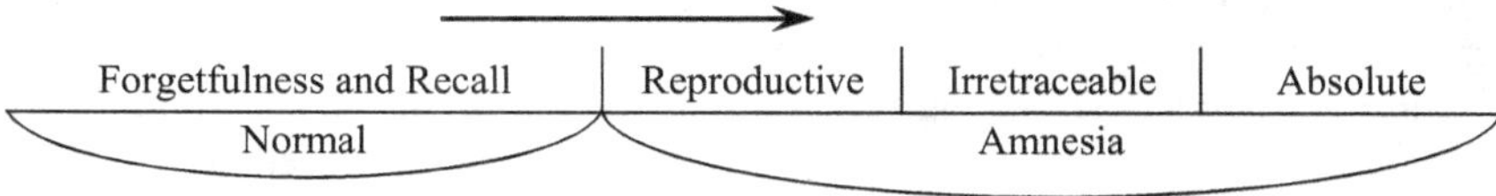

Figure 2.2 The Progression of Disaggregation.

Source: Adapted from Sidis (1898, p. 232).

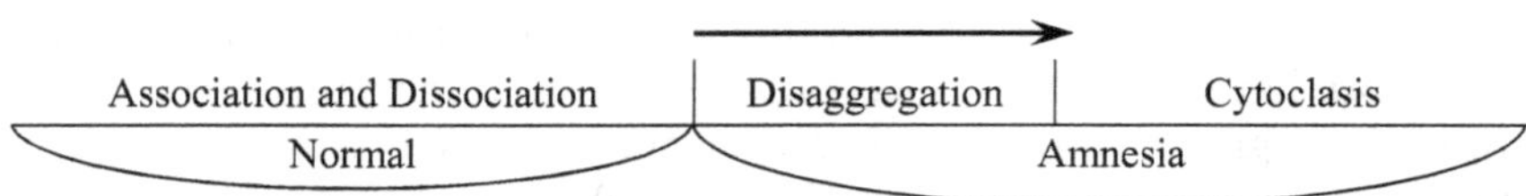

Figure 2.3 Continuum of Normal and Abnormal Amnesia.

Source: Adapted from Sidis (1898, p. 233).

1889/2022b) when referring to a problematic phenomenon indicative of the modern-day DDs. Normal association and dissociation (learning) is delineated from cell disaggregation, ranging from lesser to greater severity, and, to the right of this, we see *cytoclasis*. This is cellular damage/destruction resulting from physical brain injury. Sidis (1898) also classifies and illustrates three types of amnesia: *Reproductive amnesia*, *irretraceable amnesia*, and *absolute amnesia*. These are represented by Sidis as shown in Figure 2.3.

On the far left in Figure 2.3, we see normal, everyday forgetfulness and recall. Further along the continuum, we see *reproductive (recurrent) amnesia*, in which a person "must make a special effort to bring out the dissociated experiences, and the strength of the effort is proportional to the amount [degree] of dissociation" (Sidis, 1898, p. 233). In *irretraceable amnesia*, a person "can by no effort of will bring back the lost memories, but they emerge under artificial conditions, such as in the state of hypnosis [...]" (p. 233). This is evidence of the fact that the memories are disaggregated to some degree. Sidis's writings suggest that irretraceable amnesia may also underlie partially dissociated actions and some kinds of flashbacks for which the central executive self has no context. (Michael discusses the latter in some depth in Chapter 11. In *absolute amnesia*, "there are no means by which the lost memories may be restored; no psychic condition can reinstate them into consciousness. They are gone and lost, never to return. They are utterly destroyed" (p. 234). We pair these two illustrations, reproduced from Sidis (1898), in Figure 2.4.

Sidis (1898) advised that, "The clinician [...] must bear in mind that a case of amnesia where the lost memories lie beyond the control of the patient, may be irretraceable, disaggregative, and therefore curable, or absolute, cytoclastic, and therefore completely incurable" (p. 234). Although it may seem in Figure 2.4 that cytoclasis and absolute amnesia should perfectly overlap, based on the assumption that cell destruction would always result in absolute amnesia, this is not so. Indeed, Sidis highlights that cell destruction (i.e., 'cytoclastic' damage) *may* result in irretraceable rather than absolute amnesia. In the former instance, although

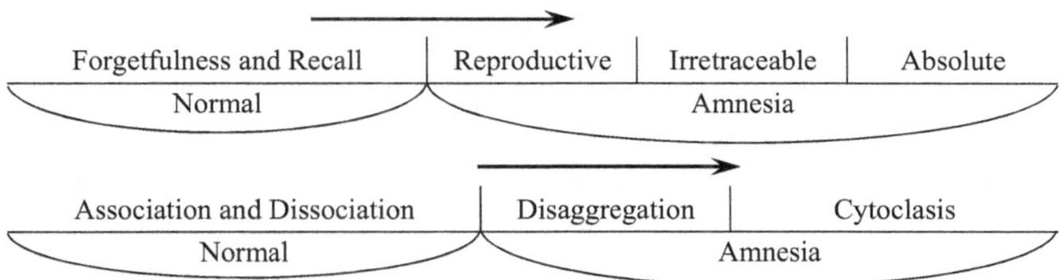

Figure 2.4 Overlap of Progression of Disaggregation and Amnesia Continuum.
Source: Adapted from Sidis (1898, p. 233).

a more obvious route to access dissociated memory may be cut off (due to cellular damage), other neural pathways may be available through which to access the disaggregated material. In other words, one or more 'bridges' may be destroyed, but detours may yield access to the destination. This assessment seems consistent with Shapiro (2018, p. 90) regarding the use of EMDR therapy methods in cases of neurological impairment due to brain damage.

We already know that a client's amnesia for their history can pose serious challenges for employing 'standard' EMDR therapy, which relies heavily upon the identification and processing of consciously available memory material. Sidis's granular approach to evaluating a client's absence of awareness (i.e., amnesia) in all its dimensions provides a useful means for clinicians to consider how 'deep,' intense, and enduring a client's traumatic cut(s) have been and, by extension, the complexity of their dissociative experiences. (For Sidis's complete typology of amnesia, refer to Sidis, 1898, pp. 242–244.)

On Multiplicity

If the trauma-induced, functional separation of neural networks begins at a comparatively rudimentary (early) stage of brain development, then there may be a significant (though not necessarily total) absence of connection between groupings and clusters of neurons as the child develops. As Bruce Perry (2002, p. 88) highlights,

> While experience may *alter the behavior of an adult, experience literally provides the organizing framework for an infant and child*. Because the brain is most plastic (receptive to environmental input) in early childhood, the child is most vulnerable to variance of experience during this time [emphasis added].

Perry is alluding to wide-scale, traumagenic alterations in neurons' natural affinities and associations with one another at elementary levels (e.g., Cheng et al., 2021; Mualem et al., 2024).

If isolated aggregations of cells began to develop in childhood, in infancy, perhaps even in utero or intergenerationally (Buss et al., 2017; Diniz & Crestani, 2023), then individuals with such experiences might have both a genetic/epigenetic predisposition toward and a higher likelihood of developing severe forms of dissociative experience (Becker-Blease et al., 2004; Bonsu et al., 2023; Rajkumar, 2022). Here, we refer to the development of highly isolated states that are varyingly aware of one another and the memory material that each holds (and may continue to synthesize) with only limited recognition or co-ownership of a single body and mind. If two or more of these isolated, subconscious states are repeatedly activated (either accidentally or intentionally) to emerge into executive functioning, they could develop increasingly sophisticated, central executive-level capacities, as is the case in dissociative identity disorder (DID).

Mending the Gaps, and Healing the Traumatized Self

The AIP model emphasizes an inherent tendency toward health and healthy functioning and offers three central precepts that guide the healing process:

1. activating and relying upon the brain's physical information processing system – the anatomical structures that facilitate processing of one's lived experience;
2. resolving the 'blocks' that are created by dysfunctionally stored memories of adverse (i.e., overwhelming) experience, and the maladaptive functioning that results from this; and
3. the restoration of adaptive functioning via processing of dysfunctionally stored memories (Shapiro, 2006, 2018).

Shapiro states that healthy functioning may be *restored* using EMDR therapy methods: "The processing of a targeted memory allows the appropriate connections to be made to the adaptive networks" (Shapiro, 2006, p. 9). This facilitates a "simultaneous shift in the components of the memory" and in "symptoms, characteristics and sense of self" (p. 10). This hypothesis seems to assume that a person *had* a coherent, relatively unified sense of self and healthy functioning prior to the traumatic experience and, therefore, processing memories and inviting associations will *restore* healthy functioning.

Sidis (1898) emphasizes the *"removal [...] of the hurtful stimuli,"* [emphasis added] after which he observes "once more a tendency, on account of the habit acquired from previous combination [of neurons], to form old associations, and the old relations and functions are gradually restored" (p. 214). Sidis elsewhere offers that, "In my own work I have insisted again and again on the important psychopathological principle, namely, that *re-association of dissociated systems effects a cure of the psychopathic disease*" (p. 246) [emphasis added]. He goes on to state that "The cure is effected by so-called 'suggestive methods' during the hypnotic state, the hypnoidal state [a liminal state between waking and sleeping] and *by various other 'associative methods'* [...]" (p. 247) [emphasis added]. These methods are employed in the service of both removing (i.e., metabolizing) the toxic agent(s) that led to traumagenically dissociated networks in the first place and facilitating their (re)association.

Although Shapiro's and Sidis's views are not dissimilar, the framing offered by Sidis allows for a more 'bottom up' conceptualization that begins at the neuronal level and proceeds up to the central executive level – as compared to Shapiro's sole focus on the memories. Additionally, Sidis's idea that harmful stimuli can lead to 'gaps' in functional connectivity between neural networks allows us to conceptualize our work with clients as one of metabolizing toxins and (re)establishing connectivity at *multiple levels* of synthesis. This seems to us more inclusive of more complex forms of dissociative experience and reduces the risk inherent in conceptualizing only in terms of resolving 'blocks' that separate memory networks.

Being a developmental framework, Sidis's (1898) model is 'bottom-up,' with experiential *moments-content* being the raw material from which memory is forged. Through an ongoing, dynamic process of association and dissociation, a person's experience is synthesized over time into more sophisticated, higher-level neural configurations of a sort that we might think of as ego states, which exist at the subconscious level. Whatever we call them, the interconnectivity of these increasingly sophisticated neural networks at the subconscious level, paired with increasing brain maturation and exposure to lived experience over a period of years, contributes to the development of a central executive. That central executive's healthy functionality and top-down, (relatively) on-demand access to memory material is dependent upon adequate functional connectivity at the lower, subconscious levels of synthesis. Sidis's conceptualization appears to be consistent with modern findings on brain development, with its focus on functional connectivity and neuroplasticity – despite his lack of access to high-resolution brain scans (Dennis & Thompson, 2013; Diniz & Crestani, 2023; Mualem et al., 2024; Sherman et al., 2014).

We suggest that the AIP model's conception of the individual is based on an essentially 'vertical' idea of pathology. Its emphasis on memories, to the exclusion of identity (beyond personality traits), presumes that a person has achieved a certain degree of personality development and self-organization *prior* to the onset of adverse experience. Furthermore, that adverse experience is presumed to intrude upon a (sole) central executive from the subconscious. And, if we can identify, access, and reprocess that material in the subconscious, then it will connect with adaptive information available at the executive level of functioning and a previous baseline of health can be restored. EMDR therapy practice does not always carry forward the assumption of a more fully formed self, as evidenced by Shapiro's (2018) enjoinder to identify a client's 'developmental deficits' so that these may be addressed in treatment. Shapiro also acknowledges that some people with complex trauma histories may have limited or no (accessible) adaptive material from which to draw.

However, the AIP model has nothing to say about the impact of this on a person's self-organization, and how this may impact the relationship between the subconscious and central executive level of awareness. Hence, we discern in AIP an implicit assumption of an already developed and unified sense of self that is intruded upon by maladaptively stored memory material (see Chapter 9 for further discussion). One of the main attractions of Sidis's work is that he makes no such assumption, and in fact proposes that memories are synthesized in the *first* stage of self-development and are the building blocks of increasingly sophisticated layers of consciousness. According to Sidis (1898), the impact of exposure to painful experience depends upon both (1) the intensity and duration of the pain and (2) the integrity/stability of the cluster(s) of neurons affected by it. Sidis's conceptualization allows us to consider disruptions in both vertical (connections between conscious/explicit and subconscious/implicit) and horizontal/lateral (connections among subconscious memory networks) dimensions of self-organization. Rudimentary though it may be (owing to its roots in the late-1800s), it seems surprisingly consistent with contemporary neuroscientific understandings.

Conclusion

The sole focus of etiology in the AIP model is dysfunctionally stored (i.e., inadequately processed) memories that impede an intrinsic progression toward health. EMDR therapy carries this forward by employing BL-DAS to facilitate an associative process among neural networks, which allows for the metabolization of painful memories that have disrupted a person's emotional health. We propose that the AIP model must take into account both the presence and *pervasive, functional absence or inaccessibility* of explicit memory – in the form of full or partial amnesia. It must also account for the clinical implications of introducing a rapid, associative process to resolve what may be something different, and more complex, than simply 'blocked' access to memory networks.

AIP cannot and should not only focus on the treatment of memories and associating memory networks in the conceptualization and treatment of DDs. AIP must also consider the organization (and disaggregation) of self as a factor in the success (or failure) of EMDR therapy methods. Our observation is that many clients do not present with simple, adult-onset trauma, and AIP is at best woefully inadequate in conceptualizing the treatment of more complex cases. Practitioners must understand the implications of the disconnections among neural networks that may have been precipitated by a need to distance from early, painful experiences. We need to conceptualize treatment accordingly, using a model that can accommodate dissociative complexity.

Notes

1 Reproductive consciousness, aka desultory self-consciousness, would also be the level at which Ernest Hilgard's (1984) so-called *hidden observer* phenomenon manifests. According to Hildgard (1984), the hidden observer is "an organized cognitive structure of recent information acquired covertly [i.e., outside conscious awareness] that could be made available only through special [hypnotic] procedures (Hilgard, 1984)" (p. 299). Coy (2025) notes that "Hilgard (1986) stressed both that this state is 'temporary' and that his conceptualization (and demonstration of the phenomenon) were not intended to suggest the more pronounced and abiding division seen in persons with dissociative disorders" (p. 95).

2 Unsurprisingly, Sidis's ideas on dissociation and the development of the self bear similarities to those of his contemporaries – they were all investigating similar phenomena, happening upon some of the same discoveries, and sharing them with one another either directly or through their writings, etc. Sidis was reportedly inspired by the work of Janet (Bliss, 1986). Available evidence suggests that Sidis was pretty good about citing his influences, sometimes even quoting them extensively. However, late in the writing of this book, we stumbled upon a discussion of the work of British neurologist John Hughlings Jackson (1835–1911). Hughlings Jackson's ideas reportedly influenced Freud and predated Janet's work. We could only find one citation of Hughlings Jackson by Sidis in the numerous works we reviewed, that being a casual reference to "Jacksonian epilepsy' (Sidis & Goodhart, 1904/1968, p. 270), also known as a 'Jacksonian March.' Today, we refer to this phenomenon as a simple partial seizure. See Meares (1999) for an introduction to Hughlings Jackson's discoveries and understanding of dissociation.

References

American Psychiatric Association. (2022). *DSM-5-TR – Diagnostic and statistical manual of mental disorders* (5th ed., text revision). American Psychiatric Publishing.

Baek, J., Lee, S., Cho, T., et al. (2019). Neural circuits underlying a psychotherapeutic regimen for fear disorders. *Nature, 566*, 339–343. https://doi.org/10.1038/s41586-019-0931-y

Becker-Blease, K. A., Deater-Deckard, K., Eley, T., Freyd, J. J., Stevenson, J., & Plomin, R. (2004). A genetic analysis of individual differences in dissociative behaviors in childhood and adolescence. *Journal of Child Psychology and Psychiatry, and Allied Disciplines*, *45*(3), 522–532. https://doi.org/10.1111/j.1469-7610.2004.00242.x

Beckman, D. (2001). An interview with Francine Shapiro, Ph.D. *The Milton H. Erickson Foundation Newsletter, 21*(1), 1, 20–22, 24. erickson-foundation.squarespace.com/newsletter-archive

Bliss, E. L. (1986). *Multiple personality, allied disorders, and hypnosis*. Oxford University Press.

Bonsu, N., Sreeram, V., & Hasan, F. M. (2023). Genetics and dissociative identity disorder (DID). In H. Tohid & I. H Rutkofsky (Eds.), *Dissociative identity disorder: Treatment and management* (pp. 133–135). Springer Publishing Company. https://doi.org/10.1007/978-3-031-39854-4_22

Bridge, D. J., & Paller, K. A. (2012). Neural correlates of reactivation and retrieval-induced distortion. *The Journal of Neuroscience*, *32*(35), 12144–12151. https://doi.org/10.1523/JNEUROSCI.1378-12.2012

Buss, C., Entringer, S., Moog, N. K., Toepfer, P., Fair, D. A., Simhan, H. N., Heim, C. M., & Wadhwa, P. D. (2017). Intergenerational transmission of maternal childhood maltreatment exposure: Implications for fetal brain development. *Journal of the American Academy of Child and Adolescent Psychiatry*, *56*(5), 373–382. https://doi.org/10.1016/j.jaac.2017.03.001

Chamberlin, D. E. (2019). The network balance model of trauma and resolution—Level I: Large-scale neural networks. *Journal of EMDR Practice and Research, 13*(2), 124–142. https://doi.org/10.1891/1933-3196.13.2.124

Cheng, T. W., Mills, K. L., Miranda Dominguez, O., Zeithamova, D., Perrone, A., Sturgeon, D., Feldstein Ewing, S. W., Fisher, P. A., Pfeifer, J. H., Fair, D. A., & Mackiewicz Seghete, K. L. (2021). Characterizing the impact of adversity, abuse, and neglect on adolescent amygdala resting-state functional connectivity. *Developmental Cognitive Neuroscience*, *47*, 100894. https://doi.org/10.1016/j.dcn.2020.10089

Corrigan, F. M., Young, H., & Christie-Sands, J. (2025). *Deep brain reorienting: Understanding the neuroscience of trauma, attachment wounding, and DBR psychotherapy*. Routledge. https://doi.org/10.4324/9781003431695

Cotraccia, A. J. (2022). Trauma as absence: A biopsychosocial-AIP definition of trauma and its treatment in EMDR therapy. *Journal of EMDR Practice and Research, 16*(3), 145–155. https://doi.org/10.1891/EMDR-2022-0011

Cotraccia, A. (2012). Adaptive information processing and a systemic biopsychosocial model. *Journal of EMDR Practice and Research, 6*(1), 27–36. https://doi.org/10.1891/1933-3196.6.1.27

Coy, D. M. (2025). The autohypnotic model of dissociation. In A. M. Gomez & J. Hosey (Eds.), *The handbook of complex trauma and dissociation in children: Theory, research and clinical applications* (pp. 89–106). W. W. Norton & Company. https://doi.org/10.4324/9781003350156

De Jongh, A., de Roos, C., & El-Leithy, S. (2024). State of the science: Eye movement desensitization and reprocessing (EMDR) therapy. *Journal of Traumatic Stress, 37*, 205–216. https://doi.org/10.1002/jts.23012

Dennis, E. L., & Thompson, P. M. (2013). Mapping connectivity in the developing brain. *International Journal of Developmental Neuroscience*, *31*(7), 525–542. https://doi.org/10.1016/j.ijdevneu.2013.05.007

Diniz, C. R. A. F., & Crestani, A. P. (2023). The times they are a-changin': A proposal on how brain flexibility goes beyond the obvious to include the concepts of "upward" and "downward" to neuroplasticity. *Molecular Psychiatry*, *28*(3), 977–992. https://doi.org/10.1038/s41380-022-01931-x

EMDR International Association. (2025). *Standards for EMDR basic training.* www.emdria.org/wp-content/uploads/2025/03/Standards-for-EMDRIA-Basic-Training.pdf

Federn, P. (1952). *Ego psychology and the psychoses.* (E. Weiss, Ed.). BasicBooks.

Ferenczi, S. (1994). *Final contributions to the problems and methods of psychoanalysis*. Routledge. (Original work published in 1929)

Harper, M. L., Rasolkhani-Kalhorn, T., & Drozd, J. F. (2009). On the neural basis of EMDR therapy: Insights from qEEG studies. *Traumatology, 15*(2), 81–95. https://doi.org/10.1177/1534765609338498

Hebb, D. O. (1949). *The organization of behavior: A neuropsychological theory.* John Wiley & Sons.

Hilgard, E. R. (1984). The hidden observer and multiple personality. *International Journal of Clinical and Experimental Hypnosis, 32*(2), 248–253. https://doi.org/10.1080f,()0207I48408416014

Hilgard, E. R. (1986). *Divided consciousness: Multiple controls in thought and action* (Expanded ed.). WiIey-Interscience.

Janet, P. (2022a). *Subconscious acts, anesthesias and psychological disaggregation in psychological automatism: Partial automatism* (G. Craparo & O. Van der Hart, Eds.; A. Crabtree & S. Osei-Bonsu, Trans.). Routledge. (Original work published 1889) https://doi.org/10.4324/9781003198727

Janet, P. (2022b). *Catalepsy, memory and suggestion in psychological automatism: Total automatism* (G. Craparo & O. Van der Hart, Eds.; A. Crabtree & S. Osei-Bonsu, Trans.). Routledge. (Original work published 1889) https://doi.org/10.4324/9780429287671

Jeong, J. H., Kim, D. K., Chung, S., Han, J. W., Han, J., & Mook-Jung, I. (2025). Long-term exposure to excessive norepinephrine in the brain induces tau aggregation, neuronal death, and cognitive deficits in early tau transgenic mice. *Aging Cell, 24*(3), e14420. https://doi.org/10.1111/acel.14420

Khalfa, S., Touzet, C. F. (2017). EMDR therapy mechanisms explained by the theory of neural cognition. *Journal of Traumatic Stress Disorders Treatment, 6*(4). https://doi.org/10.4172/2324-8947.1000179

Landin-Romero, R., Moreno-Alcazar, A., Pagani, M., & Amann, B. L. (2018). How does eye movement desensitization and reprocessing therapy work? A systematic review on suggested mechanisms of action. *Frontiers in Psychology, 9*, 1395. https://doi.org/10.3389/fpsyg.2018.01395

Lanius, U. F., Paulsen, S. L., & Corrigan, F. M. (2014). *Dissociation: Cortical deafferentation and the loss of self.* In U. F. Lanius, S. L. Paulsen, & F. M. Corrigan (Eds.), *Neurobiology and treatment of traumatic dissociation: Towards an embodied self* (pp. 5–28). Springer Publishing Company.

Lazrove, S., & Fine, C. G. (1996). The use of EMDR in patients with dissociative identity disorder. *Dissociation, 9*(4), 289–299. hdl.handle.net/1794/1778

Leeds, A. M. (2016, August 25–28). *Mediators, mechanisms and moderators of action for EMDR therapy: A review of multiplex effects in modes of bilateral stimulation* [Conference presentation]. 21st Annual Conference of the EMDR International Association. Minneapolis, Minnesota, United States.

Luber, M., & Shapiro, F. (2009). Interview with Francine Shapiro: Historical overview, present issues, and future directions of EMDR. *Journal of EMDR Practice and Research, 3*(4), 217–231. https://doi.org/10.1891/1933-3196.3.4.217

Maxfield, L. (2019). A clinician's guide to the efficacy of EMDR therapy. *Journal of EMDR Practice and Research, 13*(4), 239–246. https://doi.org/10.1891/1933-3196.13.4.239

Meares, R. (1999). The contribution of hughlings jackson to an understanding of dissociation. *American Journal of Psychiatry, 156*(12), 1850–1855. https://doi.org/10.1176/ajp.156.12.1850

Menon, V. (2011). Large-scale brain networks and psychopathology: A unifying triple network model. *Trends in Cognitive Sciences, 15*(10), 483–506. https://doi.org/10.1016/j.tics.2011.08.003

Mualem, R., Morales-Quezada, L., Farraj, R. H., Shance, S., Bernshtein, D. H., Cohen, S., Mualem, L., Salem, N., Yehuda, R. R., Zbedat, Y., Waksman, I., & Biswas, S. (2024). Econeurobiology and brain development in children: key factors affecting development, behavioral outcomes, and school interventions. *Frontiers in Public Health, 12*, 1376075. https://doi.org/10.3389/fpubh.2024.1376075

Olivé, I., Densmore, M., Harricharan, S., Theberge, J., McKinnon, M. C., & Lanius, R. (2018). Superior colliculus resting state networks in post-traumatic stress disorder and its dissociative subtype. *Human Brain Mapping, 39(*1), 563–574. https://doi.org/10.1002/hbm.23865

Pagani, M., & Carletto, S. (2017). A hypothetical mechanism of action of EMDR: The role of slow wave sleep. *Clinical Neuropsychiatry: Journal of Treatment Evaluation, 14*(5), 301–305. www.clinicalneuropsychiatry.org/download/a-hypothetical-mechanism-of-action-of-emdr-the-role-of-slow-wave-sleep/

Pagani, M., Amann, B. L., Landin-Romero, R., & Carletto, S. (2017). Eye movement desensitization and reprocessing and slow wave sleep: A putative mechanism of action. *Frontiers in Psychology, 8*, 1935. https://doi.org/10.3389/fpsyg.2017.01935

Paulsen, S. (1995). Eye movement desensitization and reprocessing: Its cautious use in the dissociative disorders. *Dissociation, 8*(1), 32–44. hdl.handle.net/1794/1592

Paulsen, S. L. (2009). *Looking through the eyes of trauma and dissociation: An illustrated guide for EMDR clinicians and clients*. Booksurge.

Perry, B. D. (2002). Childhood experience and the expression of genetic potential: What childhood neglect tells us about nature and nurture. *Brain & Mind, 3*(1), 79–100. https://doi.org/10.1023/A:1016557824657

Rajkumar R. P. (2022). The molecular genetics of dissociative symptomatology: A transdiagnostic literature review. *Genes, 13*(5), 843. https://doi.org/10.3390/genes13050843

Rameckers, S. A., Van Emmerik, A. A. P., Boterhoven de Haan, K., Kousemaker, M., Fassbinder, E., Lee, C. W., Meewisse, M., Menninga, S., Rijkeboer, M., Schaich, A., & Arntz, A. (2024). The working mechanisms of imagery rescripting and eye movement desensitization and reprocessing: Findings from a randomised controlled trial. *Behaviour Research and Therapy, 175,* 104492. https://doi.org/10.1016/j.brat.2024.104492

Richards, A., Kanady, J. C., & Neylan, T. C. (2020). Sleep disturbance in PTSD and other anxiety-related disorders: an updated review of clinical features, physiological characteristics, and psychological and neurobiological mechanisms. *Neuropsychopharmacology, 45*(1), 55–73. https://doi.org/10.1038/s41386-019-0486-5

Rydberg, J. A., Virgitti, L., & Tarquinio, C. (2024). Bolstering the adaptive information processing model: A narrative review. *Frontiers in Psychiatry, 15,* 1374274. https://doi.org/10.3389/fpsyt.2024.1374274

Shapiro, F. (1989). Efficacy of the eye movement desensitization procedure in the treatment of traumatic memories. *Journal of Traumatic Stress, 2*(2), 199–223. https://doi.org/10.1002/jts.2490020207

Shapiro, F. (1995). *Eye movement desensitization and reprocessing: Basic principles, protocols, and procedures*. The Guilford Press.

Shapiro, F. (2001). *Eye movement desensitization and reprocessing: Basic principles, protocols, and procedures* (2nd ed.). The Guilford Press.

Shapiro, F. (2006). *EMDR: New notes on adaptive information processing with case formulation principles, forms, scripts and worksheets* (version 1.1). EMDR Institute.

Shapiro, F. (2018). *Eye Movement Desensitization and Reprocessing (EMDR) therapy: Basic principles, protocols and procedures* (3rd ed.). The Guilford Press.

Sherman, L. E., Rudie, J. D., Pfeifer, J. H., Masten, C. L., McNealy, K., & Dapretto, M. (2014). Development of the default mode and central executive networks across early adolescence: a longitudinal study. *Developmental Cognitive Neuroscience, 10*, 148–159. https://doi.org/10.1016/j.dcn.2014.08.002

Sidis, B. (1898). *The psychology of suggestion: A research into the subconscious nature of man and society*. D. Appleton and Company.

Sidis, B. (1909). Studies in psychopathology: The psychotherapeutic value of the hypnoidal state. *Boston Medical and Surgical Journal, 161*(11), 356–360. www.nejm.org/doi/full/10.1056/NEJM190909091611103

Sidis, B. (1914). *The foundations of normal and abnormal psychology*. Richard G. Badger.

Sidis, B., & Goodhart, S. P. (1968). *Multiple personality: An experimental investigation into the nature of human individuality*. Greenwood Press. (Original work published 1904)

Sodré, M. E., Wießner, I., Irfan, M., Schenck, C. H., & Mota-Rolim, S. A. (2023). Awake or sleeping? Maybe both… A review of sleep-related dissociative states. *Journal of Clinical Medicine, 12*(12), 3876. https://doi.org/10.3390/jcm12123876

Szeska, C., Mohrmann, H., & Hamm, A. O. (2023). Facilitated extinction but impaired extinction recall by eye movement manipulation in humans – Indications for action mechanisms and the applicability of eye movement desensitization. *International Journal of Psychophysiology, 184*, 64–75. https://doi.org/10.1016/j.ijpsycho.2022.12.009

Van Ast, V. A., Cornelisse, S., Marin, M. F., Ackermann, S., Garfinkel, S. N., & Abercrombie, H. C. (2013). Modulatory mechanisms of cortisol effects on emotional learning and memory: Novel perspectives. *Psychoneuroendocrinology, 38*(9), 1874–1882. https://doi.org/10.1016/j.psyneuen.2013.06.012

Weathers, F. W., Bovin, M. J., Lee, D. J., Sloan, D. M., Schnurr, P. P., Kaloupek, D. G., Keane, T. M., & Marx, B. P. (2018). The clinician-administered PTSD scale for DSM–5 (CAPS-5): Development and initial psychometric evaluation in military veterans. *Psychological Assessment, 30*(3), 383–395. https://doi.org/10.1037/pas0000486

Chapter 3

New Considerations

Expanding the Frame for Ethical Practice

Jennifer A. Madere and D. Michael Coy

Introduction

Scientific interest in dissociation peaked in the early 1900s but declined sharply thereafter. This can be attributed to several practical and ethical issues faced by practitioners, in addition to the social and political disruptions of the scientific community precipitated by World Wars I and II. Treatments facilitated via hypnosis by Pierre Janet (1889/2022a, 2022b) and others illuminated the possibilities for revealing and treating dissociative states. However, Boris Sidis observed that few practitioners could master the hypnotic methods necessary to do so. Alongside that, treatment provoked serious side effects, such as sleepwalking and decompensation, for some clients (Sidis, 1909). Around this time, Breuer and Freud's psychoanalytic method gained popularity (1895/1955). Psychoanalysis offered a model that was both easier to employ and more profitable, although Boris Sidis commented that this was "not a new discovery" as it relied on concepts known to "every psychopathologist of note" (Sidis, 1909, p. 246). Parallels with the (later) emergence of EMDR therapy are striking, as EMDR has potentially posed all the combined benefits and risks in its promise of being 'easy to master,' not being a wholly new discovery, *and* resulting in decompensation when employed injudiciously to treat complex dissociative symptoms. The challenges for establishing an ethical, effective, and accessible model for treating complex trauma and dissociative disorders (DDs) are real.

Students and professionals in the mental health disciplines have been eager to learn how to treat posttraumatic presentations using EMDR therapy. Post training, some have voiced concerns that EMDR is too cognitive and does not adequately attend to emotion, body awareness, or present-day symptoms that matter to the client. These concerns have led to the development of 'new' modifications of EMDR or disillusionment with EMDR therapy in general. When Jennifer encounters these perspectives in work with consultees, one of her first questions is "Help me to

DOI: 10.4324/9781003410201-4

understand your approach: What is the theory that guides your practice in general, before or since training in EMDR therapy?" Frequently, consultees struggle to answer this question. Some even discover gaps in their conceptual understanding of EMDR therapy and the AIP model. Having a solid theoretical and/or conceptual framework is essential to guide our thinking and practice. It provides a compass and a sense of which direction we might *look* next, even while we are still unclear about what to *do* next.

The 'standard of care,' which comprises many elements, offers further guidance on how to think and what to do. These elements include:

- usual and customary professional practice standards (of peer professionals with the same educational level, license, and training);
- practitioner- and treatment-dependent qualities and conditions that prevail, or should prevail, in the provision of 'reasonable and prudent' care,
- ethics codes within different professional disciplines;
- laws, regulatory requirements, and organizational policies; and
- treatment or practice guidelines outlining best practices within a given clinical domain (e.g., for complex trauma and DDs).

The standard of care is contextual rather than absolute; thus, it is flexible and allows for common, unavoidable, or simple mistakes during the course of treatment (Brown et al., 1998; Zur, 2022)."Practitioners who work in isolation from their peers and whose treatment is markedly different from that of their peers are more at risk than the average practitioner of providing substandard care" (Brown et al., 1998, p. 498).

Treatment and practice guidelines summarize the wisdom- and/or research-based norms associated with the treatment of specific populations and clusters of symptoms. In this chapter, we invite you to hold your theoretical framework – if you have one – lightly, alongside the perspective we will offer, and consider the following questions:

- How did you arrive at your current approach to treating complex trauma and dissociation?
- How does that approach align with or diverge from the standard of care?
- Was any alignment or divergence an intentional choice or merely coincidental? If it was the former, what information informed that intention? If it were the latter, what are the implications of that for your clients?
- In what ways might the framework that we will offer expand, deepen, or challenge your thinking?

The ethical, impactful, and meaningful practice of EMDR therapy – especially with dissociation – is multifaceted. This chapter delves into the standard of care for treatment of complex trauma and DDs, which prescribes that EMDR therapy be situated within a broader framework. We will introduce a multilayered theoretical framework here and expand upon it throughout this book. The individual layers of this framework are not new. The new perspective that we offer is a nuanced, informed approach to integrating conceptual and practical elements. It is an invitation for you to consider deepening the thinking that guides your practice. Finally, we will discuss the scope of treatment, including the ways that EMDR may be employed within a broader treatment frame.

The Standard of Care

Consulting the standard of care will help us develop answers to many of the questions we raised in Chapters 1 and 2. The elements of the standard of care are sorted into three pillars: codes of ethics, legal and regulatory policies, and treatment and practice guidelines, as relfected in Figure 3.1.

Guidance specific to EMDR therapy and dissociation is found in the treatment and practice guidelines. However, there is no comprehensive guideline for employing EMDR therapy when severe dissociative symptoms are present. Francine Shapiro's texts have been inconsistent on the topic of dissociation. For instance, she states that "*Any* inappropriate dissociative response, either an over- or underreaction to a traumatic event, is considered indicative of a blocked memory network and is therefore an appropriate target for EMDR processing" (Shapiro, 2018, p. 49, emphasis in original). Later sections of the text that discuss readiness (pp. 95–97), treating persons with DDs as a special population (pp. 342–345), and client safety (*Appendix E* in Shapiro, 2018) articulate a more reserved and cautionary perspective. Shapiro describes what we refer to as the 'red flags' associated with client readiness for (standard) EMDR therapy:

Figure 3.1 The Standard of Care.

> Within a standard mental status exam, the following clinical signs should suggest to the interviewer that the client may have a dissociative disorder: (1) intractable, unexplained somatic symptoms, (2) sleep problems, (3) flashbacks, (4) derealization and depersonalization, (5) Schneiderian symptoms (e.g., voices, unexplainable feelings), (6) memory lapses, (7) multiple psychiatric hospitalizations, and (8) multiple diagnoses with little treatment progress.
>
> (Shapiro, 2018, p. 97)

Notably, flashbacks are acknowledged as a possible sign of a DD (more on that in Part IV). What if one or more of these red flags are present? What if a client meets the criteria for a DD? What if those experiences are only evident in the remote history reported by the client? These questions and related dilemmas are exactly what we hope to address throughout this book.

Guidelines for Treating Complex Trauma and Dissociation

Several practice guidelines address the treatment of complex trauma, Complex posttraumatic stress disorder (PTSD), and DDs. Two types of guidelines exist: (1) those based on *consensus* of experts in the field describing best practices and (2) those based on *empirical* research or evidence-based recommendations. Due to the scarcity of randomized, controlled studies on treating dissociation, all of the applicable guidelines hew toward expert consensus, with empirical support included where available.

The currently available consensus guidelines are described briefly below, and we recommend that readers become familiar with the guidelines themselves rather than relying on summaries. Most of these resources are available free of charge via their publisher. A recommendation common to all of these is that treatment ought to occur within a three-stage model or triphasic approach.

Complex Trauma

The term 'complex trauma' refers to traumatic experiences that are interpersonal, long-term, repeated, and severe in nature. These include various forms of neglect and/or abuse. People who have experienced complex trauma may meet criteria for a variety of diagnoses and may not meet criteria for PTSD or a DD. However, specific clinical guidance related to this category of experience is warranted.

- The *American Psychological Association Guidelines for Working with Adults with Complex Trauma Histories* (American Psychological Association (APA), 2024) is the product of a joint effort by APA Division 56 and the International Society for the Study of Trauma and Dissociation (ISSTD). Personalized care and the need for flexible sequencing of treatment are emphasized. EMDR is mentioned, but no particular modalities are endorsed.
- The Blue Knot Foundation was established in Australia in the 1990s to promote advocacy and professional training related to complex trauma and has published *Practice Guidelines for Clinical Treatment of Complex Trauma* (2019a, 2019b). These guidelines offer a comprehensive literature review addressing complex trauma and various treatment modalities (including EMDR) and describe overarching best practice considerations.

Both sets of guidelines acknowledge the stabilization debate (summarized in Rydberg, 2017). On one side of the debate is the potential risk of *de*stabilization when 'targeted' trauma work begins prematurely. On the other side is the argument that already-limited treatment resources are being withheld or 'wasted' when trauma-focused work is delayed by an unnecessary 'stabilization' phase. We will further discuss this debate below.

Complex Posttraumatic Stress Disorder (C-PTSD)

Complex PTSD was added to the International Classification of Diseases in 2018. A diagnosis of C-PTSD requires that the criteria for PTSD be met, in addition to various disturbances in self-organization (World Health Organization [WHO], 2018). Dissociative symptoms may be included but are not essential criteria for C-PTSD.

- The *Evidence-based Psychological Interventions of the Treatment of Mental Disorders: A Literature Review, Fifth Edition* (Australian Psychological Society, 2024) addresses literature associated with the treatment of C-PTSD. This review mentions EMDR therapy among the recommended approaches, while observing "reduced efficacy of treatment for people who had experienced childhood trauma" (p. 108). The text indicates that effective treatment should include more than solely trauma processing approaches.

Two other publications immediately preceded or coincided with the officialization of C-PTSD as a diagnosis by the World Health Organization.

They describe the experiences of people with C-PTSD and considerations for treatment and research.

- *International Society for Traumatic Stress Studies Guidelines Position Paper on Complex PTSD in Adults* (ISTSS, 2018). This paper reviews the case for C-PTSD as a distinct presentation, and acknowledges various enduring controversies related to this and whether modification of established treatments for PTSD is necessary.
- *Guideline for the Treatment and Planning of Services for Complex PTSD in Adults* (United Kingdom Psychological Trauma Society, 2017). This task force recommended EMDR therapy as a trauma processing modality, within a three-phase/stage model.

Dissociative Identity Disorder

For DDs, the lone source is the *Guidelines for Treating Dissociative Identity Disorder in Adults, Third Revision,* published by the ISSTD (ISSTD, 2011). EMDR therapy is cautiously included as an adjunctive approach that may be employed during the trauma processing stage of treatment. ISSTD emphasizes the importance of practicing within a psychodynamic frame and with knowledge of established adaptations of EMDR for dissociation. We contributed to the fourth revision, which remains in process as of this writing.

The Three-Stage Model

All treatment guidelines listed above refer to the three-stage model in some way as an essential framework for treatment. This model has been around for a long time, with elements of it evident in the work of Pierre Janet, Boris Sidis, and others in the late 1800s and early 1900s. The three-stage model as we know it was brought to popular awareness by Judith Herman (1992) and more fully articulated by Van der Hart et al. (1989). *Note: This approach is also referred to as the phase-oriented, triphasic, or three-phase model. To avoid confusion with the phases of EMDR therapy, in this book, we use the term 'stages.'* The stages and essential tasks of each are depicted in Figure 3.2.

In this model, movement among *the stages of treatment is guided by what is happening for the client*, providing a framework of personalized care that is recursive, flexible, relational, and integrative. Part II of this book will discuss ways in which the eight phases and three prongs of EMDR therapy may be integrated into this model. *Stabilization* usually

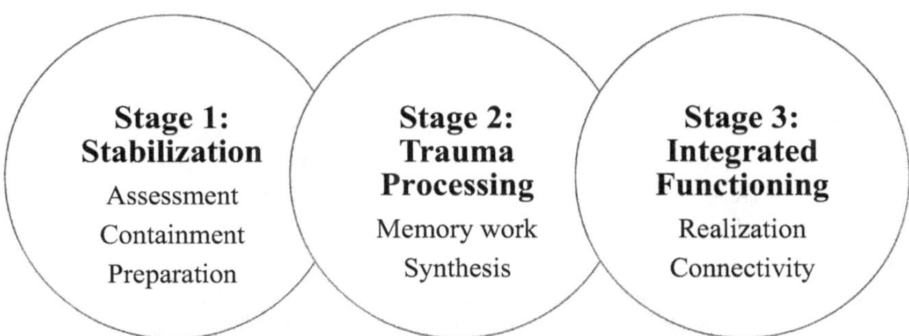

Figure 3.2 The Three-Stage Model of Treatment.

involves models other than EMDR, aside from the essential tasks of screening for dissociation and determining readiness for trauma-focused work. (See Chapters 7 and 8 for further discussion).

Integration, synthesis, or some variation of these terms is often used to characterize *Stage 3* work. However, for DID, this does not *necessarily* mean that integration (i.e., fusion) of self-states (also known as alters) is the client's desired goal or preferred treatment outcome. Rather, increasingly *integrated functioning* is an expected marker of intrapsychic health and is almost invariably an organic result of effective stabilization and trauma processing. For this reason, we chose the term 'integrated functioning' to represent clients' gradual process of building and/or restoring functional connectivity. Through this process, clients begin to perceive both their self and their social environment in more cohesive, consonant, and present-day oriented ways.

The writings of Janet and Sidis endorse the importance of integrated functioning for ensuring psychological health. Both viewed the process of psychic synthesis as oriented toward health, and dissociation (disaggregation) as the basis of psychopathology (Janet, 1889/2022a, 2022b; Sidis, 1898; Sidis & Goodhart, 1904/1968). Consistent with Janet, Sidis stated that "the very nature of mental activity is synthesis" (Sidis, 1898, p. 210) and noted that absent disruption, mental development and functioning will proceed in the direction of health. For Sidis, this comes to bear in clients' view and experience of their history: "[A] fully developed personal system *must have a continuous personal history* [sic]" (Sidis & Goodhart, 1904/1968, p. 57). Sidis (1898, 1909) suggests that integrated functioning can be restored by removing harmful stimuli and facilitating (re)association.

Is Stabilization Necessary?

Even before the development of EMDR therapy, many have debated whether, when, and for whom a stabilization phase necessarily precedes trauma processing. Jenny Ann Rydberg (2017) noted a false dichotomy posed by those who argue against a stabilization phase: "Either we accept the findings of this study demonstrating that stabilisation [sic] is unnecessary, or we must admit that we are acting unprofessionally and harming patients by denying them access to effective trauma treatment" (p. 91). We suggest that modern controversy has been fueled by both misunderstandings of what stabilization entails in the context of the three-stage model and the reality that some therapists err on the side of lengthy stabilization to avoid doing harm. What is all the controversy about? Essentially, it is about whether the complexity and/or the presence of severe dissociation indicates that therapy (specifically, EMDR therapy) should proceed differently than treatment-as-usual. The answer to this question is unavoidably context-specific – just as *every* form of individualized treatment should be.

As early as the first edition of the standard EMDR therapy text, Francine Shapiro (1995) offered this about accessing dissociated memory material:

> [T]he clinician must assess the *client's readiness and ability to uncover and withstand the information* [emphasis added] in order to ascertain whether or not the client can be guided through the disturbance that may emerge as the memory is treated.
>
> (p. 90)

Further along, speaking to readiness for processing via EMDR therapy, Shapiro (1995) asserts that if a client feels pressured to proceed with EMDR reprocessing, then "negative results may occur" (p. 129). Shapiro states that such a client "may remain anxious during the entire session, break off treatment during an abreaction, or dissociate in order to escape the ordeal" (p. 129). Why might this happen? Shapiro alluded to the reasons: Inadequate consent, and difficulty accessing and tolerating the emergence of previously dissociated affect, sensation, and knowledge.

Shapiro's understanding of dissociative phenomena does not seem to have evolved, as suggested by a statement that survived all three editions of her EMDR therapy text. While discussing the potentially distressing emergence of new emotions during reprocessing, Shapiro offers that "...the client should be appropriately screened for a DD before starting EMDR processing. *If this has been adequately done, feelings of dissociation are viewed as the next layer of emotion that needs to be processed*" [emphasis added] (2018, p. 149). This statement seems at the same time both very logical and extremely uninformed. It suggests that clients being aware that they meet criteria for a DD is equivalent to clients knowing how to navigate their dissociated experience. *This framing implicitly places the burden on the client to deal with any dissociative reactions.*

Some voices in the EMDR literature (e.g., Zoet et al., 2018) claim that participants with self-reported symptoms of depersonalization and derealization benefit from unmodified EMDR protocols without a preceding stabilization phase. While some studies report that reprocessing of past traumatic memories can result in a significant reduction in dissociative symptoms (e.g., Molero-Zafra et al., 2024), *the type and severity of dissociative symptoms are often neither thoroughly investigated nor reported.* In a recent study exploring the quality of processing in EMDR, dissociation (measured by DES-II mean scores) was negatively correlated with "good processing," and positively correlated with "indicators of a loss of dual attention" but not "lack of generalization or change" (Ramallo-Machín et al., 2024, p. 7). How confusing. Reducing a multidimensional construct such as 'dissociation' to a single factor in this way poses serious limitations and obstacles to discerning differential treatment responses (Hoeboer et al., 2020). This kind of reductivism happens when researchers and practitioners (1) fail to differentiate between the presence of dissociative symptoms more broadly and specifically meeting criteria for a DD (i.e., dissociation vs. disaggregation), (2) conflate symptom frequency with symptom severity, and (3) look no further at symptoms beyond those that indicate C-PTSD. The importance of using valid diagnostic assessments to rule in or rule out pathological dissociation (disaggregation) cannot be understated. To our knowledge, no study to date has conducted a formal diagnostic evaluation for dissociation nor specifically recruited individuals with DDs, then employed standard EMDR therapy to prove its safety and efficacy with that diagnostic population.

There is, however, evidence that supports both the utility of a stabilization phase (Benincasa et al., 2025; Willis et al., 2023) and the effectiveness of a psychodynamically informed, triphasic relational psychotherapy (Yeates et al., 2024) in the treatment of DDs in adults. The 'gold standard' of randomized controlled trials (RCTs) is difficult to achieve when studying DD treatment. Nonetheless, an international team has worked to close this gap, via the Treatment of Patients with Dissociative Disorders (TOP DD) study (e.g., Brand et al., 2009, 2025; Frewen et al., 2022; www.topddstudy.com).

The Ethical Practice of EMDR Therapy with Dissociation

Mental health practitioners learning to treat DDs and clients in the process of healing and recovering from dissociation have many things in common.

One of those is the tendency for each to misjudge the scope and pacing that is needed to accomplish treatment goals. For clients, this may present as:

- non-realization or denial (What trauma? My childhood was just fine.);
- over idealization of the therapist (I'm working with an expert, so my needs will finally be met); and/or
- idealization of EMDR therapy (If I resolve my trauma, all my symptoms will go away. I heard that for EMDR, I don't have to talk about the memories.).

Practitioners may be led to believe that the 'right' EMDR protocol or advanced training will complete their toolbox (see Chapter 4). Diving into advanced training too early and deeply often yields overconfidence or overwhelm and discouragement. Appropriately scoping and pacing the work is important for practitioners and clients alike! Cultivating an informed approach that is adjusted in scope and in pacing to the capacities of both the practitioner and the client is essential.

We (authors) have each developed metaphors that illustrate our ongoing experience of learning and practicing in the world of treating dissociation. For Jennifer, the experience feels like flying by the seat of one's pants. Over time, the process of orienting to compass points and discerning the direction of the wind has become more reliable and less panicked, but it is infinitely new and recursive with each client. Michael has likened treating dissociation with EMDR to riding a unicycle uphill, blindfolded, while juggling. With much practice and many mis-takes and near misses, one may develop a general sense of balance and keep (too many) balls from dropping.

Foundational Components of Ethical, Impactful, and Meaningful Practice

Four components are identified in our experience and the literature to be critical to ethical, impactful, and meaningful practice in the treatment of dissociation.

Individual Client Factors

The treatment *goals* agreed upon by the client and practitioner at the onset of therapy help clarify the starting point of, and guide the course of, treatment. An important initial consideration is whether the client is seeking symptom relief, comprehensive treatment, or something in between.

- *Symptom relief* – When clients present after a recent disruption in functioning, the initial goal is likely focused on restoring functioning to a

previous 'baseline.' To honor this goal, practitioners will need to align the scope of treatment to allow for the best possible odds of reaching the desired outcome without dredging up more than intended.
- *Comprehensive treatment* – Sometimes clients show up in therapy ready to engage in whatever it takes to resolve long-standing symptoms and issues and symptoms with complex roots. One client said it this way: "I'm here for as long as it takes to clean up this mess and stop passing it on."
- *Something in between* can encompass a range from wishing to address an identified yet complex theme – such as an increased sense of connection in relationships – to an amorphous statement such as "I've been told that I need to work through my trauma." The former lends itself fairly well to clear conceptualization and treatment, while the latter is vague and its external focus may signal an underlying web of complex non-realization and transference potential.

The process of confirming *consent* in trauma-focused treatment, especially in the context of complex trauma and dissociation, is necessarily recursive. Consent applies equally to the client *and* the practitioner. We need to continually assess clients' capacities to consent to goals and interventions as a *whole person*. This includes whether clients can say 'no' or speak up if something isn't okay (e.g., utilizing the 'stop signal,' Shapiro, 2018, p. 121). Consent is also critical when clients are either disproportionately invested in pleasing the therapist or motivated by secondary gains. Secondary gains are treatment-impacting factors such as legal or disability claims, problematic relational binds (e.g., maintaining a victim/sick role to avoid abandonment), or transferential dynamics to steer the focus of therapy toward or away from particular issues.

Speaking of *transference*, a multitude of psychodynamics are likely alive in the therapeutic relationship from the outset. Clients who have experienced profound attachment wounding inevitably perceive the practitioner and the therapy in ways that are filtered by their past and present subjective experience. EMDR has the potential to be a relational, two-person therapy when that reality is embraced by the therapist (Dworkin, 2005; Dworkin & Errebo, 2010; Wachtel, 2002). Moments of idealization and guardedness, for instance, can serve to respectively aid building trust or forward movement and slow the pace of treatment in ways that may ultimately benefit the client. When transference dynamics are intractable and rigid, and the therapist does not have the capacity to address them therapeutically, these can thwart or entirely halt progress. The more complex a person's self-system functioning, the more complex transference dynamics can become (see below, as well as Chapters 9 and 11).

Trauma-focused therapists must develop keen observational and listening skills, as well as their intuition, to attune to what clients share and *how* they share it, what they *don't* say or do, and implicit signs of what is yet to be discovered beneath the conscious surface. The practitioner's discernment of incongruencies and unexplained knowing or feeling too much or too little (on the part of client or therapist), among other factors, will guide the pace and depth of all phases and stages of therapy – EMDR or otherwise.

Core Ethical Principles

Several ethical principles are of heightened relevance for the treatment of complex trauma and dissociation with EMDR therapy. The primary principle to do no harm, or *non-maleficence*, is highly emphasized in our field – and rightly so. This entails our obligation to avoid harming clients; in practice, practitioners must "weigh the benefits against burdens of all interventions and treatments, to eschew those that are inappropriately burdensome, and to choose the best course of action for the patient" (Varkey, 2021, p. 18). Unfortunately, some clients have incurred (additional) harm in the context of psychotherapy resulting from the misapplication of EMDR therapy, practitioners being unable or unwilling to offer the proper treatment, and other negligent actions or inactions. There is no unilateral 'do this' or 'don't do that' that applies unequivocally to non-maleficence in EMDR therapy. A deep understanding of the concept(s) and model(s) being employed and of the experience of the person who is seeking therapy will be the best guide. Let's review the working definitions of essential principles that we will explore more deeply in later chapters.

Professional *negligence* results from the unjustified departure from usual practice or failing to exercise proper care in fulfilling our responsibilities as practitioners (Corey et al., 2023, p. 222), thus acting in ways that are unreasonable given the circumstances, laws, and standards of care associated with our profession and areas of clinical practice (Brown et al., 1998). Substandard care can result from commission or omission. Negligence is more about the process of treatment than the outcome and is most likely to occur when therapists utilize an approach, methodology, or theoretical orientation that does not fall within the standard of care. Examples of negligence in the use of EMDR therapy for treatment of complex trauma and DDs include:

- providing or knowingly participating in an EMDR therapy course that is unaccredited, does not meet the widely accepted training standards, and/or disregards the standard of care for a specific population;

- failing to appropriately detect or evaluate dissociative symptoms prior to administering bilateral dual attention stimulation (BL-DAS); and
- employing standard, unmodified EMDR therapy methods with fidelity without regard for well-known risks of treating dissociation in this way.

Treatment *fidelity*, or integrity, refers to one's adherence to a treatment model or protocol when applied in clinical practice (Waltman et al., 2016). In EMDR therapy, this is the practitioner's ability to administer the standard protocol. Fidelity rating scales are used to ensure reliability in treatment, empirical studies, and to measure proficiency (e.g., Cooper et al., 2019). Fidelity is generally a good thing, except when it ignores individual client factors. So, "one might practice competently without adherence to the model as a whole" (Waltman et al., 2016, p. 179) if the divergence from treatment-as-usual can be justified according to the standard of care and the practitioner's knowledge and skills (Corey et al., 2023).

Proficiency refers to "a distinct procedure, technique, or applied skill set used in psychological assessment, treatment and/or intervention within which one develops competence" (American Psychological Association, 2020). Practitioners can become proficient in applying a circumscribed activity, or in the case of EMDR therapy, in applying the standard protocol and procedures. Developing a specific proficiency both builds upon one's basic competency as a practitioner and is a component of advanced practice.

Competence refers to one's degree of skill in clinical practice (Waltman et al., 2016). Three domains are critical to practitioners' development of competence:

a. Attaining requisite knowledge through academic learning and clinical experience;
b. Acquiring clinical skills based upon empirical evidence and being able to apply those effectively and appropriately; and,
c. Cultivating and maintaining personal behavior and professional conduct as expected in our profession (Homrich & Henderson, 2018, pp. 12–13).

Growth in competence transforms 'requisite knowledge' into the ability to think critically and conceptualize effectively. That knowledge informs our application of clinical skills (*how to be*) within the conceptual frame and treatment plan. This frame informs our conduct, or what we *do* in session – in particular, the distinction between engaging in therapy 'with' our clients as opposed to 'doing therapy to' them. *Being with* our clients requires a relational frame, whereas viewing a memory network as a mole to be removed or a tooth to be extracted is a merely procedural practice, and risks feeling as such.

Specialized practice is characterized by proficiency in treating a specific problem or population, which "requires advanced knowledge and skills acquired through an organized sequence of education and training" (American Psychological Association, 2020). Treatment of clients with complex trauma and DDs is an area of specialized practice, no less so when employing EMDR therapy. The practitioners' process of development toward specialized practice will be addressed further in Chapter 5.

Having defined these concepts, let's contextualize them in EMDR therapy practice specifically. Basic training in EMDR therapy is the setting in which practitioners learn the standard protocols and procedures applied within the three prongs and eight phases. One aims to develop proficiency in EMDR therapy as a protocolized intervention throughout the required practicum and consultation hours within accredited training programs. In North America, the designation 'EMDR trained' indicates that a practitioner has completed an accredited training program. However, without an evaluative process, there is no guarantee that practitioners will apply EMDR therapy at any level of competence or proficiency. Other components are needed to develop a specialization, whether that be in seeking advanced designations in EMDR therapy or specializing in the treatment of trauma, complex trauma, or dissociation.

Therapist Factors

Appendix E: Client Safety in Shapiro (2018, pp. 498–503) describes several practitioner-specific considerations for employing EMDR therapy to treat DDs. If you are not familiar with this section of the standard textbook for EMDR therapy, we strongly recommend that you read it. The task force that developed these guidelines emphasized the importance of formal training and supervision/consultation in the treatment of dissociative clients. Additionally, the task force states that practitioners "should have considerable experience using EMDR on patients without dissociative disorders before attempting it on highly dissociative patients" (Shapiro, 2018, p. 500).

A high degree of competence and nuanced conceptualization skills are critical when treating complex trauma and DDs. Conversance with several theories and models, including and beyond EMDR therapy, enhances our capacity to pragmatically and flexibly attune to our clients' capacities and needs. A keen awareness of ourselves, our clients, and our conceptual frame, and being able to respond based on all three, requires a capacity called *mentalization*. All these attributes are most associated with advanced levels of practitioner development, and as such, cultivating them is often the focus and aim of professional consultation (see Chapter 5).

Treatment logistics and interpersonal boundaries can get messy when practitioners who are new to treating dissociation allow the therapy to go too far too fast. One perennial issue we encounter in our consultation practices is therapist-client contact between or outside of therapy sessions. In a common scenario, practitioners have begun tapping into traumatic material and then struggled to adequately restabilize the client during closure of the session. To assuage their own anxieties and meet the perceived needs of the client, practitioners have offered phone or text conversations after sessions in ways that are contrary to their established practice policies. We consider this to be a violation of the treatment frame on multiple levels – one that is often driven by countertransference, of which these practitioners are often, at best, minimally aware.

Experiences of *countertransference* are ubiquitous in the treatment of complex trauma and dissociation. Like transference, countertransference can be incredibly useful when understood (Dalenberg, 2000; Danylchuk & Connors, 2024). However, it is dangerous to both practitioners and clients if unrecognized and inadequately addressed. Psychotherapists invariably have prior experiences, needs, desires, and skills that inform their choices and advancement in our profession (Maroda, 2022). Karen Maroda has written extensively about the unrecognized and unrealized needs of psychotherapists from the analytic perspective and emphasizes the importance of (a) recognizing our needs so that they may be consciously navigated and (b) substituting self-idealization and positions of defense or power for authenticity. Often, we fear disappointing our clients – or ourselves – to the extent that an impasse or even harm can occur. Instead of striving to be the 'ideal parent' and perfectly attune to every need that we perceive in our clients, Maroda encourages us to model self-possessed authenticity in ways that promise to support clients' recovery and our own well-being. (See Chapters 9 and 11 for additional discussion of transference-countertransference dynamics.)

Several authors have specifically addressed countertransference phenomena as they arise in EMDR therapy practice, noting how it can both benefit the therapeutic process and contribute to 'blocked' processing or inadvertent harm of the client. Olivier Piedfort-Marin (2018) reviewed numerous examples of how psychodynamics such as countertransference may arise and be addressed within standard EMDR therapy. Mark Dworkin and Nancy Errebo (2010) expounded upon an earlier recommendation by Wachtel (2002) that EMDR ought to be taught and practiced as a two-person therapy. They describe a two-person therapy as follows:

> Therapies that employ dialogue between clinician and client about the resonance, attunement, and intention of their relationship are called two-person therapies. Two-person therapies are co-created by clinician and client. In contrast, in one-person therapies, a clinician creates rapport and trust with a client and applies a treatment; in one-person therapies the interaction between the brains of the clinician and client remains implicit.
>
> (Dworkin & Errebo, 2010, p. 114)

Fidelity to EMDR therapy procedures prescribes that practitioners closely follow the standard protocol and 'stay out of the way' of the processing, intervening only when processing appears to have stalled. Unless a practitioner is trained in a relational psychotherapy approach and receives support in integrating EMDR into a relational frame, they are likely to default to employing EMDR as a one-person (i.e., 'do to' rather than 'be with') therapy (Wachtel, 2002). Regardless of whether practitioners recognize the relational dynamics with clients, those dynamics still exist and influence the work. When we do not consider the role of intersubjectivity in the therapeutic space, we may fail to pick up on a lot of information about our clients and ourselves. That missed information can either enhance or diminish the progress and quality of therapy, particularly in work with clients with histories of attachment and/or relational trauma.

Many other therapist factors are relevant to the process of treating complex trauma and dissociation. Therapists' personal history of trauma, which is common, may put them at greater risk of vicarious traumatization (Henderson et al., 2025). Susceptibility to trance and therefore vulnerability to the clients' autohypnotic trance states is also noteworthy (Loewenstein, 1993; see also Part IV of this book). Various considerations drawn from the psychodynamic and Ego State Therapy traditions, such as the practitioner's own ego strength, are relevant and can impact treatment and the therapeutic relationship. Here, we are speaking of the often-unseen interactions between the intensity and complexity of the client's trauma material and the practitioner's own personal experience (Gartner and contributors, 2016; Watkins & Watkins, 1997).

Conceptualization

The ethical and effective application of *any* theoretical model or psychotherapy approach depends upon practitioners' ability to hold the information provided by their clients alongside or within the theoretical frame. *Conceptualization* involves the development of a coherent explanation for the present symptoms or distress and using the model to guide the direction, scope, and pace of the treatment plan – all in collaboration with the client. Conceptualization is an iterative process that evolves as new information is revealed, symptoms change, life happens, and feedback is received that instructs a reorienting or reevaluation of the current approach, goal, or intervention.

Recent trends in our field have led to an underemphasis on developing this core clinical competency in favor of a focus on interventions and techniques (Gilboa-Schechtman, 2024). Deep knowledge of a theory/approach, combined with the ability to form an effective case conceptualization, is the result of dedicated study, practice, and supervision/consultation. When practitioners are in the beginning stages of learning an approach, it is normal for attempts at conceptualization to be limited and often rigid, perhaps like a cookie-cutter that discards whatever does not fit within its frame. If we neglect to establish a conceptualization, treatment will proceed without a clear frame and lack both shape and boundaries. Adequate conceptualization operates more like a sandbox, a frame that both provides containment for its contents (the sand, tools, toys) and allows for freedom of movement within that frame. Displacement of the contents, however, may still happen due to extreme conditions, deliberate actions, or accidents.

Conceptualizing Comprehensive Treatment: A Nuanced, Integrative Approach

Comprehensive treatment of complex trauma and DDs is unavoidably integrative and requires dynamic conceptualization skills. The frame of treatment is held by the largest or broadest conceptualizing theory. It provides the boundaries of the therapeutic relationship, the stance and role of the therapist, and the job/role of the client. The framing provided by EMDR and the AIP model *may* be sufficient to guide treatment, typically when the scope of treatment is brief and focused on relief of specific symptoms. Often, employing EMDR therapy in the treatment of DDs requires multiple levels of framing. In comprehensive treatment, other approaches will be necessary, all anchored within the broader frame. This calls for a *synthesis* of theories that together comprise the treatment frame and provide nuanced options to adjust the focus and scope of therapy when navigating complex terrain.

We propose the framework represented in Figure 3.3, which visually depicts the conceptual layers of comprehensive treatment as we are presenting it in this book. Movement between layers is facilitated according to the current stage or focus of treatment. We may initially progress from the outside in, when first developing the therapeutic alliance (relational frame), conducting a diagnostic assessment (theories of dissociation), engaging in mapping of self-states (ego state therapies), and determining

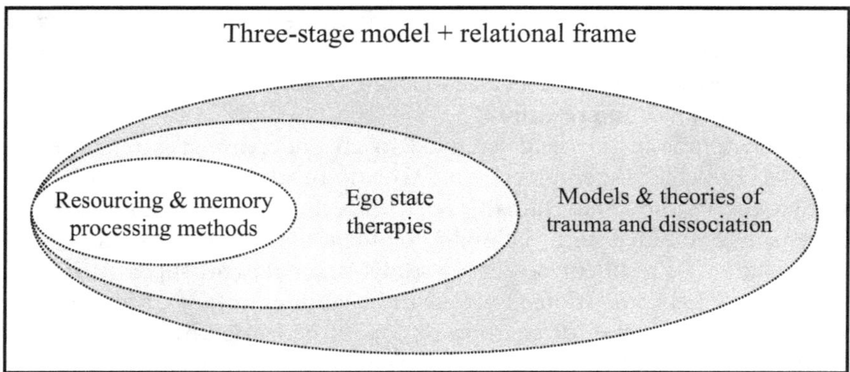

Figure 3.3 Our Conceptualization and Treatment Frame.

Sources: ISSTD (2011); Yeates et al., (2024).

the necessity of and readiness for trauma processing (resourcing and memory processing methods). Later on, as therapy progresses and treatment goals are refined or reevaluated, we may move in or out accordingly. When we move between layers of the treatment frame, the therapy usually looks different – in this case, the most obvious contrast is the reduction in verbal dialogue and addition of scripted protocols when moving into EMDR therapy. The primacy in selection of one or more layers of the frame is guided by the client and therapist factors discussed above, and the current stage of treatment.

Layer 1: Three-Stage Model + Relational Frame

In this book, we utilize a three-stage model of trauma-focused treatment, referred to as *psychodynamically informed psychotherapy* in a recent systematic review by Yeates et al. (2024), which is consonant with the ISSTD treatment guidelines (2011). In this model, the stage of treatment is dictated by what is happening for the client. Care is personalized, flexible, relational, and recursive amongst the stages. As such, it requires weaving in other theories, models, and interventions. Hence, the model has been presented differently by various authors over time, always adapted to the preferred theory of dissociation (e.g., Herman, 1992; Steele et al., 2017).

A relational approach facilitates the navigation of psychodynamics and the client's comprehensive treatment needs and goals. A multitude of psychological issues, including complex trauma and DDs, are repeatedly shown to be born out of relational trauma and neglect (e.g., Xiao et al., 2023). So, approaching the work within a relational frame seems unavoidable. Being prepared to utilize and work with transference and countertransference dynamics is essential, even when employing otherwise standard EMDR therapy (Piedfort-Marin, 2018).

Despite a general consensus among experts in the fields of complex trauma and dissociation on the necessity of the three-stage model, the specifics embedded within that frame may – or may not – pose challenges for treatment. The type and degree of challenge will depend on the complexity posed by the client's experience, and the models and methods in which you, the practitioner, are trained and competent in utilizing. For this reason, we will explicate the layers embedded within our frame.

Layer 2: Models and Theories of Trauma and Dissociation

Multiple models and theories of dissociation are useful to develop our conceptualization of clients' dissociative experiences. These include conceptual models such as the subjective-phenomenological model, the AIP model (aided by Boris Sidis's work; see Chapter 2), diagnostic criteria, and neurobiological models and markers for dissociation. This second layer influences the pace and scope of treatment and how and when other layers will best serve our treatment plan. According to Shapiro (2018), "Adopting the Adaptive Information Processing model can facilitate the ability of many EMDR-trained clinicians to achieve both substantial and comprehensive treatment effects" (p. 17). While referring to a more comprehensive approach, her description of comprehensive treatment is limited to the integrative nature of EMDR and the AIP model. Because of this, we have concluded that AIP must be intregrated within other models to conceptualize and treat dissociation.

Layer 3: Ego State Therapies

Ego state therapies are depicted as the third layer in the frame. These therapies help us know enough about the client's self-system to determine treatment goals, address internal dynamics, obtain multifaceted consent for any form of resourcing and memory processing, and more. Two prominent ego state approaches are Ego State Therapy (Watkins & Watkins, 1997) and Internal Family Systems (Schwartz, 1995). These will be discussed in later chapters, and especially in Part IV of this book.

Layer 4: Resourcing and Memory Processing Methods

Resourcing and memory processing methods are embedded within the outer layers and employed to facilitate stabilization, process traumatic memory material, restore or foster connectivity synthesis, and movement toward integrated functioning, etc. In this book, this layer of the frame draws upon the three prongs and eight phases of EMDR therapy (Shapiro, 2018). Because EMDR is an adjunctive rather than the primary or sole approach for treating complex trauma and dissociation, most interventions we discuss in this book – and specifically in Parts III and IV – reflect a more granular application or modification of the standard protocols and procedures.

Reconceptualizing 'Comprehensive' Treatment

By now, it is probably evident that there are multiple ways to think about comprehensive treatment. There is no recipe. Some clients may not present on paper with a DD, and yet a unidimensional or unorganized 'eclectic' approach may be conceptually and practically inadequate for treatment. Comprehensive treatment may involve the incorporation of conceptual pieces of EMDR and the AIP model – for example, the three domains of experience (responsibility/worth, safety, and control/choice) and three prongs (past, present, future) – and may or may not reach the point of using BL-DAS or approaching a target memory directly.

Other models have been proposed (e.g., Paulsen, 2018) that situate similar elements within the AIP model as the broadest frame. For reasons discussed in Chapter 2, we propose a different hierarchy. We invite you to think critically about the layers of *your* treatment frame, how they are similar to or differ from what we have proposed, and consider the depth and scope of your knowledge and skills to conceptualize and treat complex trauma and dissociation.

Scope and Sequence of Treatment Using EMDR Therapy

With the above multilayered framework in mind, let's consider the scope and sequence of treatment within the EMDR therapy level of the frame. While symptom relief may be what motivates a client to begin psychotherapy, we consider comprehensive treatment to be the ideal course of treatment when complex posttraumatic and dissociative symptoms are present. Nonetheless, this is not always possible. There are often limitations of frame, skills of the practitioner, and client resources such as time and means to pay for treatment. Addressing and reducing symptoms can be consonant with *Stage 1: Stabilization* and sometimes *Stage 2: Trauma Processing* work. However, if treatment ends there, the source of those symptoms may remain to spring forth again. Symptom relief does not often yield integrated functioning or long-term change.

When establishing a treatment plan and specific proximate goals with a client, the type of change that we are hoping to affect is one component that will guide the scope of treatment, and the theories, models, and interventions employed. Two general categories of symptoms (and of change) are discussed in the trauma-focused literature: state and trait. *States* have been conceptualized as transitory and fluctuating moods and other affective, somatic, and neuronal responses to internal or environmental experience – in this case, traumatic or overwhelming experience. *Traits*, in contrast, are relatively stable dispositions, skills, or habitual patterns of behavior, thought, and emotion that differ across individuals and influence behavior (Schöller et al., 2018). Shapiro's AIP model views dysfunctional traits as among the manifestations of unprocessed memories and infers that these can and should change as a result of reprocessing (Shapiro, 2018, p. 39). This view emerged from the accumulating literature; we argue that it is not unique to the AIP model and is incomplete when applied to complex trauma and DDs.

Bruce Perry et al. (1995) described how unhealed childhood trauma (acute states) may result in the development of maladaptive personality traits through their influence on the developing brain, repetition, and the resulting view of self and the world. Shapiro cites this and other papers authored by Perry in both the 2018 and the 2001 editions of her text, though not in relation to the AIP model. Additionally, Shapiro refers to how EMDR therapy works by accessing and reprocessing experiences that are stored in 'state-dependent' memory networks; she even goes so far as to say that "dissociated material may be nothing more than information that is unavailable to awareness because it is stored in state-dependent form in an isolated neural network" (Shapiro, 2018, p. 48). Shapiro seems to equate dissociated ego states, or self-states, with memory networks. We disagree, based on the observation that aspects of a traumatic memory can be shared across multiple self-states. So, does reprocessing the past memory or memories yield state change, trait change, or both? Shapiro seems to argue that the answer is 'both.'

Psychological theory and research point to a circular causality between states and traits, both in the building of and deconstructing of traits. This was illustrated in a longitudinal study by Schöller et al. (2018) in which the dynamics of client states (behaviors, cognitions, and emotions) were observed to trigger transitions (changes in patterns) and modify traits. According to their results, "long-term stabilization of treatment effects requires a change in the levels of traits" (Schöller et al., 2018, p. 456). Moreover, their results indicated that longer, more continuous treatment was more likely to effect pattern/trait change over time as compared to more 'punctual' interventions. Distinctions between states and traits have also been drawn in neuroimaging studies examining anxiety; for example, Saviola et al. (2020) found state and trait anxiety to be distinct, both neuroanatomically and in functional connectivity measurements. This, along with the neuroimaging studies on dissociation showing the neuroanatomical and functional manifestations of dissociation, supports the idea that state change and trait change are distinct.

Both states and traits are implicated in explanations for dissociative symptoms and disorders. As discussed in Chapter 1, dissociation can refer to a state (e.g., hypoarousal) or a sequela of traumatic experience that has reached the level of a pattern of behavior, or a trait, that is reflective of a pattern of internal or external responses that have become maladaptive. Non-pathological dissociation (e.g., absorption) has been termed 'trait dissociation' and is observable in the default mode network – see, for example, Badura Brak et al. (2022). A three-stage relational model accounts for working toward both state and trait change. However, we need a model – or a strategic combination of models – that can fully account for the complexity of relational trauma and DDs in order to engage in comprehensive treatment with clients who are holding those experiences.

Keeping in mind the framework described above and depicted in Figure 3.3, we now consider the scope of treatment as it pertains to EMDR therapy in comprehensive treatment. For purposes of our discussion, the three delineations of scope, ranging from most narrow to most broad, are symptom relief, issue-focused, and comprehensive.

Symptom Relief

The narrowest or most zoomed-in scope of treatment focused on symptom relief is depicted in the darkest, segmented circle in Figure 3.4. An example of this scope of treatment in EMDR therapy is when a single incident, or a fractionated segment of a single incident, is targeted. Reprocessing may be restricted to minimize associations and generalization to other memory networks. Shapiro's original EMD procedure may be employed "for symptom reduction stemming from a memory, or part of a memory, for selected clients who might otherwise become emotionally overwhelmed and dysregulated" (2018, pp. 221–222). In this scope, *Phase V: Installation* and *Phase VI: Body Scan* may not be fully completed, and it is unlikely that all three prongs will be fully addressed.

Within a comprehensive treatment plan, EMD or fractionated processing may be employed toward symptom relief at the service of *Stage 1: Stabilization*, or as a brief foray into *Stage 2: Trauma Processing*. In such cases, the focus is on a specific symptom or memory fragment that is destabilizing, impairing functioning, and/or intrusive.

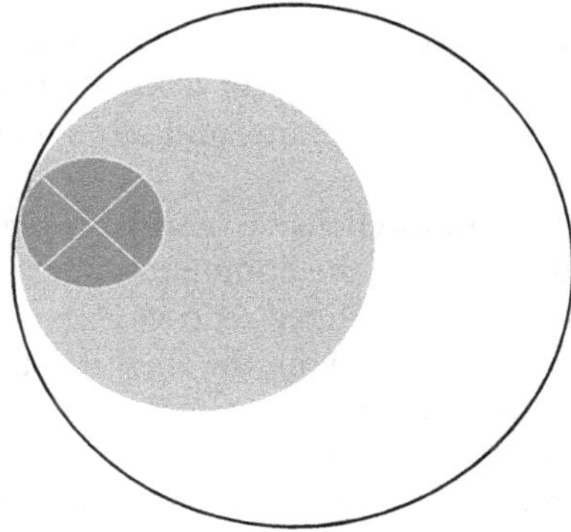

Figure 3.4 Scope of Treatment.

Issue-Focused

When the focus of treatment is to address a specific present-day issue such as performance anxiety or angry outbursts in response to relational triggers, a medium-sized scope is indicated, as represented by the mid gray circle in Figure 3.4. In the EMDR therapy frame, this involves utilizing Floatback or Affect Scan to identify the *Past* prong experience(s) associated with the issue that is showing up in *Present* prong. Some containment or restriction of reprocessing may be done, but generally it is assumed that all phases and prongs are completed whenever possible, and that this must occur for the issue to be resolved.

Within our framework, an issue-focused EMDR treatment plan most certainly represents *Stage 2: Trauma Processing* work. Diagnostic assessment and models of dissociation guide the selection and pacing of this treatment focus. Ego state therapies or other interventions may be employed prior to this work, during EMDR sessions, or to address internal conflicts or gaps in connectivity at the service of resolving the issue or symptom pattern. *Stage 1: Stabilization* and *Stage 3: Integrated Functioning* also apply, and outcomes in both state-change and some trait-change are expected.

Comprehensive Treatment

Clients may also seek therapy with a broad goal in mind – such as wanting to have more fulfilling relationships. When the information gathered in history taking and diagnostic evaluation points to a complex web of internal and external factors contributing to this issue, a comprehensive treatment scope is indicated, corresponding to the largest/outer circle in

Figure 3.4. Assuming that the client and setting allow for it, the duration of treatment is likely to be on the longer side. Within a comprehensive treatment framework, progressive areas of focus may be established to address specific symptoms, states, traits, and self-states toward the goal of more fulfilling relationships.

For Shapiro (2018), a comprehensive treatment plan for someone with PTSD assumes EMDR therapy is the dominant approach, entailing a three-prong treatment plan with unrestricted reprocessing of multiple past prong targets, as discussed above. Following the identification and reprocessing of multiple past prong targets, present triggers are checked and addressed to ensure resolution, and future templates are completed to ensure generalization. State- and trait-change are thought to occur organically, in a circular fashion, as memory networks are consolidated and reach adaptive resolution. Regarding complex PTSD, Shapiro states, "It is important that clients with complex PTSD receive comprehensive treatment to address all areas of dysfunction after a thorough assessment and adequate stabilization has been achieved" (2018, p. 347). That implies that (a) interventions in addition to the standard EMDR protocol are needed and (b) multiple treatment plans may be required to address 'all areas of dysfunction.'

Comprehensive Treatment Example

In real life, we find that comprehensive treatment for persons with complex trauma and/or dissociation looks something like Figure 3.5. Multiple issues and symptoms, both directly related/adjacent to each other and distinct, will invite iterative treatment plans of various scope with recursive movement through the three stages of trauma-focused treatment and, within some iterations, all phases and prongs of EMDR therapy. Let's imagine comprehensive treatment for a client presenting with the goal of having more stable and fulfilling relationships. The following sequence assumes an initial completion of *Stage 1: Stabilization*, diagnostic assessment of complex trauma without full meeting criteria for a DD, and *Phases I* and *II* of EMDR therapy.

1. The treatment goal is to have more stable and fulfilling relationships. This is represented by the largest, unshaded circle.
2. The breakup of a recent relationship is represented by the segmented mid-gray circle, on the upper right of the diagram. This experience, though recent, looms large. Alongside ensuring consent and readiness of the client's self-system, the practitioner fractionates this into multiple targets for EMD, based on a chronological timeline, to contain reprocessing and prevent activation of associated memory

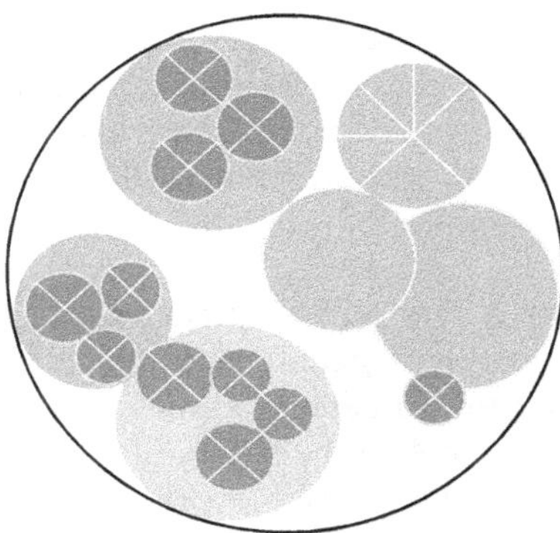

Figure 3.5 Comprehensive Treatment Example.

networks. As such, this represents an initial foray into *Stage 2: Trauma Processing* work.

3. Near-resolution of the distress associated with the recent breakup clarifies and reveals a pattern of anxious-avoidant attachment, highlighted by a recent trigger that evoked internal conflict in response to receiving or not receiving attention. Psychodynamics in the therapist-client relationship raised this issue to prominence, though the patterns were quite familiar to the client. A lineage of six incidents associated with the client's parental relationships are identified via Affect Scan and ego state work – represented by the two mid-gray circles and seven dark and segmented circles in the shape of an 'S.' Understanding this as primarily *Stage 2* work, several targets required fractionation and/or ego state work to reprocess fully, due to internal dynamics associated with attachment to caregivers.
4. Upon addressing the most charged memories and internal dynamics associated with early attachment experience, the need to develop emotional regulation skills became apparent. Now, the client as a whole self was more able and willing to practice simple grounding skills, etc. This represents a revisiting of the largest, unshaded circle, and various interventions situated within *Stage 1: Stabilization* and *Stage 3: Integrated Functioning*.
5. Reevaluation of the client's symptoms and functioning identified a gap in the development of close peer relationships, represented toward the top of the diagram by the larger mid-gray circle and three segmented dark circles within it. Past incidents and associated ego states were identified as related to bullying and loss of friendships in adolescence and young adulthood. As before, fractionation and/or ego state work

> was required to fully reprocess these experiences in EMDR therapy. This treatment episode represented both *Stage 2: Trauma Processing* work and *Stage 3: Integrated Functioning* and supporting the client in building a full spectrum of developmentally appropriate relationships in present life.

You might notice that two mid-gray circles and one dark segmented circle have not yet been mentioned. The process of comprehensive treatment within a multilayered framework allows for the flexible and gradual identification of and response to the issues and symptoms that rise to the top priority as treatment progresses. Sometimes comprehensive treatment continues until planned termination; sometimes it is interrupted or ends prematurely.

Conclusion and Recommendations

In this chapter, we have discussed a few of the complexities of deep and often long-term psychotherapy with persons with complex trauma and DDs. Ethical practice in this context is nuanced, flexible and requires practitioners to persist beyond the beginning stages of learning and competency toward mastery and specialized practice.

We are in favor of including EMDR within the framework of comprehensive treatment for persons with complex trauma and DDs *when it is applied judiciously* and nuanced to fit the goals and readiness factors presented by the individual client. In general, if the client meets criteria only for the dissociative subtype of PTSD or C-PTSD, EMDR can sometimes occupy the primary frame; for symptom relief, this is certainly the case – though not necessarily for comprehensive treatment. For some dissociative clients, EMDR may serve as a primarily *Stage 2: Trauma Processing* approach and be embedded within other models. An exception to this could be treatment of acute stress symptoms following a recent incident – which would be focused on discrete symptom relief. When the client meets criteria for DID, EMDR ought to be an adjunctive approach within a larger network of frames and models, with the scope of reprocessing adjusted to fit the consent, preparedness, and complexity of the person's self-system. Sometimes things are not clear – diagnostically and otherwise. In such circumstances, elements of EMDR therapy and the expanded AIP model that we proposed can still be useful conceptually.

Symptom relief and comprehensive treatment are not necessarily either/or choices. Our scope and direction at any point in therapy will guide and be guided by a number of factors, including and in addition to Shapiro's 'red flags.' Many of those listed below are discussed in more depth in other chapters.

- Pacing and addressing trauma-specific barriers to continuing treatment, such as phobias of internal experience or traumatic memories. Too much too soon can increase drop-out rates (Nester et al., 2022).
- Complexity of the dissociation and the severity of the dissociation (see Chapters 2 and 6).
- Needs/goals of the client – and of different self-states. Informed consent must be discerned accordingly to determine whether the client has the capacity to say 'no' when it is not okay to proceed.
- Training, experience, and abilities of the practitioner (Nester et al., 2022).
- Treatment setting and third-party factors. Timing and number of sessions may be dictated or influenced by the payor or the setting in which the practitioner works. Goals and focus of treatment may also be directed by these.
- The therapeutic alliance. Short, symptom-focused episodes of standard EMDR therapy *may* be less dependent upon client-therapist fit. Longer, deeper treatment within a relational frame requires a robust therapeutic alliance and a good fit between client and practitioner. This includes considering whether (and how) different states perceive the practitioner.
- Client *and* practitioner tolerances of trauma-related behavior affect, sensation, and knowledge (BASK material; Braun, 1988a, 1988b – see Chapter 10) impact the pace and scope of treatment. These may contribute to impasses and halt the progress of therapy – especially if either one continually turns away from what needs to be felt or known (e.g., Chefetz, 2017).
- The ability of both client *and* practitioner to tolerate trauma-related BASK material directly shapes the pace and depth of treatment. When either continually struggles to face what must be felt or known, progress can stall, and impasses are likely (e.g., Chefetz, 2017).
- Issues of secondary gain. Some clients experience some benefit associated with their symptoms, such as financial support, decreased pressure to earn an income, or sympathy from others. They may desire only stabilization of symptoms and a supportive relationship rather than the change or recovery that comprehensive treatment can facilitate.

Other internal/interoceptive factors and external/exteroceptive factors may emerge that are unique to the individual at the outset of treatment, or later. If the client does not yet realize their dissociative experience, the anticipated scope and frame may need to be intentionally adjusted from what the client *and* the practitioner originally expected. Relying upon thinkers and mentors who have gone before, and staying close to the standard of care, will help practitioners who are new(er) to treating complex trauma and dissociation to apply their skills and navigate the unique situations that each client brings.

References

American Psychological Association. (2020, August). *Principles for the recognition of proficiencies in professional psychology*. Commission for the recognition of proficiencies and specialties in professional psychology (CRSSPP). www.apa.org/about/policy/recognition-principles.pdf

American Psychological Association. (2024). *Guidelines for working with adults with complex trauma histories*. www.apa.org/practice/guidelines/adults-complex-trauma-histories.pdf

Australian Psychological Society. (2024). *Evidence-based psychological interventions of the treatment of mental disorders: A literature review* (5th ed.). psychology.org.au/for-the-public/psychology-topics/evidence-based-psychological-interventions

Badura Brack, A. S., Marklin, M., Embury, C. M., Picci, G., Frenzel, M., Klanecky Earl, A., Stephen, J., Wang, Y. P., Calhoun, V., & Wilson, T. W. (2022). Neurostructural brain imaging study of trait dissociation in healthy children. *BJPsych Open, 8*(5), e172. https://doi.org/10.1192/bjo.2022.576

Benincasa, C. A., O'Connor, S., Pierorazio, N. A., Wentling, S. S., Brand, B. L., Israel, B. S., & Schielke, H. J. (2025). Inpatient outcomes following admission to stabilization-focused complex trauma- and dissociation-specific unit. *Psychological Trauma: Theory, Research, Practice and Policy, 17*(8), 1728–1735.https://doi.org/10.1037/tra0001748

Blue Knot Foundation. (2019a). [Kezelman, C., & Stavropoulos, P.]. *Practice guidelines for clinical treatment of complex trauma*. National Centre for Excellence for Complex Trauma.

Blue Knot Foundation. (2019b). [Kezelman, C., & Stavropoulos, P.]. *Complementary guidelines to practice guidelines for clinical treatment of complex trauma*. National Centre for Excellence for Complex Trauma.

Brand, B. L., Classen, C. C., Lanius, R., Loewenstein, R. J., McNary, S. W., Pain, C., & Putnam, F. W. (2009). A naturalistic study of dissociative identity disorder and dissociative disorder not otherwise specified patients treated by community clinicians. *Psychological Trauma: Theory, Research, Practice, & Policy, 1*(2), 153–171. psycnet.apa.org/doi/10.1037/a0016210

Brand, B. L., Schielke, H. J., Putnam, K., Pierorazio, N. A., Nester, M. S., Robertson, J., Myrick, A. C., Loewenstein, R. J., Putnam, F. W., Steele, K., Boon, S., & Lanius, R. A. (2025). A randomized controlled trial assists individuals with complex trauma and dissociation in Finding Solid Ground. *Psychological Trauma: Theory, Research, Practice, and Policy*. Advance online publication. https://doi.org/10.1037/tra0001871

Braun, B. G. (1988a). The BASK model of dissociation. *Dissociation, 1*(1), 4–23. hdl.handle.net/1794/1276

Braun, B. G. (1988b). The BASK model of dissociation: Part II – treatment. *Dissociation, 1*(2), 16–23. hdl.handle.net/1794/1340

Breuer, J., & Freud, S. (1955). Studies on hysteria (J. Strachey, Trans. & Ed.). In J. Strachey (Ed.), *The standard edition of the complete psychological works of Sigmund Freud* (Vol. 2, pp. 1–305). Hogarth Press. (Original work published 1895).

Brown, D., Scheflin, A. W., & Hammond, D. C. (1998). *Memory, trauma treatment, and the law*. W. W. Norton & Company. https://doi.org/10.1176/ps.50.11.1501

Chefetz, R. A. (2017). Issues in consultation for treatments with distressed activated abuser/protector self-states in dissociative identity disorder. *Journal of Trauma & Dissociation, 18*(3), 465–475. https://doi.org/10.1080/15299732.2017.1295428

Cooper, R. Z., Smith, A. D., Lewis, D., Lee, C. W., & Leeds, A. M. (2019). Developing the interrater reliability of the modified EMDR fidelity checklist. *Journal of EMDR Practice and Research, 13*(1), 32–50. https://doi.org/10.1891/1933-3196.13.1.32

Corey, G., Corey, M. S., & Corey, C. (2023). *Issues and ethics in the helping professions* (11th ed.). Cengage Learning.

Dalenberg, C. J. (2000). *Countertransference and the treatment of trauma*. American Psychological Association. https://doi.org/10.1037/10380-000

Danylchuk, L. S. & Connors, K. J. (2024). *Treating complex trauma and dissociation: A practical guide to navigating therapeutic challenges* (2nd ed.). https://doi.org/10.4324/9781003217541

Dworkin, M. (2005). *EMDR and the relational imperative: The therapeutic relationship in EMDR therapy*. Routledge.

Dworkin, M., & Errebo, N. (2010). Rupture and repair in the EMDR client/clinician relationship: Now moments and moments of meeting. *Journal of EMDR Practice and Research, 4*(3), 113–123. https://doi.org/10.1891/1933-3196.4.3.113

Frewen, P., Brand, B. L., Schielke, H. J., McPhail, I. V., & Lanius, R. (2022). Examining the 4-D model in persons enrolled in the TOP DD internet intervention. *Journal of Trauma & Dissociation, 23(5), 559–577.* https://doi.org/10.1080/15299732.2022.2079794

Gartner, R. B. (Ed.) (2016). *Trauma and countertrauma, resilience and counterresilience: Insights from psychoanalysts and trauma experts*. Routledge. https://doi.org/10.4324/9781315716213

Gilboa-Schechtman E. (2024). Case conceptualization in clinical practice and training. *Clinical Psychology in Europe*, *6*(Special Issue), e12103. https://doi.org/10.32872/cpe.12103

Henderson, A., Jewell, T., Huang, X., & Simpson, A. (2025). Personal trauma history and secondary traumatic stress in mental health professionals: A systematic review. *Journal of Psychiatric and Mental Health Nursing, 32*(1), 13–30. https://doi.org/10.1111/jpm.13082

Herman, J. L. (1992). *Trauma and recovery*. Basic Books.

Hoeboer, C. M., De Kleine, R. A., Molendijk, M. L., Schoorl, M., Oprel, D. A. C., Mouthaan, J., Van der Does, W., & Van Minnen, A. (2020). Impact of dissociation on the effectiveness of psychotherapy for post-traumatic stress disorder: Meta-analysis. *British Journal of Psychiatry Open, 6*(3), e53. https://doi.org/10.1192/bjo.2020.30

Homrich, A. M., & Henderson, K. L. (Eds.). (2018). *Gatekeeping in the mental health professions.* American Counseling Association.

International Society for the Study of Trauma and Dissociation. (2011). Guidelines for treating dissociative identity disorder in adults, third revision. *Journal of Trauma & Dissociation, 12*(2), 115–187. https://doi.org/10.1080/15299732.2011.537248

International Society for Traumatic Stress Studies. (2018). [Berliner, L., Bisson, J., Cloitre, M., Forbes, D., Goldbeck, L., Jensen, T., Lewis, C., Monson, C., Olff, M., Pilling, S., Riggs, D., Roberts, N., & Shapiro, F.]. *ISTSS guidelines position paper on complex PTSD in adults.* istss.org/getattachment/Treating-Trauma/New-ISTSS-Prevention-and-Treatment-Guidelines/ISTSS_CPTSD-Position-Paper-(Adults)_FNL.pdf.aspx

Janet, P. (2022a). *Subconscious acts, anesthesias and psychological disaggregation in psychological automatism: Partial automatism* (1st ed.)(G. Craparo & O. van der Hart, Eds.; A. Crabtree & S. Osei-Bonsu, Trans.). Routledge. (Original work published 1889). https://doi.org/10.4324/9781003198727

Janet, P. (2022b). *Catalepsy, memory and suggestion in psychological automatism: Total automatism* (1st ed.)(G. Craparo & O. van der Hart, Eds.; A. Crabtree & S. Osei-Bonsu, Trans.). Routledge. (Original work published 1889) https://doi.org/10.4324/9780429287671

Loewenstein, R. J. (1993). Posttraumatic and dissociative aspects of transference and countertransference in the treatment of multiple personality disorder. In R. P. Kluft & C. G. Fine (Eds.), *Clinical perspectives on multiple personality disorder* (pp. 51–85). American Psychiatric Press.

Maroda, K. J. (2022). *The analyst's vulnerability: Impact on theory and practice.* Routledge.

Molero-Zafra, M., Fernández-García, O., Mitjans-Lafont, M. T., Pérez-Marín, M., & Hernández-Jiménez, M. J. (2024). Psychological intervention in women victims of childhood sexual abuse: a randomized controlled clinical trial comparing EMDR psychotherapy and trauma-focused cognitive behavioral therapy. *Frontiers in Psychiatry, 15,* 1360388. https://doi.org/10.3389/fpsyt.2024.1360388

Nester, M. S., Hawkins, S. L., & Brand, B. L. (2022). Barriers to accessing and continuing mental health treatment among individuals with dissociative symptoms. *European Journal of Psychotraumatology, 13*(1), 2031594. https://doi.org/10.1080/20008198.2022.2031594

Paulsen, S. L. (2018). Neuroaffective embodied self therapy (NEST): An integrative approach to case formulation and EMDR treatment planning for complex cases. *Frontiers in the Psychotherapy of Trauma and Dissociation, 1*(2), 125–148. https://doi.org/10.46716/ftpd.2017.0009

Perry, B., Pollard, R., Blakley, T., Baker, W., & Vigilante, D. (1995). Childhood trauma, the neurobiology of adaptation, and "use-dependent" development of the brain: How "states" become "traits." *Infant Mental Health Journal, 16,* 271–290.

Piedfort-Marin, O. (2018). Transference and countertransference in EMDR therapy. *Journal of EMDR Practice and Research, 12*(3), 158–172. https://doi.org/10.1891/1933-3196.12.3.158

Ramallo-Machín, A., Gómez-Salas, F. J., Burgos-Julián, F., Santed-Germán, M. A., & Gonzalez-Vazquez, A. I. (2024). Factors influencing quality of processing in EMDR therapy. *Frontiers in Psychology, 15*, 1432886. https://doi.org/10.3389/fpsyg.2024.1432886

Rydberg, J. A. (2017). Research and clinical issues in trauma and dissociation: Ethical and logical fallacies, myths, misreports, and misrepresentations. *European Journal of Trauma & Dissociation, 1*, 89–99. https://doi.org/10.1016/j.ejtd.2017.03.011

Saviola, F., Pappaianni, E., Monti, A., Grecucci, A., Jovicich, J., & De Pisapia, N. (2020). Trait and state anxiety are mapped differently in the human brain. *Scientific reports, 10*(1), 11112. https://doi.org/10.1038/s41598-020-68008-z

Schöller, H., Viol, K., Aichhorn, W., Hütt, M. T., & Schiepek, G. (2018). Personality development in psychotherapy: A synergetic model of state-trait dynamics. *Cognitive Neurodynamics, 12*(5), 441–459. https://doi.org/10.1007/s11571-018-9488-y

Schwartz, R. (1995). *Internal family systems therapy*. The Guilford Press.

Shapiro, F. (1995). *Eye movement desensitization and reprocessing: Basic principles, protocols, and procedures*. The Guilford Press.

Shapiro, F. (2018). *Eye Movement Desensitization and Reprocessing (EMDR) therapy: Basic principles, protocols and procedures* (3rd ed.). The Guilford Press.

Sidis, B. (1898). *The psychology of suggestion: A research into the subconscious nature of man and society*. D. Appleton and Company.

Sidis, B. (1909). Studies in psychopathology: The psychotherapeutic value of the hypnoidal state. *Boston Medical and Surgical Journal, 161*(8), 242–247. www.nejm.org/doi/abs/10.1056/NEJM190908261610904

Sidis, B., & Goodhart, S. P. (1968). *Multiple personality: An experimental investigation into the nature of human individuality*. Greenwood Press. (Original work published 1904).

Steele, K., Boon, S., & Van der Hart, O. (2017). *Treating trauma-related dissociation: A practical, integrative approach*. W. W. Norton & Company.

United Kingdom Psychological Trauma Society. (2017). *Guideline for the treatment and planning of services for complex PTSD in adults*. ukpts.org/cptsd-guideline/

Van der Hart, O., Brown, P., & Van der Kolk, B. A. (1989). Pierre Janet's treatment of post-traumatic stress. *Journal of Traumatic Stress, 2*(4), 379–395. https://doi.org/10.1007/BF00974597

Varkey B. (2021). Principles of clinical ethics and their application to practice. *Medical Principles and Practice, 30*(1), 17–28. https://doi.org/10.1159/000509119

Wachtel, P. L. (2002). EMDR and psychoanalysis. In F. Shapiro (Ed.), *EMDR as an integrative psychotherapy approach: Experts of diverse orientations explore the paradigm prism* (pp. 123–150). American Psychological Association. https://doi.org/10.1037/10512-005

Waltman, S. H., Frankel, S. A., & Williston, M. A. (2016). Improving clinician self-awareness and increasing accurate representation of clinical competencies. *Practice Innovations, 1*(3), 178–188. https://doi.org/10.1037/pri0000026

Watkins, J. G. & Watkins, H. H. (1997). *Ego states: Theory and therapy*. W. W. Norton & Company.

Willis, N., Dowling, A. P. C., & O'Reilly, P. G. (2023). Stabilisation and phase-orientated psychological treatment for posttraumatic stress disorder: A systematic review and meta-analysis. *European Journal of Trauma & Dissociation, 7*(1), 100311. https://doi.org/10.1016/j.ejtd.2022.100311

World Health Organization. (2018). *ICD-11: International classification of diseases. 11th Revision*. https://icd.who.int/

Xiao, Z., Murat Baldwin, M., Wong, S. C., Obsuth, I., Meinck, F., & Murray, A. L. (2023). The impact of childhood psychological maltreatment on mental health outcomes in adulthood: A systematic review and meta-analysis. *Trauma Violence Abuse, 24*(5), 3049–3064. https://doi.org/10.1177/15248380221122816

Yeates, S., Korner, A., & McLean, L. (2024). A systematic review and narrative analysis of the evidence for individual psychodynamically informed psychotherapy in the treatment of dissociative identity disorder in adults. *Journal of Trauma & Dissociation, 25*(2), 248–278. https://doi.org/10.1080/15299732.2023.2293802

Zoet, H. A., Wagenmans, A., Van Minnen, A., & De Jongh, A. (2018). Presence of the dissociative subtype of PTSD does not moderate the outcome of intensive trauma- focused treatment for PTSD. *European Journal of Psychotraumatology, 9*(1), 1468707. https://doi.org/10.1080/20008198.2018.1468707

Zur, O. (2022). *The standard of care in psychotherapy and counseling*. https://drzur.com/standard-of-care-therapy/

Part II

Ethics in Action

Chapter 4

Stumbling into Dissociation with EMDR Therapy

D. Michael Coy and Jennifer A. Madere

Introduction

The relationship between the fields of EMDR therapy and dissociative disorders (DDs) has been fraught since the earliest reports of undiagnosed dissociative clients decompensating after reprocessing. Subsequently, the potential risks of using EMDR therapy received significant attention in literature, treatment guidelines, and conference presentations throughout the 1990s and into the early 2000s. The focus was twofold: (1) discernment of dissociative symptoms and disorders to avoid unwitting use of EMDR therapy with undiagnosed dissociation and (2) obtaining adequate and ongoing training and consultation to treat dissociative clients (e.g., International Society for the Study of Dissociation, 2005; Lazrove & Fine, 1996; Paulsen, 1995; Shapiro, 1995, 1996; Twombly, 2000). Since the early 2000s, attention has been devoted to modifying standard EMDR therapy to accommodate and treat dissociative symptoms and disorders. Information about EMDR therapy-driven treatment of dissociation continues to be provided *without* attention to the nuances and complexities of dissociation. This is highly problematic. EMDR therapists are recipients of the same types of foundational education as other practitioners, which may either have glossed over, entirely ignored, or outright denied dissociation as a relevant treatment concern (Brand, 2024; Steinberg & Schnall, 2001).

Despite the emphasis placed upon discernment and treatment of dissociation in the EMDR therapy field over the past 35 years, there has been a near-absence of attention given to ethical considerations specific to EMDR therapy and dissociation. In Chapter 3, we proposed an expanded conceptual frame for doing so. In this chapter, we examine the four 'schools of thought' on treating dissociation that may influence EMDR practitioners' decision-making. Following the process of Quinn, a newly trained EMDR therapist, who received a referral for a client with a complex history,

DOI: 10.4324/9781003410201-6

provides an example of the practical and ethical challenges faced by practitioners in the field.

Stumbling into Dissociation

Quinn (they/them) is an early-career, Master's-level mental health practitioner who works at a not-for-profit community health center. They love their job, but staff capacity cannot meet the high demand for mental health services. The center's management emphasizes the importance of being a 'team player' with one's colleagues. Quinn is also newly trained in EMDR therapy. In fact, they only just received their certificate of completion for basic training a few months ago. Because they are the only EMDR-trained practitioner on staff, Quinn has been designated as the center's 'EMDR expert.'

Recently, Quinn received a referral from a primary care doctor at the center to work with a young woman named Jane. The doctor noted that Jane may have posttraumatic stress disorder (PTSD) symptoms, stemming from a recent sexual assault. In the intake session, Quinn perceived a lot of complexity in their new client's history, as Jane's memory for her childhood experience seemed to be spotty. Keeping in mind EMDR's three-prong approach, Quinn asked Jane whether she sensed any connections between her present-day symptoms and her past experience. Jane quickly insisted, "That's all in the past – I'm here to deal with what happened to me recently," and expressed impatience to 'do EMDR' as soon as possible, based on the doctor's recommendation. Jane has heard from friends online and seen on social media that EMDR is 'great,' and is hopeful to 'get her life back.' Jane also offhandedly mentioned to Quinn that she expected treatment with EMDR to take "a couple of months, at most."

After just one history-taking session, Quinn sensed there may be more going on than only PTSD. Jane *did* endorse flashbacks (including nightmares) related to the recent assault. In her second session, Jane disclosed that in a couple of the nightmares she remembered seeing herself as a child rather than as an adult and still felt that way upon awakening. Jane also reported having a hard time remembering periods of time growing up and struggling with a few persistent physical symptoms for which her doctor can find no explanation. For example, Jane shared that she experiences both difficulties with swallowing at times and periodic flare-ups of genitourinary issues. She said that no doctor has been able to figure out why these symptoms are happening. The doctor did not mention these to Quinn at the time of referral. Quinn later learned that the doctor did not think these physical symptoms were relevant for PTSD treatment, particularly since they pre-dated the sexual assault. In her third session with

Quinn, Jane alluded to 'hearing voices' in her head and being bothered by day-to-day memory problems. Both experiences seemed to be frequent for Jane, as far as Quinn could tell, and appeared to predate the assault. Jane also reported that these experiences increased in frequency and intensity in the days following the assault.

Following the first few sessions, Quinn decided to focus on making sense of Jane's known symptoms. There was no doubt that Jane met the DSM diagnostic criteria for PTSD. Quinn discovered that 'hearing voices' can be a feature of PTSD, though it is seemingly not a common one, as it is mentioned only as an 'associated feature' (American Psychiatric Association, 2022). A lack of recall of an important aspect of the traumatic event makes sense, and is consistent with the PTSD criteria, but Jane's memory problems extended back to childhood and included issues with day-to-day recall. Jane's doctor was able to confirm Jane's report of no known history or evidence of traumatic brain injury that would suggest an organic basis for the memory problems. Quinn repeatedly saw the word 'dissociation' mentioned in the DSM section on PTSD. Quinn received limited information in EMDR basic training about screening for dissociation but does know that it can be problematic for reprocessing. Quinn feels conflicted but can't quite figure out why. They wanted to try to make space to think about why they felt so torn.

Working with Uncertainty: An Ethical Choice Process

Certainly, Quinn does not want to stand in the way of Jane getting relief from her symptoms. At the same time, they feel uncomfortable with the pressure to dive into reprocessing, based on both Jane's sense of urgency and what feels like an explicit order from the referring primary care doctor. Quinn also recalls the voice of their EMDR basic trainer, who was very enthusiastic and strongly urged learners to 'just do it,' echoing in their minds. The trainer stated that practicing with clients is crucial in the learning process, as it helps build confidence in using EMDR. However, Quinn was one of a handful of learners in their basic training who seemed to have a hard time getting through all eight phases and three prongs of the standard protocol with any of their clients. These clients seemed to struggle a lot with reprocessing, and using cognitive interweaves didn't seem to help much. On one hand, Quinn wants to be a 'team player' by helping Jane find relief. On the other hand, Quinn is not certain whether jumping into reprocessing with *this* client is the right course of action, especially with several unanswered questions about Jane's symptoms. And, if Jane is experiencing something more complex than 'just' PTSD, Quinn isn't certain how EMDR fits into treatment at their current level of experience. And what will Quinn's colleagues, their supervisor Tom, and even the referring doctor think if Quinn doesn't deliver EMDR therapy as prescribed?

Sitting with uncertainty can be quite challenging, regardless of a therapist's knowledge and experience, especially earlier in their career (Fewings & Quinlan, 2023; Quinlan et al., 2021). Beyond the practical aspects of this dilemma, the attachment-related anxieties stoked by feeling compelled to please – or not disappoint – clients, supervisors, and colleagues may heighten the risk of impaired clinical decision-making and, eventually, burnout (Bhattacharyya & Banerjee, 2022; McWilliams, 2021). Quinn began to recognize that their bind may involve bigger issues, beyond whether to reprocess trauma. Uncertain about how to sort out their conflicting thoughts and feelings, Quinn turned first to a book that was recommended by one of their basic training consultants, *Ethics for Psychotherapists and Counselors: A Proactive Approach* (Anderson & Handelsman, 2010).

Anderson and Handelsman (2010, p. 90) reviewed several ethical decision-making models and found that most of them included four steps:

1. identify the problem;
2. develop and analyze alternatives using relevant codes, guidelines, laws, regulations, and policies;
3. consult with other professionals; and
4. choose, implement, and evaluate the decision.

Quinn noted how the authors reframed these steps as an *ethical choice process*, stressing the terms *choice* and *process* to highlight the model's dynamic and recursive nature and the active role of the practitioner in the process (Anderson & Handelsman, 2010). Quinn liked the idea of a 'process,' because it reminded them a bit of the reprocessing phases in EMDR. They had observed in practicum that sometimes the processing didn't move in a straight line from beginning to end. Quinn decided to use this *ethical choice process* as a guide for working through their bind. (For an alternative ethical decision-making model, see Stark et al., 2024.)

Identifying the Problem

Quinn spent time considering the nature of their problem. This is what they came up with:

- A client was referred specifically for PTSD treatment with EMDR therapy.

- The therapist (Quinn) was only recently trained in EMDR and has limited experience.
- Jane may be dealing with more complex issues beyond PTSD – even though this is clearly part of the cluster of presenting issues.
- Quinn has a *very* basic understanding of screening for dissociative symptoms, but no experience with a comprehensive diagnostic evaluation to rule out a DD.
- Quinn has concerns about offering their client Jane treatment with EMDR therapy but feels pressure to do so from the referring doctor, Jane, and their colleagues and supervisor, who have named Quinn 'the EMDR expert.'

Following the guidance of Anderson and Handelsman (2010), Quinn examined how they felt about the situation. The referral itself was not bothersome. However, other aspects of the situation made them feel uncomfortable. Quinn wondered about their relative lack of experience with EMDR therapy in light of Jane's presenting symptoms, some of which Quinn didn't understand and weren't sure how to conceptualize. They didn't like the pressure – self-imposed and otherwise – to move quickly in processing the recent trauma. Jane insisted she is ready. But then Quinn recalled the words of Francine Shapiro (2018) on readiness criteria. There still seemed to be a lot Quinn didn't know about Jane. At the same time, Quinn was keenly aware that they had something Jane wanted – and *needed.* This fact, combined with Jane's sense of urgency to process, only seemed to magnify the natural power asymmetries between therapist and client (Maroda, 2022). Quinn wasn't yet sure how to balance Jane's needs alongside their own need to practice ethically and do no (more?) harm. They felt a bit stuck with only two, polarized courses of action: (1) To do nothing – an act of omission or (2) to do something potentially harmful – an act of commission. Quinn wanted a third possibility.

Developing and Analyzing Alternatives

Quinn quickly realized that they were unsure what resources they should consult in this ethical choice process, aside from their professional code of ethics. In Chapter 3, Jennifer discussed the three pillars of the standard of care for clinical practice of EMDR therapy to treat dissociation. Although Quinn hasn't read this book (it wasn't yet published), they can probably still compile resources encapsulated in those pillars: Codes of ethics, legal and regulatory policies, and treatment and practice guidelines. Quinn returned to Anderson and Handelsman (2010), who mention professional codes of ethics (check!), potential legal issues, and what else? It seemed a good idea to start with the code of ethics associated with their licensure.

Codes of Ethics

Ethics codes universally and explicitly highlight the importance of the following aspects of clinical practice:

- adequate training and education (scope of practice),
- history taking and diagnostic assessment,
- informed consent,
- appropriate treatment boundaries,
- avoiding harm to the client/patient, and
- mitigating risks associated with potential legal liability.

However, codes of ethics do not discuss:

- specific legal and regulatory issues,
- organizational and practice-specific policies, and
- working with specific diagnostic and demographic populations.

Since we do not know the nature of Quinn's clinical training and license, it might be helpful to generalize this exploration a bit. The EMDR International Association has adopted, as a default for its Professional Code of Conduct (EMDR International Association, 2025), the ethical standards promulgated by the American Psychological Association (APA, 2017). These standards have also been used as a model for ethics codes for mental health disciplines elsewhere in the world. According to APA's (2017) *Ethical Principles of Psychologists and Code of Conduct*, Quinn needed to consider the following:

A. Beneficence and Nonmaleficence
B. Fidelity and Responsibility
C. Integrity
D. Justice
E. Respect for People's Rights and Dignity

The first of these principles, *Beneficence and Nonmaleficence*, APA (2017) indicates that we as practitioners must "strive to benefit those with whom [we] work and take care to do no harm" (p. 3). In reviewing these standards, Quinn questioned whether proceeding from a place of beneficence – in this case, by moving more quickly into reprocessing with the aim to reduce a client's distress – potentially overrides the principle of nonmaleficence.

Of the second principle, *Fidelity and Responsibility*, Quinn read that practitioners must "establish relationships of trust with those with whom

[we] work," "uphold professional standards of conduct, [...], clarify [our] professional roles and obligations, [and] accept appropriate responsibility for [our] behavior [...]" (APA, 2017, p. 3). Here, recall from Chapter 3 that *professional negligence* is the result of an unjustified departure from usual practice or failing to exercise proper care in fulfilling one's responsibilities. Quinn wondered about the potential consequences of moving forward with reprocessing without being aware of the accepted 'usual practice,' or standard of care. It struck Quinn that they could not confidently exercise proper, informed judgment and could, as a result, fail to provide Jane with ethically sound treatment.

Quinn thought a lot about *Integrity*, the third principle. According to APA (2017), practitioners must "seek to promote accuracy, honesty, and truthfulness in the science, teaching, and practice" of our chosen discipline, and "strive to keep [our] promises and to avoid unwise or unclear commitments" (p. 3). Quinn wondered what could happen if they decided to proceed with 'treatment as usual' – in other words, using standard EMDR – as though Jane were only dealing with PTSD? What were the implications of failing to recognize, or even outright ignoring, potential risks to Jane, the therapeutic relationship, and even Quinn's own professional standing (Shapiro, 2018)? And what of the risk of pressing ahead with a course of treatment without adequate information?

That question led directly to *Justice*, APA's fourth ethical principle. Quinn read that practitioners must "recognize that fairness and justice entitle all persons to access to and benefit from the contributions of [our field] and to equal quality in the processes, procedures, and services being conducted [...]," and "exercise reasonable judgment and take precautions to ensure that [our] potential biases, the boundaries of [our] competence, and the limitations of [our] expertise do not lead to or condone unjust practices" (p. 4). Quinn was uncertain how to balance justice alongside the other principles. Although access to treatment is important, Quinn wondered whether reprocessing in EMDR therapy (and really, doing *any* kind of trauma processing) at this point would draw them outside the boundaries of their current competence and expertise. Would their desire to quickly relieve Jane's pain be a just reason to move forward without additional consideration?

Quinn then arrived at the fifth and final ethical principle, *Respect for People's Rights and Dignity*. On this, APA (2017) offers that we must "respect the dignity and worth of all people, and the rights of individuals to privacy, confidentiality, and self-determination" (p. 4). Quinn felt compelled to ask how far *any* client's right to self-determination extends. Does a client have the right, for example, to compel a therapist to provide a treatment for issues that are currently outside the therapist's scope of practice? What is the therapist's responsibility in that case?

Quinn did not find definite answers in these principles, but this review generated some helpful questions. It was crystal clear to Quinn, though, that they should not have to decide alone. And, Quinn most definitely wanted to avoid deciding *on Jane's behalf*. Instead, Quinn would need to have a frank discussion with Jane about this, once a plan of action had been devised. Before reaching out to anyone, Quinn decided to do a bit more research.

Having carefully reviewed the APA code of ethics, Quinn recognized the need to look elsewhere to find information about specific legal and regulatory issues, organizational and practice-specific policies, and working with specific diagnostic and demographic populations. Quinn was not certain what legal issues applied to this situation. Quinn's profession, as represented in their clinical license, was regulated by the body that issued that license. Quinn also needed to figure out where to find relevant treatment and clinical practice guidelines. Although they considered accessing academic journal articles through the university library, Quinn knew for sure they had access to the full run of the open-access *Journal and EMDR Practice & Research* (https://spj.science.org/journal/jemdr).

Legal and Regulatory Policies

Quinn's next task in developing and analyzing alternative courses of action involved examining the legal angle of their situation. Here are the questions that Quinn asked:

1. Are there any laws or regulatory considerations that I need to be aware of that could impact my decision-making process?
2. What are the policies at my agency about issues like scope of practice and employee liability? For how many sessions am I allowed to see this client?
3. If I feel like I'm in over my head – and I think I might be getting a bit close to that point – what kind of support or feedback do I need (and can I expect) from my supervisor, my colleagues, and others in my agency?
4. What (outside) resources can I access for support?

On the first of these, Quinn thought about Jane's healthcare coverage and benefits, federal and state privacy laws above all. Jane was a legal and independently functioning adult, so no age-related concerns about treating a minor or healthcare privacy applied. For professional liability, Quinn was aware that their employer provided insurance coverage – but, were there any limits to that coverage? Quinn wondered what could happen if they were ever sued directly, as an individual practitioner. Would that matter?

This was added to the list of questions Quinn had for Tom, their supervisor. What would Tom think of them for being concerned at all about this? What if Tom lost confidence in Quinn's ability to do their job with all this 'soul searching'? What was the big deal? Then, Quinn wondered why this would *not* be a big deal? That led to the last question: If professional support from *within* their agency was not available, how, where, and with whom could *outside* support be found?

Treatment and Practice Guidelines

Quinn returned to the question of where outside support might come from, particularly on the matter of treatment and clinical practice guidelines, and decided to start with a resource they already had: Shapiro's (2018) EMDR therapy textbook – specifically, *Appendix E: Client Safety*. Here, Quinn found the *EMDR Dissociative Disorders Task Force Recommended Guidelines* for using EMDR therapy with persons with DDs and a mention of the International Society for the Study of Trauma and Dissociation (ISSTD). A visit to ISSTD's website turned up several resources, including the most recent *Guidelines for Treating Dissociative Identity Disorder in Adults, Third Revision* (ISSTD, 2011). While Quinn was not sure whether Jane met the criteria for a DD, reading these guidelines did raise additional possibilities for making sense of the symptoms that did not fit neatly into a PTSD diagnosis. On the topic of complex trauma, a quick web search also pointed to the *American Psychological Association Guidelines for Working with Adults with Complex Trauma Histories* (American Psychological Association, 2024).

At this point, Quinn felt a bit confused. First, they had been under the impression that DDs were extremely rare. Second, the messages they received from the start of basic training were to move forward with EMDR processing. But that did not align with what Shapiro (2018) says. And, assuming Quinn understood the ISSTD (2011) *Guidelines* correctly, if their client ends up meeting the diagnostic criteria for a DD, then pushing ahead with trauma processing without laying more groundwork is not a good idea. Before looking at how Quinn resolved their dilemma through the ethical choice process, we would like to address the conflict Quinn is feeling between the cautionary words they have read and what they learned elsewhere. Quinn is not alone in this: The entire field of EMDR therapy is beholden to such conflict, and it's a big deal.

EMDR, BL-DAS, and 'The Big Deal'

In Chapter 2, we discussed the mechanisms of action in EMDR therapy and potential challenges posed by using bilateral dual-attention stimulation (BL-DAS) in the context of more severe dissociation. According to the Dissociative Disorders Task Force (Shapiro, 2018), "The use of BLS [BL-DAS] too early in treatment risks premature penetration of dissociative barriers, which could produce results such as flooding of the personality system, uncontrolled destabilization, and increased suicidal or homicidal risk" (p. 501). If we carry forward the expanded conceptual framework for the adaptive information processing (AIP) model informed by the work of Boris Sidis, discussed in Chapter 2, then we can think of prematurely increasing connectivity rather than of penetrating barriers. In either case, in practice, this could translate to one or more of the following:

1. Unplanned, unexpected, and uncontrollable 'flooding.' The contents of the 'flood' may include behavior, affect, sensation, and/or knowledge (BASK elements, Braun, 1988a, 1988b) previously dissociated from conscious, executive awareness and control. These may include functional neurological (conversion) symptoms. These are physiological features that appear to be medical in nature, as they lack any obvious context because the knowledge of their source(s) is unavailable to conscious awareness. Examples include paralysis, non-epileptic seizures; unexplained pain; and visual or auditory impairments.
2. The activation and emergence of previously disaggregated self-states into executive functioning and control. This emergence could manifest either partially ('intrusions') or fully (contemporaneous amnesia), and may be quite rapid. In addition to the emergence of previously unknown states, it is possible that a more resourced state might 'disappear,' becoming unavailable even to other self-states that previously had access to them. Sometimes, what comes to the fore are very underdeveloped and profoundly attachment-injured infant and child states that the therapist may feel compelled to protect, rescue, and nurture. The therapist may atypically modify their own boundaries or policies and/or transgress the client's boundaries to achieve this (e.g., Davies & Frawley, 1994; Sachs, 2013; Watkins & Watkins, 1988; see also Chapters 5 and 11).
3. Self- and other-directed aggression arising from anger/rage-energized states. These may manifest as suicidal and non-suicidal self-directed harm (e.g., cutting, scratching, hitting); physical aggression and homicidal behavior; or psychologically/emotionally destructive behavior toward the therapist and important others (e.g., Chefetz, 1997;

Moskowitz & Evans, 2009; Trumbull, 2017; Watkins & Watkins, 1984, 1988).

There is no question that the rapid associations facilitated by BL-DAS can be demonstrably overwhelming and potentially harmful for persons with DDs (Lazrove & Fine, 1996; Paulsen, 1995; Twombly, 2000). Although EMDR has been a long-standing target of criticism from many practitioners in the DD fields, we would like to stress that the risk of premature (over-)connection with traumatic material is inherent in *any* therapeutic approach that plumbs the depths of the human mind (Fine, 2012; ISSTD, 2011; Kluft, 2006; Steele et al., 2017; Van der Hart et al., 1993).

EMDR and Dissociation: Four Schools of Thought

Everyone seems to have at least one opinion on the topic of EMDR and dissociation, whether informed or not, fed by any number of influences both within and beyond the EMDR therapy field. The gravitational pull of opinion, regardless of its source, can be difficult to escape – the mouths (or keyboards) of experts, trainers, consultants, authors, presenters, colleagues, even information gleaned from the Web and (social) media outlets. We might not even be able to explain how our assumptions about EMDR and dissociation first came to be. Observation and experience over a number of years have led us, the authors, to classify the opinions that inform the most common assumptions into four schools of thought:

1. Never use EMDR with a person with a dissociative disorder!
2. You just need the 'right' EMDR protocols to treat dissociation.
3. Break through the dissociation and it'll go away.
4. Cultivate an informed and thoughtful approach to treatment.

Never use EMDR with a Person with a Dissociative Disorder!

Many of us have stories about our early, often unwitting and unintentional use of EMDR with someone with severe, undiagnosed, dissociative symptoms. Some trainers and practitioners, scared by either direct experience or what they have read or heard, avoid using EMDR (or BL-DAS) entirely in the context of 'dissociation.' This avoidance is then passed along to others. While the commitment to 'do no (more) harm' is well-meaning, this mindset can have the unfortunate outcome of withholding appropriate treatment. Examples of this include the practitioner remaining in 'resourcing' because they do not know what else (or what next) to do, without seeking training/consultation or offering a referral. Or they may detect 'red flags' for reprocessing (see Chapter 3), including indicators of dissociative symptoms, and tell the client, "You're not a candidate for EMDR." Both responses could be signs of negligence, with the practitioner focusing only upon avoiding the *commission* of harm without considering the deleterious impact of the act of *omission*. Too little treatment is not necessarily better than too much. The context informing a practitioner's decisions matters.

Given the mixed messages in Shapiro's texts and the broader EMDR therapy literature, it is no wonder that practitioners struggle to know when and how to move forward. On the one hand, the message in Shapiro's AIP model says that relief comes when the maladaptively stored or unprocessed material is reprocessed to adaptive resolution. On the other hand, screening, assessment, and stabilization are emphasized. As the Dissociative Disorders Task Force states in *Appendix E: Client Safety* (Shapiro, 2018), destabilization can occur for dissociative clients if eye movements (or other forms of BL-DAS) are introduced into treatment before it is clear the client is prepared to tolerate what may surface. Moreover, BL-DAS is used in *Phase II: Preparation* as well as in the reprocessing phases, so this is not exclusively about trauma processing. As we discussed in Chapter 2, it's about too much or too little neural network connectivity.

As mentioned above and elsewhere (perhaps ad nauseum, at this point), the relationship between the EMDR therapy and DDs fields has always been complicated. Some practitioners who hail from the DDs field have seen the worst of what EMDR has to offer and, as a result, detest EMDR therapy, period. In rebuttal, we ask: Is it reasonable to expect that an orthopedic surgeon would know how to conduct brain surgery just because they know how to use a scalpel? Is it the therapy, the therapist, or both that poses the risk and under what circumstances? Bliss (1986) notes that it is not possible to plan for everything when treating DDs. Even with the most careful planning, clients may still over-access and at least temporarily decompensate. When a flight is turbulent, is the pilot knowledgeable and skilled enough to both reduce the risk of acute air sickness and land the plane safely?

When practitioners are not well-versed in the ins and outs of EMDR *and* dissociation, both educationally and experientially, the tensions between these conflicting messages can be immobilizing. We have learned and emphasized the importance of conceptualization, depth of understanding, and development toward mastery and specialized practice. The standard of care and scholarly literature tell us that people with DDs face a good prognosis in many cases when practitioners are well-trained and follow treatment guidelines (Brand et al., 2016; Yeates et al., 2024). The principle of nonmaleficence is good and is reinforced when coupled with strategies for ensuring that clients can receive safe and effective treatment from a practitioner who is sufficiently proficient and/or specialized.

You Just Need the 'right' EMDR Protocols to Treat Dissociation

In consultation, we field all sorts of questions about EMDR and dissociation. Here are two common questions:

> "I heard about such-and-such a protocol. Could that work for my dissociative client?"
>
> "I attended a workshop on such-and-such an approach. The presenter said it's great (safe) with dissociation... Should I use it?"

Great questions. Let's think about this. First, do we have enough context to say whether this is an appropriate fit for your client's needs at your level of knowledge and skill? We need to know more about the client, and how you are conceptualizing this case, before we can discuss the merits of using a particular protocol. Second, maybe that approach *could* be helpful, but there may be more context for the *presenter's* success with that approach. Did they share a conceptual framework for using this approach with dissociative clients who have autonomous or semi-autonomous self-states? Always consider the implications and potential impact of using any protocol with *your* clients.

For all the advanced EMDR training and approaches out there for employing EMDR with DDs, none have robust research supporting their use. Some have no supporting evidence for use with people with DDs, while others have no empirical evidence at all, with any population. As discussed earlier, a few studies have attempted to test the need for stabilization and efficacy of EMDR in persons with dissociative symptoms. However, these studies have tended to use DES-II mean scores, which we know to be imprecise, as a definitive measure of dissociation. By definition (see Chapter 2), dissociation is not a unidimensional construct and how it manifests – and, by extension, how it needs to be treated – will vary from client to client. We advocate instead for a clear and nuanced conceptual framework, and a deep understanding of the model(s) being employed and of your client.

Break Through the Dissociation and It'll Go Away

This school of thought may be communicated either implicitly or explicitly. It unavoidably overlaps with the second school of thought (above).

Proponents of EMDR 2.0 (e.g., De Jongh et al., 2013; Matthijssen et al., 2021) argue that a stabilization phase is not needed before memory processing. The importance of screening for dissociative symptoms is glossed over or dismissed. The authors who promote this approach also advocate for increased, multimodal dual-attention stimulation (the DAS of BL-DAS), stating that it will both keep clients 'present' (i.e., not depersonalized) and plow through the dissociative barriers, ostensibly toward health. As discussed in earlier chapters, Francine Shapiro expressed a rather similar mindset in some of her own writing.

Other practitioners may go forward more blithely. For example, they may facilitate *Phase I: History Taking* by allowing (or even inviting) a client to share about past traumatic experiences in detail while the therapist administers 'passive' BL-DAS via electronic 'tappers.' This leads to unprocessed memory material becoming activated, but without the therapist intending or being prepared to resolve it at that time. We have heard this recommendation issued directly from the mouths of long-time EMDR therapy trainers and consultants who themselves were trained by Francine Shapiro. In reprocessing (*Phases IV–VI*), this may manifest in the practitioner staying out of the way, a bit too much, by using unrestricted reprocessing of remote or recent memories. This manner of practice also aligns with offering insufficient closure of incomplete sessions – relying on the client's possibly maladaptive dissociative capacities rather than intentional containment, etc. This school of thought can also encompass practicing EMDR therapy with 'blind fidelity' – that is, without consideration of unique client factors – in the name of 'trusting' the model. Treatment guidelines call for knowledge of and proficiency in modifications to standard EMDR therapy for persons with DDs, toward the standard of personalized care.

We would like to pose a question regarding the ongoing pushback against stabilization. Why, exactly, has it become so important to 'prove' that a stabilization phase is unnecessary? How does it serve practitioners working with complex clients in an outpatient treatment setting to forgo stabilization for any client with dissociative symptoms? This question seems particularly salient considering recent, if only exploratory, data that point to clinical challenges posed using EMDR/BL-DAS in the face of more severe dissociative symptoms (Keltgen-Lo, 2024).

Is it true that a preparation phase is unnecessary even with people who meet the criteria for a DD? If so, then we invite the researchers who argue this to go the extra kilometer and design a study of this topic that replaces the DES-II with a formal diagnostic instrument. Taking the time to thoroughly evaluate a full range of dissociative symptoms, rather than depending upon speculation about whether someone may meet criteria for DD based on the 28-item DES, would go some distance toward legitimizing the case that stabilization in the face of any form of dissociation is unnecessary. The researchers pursuing this issue may not actually be focused on ensuring client safety and stability throughout a longer-term treatment, or even on treatment efficacy. Framing of the arguments in this literature suggests to us that the author(s) are determined to prove that DDs do not exist as a separate set of diagnostic features with their own treatment considerations. And that would pose a problem, as we know they do exist, per contemporary research (e.g., Dorahy et al., 2014; Fung et al., 2024; Lebois et al., 2022, 2023; Reinders et al., 2003, 2012, 2019; Schlumpf, 2014; see also Chapter 1).

Cultivate an Informed and Thoughtful Approach to Treatment

In our opinion, this school of thought represents the only ethical path to treating complex trauma and DDs. Our reading of the established treatment guidelines supports this (see Chapter 3). When we approach *Stage 2: Trauma Processing* work, fractionation, titration, containment, etc. will reduce the risk of flooding via associations that breach dissociative barriers or gaps that were once functional (ISSTD, 2011, p. 160). Part III of this book will elaborate upon the EMDR therapy layer of our treatment frame. Treatment occurs within a broader relational frame and model(s) of understanding complex dissociation (ISSTD, 2011; see also Chapter 3).

One practice is recommended unilaterally: Every client must be screened for the presence of an underlying DD. "Monitoring for evidence of 'switching' in session is not sufficient. If suspicion of a dissociative disorder, conduct further diagnostic evaluation" (Shapiro, 2018, p. 499). What was the purpose of administering the screening or assessment tool if it is not applied to shape the treatment plan? If we don't ask, clients may not think it is safe or important to tell us about their experience. In screening and assessment, what 'red flags' might be missed if a follow-up interview is not conducted? (We will discuss the screening and assessment process further in Chapter 6.) We can facilitate the necessary and recursive process of informed consent when we know what we are asking or offering to the client as a whole person while considering the presence of dissociation. Safety and predictability are foundations of the therapeutic relationship – both within and between sessions. This is essential to establish roles and trust for all stages and phases of psychotherapy.

Enhanced connections among different self-states and awareness of the body are inevitable treatment outcomes – whether accidental or intentional – using BL-DAS. EMDR therapy is seen among many as 'dangerous' for treating persons with DDs largely because BL-DAS has been used injudiciously by practitioners who did not understand and have an adequate understanding of how to work with the complexities of dissociation. Thus far, we have only discussed the problems of *over*-access. What, though, about *under*-access?

Under-accessing seems most obvious when a client has limited or no connection to their felt experience. Additionally, under-accessing may be marked by the 'blocks' (aka 'looping') that surface – sometimes repeatedly – during reprocessing (EMDR *Phases IV–VI*). Looping is an indicator of stalled or 'stuck' processing, as evidenced by the client's reported experience, whether cognitive, emotional, or somatic, after two successive sets of BL-DAS. Typically, it is possible to find a detour around the 'block' via either 'mechanical' means (e.g., changing the speed or direction of eye movements, and returning to target) or an interweave.

However, under-accessing can be much more subtle, such as when the spontaneous connections among different, associated memories do not happen as we would expect. It may appear that we are reprocessing a truly isolated, single-episode trauma, even when we know that the client has a complex history. The client's between-set reports all seem to be associated with the target memory. There may be no random 'pings' to seemingly off-topic ideas. Somatic and cognitive linkages to other experiences are absent. Or, the processing may be prolonged, with many more associations surfacing than we might expect with a single-episode trauma. This could occur if the client is reprocessing multiple experiences, which may not have come to light during history taking, without us realizing it. Reprocessing in this case may look very 'clean and neat', but only because we are unknowingly working with a self-state that is isolated enough from other self-states that they cannot connect with any material beyond their own experience. (This may mean we are working with a fragmentary state. See Chapter 10.) Depending on the client, unrestricted processing (EMD-big R) will instead resemble and 'behave' like either EMD (restricted processing) or EMDr (contained processing). Michael learned this by accident with one of the earliest dissociative clients with whom he unwittingly reprocessed. What he drew from this experience was: "You will be lucky until you're not." Whether we run the risk of over- or under-accessing with a client may depend upon several factors unique to that individual (see Chapter 6 and Part IV). With that, let's return to Quinn's unfolding process.

A Hypothetical Situation, an Ethical Solution

Consult with Other Professionals

After doing a lot of research, Quinn was finally able to consult with Tom, their supervisor. Although Tom did not understand EMDR or the concerns related to dissociation, he did appreciate the bind in which Quinn found themselves and the paramount importance of avoiding harm. Quinn shared the information they gathered related to the standard of care. Tom asked Quinn to bring this issue to the weekly team meeting for everyone to discuss.

Choose, Implement, and Evaluate the Decision

During the team meeting, Quinn received some support from their colleagues, though they, too, were uncertain about the 'dissociation thing.' Following the meeting, Tom worked with Quinn to develop a short-term plan of action, which included obtaining outside consultation on complex trauma and dissociation – assuming an affordable option could be found. This plan was briefly discussed with the doctor who originally referred Quinn's client for treatment. The doctor expressed annoyance but didn't object.

Quinn subsequently discussed concerns about 'doing EMDR,' at least at this point, with Jane, and shared their 'rough sketch' plan for moving forward. This included a thorough evaluation of dissociation before developing a treatment plan – as thorough as Quinn could provide. Jane expressed frustration about treatment taking longer, especially given her impression that EMDR was 'fast,' but she was willing to collaborate on the proposed plan. Although Jane expressed tentative interest in learning more about dissociation, she continued to insist that the past couldn't possibly have anything to do with her PTSD symptoms.

Conclusion

Codes of ethics are intentionally broad and open to interpretation. As such, they do not, and cannot, speak to the complexities of treating dissociation. We saw Quinn cobble together resources to navigate a common ethical bind in EMDR therapy practice. What was illuminated in the process of discovery was a glaring lack of awareness that easily could have resulted in harm to their client, despite good intentions. Quinn was relatively fortunate, being curious and resourceful, and they had in Tom a sympathetic and reasonable supervisor who was willing to work with them to develop a plan. This is not always so, based on our experience of consulting with hundreds of EMDR therapists over the years. More often, EMDR therapists know only what they learned about dissociation in basic training, and from participating in advanced workshops on dissociation – which tend to emphasize treatment over conceptualization. This fosters a dichotomy of stereotypes among EMDR practitioners. They either "don't know what they don't know yet" and stumble upon severe dissociation accidentally, or they believe they know more than they do, increasing the risk of making a mess for their clients and themselves.

The pervasive dearth of foundational acknowledgement, recognition, and understanding of dissociation poses a significant obstacle for EMDR therapists who could benefit from continuing professional development on this important topic. Limited time and financial resources create additional barriers to access. Without education-informed experience, approaches as represented by the first three schools of thought discussed in this chapter can easily take hold. Unfortunately, this only widens the chasm separating EMDR therapy and DD fields. In the next chapter, Jennifer will discuss ways of identifying and addressing educational and experiential gaps in the interest of building bridges across that chasm.

References

American Psychiatric Association. (2022). *DSM-5-TR – Diagnostic and statistical manual of mental disorders* (5th ed., text revision). American Psychiatric Publishing.

American Psychological Association. (2017). *Ethical principles of psychologists and code of conduct.* Retrieved May 26, 2025, from www.apa.org/ethics/code

American Psychological Association. (2024). *Guidelines for working with adults with complex trauma histories.* www.apa.org/practice/guidelines/adults-complex-trauma-histories.pdf

Anderson, S. K., & Handelsman, M. M. (2010). *Ethics for psychotherapists and counselors: A proactive approach.* John Wiley & Sons.

Bhattacharyya, B., & Banerjee, U. (2022). Exploring burnout in clinical psychologists: Role of personality, empathy, countertransference and compassion fatigue. *Indian Journal of Psychiatric Nursing, 19*(2), 117–124. https://doi.org/10.4103/iopn.iopn_62_21

Bliss, E. L. (1986). *Multiple personality, allied disorders and hypnosis.* Oxford University Press.

Brand, B. L. (2024). *The concise guide to the assessment and treatment of trauma-related dissociation.* American Psychological Association. https://doi.org/10.1037/0000386-000

Brand, B. L., Sar, V., Stavropoulos, P., Krüger, C., Korzekwa, M., Martínez-Taboas, A., & Middleton, W. (2016). Separating fact from fiction: An empirical examination of six myths about dissociative identity disorder. *Harvard Review of Psychiatry, 24*(4), 257–270. https://doi.org/10.1097/HRP.0000000000000100

Braun, B. G. (1988a). The BASK model of dissociation. *Dissociation, 1*(1), 4–23. hdl.handle.net/1794/1276

Braun, B. G. (1988b). The BASK model of dissociation: Part II – treatment. *Dissociation, 1*(2), 16–23. hdl.handle.net/1794/1340

Chefetz, R. A. (1997). Special case transference and countertransference in the treatment of dissociative identity disorder. *Dissociation, 10*(4), 255–265. hdl.handle.net/1794/1814

Davies, J. M., & Frawley, M. G. (1994). *Treating the adult survivor of childhood sexual abuse: A psychoanalytic perspective.* Basic Books.

De Jongh, A., Ernst, R, Marques, L. & Hornsveld, H. (2013). The impact of eye movements and tones on disturbing memories of patients with PTSD and other mental disorders. *Journal of Behavior Therapy and Experimental Psychiatry, 44*(4), 447–483. https://doi.org/10.1016/j.jbtep.2013.07.002

Dorahy, M. J., Brand, B. L., Sar, V., Krüger, C., Stavropoulos, P., Martínez-Taboas, A., Lewis-Fernández, R., & Middleton, W. (2014). Dissociative identity disorder: An empirical overview. *Australian and New Zealand Journal of Psychiatry, 48*(5), 402–417. https://doi.org/10.1177/0004867414527523

EMDR International Association. (2025, March 4). *Standards for EMDR basic training.* www.emdria.org/wp-content/uploads/2025/03/Standards-for-EMDRIA-Basic-Training.pdf [proprietary link]

Fewings, E., & Quinlan, E. (2023). "It hasn't gone away after 30 years." Late-career Australian psychologists' experience of uncertainty throughout their career. *Professional Psychology: Research and Practice, 54*(3), 221–230. https://doi.org/10.1037/pro0000511

Fine, C. G. (2012). Cognitive behavioral hypnotherapy for dissociative disorders. *American Journal of Clinical Hypnosis, 54*(4), 331–352. https://doi.org/10.1080/00029157.2012.656856

Fung, H. W., Yuan, G. F., Liu, C., Lin, E. S. S., Lam, S. K. K., & Wong, J. Y. (2024). Prevalence and clinical correlates of dissociative symptoms in people with complex PTSD: Is complex PTSD a dissociative disorder? *Psychiatry Research, 339*, 116076. https://doi.org/10.1016/j.psychres.2024.116076

International Society for Study of Dissociation. (2005). Guidelines for treating dissociative identity disorder in adults (2005). *Journal of Trauma & Dissociation, 6*(4), 69–149. https://doi.org/10.1300/j229v06n04_05

International Society for the Study of Trauma and Dissociation. (2011). Guidelines for treating dissociative identity disorder in adults, third revision. *Journal of Trauma & Dissociation, 12*(2), 115–187. https://doi.org/10.1080/15299732.2011.537247

Keltgen-Lo, J. (2024). *Uncovering adverse eye movement desensitization and reprocessing events: A descriptive study among approved consultants* [Master's thesis, University of Washington]. Collections: Nursing – Tacoma. hdl.handle.net/1773/51743

Kluft, R. P. (2006). Dealing with alters: A pragmatic clinical perspective. *Psychiatric Clinics of North America, 29*(1), 281–304. https://doi.org/10.1016/j.psc.2005.10.010

Lazrove, S., & Fine, C.G. (1996). The use of EMDR in patients with dissociative identity disorder. *Dissociation, 9*(4), 289–299. hdl.handle.net/1794/1778

Lebois, L. A. M., Kaplan, C. S., Palermo, C. A., Xi, P., & Kaufman, M. L. (2023). A grounded theory of dissociative identity disorder: Placing DID in mind, brain, and body. In M. J. Dorahy, S. N. Gold, & J. A. O'Neil (Eds.), *Dissociation and the dissociative disorders: Past, present, future* (2nd ed.)(pp. 392–407). Routledge. https://doi.org/10.4324/9781003057314

Lebois, L. A. M., Kumar, P., Palermo, C. A., Lambros, A. M., O'Connor, L., Wolff, J. D., Baker, J. T., Gruber, S. A., Lewis-Schroeder, N., Ressler, K. J., Robinson, M. A., Winternitz, S., Nickerson, L. D., & Kaufman, M. L. (2022). Deconstructing dissociation: A triple network model of trauma-related dissociation and its subtypes. *Neuropsychopharmacology, 47*(13), 2261–2270. https://doi.org/10.1038/s41386-022-01468-1

Maroda, K. J. (2022). *The analyst's vulnerability: Impact on theory and practice.* Routledge.

Matthijssen, S. J. M. A., Brouwers, T., Van Roozendaal, C., Vuister, T., & De Jongh, A. (2021). The effect of EMDR versus EMDR 2.0 on emotionality and vividness of aversive memories in a non-clinical sample. *European Journal of Psychotraumatology, 12*(1), 1956793. https://doi.org/10.1080/20008198.2021.1956793

McWilliams, N. (2021). *Psychoanalytic supervision.* The Guilford Press.

Moskowitz, A., & Evans, C. (2009). Peritraumatic dissociation and amnesia in violent offenders. In P. F. Dell & J. A. O'Neil (Eds.), *Dissociation and the dissociative disorders: DSM-V and beyond* (pp. 197–207). Routledge. https://doi.org/10.4324/9780203893920

Paulsen, S. (1995). Eye movement desensitization and reprocessing: Its cautious use in the dissociative disorders. *Dissociation, 8*(1), 32–-44. hdl.handle.net/1794/1592

Quinlan, E., Schilder, S., & Deane, F. P. (2021). "This wasn't in the manual": A qualitative exploration of tolerance of uncertainty in the practicing psychology context. *Australian Psychologist, 56*(2), 154–167. https://doi.org/10.1080/00050067.2020.1829451

Reinders, A. A. T. S., Marquand, A. F., Schlumpf, Y. R., Chalavi, S., Vissia, E. M., Nijenhuis, E. R. S., Dazzan, P., Jäncke, L., & Veltman, D. J. (2019). Aiding the diagnosis of dissociative identity disorder: Pattern recognition study of brain biomarkers. *The British Journal of Psychiatry, 215*(3), 536–544. https://doi.org/10.1192/bjp.2018.255

Reinders, A. A., Nijenhuis, E. R., Paans, A. M., Korf, J., Willemsen, A. T., & den Boer, J. A. (2003). One brain, two selves. *NeuroImage, 20*(4), 2119–2125. https://doi.org/10.1016/j.neuroimage.2003.08.021

Reinders, A. A. T. S., Willemsen, A. T., Vos, H. P., den Boer, J. A., & Nijenhuis, E. R. (2012). Fact or factitious? A psychobiological study of authentic and simulated dissociative identity states. *PloS One, 7*(7), e39279. https://doi.org/10.1371/journal.pone.0039279

Sachs, A. (2013). Boundary modifications in the treatment of people with dissociative disorders: A pilot study. *Journal of Trauma & Dissociation, 14*(2), 159–169. https://doi.org/10.1080/15299732.2012.714677

Schlumpf, Y. R., Reinders, A. A., Nijenhuis, E. R., Luechinger, R., Van Osch, M. J., & Jäncke, L. (2014). Dissociative part-dependent resting-state activity in dissociative identity disorder: A controlled fMRI perfusion study. *PloS One, 9*(6), Article e98795. https://doi.org/10.1371/journal.pone.0098795

Shapiro, F. (1995). *Eye movement desensitization and reprocessing: Basic principles, protocols, and procedures.* The Guilford Press.

Shapiro, F. (1996, November 7–10). *Dissociative disorders task force position paper* [Conference presentation]. 13th Annual Conference of the International Society for the Study of Dissociation. San Francisco, California, United States.

Shapiro, F. (2018). *Eye movement desensitization and reprocessing (EMDR) therapy: Basic principles, protocols and procedures* (3rd ed.). The Guilford Press.

Stark, C., Rogalla, K., Tapia, J. L., & Bunch, K. (2024). Introduction to the principles of trauma-informed ethical practice. In C. Stark, J. L. Tapia, Jr., K. Rogalla, & K. Bunch (Eds.), *Professional's guide to trauma-informed decision making* (pp. 3–18). Springer Nature Switzerland AG. https://doi.org/10.1007/978-3-031-54626-6_1

Steele, K., Boon, S., & Van der Hart, O. (2017). *Treating trauma-related dissociation: A practical, integrative approach*. W. W. Norton & Company.

Steinberg, M., & Schnall, M. (2001). *The stranger in the mirror: Dissociation – the hidden epidemic*. Harper-Collins.

Trumbull, D. (2017). Seeing through the eyes of the perpetrator: A goal-directed function of introjection. *Neuropsychoanalysis, 19*(2), 143–157. https://doi.org/10.1080/15294145.2017.1366280

Twombly, J. H. (2000). Incorporating EMDR and EMDR adaptations into the treatment of clients with dissociative identity disorder. *Journal of Trauma & Dissociation, 1*(2), 61–81. https://doi.org/10.1300/J229v01n02_05

Van der Hart, O., Steele, K., Boon, S., & Brown, P. (1993). The treatment of traumatic memories: Synthesis, realization, and integration. *Dissociation, 6*(2–3), 162–180. hdl.handle.net/1794/1633

Watkins, J. G., & Watkins, H. H. (1984). Hazards to the therapist in the treatment of multiple personalities. *Psychiatric Clinics of North America*, 7(1), 111–119. https://doi.org/10.1016/S0193-953X(18)30784-6

Watkins, J. G., & Watkins, H. H. (1988). The management of malevolent ego states in multiple personality disorder. *Dissociation, 1*(1), 67–72. hdl.handle.net/1794/1333

Yeates, S., Korner, A., & McLean, L. (2024). A systematic review and narrative analysis of the evidence for individual psychodynamically informed psychotherapy in the treatment of dissociative identity disorder in adults. *Journal of Trauma & Dissociation, 25*(2), 248–278. https://doi.org/10.1080/15299732.2023.2293802

Chapter 5

Development of the Practitioner

Jennifer A. Madere

Introduction

This chapter follows many layers of conceptual, theoretical and practical discussion. Have you ever thought, *why didn't they teach us this in graduate school?* I certainly have – many times. Graduate-level training programs for mental health professionals must meet numerous accreditation requirements. New graduates are thus more likely to enter the field with a foundation of general knowledge but little in-depth training in any specific theory or approach. Whether a practitioner develops proficiency in at least one therapeutic modality depends on the individual's determination and effort, as well as the quality of guidance received from supervisors, trainers, and consultants. Gaps in knowledge are inevitable and can persist.

When practitioners pursue EMDR therapy training, existing gaps are highlighted in their (lack of) understanding of how trauma-related issues are conceptualized and treated. The burden then falls on the specialist therapy training to make up the difference, with practitioners sometimes expecting they will learn 'all they need to know,' not only about the approach itself but also about how to understand and treat trauma. In basic EMDR training programs, foundational skills, such as using screening and assessment tools to identify dissociative symptoms, are taught inconsistently. Training standards and the application of best practices, as outlined in Shapiro's foundational text, vary (Leeds et al., 2022). Only in the third edition of Shapiro's text (2018) was it *explicitly* stated in the main body of the text that screening for dissociative features is a *mandatory* prerequisite to better ensure safe reprocessing. In North America, EMDR training standards have been slow to catch up to this change. As discussed in earlier chapters, the EMDR International Association (EMDRIA) has updated its training standards to include the requirement that "assessment tools and procedures for screening dissociation" be taught as part of *Phase I: History Taking, Case Conceptualization, and Treatment Planning*

DOI: 10.4324/9781003410201-7

(EMDRIA, 2022/2025, p. 17). Similar updates have been made by EMDR organizations outside North America, such as in Europe and Australia, and globally (EMDR Global Alliance, 2024), in accord with changes in Shapiro's 2018 text. However, these new standards do not automatically equip trainers and consultants, who may not be versed in the screening and assessment of dissociation, to teach and consult in these areas. Given these recent changes, along with Michael's and my observations through consultation and discussions with other professionals, understanding and implementation of these new standards remain inconsistent. In one recent consultation session, a consultee stated, "My EMDR consultant for Certification told me not to worry about screening for dissociation – he said to 'just work with how the client shows up.' "

Despite messages like this, awareness of the need to address dissociation in EMDR therapy training and consultation is growing. According to a survey presented during EMDRIA's Consultant Day training in August 2023, 'dissociation' was identified as the most common issue raised by consultees. The survey also revealed that, from consultants' perspective, the most significant barrier to practitioner growth was consultees' approach or attitude, particularly the extremes of "I know nothing" and "I know everything" (i.e., the Dunning-Kruger effect; Kruger & Dunning, 1999). This combination with the widespread prevalence of dissociation (e.g., Kate et al., 2020; Şar, 2011; Simeon & Putnam, 2022; Swart et al., 2020), the importance of screening for dissociation to ensure client safety (Leeds et al., 2022), and the significant learning gaps surrounding dissociation in EMDR therapy is concerning – and has potentially severe consequences.

Post-EMDR training, many practitioners rely on their experience and peer consultation. This can sometimes lead to two problematic tendencies: (1) applying standard EMDR therapy or adapted protocols without enough discretion, or (2) avoiding trauma processing for individuals with complex symptoms and histories. Both can be detrimental.

EMDR therapy, in its standard form, is a protocol-based approach that requires clinical judgment to be implemented well (Laliotis et al., 2021; Shapiro, 2018). The practitioner's ability to adhere to the protocol, establish and maintain a strong therapeutic alliance, and to continuously conceptualize and adjust the pace and direction of therapy are all crucial elements of EMDR therapy practice. To effectively use EMDR, practitioners must apply their foundational knowledge of psychotherapy and trauma treatment – assuming there is a solid foundation from which to draw.

A central focus of EMDR consultation is helping practitioners integrate new learning and treatment models into their existing foundational knowledge and experience. Robin Logie offers an excellent discussion of this process in *EMDR Supervision: A Handbook* (Logie, 2023). Practitioners with experience in other models may require support to shift their language and conceptualization to align with the framework of the adaptive information processing (AIP) model and EMDR therapy. On the other hand, beginning practitioners often need guidance to build new competencies for treating trauma and learning how to tolerate clients' processing of intense emotions (e.g., Soma et al., 2020) and disturbing memories.

Working, teaching, and learning within a chosen theory is of utmost importance because it provides a framework with clear boundaries that help practitioners and consultants to be better aware of what they *can* explain and conceptualize within that theoretical lens, and what cannot be fully explained or understood within that theoretical lens. Conceptualization is much more than choosing the right protocol for a certain 'problem.' When practitioners discover the gaps in their knowledge and skills, they become able to address them (Falender & Shafranske, 2016; Logie, 2023). In our multilayered treatment frame, we have expanded AIP to be a more comprehensive trauma-dissociation model (see Chapters 2 and 3). To treat complex trauma and dissociative disorders (DDs) effectively, we must be able to conceptualize both within and beyond the AIP level of the frame. The initial case conceptualization for a client's treatment will be modified as new information is gained and the path to facilitating connectivity and integrated functioning evolves.

This chapter will examine how practitioners, consultants, and trainers can identify and address gaps in training, conceptualization skills, and clinical development that may hinder effective treatment and contribute to professional burnout and a reduced career lifespan. Building blocks for conceptualization are gained in training and gelled through practice and consultation. Honing these conceptualization skills is essential to moving within the AIP model and other layers of the treatment frame (see Figure 3.3).

Stages of Practitioner Development

We all started somewhere. When in your professional journey did you enter EMDR therapy training? Did you encounter learning about DDs before or after that? One's stage of professional development upon entry to EMDR therapy training impacts how practitioners learn initially, and their trajectory of development as an EMDR therapist throughout the training and consultation process.

I would like to utilize the stages of practitioner development proposed by Stoltenberg and McNeill (2010) as a framework for discussing the EMDR basic training and professional development process. They propose four developmental levels: beginner, intermediate, experienced, and master.

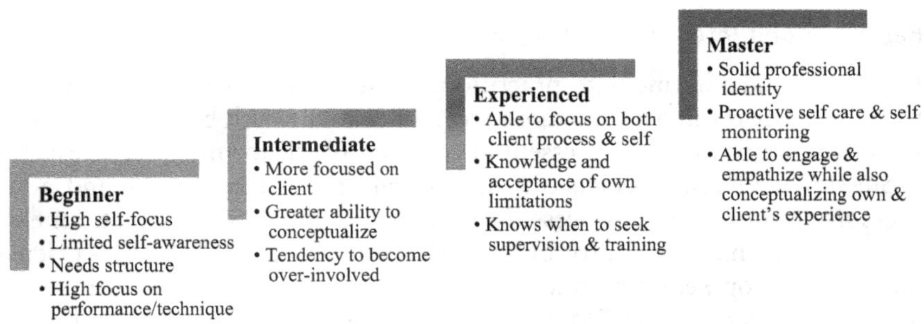

Figure 5.1 Stages of Practitioner Development.

Sources: Adapted from Stoltenberg and McNeill (2010) and Calvert et al. (2018).

Within these stages, there are three overriding structures: (1) self and other awareness; (2) motivation; and (3) autonomy (McNeill & Stoltenberg, 2016). When you attended your first day of EMDR therapy training, you entered from your current developmental level. Maybe you felt excited, anticipating that you would learn something new – something that would help your clients, advance your practice, and help you meet your professional goals. At the same time, you also became a beginner (again), this time in relation to EMDR therapy. During the supervised practice sessions, you probably fumbled with the script, either getting overwhelmed by trying to follow it exactly or giving up on the script and trying to 'wing it.' The scripts feel uncomfortable or unnatural, especially at first, and new learners often feel insecure. All new learners of EMDR therapy are beginners again.

At some point during each training cohort that I teach, trainees encounter something that makes them feel uncertain. I invariably hear someone exclaim, "The worksheet is so confusing – I don't know what to do!" or encounter something that makes them feel uncertain. This is likely an expression of the tension in the sense of motivation and autonomy that the learner feels at that moment. Doesn't this sound familiar? We thought of Erikson's 'autonomy versus shame and doubt' that children experience when they begin to explore the environment (Erikson, 1959/1980). Poor tolerance of uncertainty has been linked to higher levels of stress and risk of burnout – especially among new professionals (Quinlan et al., 2021). Consultants and trainers can support new (or newly trained) practitioners in growing their tolerance of uncertainty by focusing on *how to think* rather than what to do. Let's more closely examine these stages of practitioner development to see how they can guide us.

Beginning and Intermediate Stages

Beginning and intermediate practitioners often feel overwhelmed in the training process but are also more recently familiar with being a beginner. EMDR therapy may be an essential building block forming the learner's professional identity, which can be a strong motivating factor and add pressure to the learning process. Beginning and intermediate practitioners are also at the highest risk for burnout (Calvert et al., 2018). So, it is essential that development continues to progress during and following training in a new model such as EMDR therapy, upon encountering dissociation for the first time in practice, and in general.

It is normal for beginners to be highly focused on technique –what to do, and whether they are doing it right. New learners are often heavily focused on the script and may lack mentalization skills or the ability to focus on self and others during the session to the extent that practitioners may miss cues that clients are not following eye movements, or that the client's affect has shifted dramatically. This is not necessarily a learner deficit – it is inherent to the learning and development process.

Structures such as worksheets, case presentation forms, and other assignments aim to help the new learner absorb and practice new knowledge and skills. Practice, supervised practice, and consultation lend to the growth in self-awareness and the ability to conceptualize – in organizing case material according to the AIP model, navigating the EMDR protocol, and learning to discern choice points in vivo based on this conceptualization. Eventually, new learners become aware of when to check the target, etc., without overthinking the technique or becoming overly involved with the client's processing.

Experienced and Master Stages

While experienced or master clinicians may strongly desire to engage in EMDR therapy training, this motivation may be balanced with a sense that their professional identity is being shaken as they attempt to accommodate a new model. From this perspective, they may eschew the scripted worksheets, preferring to do EMDR in their own way. My observation is that experienced or master clinicians often feel deskilled and frustrated as they find themselves suddenly regressed to the beginner stage of development – temporarily. This self-imposed expectation to continue to function at an advanced level of practice while learning something very new and different is a common challenge.

Supporting seasoned practitioners to integrate new learning into their existing knowledge and practice is particularly vital to continued use of EMDR therapy in their practice post-training (Grimmett & Galvin, 2015;

Logie, 2023). Without that, experienced practitioners are prone to discard EMDR therapy for more familiar approaches. When practitioners have a robust understanding of themselves and the psychotherapeutic process, coaching them to access their established clinical and conceptualization skills is helpful. For example, the consultant may ask a series of questions:

> Okay, let's zoom out for a moment. What is your clinical brain seeing right now, in general? Put on your AIP model glasses... what stands out now? Do you know which of the eight phases you are in? According to your understanding of the AIP model and EMDR therapy so far, what could be next in this phase? What are you observing in your client that informs this decision-point? What does that mean that you might do next?

Adding Dissociation into the Mix

Throughout the training process and beyond, most learners, regardless of their starting level of development, struggle to integrate EMDR therapy into their practice. This seems particularly to be the case when they are working with more complex or less straightforward cases. Many practitioners have shared that they first encountered dissociative symptoms in their clients during or after EMDR therapy training. This may be due to their adherence to the procedures of *Phase I: History Taking and Diagnostic Evaluation*, which include screening or assessment for dissociative symptoms. The mechanisms of EMDR therapy – specifically, bilateral dual-attention stimulation – can act as what Sandra Paulsen described as a 'divining rod' for identifying DDs (Paulsen, 1995). These, among other reasons, lead many newly trained EMDR practitioners into the frontier of dissociation.

The discovery of the reality that a person with a DD is on one's caseload *also* leads many practitioners to feel deskilled. Not everyone wants to – or is able to – do the hard, sustained work to learn and acquire new competencies that align with a more complex client's needs. The prospect of either not being able to help a client with whom they had hoped to use EMDR or adding another substantial area of study to one's plate is indeed a lot to process. We saw this happen with the example therapist Quinn in Chapter 4.

Consultants and trainers can normalize that this is an area where almost everyone gets to be a 'beginner' again. Balancing awareness and caution to ensure the safety of clients while encouraging practitioners to rely on their foundational skills *and* identify specific and proximate next steps in learning about dissociation is quite challenging. If consultants have seen the harm that injudicious use of standard EMDR can cause, it is easy to become activated and react strongly. Conversely, some consultants and trainers do appreciate the relevance of dissociation and elect not to address their own learning gaps. Those consultants may simply advise the consultee that "this client is not a good fit for EMDR," or share another school of thought we identified in Chapter 4. I hope that this and other chapters will illuminate alternative and more helpful ways forward.

Food for Thought

If you are reading this book for your own professional development, I invite you to consider the following questions. If you are reading this book as a consultant who wishes to better help others in reaching their professional goals, then think of a current consultee or supervisee and how they might respond.

- How do I think through and conceptualize my approach to treatment with complex trauma and dissociative presentations? What is my process?
- What knowledge and skills help me to determine proximate next steps to proceed safely in a current treatment plan with my client(s)?
- Do I know who to ask, or what questions to ask to begin building my competencies and proficiencies to better work with dissociative symptoms and disorders?

Common Learning Gaps and Other Challenges

Some practitioners seek EMDR therapy training in hopes that it will help them feel more capable or confident as a therapist. These expectations may be met, especially when a competent practitioner and motivated learner engages with a solid training team, is supported to use EMDR therapy in their practice setting, and continues their development as an EMDR therapist after training (Grimmett & Galvin, 2015). Just as EMDR has been described as a 'divining rod' for dissociation (Paulsen, 1995), it is such a powerful and technical therapy that it often pushes the edges of practitioners' window of tolerance, revealing gaps in prior learning, weaknesses in foundational competencies, and their readiness and ability to learn. We will now discuss some of those common learning gaps.

Knowledge of Trauma and Dissociation

Despite the best efforts of many who came before us, gaps in knowledge about the realities of trauma, dissociation, and their complexities, prevalence, and effects persist. In clinical practice, encountering individuals who suffer the effects of trauma is inevitable, regardless of one's setting. Yet only 8% of graduates from doctoral programs in psychology accredited by the American Psychological Association report having been required to take a course on trauma (Foltz et al., 2023). As Bethany Brand, PhD, stated, "the lack of systematic training for mental health professionals in trauma and dissociation is alarming" (2024, p. 18). While I understand that graduate programs cannot prioritize everything, it seems that some authors, professors, and programs are contributing to this issue willfully by what they write and teach and by neglecting to verify or deepen the information that they impart.

Misinformation abounds in academic programs. A recent analysis of undergraduate psychopathology textbooks found that in the discussion of trauma, sexual abuse was likely to be mentioned – rather than a more comprehensive description of forms of abuse or neglect, adverse childhood experiences, etc. Regarding dissociation, the false memory controversy and media portrayals of DID were likely to be mentioned – rather than any consideration of trauma and other factors that may contribute to someone developing a DD (Nester et al., 2025). In the discussion of the findings, the authors observed:

> It was also striking that many textbooks shared nearly identical language in some portions of the textbook; this was particularly noticeable in the sections about dissociation. Perhaps the authors of textbooks lack systematic training in dissociation as do most mental health professionals, with this lack of knowledge being reflected in their texts.
>
> (Nester et al., 2025, p. 1,000)

There seems to be evidence of intergenerational transmission of professional non-realization when it comes to dissociation (see Chapter 4). Apparently, some of us prefer not to know about these things. Consequently, *we were taught that they are irrelevant.* While the horrors of sexual abuse and exploitation are real and valid, emotional neglect and abuse are found to be vastly more common and bear similar risk to developing psychopathology (e.g., Xiao et al., 2023).

In combination, these realities lead some members of the mental health professions to view chronically traumatized persons as 'difficult' or 'difficult to treat' when they do not respond to us or to treatment in ways that are optimal or expected. Our immediate responsibility is to identify and accept the knowledge gaps and biases that we as practitioners contribute to.

Establishing the Therapeutic Frame

The *therapeutic frame* refers to the expectations and boundaries that define the roles of the practitioner and the client within the professional relationship, including psychotherapy sessions themselves, between sessions. This frame and the tasks of the therapy are largely informed and prescribed by one's theoretical orientation – that is, the theory that is guiding the treatment – though distinct from the case conceptualization (Cherry & Gold, 1989). In Chapter 3, we introduced the layers of the conceptual and therapeutic frame that we are using in this book.

Today, many essential aspects of the 'standard' therapeutic frame are codified in our professional ethics codes and the statutes that govern our license/registration to practice psychotherapy. However, those codes do not delineate or prescribe *how* practitioners are to best apply them within a certain theoretical framework or modality, or with a particular clinical population. Practitioners come to EMDR therapy with whatever has been impressed upon them in prior training and experience, and that informs how they 'do' EMDR.

This matters greatly for EMDR therapy and dissociation. In the development of the AIP model, protocols, and procedures of EMDR, Francine Shapiro may have been operating under the assumption that learners already know how to handle the difficult interpersonal and intrapersonal issues that arise during treatment – especially in treatment with individuals who have experienced profound relational trauma. An alternate viewpoint is that attention to the therapeutic frame may have been discarded due to the disfavor of psychodynamic models and increased focus on interventions and brief therapy that leaves less room for relational issues to emerge.

EMDR therapy offers a structural framework of prongs, phases, protocol, and procedures; however, these provide little guidance regarding how to think or what to do when things get complicated. New EMDR practitioners struggle to assess whether the client has the capacity to use any stop signal rather than shutting down due to freezing or pleasing patterns, or how to determine consent to work on a target memory beyond "the client wanted to work on this incident." Regarding *Phase VII: Closure*, many practitioners do not understand that this applies to <u>every</u> session in the EMDR therapy frame, as part of the therapeutic frame that is intentionally constructed – from the beginning – to support trauma processing. Richard Kluft, MD, proposed the 'rule of thirds' for structuring a session (Kluft, 1991).

- 1st third: Prepare for the work of the session, address containment, consent, and regulation as applicable.

- 2nd third: Intensive work, to include accessing self-states, trauma accessing or processing.
- 3rd third: Closure, tending to grounding, orienting, containment, and cognitive focus in the present.
- Time between sessions for self-care. Starting and ending on time is essential for the therapeutic process.

Establishing a clear and consistent therapeutic frame is important to allow the best chance for continuance and completion of a treatment plan. Some instances of mis-attunement, rupture in the therapeutic alliance, and (re)enactment of trauma-based patterns are an inevitable and expected part of the treatment process – despite our best efforts to curtail them. Ben Israel, MD, emphasized the distinctions between the interpersonal and defensive patterns of non-traumatized individuals, and the "characteristic constellation of mental defenses, coping strategies and reality testing heuristics" that emerge from a life of survival honed by early, repeated relational trauma (Israel, 2023).

Educating clients about and maintaining the therapeutic frame can involve conflict as we articulate and honor boundaries related to time, behavior, etc. This includes confronting our own idealization of ourselves as helpers. Karen Maroda, PhD, reviewed the trends in psychotherapy from being a male-dominant field to a female-dominant field, alongside the rise of attachment theory and trauma-informed care, and how this has (re)shaped our views and ideals of the therapeutic frame (Maroda, 2022). Regardless of anyone's fantasy, we cannot be the ideal parent to our clients. Being a 'good enough' therapist involves providing both a caring environment that may have been lacking, and clear limits to protect the client, practitioner, and the therapeutic relationship (Kinsler, 2017; Steele et al., 2017). There are many valuable resources within our field regarding the establishment and maintenance of the therapeutic frame when working with chronically traumatized individuals. Such work often extends over several years, rather than just a few months. Becoming familiar with the extant literature, as well as pursuing ongoing training and consultation, can help practitioners anticipate and navigate important junctures, such as:

- managing contact between sessions,
- adjusting the treatment plan when new symptoms or historical information emerge, and
- when, if ever, to consider meeting multiple times per week in an outpatient setting.

Screening for Severe Dissociation

At a minimum, EMDR trainers and consultants must ensure that EMDR Trained practitioners know how to screen for complex dissociative symptoms. This includes conducting a follow-up interview to confirm and discern symptom features, which will be discussed in greater detail in Chapter 6.

Trainers are now required to teach this within accredited basic training programs (e.g., EMDRIA, 2022). Given that this may be the first time that practitioners are learning that dissociation is relevant to their practice, more attention is necessary to develop this competency. Some basic training programs include a practicum segment focused on administering and scoring a screening tool and utilizing the results of these screening tools during consultation groups to further advance learners' skills in determining readiness for later phases of EMDR therapy. This is a good start.

For most practitioners, this gap will not be fully addressed within their EMDR training program. Consultants can expect to dedicate time to helping others cultivate this skill and direct learners to other means to deepen their learning in recognizing and assessing dissociative symptoms – both in general and for purposes of determining readiness for EMDR therapy.

Mentalizing

Mentalizing, often synonymous with reflective functioning, refers to the capacity to understand and interpret – implicitly and explicitly – one's own and others' behaviors as an expression of specific feelings, desires, thoughts, attitudes, or goals (Brugnera et al., 2021). Development of the psychotherapist beyond the 'beginner' stage (see Figure 5.1) relies heavily upon one's ability to mentalize. Practitioners' ability to recognize and attend to their own experience and that of the client depends upon their self-reflective abilities and self-awareness; this, in turn, impacts practitioners' ability to provide quality care. When practitioners arrive at EMDR therapy training with prior learning focused heavily on what to do and how to behave as mental health professionals, their capacity to mentalize may be underdeveloped.

This matters in the practice of trauma-focused therapy for several reasons. First, reflective functioning has been found to mediate attachment (in)security and well-being of psychotherapists (Brugnera et al., 2021). Said plainly, the ability to mentalize is essential to the ability to notice what I am thinking and feeling and discern what is 'mine' and what is 'not mine.' When practitioners can recognize what is 'mine,' this minimizes the likelihood and extent to which our unresolved issues will negatively impact clients (Abargil & Tishby, 2021), especially those who have experienced attachment wounding and developed a DD. Mentalizing also helps us to notice our own window of tolerance, to be with others' strong emotions that arise in trauma processing, and aids in preserving our professional and personal resources.

Second, the ability to conceptualize, think, and operate from a theory in a manner that is personalized to the client relies on our mentalizing capacity. Observations of what seemed to go well in initial sessions, interpreting the results of screening or assessment tools, considering unexpected responses to containment, and determining what is needed to achieve the goals of any phase of EMDR therapy depend upon these skills. Knowledge of theory and research then combines via mentalization to integrate all available information to construct a case conceptualization and treatment plan – and to facilitate informed consent at each turn.

Greater understanding of our own mental states and those of our clients can increase our capacity to tolerate and manage emotions common in countertransference (Abargil & Tishby, 2021). Deep knowledge of our treatment model(s) allows us to consider all available options within our frame at a moment's notice. Together, these abilities increase our tolerance of uncertainty and can improve our overall bandwidth and attunement in the session.

Relational Competency

Relational competency refers to our ability to understand relational data in the moment and speak directly about the therapeutic relationship with the client (Calvert et al., 2018). This skill builds upon our mentalizing capacities and our overall developmental level as a practitioner. In its early days, EMDR was criticized by scholars in the psychodynamic and psychoanalytic fields as a "one-person therapy" because of how the person of the therapist seemed to be reduced to a technician reading a script (Wachtel, 2002). Nonetheless, the therapeutic relationship is a core element of EMDR therapy (e.g., Hase & Heinz Brisch, 2022). When implemented as an intervention, EMDR can easily lean toward a one-person stance of reading a script and implementing a protocol rather than a process of engaging *with* the client in the frame of EMDR therapy. When employing EMDR therapy to treat clients who have been harmed in relationships, this one-person stance of 'doing EMDR to' someone runs the risk of the practitioner unwittingly causing harm to the client.

As a transtheoretical concept, relational competency often overlaps with what we also know as transference and countertransference. Some practitioners find that their foundational learning is insufficient for "navigating the intersubjective phenomena that are active during EMDR therapy, especially in the treatment of complex cases" (Piedfort-Marin, 2018, p. 159).

Those with psychodynamic training are better prepared to navigate the relational complexity of trauma processing – via EMDR therapy or otherwise. When gaps exist in this area, case review in consultation and supervision is a prime opportunity to learn about, identify, and process the psychodynamics that are impacting the EMDR therapy process.

When Professional Learning is a Parallel Process

There are many parallel processes in the practice and learning of psychotherapy. Working in this profession serves as a mirror in which we can learn a lot about ourselves. In EMDR therapy, the parallel processes are between the training material and the learner, and between the client and the practitioner.

In basic EMDR therapy training, the standard protocol and its variants are the 'client.' Due diligence may be considered here, in estimating whether the learning practitioner has the capacity and the willingness to adequately learn about the 'client' so that they can apply that learning in an informed way. Sufficient information is needed to accurately and effectively conceptualize. Therapists' tolerance of intense affect may come into play as well. Self-awareness in the training setting impacts whether or how someone becomes activated by the training material or faculty members, especially when the learner has not done (enough of) their own personal psychotherapy. Impatience with oneself or the 'client' may show up as wanting to skip ahead and learn modified or adapted protocols for specific situations or populations – without first learning and becoming proficient in the basic, standard protocol. When new learners allow themselves to engage in developing proficiency in the standard protocol, they invariably find it to be complicated enough!

The task of establishing treatment goals is another common parallel process challenge, especially for beginner and intermediate practitioners. In psychotherapy, treatment goals are primarily determined by the client, while the therapeutic frame is determined by practitioners – according to what they are trained to provide, professional standards, and what they discern best corresponds to the symptoms and goals presented by the client. Beginning practitioners and newly trained EMDR therapists are prone to be more self-focused, lower in self-awareness, and highly focused on technique. Presumably, the EMDR therapist wants to practice new skills, and the client wants to try a new approach. Listening for slips in speech that indicate "I think the client needs to…." or selecting target memories based solely upon the practitioner's perspective are red-flag indicators that the therapeutic alliance may be at risk.

When practitioners rigidly follow the protocol and worksheets and yet struggle to share the observations that inform their decision points, various parallel processes may be occurring beneath the surface. Is this an issue of mentalizing capacity, relational competency, professional development, or something else? The careful listening and insight of a consultant or supervisor can help to clarify the situation and balance practicing fidelity to the protocol with attuned client care.

Types of Consultation and Training

Consultation here refers to a situation in which the consultant has advanced knowledge and skills in a particular area that may benefit the consultee, but the consultant holds no legal liability for the treatment of the client. (In some countries, the terms 'supervision' and 'consultation' are used interchangeably, but in the USA the distinction is an important one for legal liability.) Learning predominantly focused on interventions and what-to-do-when can leave practitioners without a clear orientation or direction, and unable to explain why they chose an intervention or why they think clients responded well or poorly to it. Consultation and supervision are crucial in supporting the development of dynamic conceptualization skills to both anticipate and respond to situations that arise in practice (Gilboa-Schechtman, 2024).

So many options are available for consultation and training – and many of them are good. Without intentional consideration, practitioners can easily become lopsided in their learning or unintentionally neglect gaps that interfere with their well-being or therapeutic outcomes for their clients. The following sections describe specific goals for learning in consultation and training, and ways that practitioners and their consultants may navigate the process of continued development toward specialized practice. Knowing what one needs is an essential step to being an informed and intentional seeker and consumer of consultation and training. Different types of consultation and training may correspond to different gaps and needs of the practitioner.

To Gain Competence and Proficiency

Further learning in the knowledge, skills, and behaviors that comprise competency in a specific model or area of practice – such as EMDR therapy – builds upon the initial foundational competencies developed in a practitioner's graduate program and supervision process. Any gaps that remain in that foundation will need to be identified and addressed, or else they may continue to proliferate outside of the practitioner's awareness.

Proficiency in the basic protocols and procedures of EMDR therapy involves being able to implement those elements to reasonable fidelity. Practitioners who become aware of struggling to implement the basic protocols and procedures of EMDR therapy may seek consultation beyond the required hours associated with their basic training program. They may further deepen their understanding by (re)reading the Shapiro textbook (2018) and/or auditing a training course. Peer consultation may be helpful at this stage, depending upon the peer group. If values of the group include review of work samples and adherence or fidelity to the standard protocol, peer consultation may help in bolstering foundational learning (Calvert et al., 2018). However, without those elements, peer consultation is likely to pose a risk for drift from the treatment model and standard of care (Waltman et al., 2016).

Practitioners who are still struggling with the implementation of Shapiro's AIP model and basic protocols and procedures are encouraged to patiently develop those skills before proceeding to advanced training. One exception may arise when further training is essential to implementing EMDR therapy with a special population that comprises the majority of the practitioner's client base (e.g., clients with complex trauma and DDs, or children and adolescents). A good level of proficiency in the standard EMDR protocol and procedures is needed before learning modified EMDR protocols to support work with DDs.

To Meet Requirements for an Advanced Designation

When practitioners pursue an advanced designation such as certification, accreditation, or consultant status, this involves the evaluation of their clinical work by a senior practitioner-consultant. Specific requirements are determined by the professional organization that accredits EMDR therapy designations in one's geographical region. The focus of this consultation is intended to be on implementing the standard EMDR protocol with proficiency and fidelity. Best practices for this type of consultation have been discussed in several publications (EMDRIA, 2020; Leeds, 2016; Logie, 2023; Madere et al., 2020). Nonetheless, individual consultants vary considerably in their means, rigor, and emphasis on evaluation of practice fidelity, competency, and proficiency.

Competent and proficient implementation of *Phases I and II* of EMDR therapy includes determining readiness for trauma accessing and reprocessing via skillful use of a screening or assessment tool for identifying dissociative symptoms and disorders (Shapiro 2018, p. 96). Careful history taking, screening, or assessing dissociative symptoms, and gauging affect tolerance and other factors of readiness ought to be among every consultant's areas of emphasis and evaluation of competency in EMDR therapy.

All EMDR consultants and certified/accredited practitioners are strongly urged to become adept at utilizing at least one diagnostic assessment tool for dissociative symptoms and disorders. This is not an ancillary skill – which would not be the proper focus of consultation for advanced designations – but rather an essential area of competency and proficiency to develop. When a client scores highly on the Dissociative Experiences Scale (DES-II, Carlson & Putnam, 1993) or other screening measures, knowing how to follow up on the answers given and how to assess further has become an integral part of practice as an EMDR therapist (Leeds et al., 2022).

For General Professional Development

Trauma-focused psychotherapists are at a higher risk for burnout and deviating from the standard of care if they lack a supportive group of peers or appropriate continued professional development (Hensel et al., 2015). Consultation may enhance mentalization and conceptualization skills, which, as discussed above, are both essential for trauma therapists. Practitioner growth in the area of relational competencies has been shown to improve practitioner well-being and client outcomes (Brugnera et al., 2021; Calvert et al., 2018).

To Gain Specialized Knowledge

Perhaps because psychotherapy is a *practice*, much can be learned interpersonally – in a group or 1:1 setting – that can be difficult to learn from a book or in a purely didactic format. To this end, practitioners may seek out peers or advanced practitioners with specialized knowledge for consultation focused on learning from them. After completion of EMDR therapy training, practitioners often seek specialized knowledge in the treatment of a particular population, issue, and/or how to integrate EMDR with another theory or model (e.g., ego state therapies).

According to the third revision of the *Guidelines for Treating Dissociative Identity Disorder in Adults* (ISSTD, 2011), "expert consultation can be particularly helpful in development of the treatment frame and anticipation and management of boundary-related dilemmas" (p. 164). The 'expert' or specialized consultant may not also be an advanced/master clinician in the practice of EMDR therapy. Both the practitioner and the consultant ought to clarify the goals of consultation and the scope of their expertise.

To Consult on a Particular Case (vs a Type of Case)

Often, practitioners are motivated to reach out for consultation based upon a need or concern raised by experiences with a particular client. It can be helpful to clarify – for both the practitioner and the consultant – whether they agree to engage in consultation on an individual case, or on clinical work with a *type* of case.

Consultation focused on a particular case – one person, and clinical questions associated with that client's treatment plan – tends to be narrower and may pose challenges. The consultant does not know this person, so any feedback or recommendations given are based upon the report of the practitioner or data provided by the practitioner. This narrow focus can be helpful and necessary in situations where legal and ethical ramifications are imminent, such as safety issues, boundary crossings or violations, and transference or countertransference issues that are unique to this practitioner-client dyad. The consultant may support the practitioner in forming a case conceptualization, providing knowledge related to the standard of care, determining what to do next, and how to best accomplish it. The consultant can ask the practitioner questions such as "how did you select this target?" or "when you followed up on this assessment item, what qualitative data was provided by the client?" This information will contribute to the context of learning for the practitioner – regarding how to think about and navigate the clinical work with this *type* of situation in their practice.

To Adhere to Best Practices and Ethical Standards

Seeking consultation with a specialized and/or master practitioner is one way to ensure that one is practicing within the standard of care associated with the application of a particular model, or working with a particular population (Brown et al., 1998). This can be in conjunction with other types of consultation discussed above. When venturing into new clinical territory, such as working with complex trauma and dissociation, many practitioners find themselves naive and without guideposts to tell them if they are on track, or not. Practitioners may have questions such as "is this normal?" or "what are the appropriate steps to take in this scenario?" In this context, one purpose of consultation is to ensure that treatment is congruent with the relevant best practices, established literature, and treatment guidelines.

If this is the goal – or a goal – of consultation, the consultant ought to be knowledgeable of the relevant treatment and practice guidelines, associated ethical codes, and steeped in the professional community of practitioners who specialize in this area. The consultant's qualifications can be substantiated via years of membership in professional organizations, participation in those organizations, and other professional work such as presentations and publications on the topic that are peer-reviewed by the association, academic journal, or publisher.

Food for Thought

- As a consultant – What kind of consultation is this practitioner seeking? Do they want my opinion, or to help them grow? In what way(s)? How am I qualified to do that? What is the scope of my knowledge and skills in this area?
- As a practitioner seeking consultation – What kind(s) of consultation am I seeking? How do I know that a consultant is qualified to offer what I need? How will I know when I have reached my goals or the limits of what this consultant can offer me?

Specialized Practice

Trauma-focused therapy, treating people with DDs, and especially doing so in a framework that includes the AIP model and EMDR therapy, is an area of specialized practice. The American Psychological Association offers this definition of specialized practice:

> a specialty ... is a defined area of ... practice characterized by a distinctive configuration of competent services for specified problems and populations. Practice in a specialty requires advanced knowledge and skills acquired through an organized sequence of education and training.
>
> (APA, 2020)

This definition offers a framework for understanding the process of developing a specialization. The title of this book, *EMDR, Dissociation and Beyond,* designates a 'problem and population.' Given how most graduate programs do not offer much – if any – training in trauma, dissociation, or EMDR, these areas of practice constitute advanced knowledge and skills. An organized sequence of training and learning can be found via accredited training in EMDR therapy, and courses of study offered via the International Society for the Study of Trauma and Dissociation or equivalent. Practitioners who have developed a specialization in treating dissociation, and who use EMDR therapy within that broader framework offer a distinctive configuration of competent services.

Figure 5.2 depicts specialized practice as a process. Notice how the arrows along the bottom of the diagram are bidirectional. This is because specialized and integrated practice requires a journey of ongoing learning. We gradually discover the need to learn and/or have the interest piqued by a research article, a stuck point with a client, or a conversation with a colleague. Cultivating a specialty is ultimately about

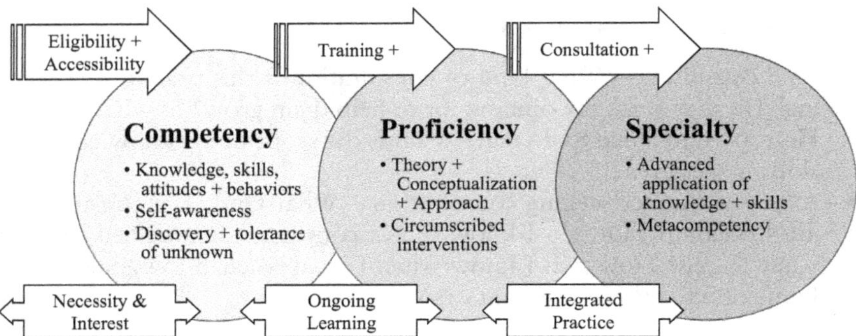

Figure 5.2 Specialized Practice as a Process.

meta-competence – knowing what one knows, and what one does not know. Perhaps 'humility' ought to be added as a criterion for being a specialist.

Specialized Consultation

What makes one qualified to provide specialized supervision or consultation? Broadly speaking, it seems that the professional must be an advanced or master practitioner, have demonstrable and advanced competence in the area of specialization, *and* have knowledge and skills in providing consultation. Figure 5.3 depicts the stages of development for supervisors and consultants.

There is quite a lot of correspondence between the levels of practitioner development and the levels of supervisor/consultant development. Meta-competency – knowing what one knows and the limits of one's knowledge – also applies to the practice of supervision and consultation. This framework can guide practitioners in selecting a consultant. For a beginner practitioner, a Level 2 consultant may be just the right match to help surpass feeling overwhelmed and become excited about learning again. The same Level 2 consultant may not be the best fit for an advanced or master practitioner who desires to grow toward specialization or to develop advanced conceptualization skills.

Finding a good fit in a consultant is quite multifaceted. When searching for a new consultant, consider identifying your highest priorities. The list below offers a summary of approaches and qualifications of consultants referenced in the preceding sections.

- Advanced qualification(s) in clinical practice
- Evidence of specialized training and expertise

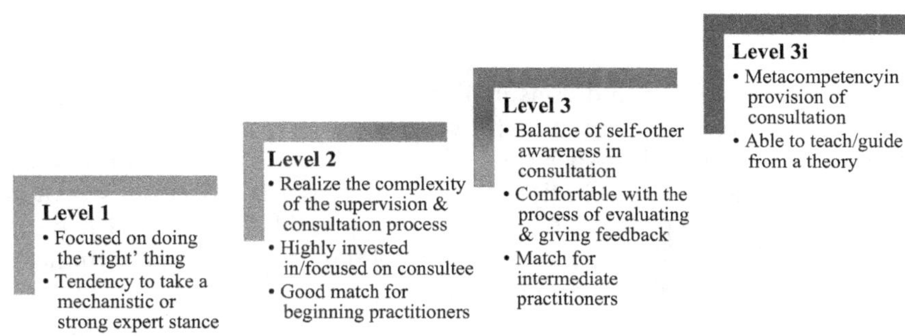

Figure 5.3 Stages of Supervisor/Consultant Development.

Sources: Adapted from Stoltenberg and McNeill (2010) and Logie (2023).

- Clear alignment with at least one relevant credentialing body, professional organization, etc.
- Evidence of ongoing professional development in the topic or approach in question
- Utilization of established resources such as fidelity rating scales, treatment/practice guidelines
- Deep knowledge of the standard of care related to the subject of consultation
- Trained/qualified in providing clinical supervision
- Utilizes a written consultation agreement
- Awareness of the scope/limits of their own expertise

When looking for specialized consultation on a particular model, theory, or ad hoc consultation on a specific and time-limited issue, consulting with someone who is trained in clinical supervision may not be as important. However, if you want to develop your skills in treating complex trauma and DDs with EMDR therapy, ensuring that your consultant is an established and involved member of the professional organization(s) associated with each area of practice ought to be a minimum requirement.

For consultants and supervisors, I invite you to evaluate your toolbox. Considering the above list, what are your greatest strengths? What is your level of familiarity with the guidelines associated with EMDR therapy, treatment of complex trauma, and treatment of DDs? What literature, theories, and adjunctive therapies have you studied at an advanced or master's level? How do you keep up with the evolving literature? Awareness of these areas is a great place to start to ensure that we are each doing our part to advance the standard of care and offer competent and healing psychotherapy.

Conclusions

Postgraduate training and consultation play vital roles in bridging gaps in knowledge and skills essential for conceptualizing and treating trauma, complex trauma, and dissociation – both within the EMDR framework and more broadly. Consultation naturally invites self-reflection, which is a growth-promoting practice in itself (Knapp et al., 2017), and it must be paired with specialized input to meaningfully support a practitioner's development toward advanced practice.

A principal marker of advanced clinical practice is meta-competence. Growing beyond foundational training is critical for developing the nuanced clinical judgment needed for complex case conceptualization, sustaining resilience amid the emotional demands of our work, and providing competent care for individuals with DDs. Ongoing professional development and consultation are not optional in this field – they are central to ethical, effective practice.

References

Abargil, M., & Tishby, O. (2021). Fluctuations in therapist emotions and their relation to treatment processes and outcomes. *Journal of Psychotherapy Integration, 31*(1), 1–18. https://doi.org/10.1037/int0000205

American Psychological Association. (2020, August). Principles for the recognition of proficiencies in professional psychology. *Commission for the Recognition of Proficiencies and Specialties in Professional Psychology (CRSSPP)*. https://www.apa.org/about/policy/recognition-principles.pdf

Brand, B. L. (2024). *The concise guide to the assessment and treatment of trauma-related dissociation. American Psychological Association.* https://doi.org/10.1037/0000386-000

Brown, D., Scheflin, A. W., & Hammond, D. C. (1998). *Memory, trauma treatment, and the law*. W. W. Norton & Company.

Brugnera, A., Zarbo, C., Compare, A., Talia, A., Tasca, G. A., de Jong, K., Greco, A., Greco, F., Pievani, L., Auteri A., & Lo Coco, G. (2021). Self-reported reflective functioning mediates the association between attachment insecurity and well-being among psychotherapists, *Psychotherapy Research, 31*(2), 247–257. https://doi.org/10.1080/10503307.2020.1762946

Calvert, F. L., Deane, F. P., Crowe, T. P., & Grenyer, B. F. S. (2018). Supervisor perceptions of relational competence: Core components and developmental considerations. *Training and Education in Professional Psychology*, *12*(3), 135–141. psycnet.apa.org/doi/10.1037/tep0000194

Carlson, E., & Putnam, F. (1993). An update on the dissociative experiences scale. *Dissociation*, *6*(1), 16–27.

Cherry, E. F., & Gold, S. N. (1989). The therapeutic frame revisited: A contemporary perspective. *Psychotherapy: Theory, Research, Practice, Training,* *26*(2), 162–168. https://doi.org/10.1037/h0085415

EMDR Global Alliance. (2024). *Training Standards.* https://emdrglobal.org/training-standards/

EMDRIA. (2020). *Consultation Packet.* www.emdria.org/emdr-training/become-anemdria-approved-consultant/consultation-packet/

EMDR International Association. (2022, December 27). *Standards for EMDR Basic Training.* www.emdria.org/standards-for-emdr-basic-training-2/ [proprietary link]

EMDR International Association. (2025, March 4). *Standards for EMDR Basic Training.* www.emdria.org/wp-content/uploads/2025/03/Standards-for-EMDRIA-Basic-Training.pdf [proprietary link]

Erikson, E. (1980). *Identity and the life cycle.* W. W. Norton & Company. (Original work published 1959).

Falender, C., Shafranske, E. (2016). *Supervision essentials for the practice of competency-based supervision.* American Psychological Association.

Foltz, R., Kaeley, A., Kupchan, J., Mills, A., Murray, K., Pope, A., Rahman, H., & Rubright, C. (2023). Trauma-informed care? Identifying training deficits in accredited doctoral programs. *Psychological Trauma: Theory, Research, Practice, and Policy, 15*(7), 1188–1193. https://doi.org/10.1037/tra0001461

Gilboa-Schechtman E. (2024). Case conceptualization in clinical practice and training. *Clinical psychology in Europe*, 6(Spec Issue), e12103. https://doi.org/10.32872/cpe.12103

Grimmett, J., & Galvin, M. D. (2015). Clinician experiences with EMDR: Factors influencing continued use. *Journal of EMDR Practice and Research, 9*(1), 3–16. https://doi.org/10.1891/1933-3196.9.1.3

Hase, M., & Brisch, K. H. (2022). The therapeutic relationship in EMDR therapy. *Frontiers in Psychology, 13*, 835470. https://doi.org/10.3389/fpsyg.2022.835470

Hensel, J. M., Ruiz, C., Finney, C., & Dewa, C. S. (2015). Meta- analysis of risk factors for secondary traumatic stress in therapeutic work with trauma victims. *Journal of Traumatic Stress, 28*(2), 83–91. psycnet.apa.org/doi/10.1002/jts.21998

Israel, B. (2023, April 13). Conditions for healing: Uses of the therapeutic frame and alliance for treating complex trauma-related disorders [Conference presentation]. Full-day Workshop Presented at the 40th Annual Conference of the International Society for the Study of Trauma and Dissociation. Louisville, KY.

International Society for the Study of Trauma and Dissociation. (2011). [Chu, J. A., Dell, P. F., Van der Hart, O., Cardeña, E., Barach, P. M., Somer, E., Loewenstein, R. J., Brand, B., Golston, J. C., Courtois, C. A., Bowman, E. S., Classen, C., Dorahy, M., , Sar,V., Gelinas, D. J., Fine, C. ., Paulsen, S., Kluft, R. P., Dalenberg, C. J., Jacobson-Levy, M., Nijenhuis, E. R. S., Boon, S., Chefetz, R. A., Middleton, W., Ross, C. A., Howell, E., Goodwin, G., Coons, P. M., Frankel, A. S., Steele, K., Gold, S. N., Gast, U., Young, L. M., & Twombly, J.]. Guidelines for treating dissociative identity disorder in adults, third revision. *Journal of Trauma & Dissociation, 12,* 115–187.

Kate, M.-A., Hopwood, T., & Jamieson, G. (2020). The prevalence of dissociative disorders and dissociative experiences in college populations: A meta-analysis of 98 studies. *Journal of Trauma and Dissociation, 21*(1), 16–61. https://doi.org/10.1080/15299732.2019.1647915

Kinsler, P. J. (2017). *Complex psychological trauma: The centrality of relationship* (1st ed.). Routledge. https://doi.org/10.4324/9781315651910

Kluft, R. P. (1991). Multiple personality disorder. In A. Tasman & S. M. Goldfinger (Eds.), The *a*merican *p*sychiatric *p*ress *a*nnual *r*eview, (Vol. 10, pp. 161–188). American Psychiatric Press.

Knapp, S., Gottlieb, M. C., & Handelsman, M. M. (2017). Enhancing professionalism through self-reflection. *Professional Psychology: Research and Practice, 48*(3), 167–174. https://doi.org/10.1037/pro0000135

Kruger, J., & Dunning, D. (1999). Unskilled and unaware of it: How difficulties in recognizing one's own incompetence lead to inflated self-assessments. *Journal of Personality and Social Psychology, 77*(6), 1121–1134. https://doi.org/10.1037/0022-3514.77.6.1121

Laliotis, D., Luber, M., Oren, U., Shapiro, E., Ichii, M., Hase, M., LaRosa, L., Alter-Reid, K., Tortes St. Jammes, J. (2021). What is EMDR therapy? Past, present, and future directions. *Journal of EMDR Practice and Research, 15*(4), 186–201. https://doi.org/10.1891/EMDR-D-21-00029

Leeds, A. M. (2016). *A guide to the standard EMDR therapy protocols for clinicians, supervisors, and consultants* (2nd ed.). Springer.

Leeds, A., Madere, J., & Coy, D. M. (2022). Beyond the DES-II: Screening for dissociative disorders in EMDR therapy. *Journal of EMDR Practice and Research, 16*(1), pp. 25–38. https://doi.org/10.1891/emdr-d-21-00019

Logie, R. (2023). *EMDR supervision: A handbook* (1st ed.). Routledge. https://doi.org/10.4324/9781003214588

Madere, J., Leeds, A., Sells, C., Sperling, C., & Browning, M. (2020). Consultation for EMDRIA certification in EMDR: Best practices and challenges. *Journal of EMDR Practice and Research, 14*(2), 62–75. https://doi.org/10.1891/EMDR-D-19-00052

Maroda, K. J. (2022). *The analyst's vulnerability: Impact on theory and practice.* Routledge/Taylor & Francis Group.

McNeill, B. W., & Stoltenberg, C. D. (2016). *Supervision essentials for the integrative developmental model.* American Psychological Association. https://doi.org/10.1037/14858-000

Nester, M. S., Spicher, B., Pierorazio, N. A., Brand, B. L., & McEwen, L. E. (2025). Coverage of child maltreatment in undergraduate psychopathology textbooks. *Psychological Trauma: Theory, Research, Practice, and Policy, 17*(5), 996–1003. https://doi.org/10.1037/tra0001683

Paulsen, S., (1995). Eye movement desensitization and reprocessing: Its cautious use in the dissociative disorders. *Dissociation: Progress in the Dissociative Disorders, 8*(1), 32–44.

Piedfort-Marin, O. (2018). Transference and countertransference in EMDR therapy. *Journal of EMDR Practice and Research, 12*(3), 158–172. https://doi.org/10.1891/1933-3196.12.3.158

Quinlan, E., Schilder, S. & Deane, F. P. (2021). "This wasn't in the manual": A qualitative exploration of tolerance of uncertainty in the practicing psychology context. *AustralianPsychologist, 56*(2), 154–167. https://doi.org/10.1080/00050067.2020.1829451

Sar, V. (2011). Epidemiology of dissociative disorders: An overview. *Epidemiology Research International, 2011*, 404538.

Shapiro, F. (2018). *Eye movement desensitization and reprocessing (EMDR) therapy: Basic principles, protocols and procedures* (3rd ed). Guilford.

Simeon, D., & Putnam, F. (2022). Pathological dissociation in the national comorbidity survey replication (NCS-R): Prevalence, morbidity, comorbidity, and childhood maltreatment. *Journal of Trauma & Dissociation, 23*(5), 490–503. https://doi.org/10.1080/15299732.2022.2064580

Soma, C. S., Baucom, B. R. W., Xiao, B., Butner, J. E., Hilpert, P., Narayanan, S., Atkins, D. C., & Imel, Z. E. (2020). Coregulation of therapist and client emotion during psychotherapy. *Journal of the Society for Psychotherapy Research, 30*(5), 591–603. https://doi.org/10.1080/10503307.2019.1661541

Steele, K., Boon, S., & Van der Hart, O. (2017). *Treating trauma-related dissociation: A practical, integrative approach.* Norton.

Stoltenberg, C. D, & McNeill, B. W. (2010). *IDM supervision: An integrative developmental model for supervising counselors and therapists* (3rd ed.). Routledge.

Swart, S., Wildschut, M., Draijer, N., Langeland, W., & Smit, J. H. (2020). Dissociative subtype of posttraumatic stress disorder or PTSD with comorbid dissociative disorders: Comparative evaluation of clinical profiles. *Psychological Trauma: Theory, Research, Practice and Policy, 12*(1), 38–45. https://doi.org/10.1037/tra0000474

Wachtel, P. L. (2002). EMDR and psychoanalysis. In F. Shapiro (Ed.), *EMDR as an integrative psychotherapy approach: Experts of diverse orientations explore the paradigm prism* (pp. 123–150). *American Psychological Association.* https://doi.org/10.1037/10512-005

Waltman, S. H., Frankel, S. A., & Williston, M. A. (2016). Improving clinician self-awareness and increasing accurate representation of clinical competencies. *Practice Innovations*, *1*(3), 178–188. https://doi.org/10.1037/pri0000026

Xiao, Z., Murat Baldwin, M., Wong, S. C., Obsuth, I., Meinck, F., & Murray, A. L. (2023). The impact of childhood psychological maltreatment on mental health outcomes in adulthood: A systematic review and meta-analysis. *Trauma Violence Abuse*, *24*(5), 3049–3064. https://doi.org/10.1177/15248380221122816

Part III

Dissociation-Informed Practice of EMDR Therapy

Chapter 6

Collecting History and Evaluating Symptoms

Jennifer A. Madere and D. Michael Coy

Introduction

As we begin Part III of this book, the focus turns to the fourth layer of our treatment frame (see Chapter 3), resourcing and memory processing methods. This and the following two chapters will walk through the eight phases and three prongs of EMDR in the context of complex trauma and dissociation. For the sake of clarity, we will address our third layer, ego state therapies, in Part IV, though in practice the layers are commingled.

Phase I: History Taking commonly garners minimal attention in basic and advanced EMDR training programs. In the Shapiro (2018) text, diagnostic evaluation and treatment planning are included within *Phase I*; however, this is largely implicit. There seems to be an assumption that learners of EMDR therapy are already competent in gathering a client's relevant history and evaluating symptoms. Our experience as consultants and trainers indicates otherwise. Considering how few practitioners receive foundational training in working with trauma-related issues during or after graduate school, this should be no surprise (Brand, 2024).

When complex trauma and dissociative symptoms are present, collecting history is more than identifying potential targets, organizing them into a timeline, and developing a treatment plan for EMDR therapy. Establishing safety during the initial sessions supports the process of history taking and ensures that stabilization and closure strategies are in place *before* traumatic events are actively identified. Moreover, learning a person's history is often a recursive process as practitioner and client navigate memory gaps, internal conflict, psychodynamics, and other unique challenges resulting from complex trauma and disruptions in functional connectivity that disrupt memory and one's access to it.

All EMDR therapists need to know how to evaluate symptoms and ethically and effectively care for clients who have sought their assistance. Referring to diagnostic 'assessment' in EMDR therapy can be confusing because *Phase III: Assessment* refers to activation of the target memory.

DOI: 10.4324/9781003410201-9

So, we will use terms such as 'diagnostic evaluation' for clarity. Evaluating symptoms may be facilitated concurrently with collecting history and building the therapeutic alliance. This is not about finding out what is 'wrong' with the client, or pathologizing their experience. Instead, identifying the type, frequency, and severity of symptoms will assist us in collaboratively selecting treatment goals that can be reasonably and safely accomplished within our scope of competency and consent. The process of diagnostic evaluation deepens informed consent and clarifies when consultation and/or referral are needed. Diagnostic frameworks other than the DSM and ICD can be helpful, such as the *Psychodynamic Diagnostic Manual* (PDM-II, Lingiardi & McWilliams, 2017), which contextualizes symptoms within personality functioning and mental functioning to aid practitioners in developing a theory of mind regarding each client.

> A good diagnosis operationalizes empathy.
>
> —Robert M. Gordon (2025)

The timing, selection, and process of employing screening and assessment tools for dissociative symptoms will partially depend on the intended scope and goal(s) of treatment. A brief review of screening and assessment tools for dissociation will be provided. We recommend that every practitioner become familiar with and practice administering at least one brief screening, one full screening, and one diagnostic assessment. We will discuss how these instruments correspond to treatment plans, endeavoring to accomplish symptom relief, inform comprehensive treatment, measure progress, and recognize treatment trajectories. Case examples will illustrate how assessment tools may be utilized at the outset of treatment and in reevaluation of the diagnosis and treatment plan.

Collecting History

Phase I: More Than Timelines and Readiness

Collecting history begins on the first contact with a potential client. For practitioners who advertise working with complex trauma and dissociation, clients may spontaneously share about their trauma-related symptoms and experiences because they expect that we want to know about it. Others may offer vague statements such as "I want to stop having the same relationship over and over" that hint at a history of complex trauma.

Upon completion of basic training, many EMDR practitioners adjust their intake and standard bio/psycho/social/spiritual evaluation processes to invite clients to self-identify adverse and potentially traumatic experiences.

'Red Flags' for Dissociative Disorders

- Extensive trauma, and/or substance use history
- Extensive treatment history without periods of sustained recovery/stability
- Numerous prior diagnoses such as the following, with co-occurring trauma history:
  - Bipolar I or II
  - Major depression
  - Borderline personality disorder (traits or prior diagnosis)
  - Neurodivergence (ASD, ADHD, etc.)
  - Eating disorders
- History of early medical trauma and/or attachment wounding
- Parents with significant disruptions in mental health functioning (suspected or diagnosed)
- Non-response to psychiatric medication (for panic attacks, bipolar disorder, major depression, etc.)
- Persistent, medically unexplained physical symptoms
- Blank spells (or possible indicators of amnesia)
- Voices, psychosis, or 'loud thoughts'

Figure 6.1 'Red Flags' for Dissociative Disorders.

Validated question sets, such as the Adverse Childhood Experiences Scale (ACES, Felitti et al., 1998), may be incorporated to gauge the person's overall trauma load. Some early EMDR trainers suggested that clients be given homework to prepare a timeline or a list of the '10 worst' and '10 best' experiences in their lifetime. All of these strategies may fail when clients are unable or unwilling to disclose present or past experiences. If clients *are* able to recall and endorse past traumatizing experiences, this may be destabilizing for them. Even in the best-case scenario, a list of disturbing experiences or categories of adverse experiences still only offers one dimension of their history – and it may not be complete.

Gathering a client's history and present symptoms in a way that is attuned and effective is an art form. As practitioners, we hone our skills by learning what to listen and look for, and discerning what questions to ask, and when. Awareness and recognition of the 'red flags' that someone may have an undiagnosed dissociative disorder (DD) is a skill that all EMDR practitioners need to cultivate. In addition to the general contraindications for standard EMDR therapy posed by Shapiro (2018), further evaluation is recommended when one or more of the features listed in Figure 6.1 are reported by a client (Coy et al., 2022; Leeds et al., 2022; Ross, 2015).

With these 'red flags' in mind, consider how you might approach the first sessions with the clients presented in the following vignettes.

Example A

An adult male client is struggling to return to work after a motor vehicle accident in which a passenger in the other car was seriously injured. He suffered no physical injury. Two weeks later, he is still struggling to return to work and other previous 'normal' functioning.

He has not driven since the accident and has been able to work from home sporadically. Flashbacks specific to the accident are reported, along with waking up at night crying.

In forms completed prior to the first session, he reports a history of panic attacks that responded to cognitive behavioral therapy. Family history includes being adopted shortly after birth and having a 'normal' relationship with both adoptive parents.

Example B

A young adult female client is seeking therapy to address a lack of confidence and 'social anxiety.' She reports prior psychotherapy following a suicide attempt at age 15 years, and that she did not like the practitioner chosen by her parents. She mentions, "I always wondered if I might be Autistic." EMDR therapy sounds appealing to her because it does not rely on an ability to verbalize feelings and experiences.

In forms completed prior to the first session, she reports historical non-response to various medications for 'anxiety and depression.' A history of extensive polysubstance use from ages 13–22 is reported, followed by being 'able to quit using' after graduating from college three years ago. Several 'intense relationships' are described as leading to the present social anxiety and difficulty trusting.

Example C

An adult female client reaches out in hopes of changing therapists. She reports "doing EMDR" with her current therapist, but states that it is not helping and the therapist "seems to be annoyed with me." While functioning is "much more stable now," she reports having "OCD" (obsessive compulsive disorder) symptoms of intrusive images and thoughts that get stuck in her mind. She hopes that a more advanced EMDR practitioner can help these symptoms diminish.

In forms completed prior to the first session, she endorses all ten items on the Adverse Childhood Experiences scale. A variety of mental health issues and patterns of addiction are reported for various biological family members, some of whom have received formal diagnoses and treatment. Sleep problems are reported, including night terrors from which she often wakes up with an injury or evidence of distress overnight (e.g., a bloody lip from biting it and bedding and pillows being thrown across the room).

Screening Before You Screen

Attuned, informed observation helps us survey the topography of the clients' symptoms and history, make notes about what to ask more about, and form hypotheses about what is notably absent. It's not just *what* is said, but *how* clients present before, during, and after saying it. Is the narrative fragmented or scattered? Does the client seem distracted? Do they seem to be telling a story almost as if it belongs to someone else? Do they become easily flooded and hyperaroused? Are the client's verbal content, tone, and affect congruent (e.g., softening, brightening, rising, falling appropriately)? How does the client respond to a simple reflection of *"that's hard to talk about"*? Is the reflection readily endorsed or elaborated upon by the client, or do they seem puzzled, or even defensive, in their response? Therapists may also consider their own countertransferential experience while interacting with the client, such as feeling bored, sleepy, trancey, forgetful, 'on edge' for no reason. This is screening before you screen.

In an initial session, setting expectations, pacing, and confirming consent could sound like this:

> Today we are going to cover logistics, policies, and begin to talk about what it will be like for us to work together. Then, I would like to hear more about how these struggles that brought you to therapy show up in your day-to-day life now. The other historical stuff will be there for us to come back to next time or once we have gotten to know each other better. How does that sound to you?

If that goes as proposed, a choice for how to proceed could be offered after the policies, therapeutic contract, and practical frame have been addressed.

> Now, about the recent struggles that prompted you to reach out to me… We can begin with what you think is important for me to know, or if you're not sure where to start, I can ask a few questions about what you wrote. How would you prefer to start?

Occasionally, people say that they do not remember what they wrote in the intake questionnaire. That is notable! Gently following up on a couple of entries will clarify whether their memory can be easily jogged.

When clients are motivated to engage in trauma processing and ask for homework between sessions, tracking symptoms using the TICES log can be useful (Trigger, Image, Cognition, Emotion, and Sensation; Shapiro, 2018, pp. 441–442). This will assist in discerning the client's needs for stabilization, identification of present triggers for target selection and treatment planning, and mapping of ego states. Though originally intended for use between reprocessing sessions, we find the use of the TICES log can be much broader. Asking clients to log symptoms and triggers early in therapy will yield a sense of whether they can easily identify images, self-referencing beliefs, emotions, and body sensations – or not. In *Phase I*, the TICES log or an equivalent tool may be introduced by saying:

> When I ask how you have been since our last session, these are the kinds of things that would be most useful for me to know. It's okay if you can't complete all the fields, or if you prefer to use another strategy to track these kinds of experiences between sessions. If you make a notation whenever a significant symptom or trigger shows up, that will help us to identify themes and to track when things change or don't change as we go forward.

In subsequent sessions, we may gather information about the client's family of origin, culture, and other aspects of their personal identity, and, eventually, pivotal, distressing, and/or traumatic events. The pace of gathering this content will depend on the individual client and the degree of stabilization needed, etc. Implicitly and explicitly, we will gain a sense of what kind of environment clients have lived in and what resources were available or not available when they were needed or developmentally appropriate. *If* we inquire directly about past traumatic events, orienting clients to what is intended and gaining consent is crucial. For example,

> I would like to know a bit more about those childhood experiences of neglect and abuse that you endorsed. Would that be okay? (if consent is given…) For now, it is usually best for you to share just the 'post-it-note sized' version of the story. It's okay to leave out any details that you are not ready to share or to tell me that there's more that you would prefer to share at another time. How does that sound to you?

The depth and breadth of information we collect will depend on the client's initial presenting concern or goal for treatment, whether direct inquiry into historical experience is judged to be immediately unsafe or destabilizing, and other factors we will discuss later in this chapter. We caution against employing the floatback technique or affect scan within *Phase I* when complex trauma and/or a DD is suspected. Those interventions are indeed helpful in identifying earlier experiences related to present symptoms and triggers. As such, they intentionally *activate* distress and *access* experiences that may be held by self-states before having obtained consent to do so or being ready to address them effectively (the memories or the self-states).

Safety During History Taking

Practicing containment and closure strategies from the outset is recommended. Containment is about increasing the subjective distance between the client and any distressing memory material, which can include explicit container exercises or other distancing techniques. Because we do not yet know our client, it may be helpful to ask *"Based on how you know yourself, how might it be helpful to close our sessions?"* Responses to this question reveal clients' awareness of and ability to voice their needs. Even if a plan for closure is not established in the first session, introducing a pattern of setting aside material and slowing down at the end of sessions is important. "*Now that we have about 15 minutes left in our time together today, I'm interested to check in... how has it been talking about these things?*" We are beginning to informally test how or whether clients are able to regulate flexibly, or shift in a way that seems abrupt or dismissive of their own experience, and need assistance to ground and orient themselves.

Dissociative coping during and at the end of sessions is common. When practitioners are aware of this, they can help clients become aware of their own distancing strategies that are likely trance-based. Clients and therapists who have high (auto)hypnotic capacities may need to deliberately avoid falling into trance or activation without intention. Ensuring that the client and therapist are alert, aware, consciously present with a sense of 'adultness,' and oriented (times four) can be essential in the closure ritual. The *Howard Alertness Scale* is a helpful resource to guide this process (Howard, 2017). In Part IV, we will discuss several facets of trance phenomena.

Affect intolerance and other manifestations of defendedness or gaps in functional connectivity within the self can present in various ways. Throughout early sessions, practitioners can examine clients' tolerance for each of the BASK elements: behavior, affect, sensation, and knowledge (Braun, 1988a, 1988b). Tolerance for each of the four, alone and together, individually and relationally, lends a forecast for how complicated and/or deep the disruption in functional connectivity has become in order to avoid toxins and/or distressing experience (see discussion of Sidis's work in Chapter 2). Notably, tolerance of these is relevant for the client *and* the practitioner.

Upon learning how clients demonstrate activation and function immediately after and between sessions, we can introduce tailored strategies.

Reevaluation of stabilization – or lack thereof – between sessions, and making adjustments will gradually build a sense of trust in the therapeutic relationship that will serve as a foundation for intentional accessing of distressing material later on.

Evaluating Symptoms

What feelings arise for you with the phrases 'evaluating symptoms' or 'diagnostic assessment?' Our interest in the assessment of dissociative symptoms and disorders came as a result of missing things that we didn't know to notice or know to ask early in our practices. We have come to value using valid and reliable instruments. Employing these with skill and nuance helps to minimize the 'cold' feeling and other drawbacks that previously contributed to our avoidance of them. In most contexts, diagnostic evaluation occurs within the therapeutic space, and process-oriented questions are just as important as those focused directly on evaluating symptoms (Pierorazio et al., 2025). Even if we do not assign a diagnosis, an informed treatment plan based on specific symptoms is still an ethical imperative – to identify/confirm what we are treating, and map that to the corresponding standard of care.

Why Is Diagnostic Evaluation Important for EMDR?

In EMDR therapy, diagnostic evaluation applies to *Phase I: History Taking, Phase II: Preparation*, and *Phase VIII: Reevaluation*. Diagnostic evaluation is one element of both initial and ongoing assessment processes in the context of developing a conceptualization and treatment plan. The unique combination of presenting symptoms and current and historical context that each person brings will support the personalization of the treatment goals, scope, and pacing. This also involves considering the need for specialized approaches and established modifications to the standard EMDR protocols and procedures. Understanding *what* we are treating is essential to prevent – or at least reduce – unintended harm or delay in symptom relief.

> Accurate diagnoses are critical for appropriate treatment planning.
> If DID is not targeted in treatment, it does not appear to resolve
> (Brand et al., 2016, p. 258).

As we discussed in prior chapters, clinical practice guidelines indicate that the presence of a DD should prompt the integration of EMDR therapy within a broader therapeutic framework (see Figure 3.3). The imperative to screen for dissociative symptoms was made clear in the general body of Shapiro's (2018) text:

> Because many clinicians are not educated in the treatment of dissociative disorders and greatly underestimate their prevalence, the appropriate safeguards must be stressed (see Ross, 2015).... Therefore, the clinician intending to initiate EMDR should first administer the Dissociative Experiences Scale–II (DES-II; Carlson & Putnam, 1993) and do a thorough clinical assessment with every client.
>
> (p. 96)

The results of said screening and clinical assessment inform the determination of readiness for and scope of EMDR therapy, even when *Stage 2: Trauma Processing* work may come much later in treatment.

Informed consent and goals for therapy also guide diagnostic assessment and how *Phase I: History Taking* is conducted. Clients may specifically seek relief from symptoms arising immediately following a recent event, with reported history indicating possible complexity (i.e., *Example A*, above). Or, clients such as those initially described in *Example B* or *Example C* may request comprehensive treatment and therefore are likely to be open to a thorough diagnostic evaluation to support their goals. (See Chapter 3 for a discussion on the scope of treatment.)

Right-Sizing Screening and Assessment for Dissociation

Choosing the best screening or assessment tool and employing it in an attuned and effective manner is what we aim to accomplish in *right-sizing* this process. The average EMDR practitioner is unfamiliar with the range of options that are available. Practitioners have reported that they sensed that the DES-II is not always the 'right' tool, or felt uncomfortable using it. In situations like that, some have either skipped this step or, perhaps unnecessarily, overcorrected and slowed down the process by choosing a 'gold standard' clinical interview that may be oversized for the client's initial symptoms, history, and treatment goals.

Most tools are either 'too big' for some settings (e.g., acute stress or disaster response work) and treatment plans, or 'too small' or inadequate for comprehensive treatment. Choosing the screening or assessment tool intentionally is a significant step toward both honoring the ethical imperative stated by Shapiro and preventing overwhelm for clients and practitioners.

Too BIG

When the chosen tool – or its implementation – is 'too big,' practitioners often describe it as feeling 'clunky' or overwhelming. This is likely due to some combination of three factors:

1. *The practitioner's training and approach:* The tool may be a poor match for the practitioners' level of learning or expertise. When we are doing something new, it often feels foreign – like having two feet can feel overwhelming when learning to dance! Smooth and nuanced administration of any instrument requires deepening one's skills and practicing over time. One of those skills is discerning which items to prioritize in the follow-up interview associated with any self-report measure.
2. *The choice of instrument:* A robust assessment or clinical interview might be more than is warranted by the client's history, symptoms, and treatment goals. For instance, some practices serving populations with pervasive complex trauma may choose the *Multidimensional Inventory of Dissociation* (MID, Dell, 2006) as their default tool of choice. Notwithstanding the value of the MID or any diagnostic instrument, it may be unnecessary if no red flags for DDs are evident.
3. *The setting or scope of treatment:* Settings that are focused on triage, critical incident response, or only offer short-term treatment allow minimal time dedicated to screening or assessment. Brief, direct instruments are likely to fit better. When addressing acute stress symptoms arising from a recent experience, treatment ought not be delayed unless other factors indicate it is necessary. In contrast, a practice that focuses on comprehensive treatment of attachment injury warrants a more robust diagnostic tool.

How one administers *any* tool can have a significant bearing (Pierorazio et al., 2025). Imagine that the practitioner for *Example A* administers the DES-II in session as a clinical interview, spending an entire session discussing the client's related experiences. The client reports that most items endorsed correspond to symptoms that have emerged since the accident. Using the DES might be a reasonable choice in this case but the administration is oversized. Moreover, the DES is intended to be a self-report measure – meaning that the respondent reads the items and completes the responses on their own, usually in 15 minutes or less. The DES is not intended to be a clinical interview; alternatives are available if that is the desired approach.

Too Small

When the chosen instrument does not clarify questions of diagnosis and readiness posed by the known history, symptoms, and goals of the client or is underutilized in a way that misses the point, it is 'too small.' If the treatment goal or setting is oriented toward comprehensive treatment, screening is rarely the best fit. Those same three factors apply to how 'too small' may show up in practice.

1. *The practitioner's training and approach:* The practitioner may not appreciate the meaning or significance of the process of screening, or may not utilize the tool fully. Commonly, beginning EMDR therapists have taken a red-light/green-light approach to the DES or other screening tools by relying entirely on mean scores to determine whether clients are 'good candidates' to proceed in EMDR therapy. In addition, many mistakenly rely on 'cutoff' numbers intended to inform research – not clinical use (see Carlson & Putnam, 1993). Overlooking the follow-up interview, especially when the scores are 'low,' is another way in which practitioners underutilize screening tools (Leeds, et al., 2022).
2. *The choice of instrument:* When the person's history indicates complexity, possible 'red flags' for dissociation, or dissociative experiences are observed or reported, a screening tool is not suited to provide enough information for the practitioner to determine readiness or establish a diagnostic impression. Some screening tools (including the DES) include items that are 'normal' on some level (recall Sidis's 'dissociation' in Figure 2.3). Most screeners do not provide indicators of response bias to signal whether someone may be responding in a manner that is consistent with a false-positive or false-negative impression.
3. *The setting or scope of treatment:* When comprehensive treatment is sought, or the setting serves many people with complex posttraumatic symptoms and/or histories, broader and deeper assessment is warranted. In these situations, screening tools will generally fall on the side of 'too small' unless it is accompanied by an expertly facilitated clinical interview by a practitioner versed in recognizing DDs. If that is the case, then why not start with a structured clinical interview?

Some EMDR trainers have promoted the use of the CAPS-5 (Clinician Administered PTSD Scale, Weathers et al., 2018), an instrument designed to measure symptoms of PTSD and Complex PTSD. As discussed in earlier chapters, this misses the point of screening for dissociative symptoms and reflects a misunderstanding both of dissociative experience and Shapiro's directive to screen for them.

Just Right

The 'just right' choice and administration of screening or assessment tools happens when the practitioner's selection is informed, attuned, and intentional. Client factors that may influence this choice include:

- The client's goals, symptoms, history, and tolerance of knowing and reporting on these;
- The acuity, timing (onset), and degree of distress associated with known symptoms;
- Factors which may influence how the client engages in screening or assessment, such as willingness to report;
- Language(s) known by the client and available in validated tools;
- Accessibility considerations such as reading level;
- Presence or absence of client-identified dissociative experiences or 'red flags' for undiagnosed DDs; and
- Whether a diagnosis is being sought by the client or required by the treatment setting, a third party, etc.

As with many things in this work, there is no script or universal recipe for choosing the right tool. That choice is for you to discern based upon all of these factors, and perhaps others that are unique to you, your setting, and your client. An array of brief screening, full screening, and diagnostic assessment tools will be offered below. Competency and knowledge in screening and assessment are a growth edge for most new EMDR practitioners. A nuanced and personalized facilitation of diagnostic evaluation requires knowledge and skill in recognizing dissociative symptoms, knowing about available tools, seeking training in utilizing those tools, and becoming practiced and skillful in administering them.

Screening for and Diagnosing Dissociative Symptoms and Disorders

Many screening and diagnostic tools for dissociation were originally developed in the 1980s and 1990s in response to the widespread misconceptions that dissociation was exceedingly rare and/or iatrogenic. Developers of the DES, for example, aimed to increase the probability that persons with significant dissociative symptoms would be identified by professionals who otherwise lacked the experience to recognize them (Carlson et al., 1993). Cultural variations in dissociative experience were considered from the outset, with recommendations to focus on applying or translating concepts – rather than literal experience or relying on colloquial expressions (Carlson & Putnam, 1993).

Practitioners' lack of recognition of DDs continues to present an obstacle to accessing effective treatment (Nester et al., 2022). In striking contrast, or perhaps because of this, the incidence of people arriving at self-diagnosis of DDs via social media has been noted, with some seeking verification of this diagnosis from mental health professionals (e.g., Salter et al., 2025). Understanding the distinctions between screening and diagnostic measures and becoming skilled in selecting and administering them is as important now as it ever has been.

In this section, we will review two categories of instruments used to identify dissociative experience or diagnose DDs in adolescents and adults:

1. *Screening tools.* These are sorted into two categories: brief and full. Each has different purposes and utility for clinical use.
   a. *Brief screening:* tools with 5–8 items, often measuring experience within the past week.
   b. *Full screening*: tools with 20–60 items. Most identify dissociation as a single construct and do not validly identify specific symptoms or detect response bias to signal possible false positive/negative results.
2. *Structured diagnostic assessments.* These are structured interviews and self-report measures that have more than 100 items and/or are expected to require multiple steps or sessions to complete all aspects of administration and follow-up.

The *minimum standard* for EMDR therapists, according to the Shapiro text and standard of care, is to screen for dissociative symptoms prior to administering bilateral dual attention stimulation (BL-DAS). Screening best applies when a client is seeking symptom relief, presents no/few 'red

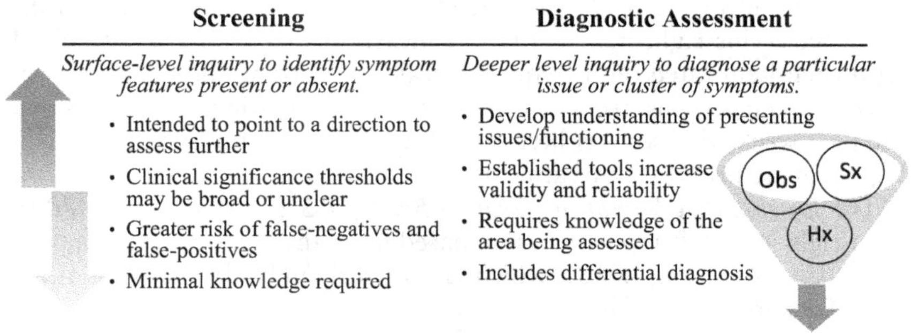

Screening	**Diagnostic Assessment**
Surface-level inquiry to identify symptom features present or absent.	*Deeper level inquiry to diagnose a particular issue or cluster of symptoms.*
• Intended to point to a direction to assess further	• Develop understanding of presenting issues/functioning
• Clinical significance thresholds may be broad or unclear	• Established tools increase validity and reliability
• Greater risk of false-negatives and false-positives	• Requires knowledge of the area being assessed
• Minimal knowledge required	• Includes differential diagnosis

Obs
Sx
Hx

Figure 6.2 Screening vs. Structured Diagnostic Assessment.

flags' for dissociation, and has a relatively low complexity of history of symptoms and treatment.

In general, a diagnostic assessment tool is better suited for clients who are seeking comprehensive treatment, reporting multiple (and/or chronic) 'red flags,' and/or a high complexity of symptoms and treatment. Thorough, multimodal assessment includes utilization of at least one diagnostic assessment tool, alongside other measures or consultation with collaborating professionals to address differential diagnosis and/or comorbidity questions. This may include or be conducted in conjunction with a full psychological evaluation, especially when complex medical, characterological, and/or forensic circumstances require it (see Brand, 2024, for a review of and recommendations for this process). If you regularly work with children and adolescents, please refer to Arbuthnott et al. (2025) for a comprehensive discussion of this topic as it applies to working with children and younger adolescents.

Screening Tools

A shorter, validated screening instrument, applied with knowledge and skill, can be the perfect fit at times. All measures included here are freely/publicly available in English to practitioners and researchers. In all cases, following up to inquire about the client's experience associated with significant items is vital to determine a) whether the reported experience aligns with pathological dissociation, and b) the timing, onset, and other context of the symptoms.

Brief Screening

The *Brief Dissociative Experiences Scale (DES-B)* was developed by Dalenberg and Carlson (2010) and is included among the online assessment measures recommended by the American Psychiatric Association to clinicians and researchers using the DSM-5 (see link associated with this reference). This eight-item self-report measure is based upon the DES-II, with each item rated on a frequency scale (0 = not at all, 4 = more than once a day) in the past week. Due to its brevity and rating experiences over the past week, this scale is best served to measure acute symptoms or to approximate progress in treatment.

The *Dissociative Symptoms Scale – Brief (DSS-B)* (Macia et al., 2023) is an eight-item self-report measure based upon the Dissociative Symptom Scale (Carlson et al., 2018), which is not freely/publicly available at this time. Each item is rated in the past week on a frequency scale (0 = not at all to 4 = more than once a day). The DSS-B items were selected by identifying the two items from each DSS subscale that were most precise in measuring above-average levels of the latent trait of dissociation among individuals from a variety of clinical and nonclinical samples (Brand, 2024, p. 118). Those four subscales are depersonalization, derealization, gaps in awareness or memory, and reexperiencing (cognitive, behavioral, sensory). The DSS and DSS-B items and scales were intentionally designed to measure these symptom sets – rather than being identified via factor analysis. As such, the DSS-B more directly and reliably measures a variety of dissociative symptoms compared to most screenings. Measuring symptoms in the past week may be effective for identifying changes in symptoms or acute stress/peritraumatic symptoms. Because of the brief nature of the instrument and the timeframe, this scale would not be appropriate for comprehensive treatment of historical experience, or for anyone who presents 'red flags' for dissociation in their history.

Full Screening

The *Dissociative Experiences Scale (DES-II)* (Carlson & Putnam, 1993) is regarded as the most valid and reliable *screening* for DDs and is the most widely used. Originally published in 1986, the second edition was modified only to standardize the method of scoring. Accessibility is a strength of the DES-II, as it is available in many non-English languages.

Results of the DES-II tend to reflect present/recent functioning despite the instructions indicating no timeframe of experience. It measures dissociation on a continuum, with a higher score indicating greater severity. A comprehensive discussion of the history, strengths, and limitations of the DES-II can be found elsewhere (Leeds et al., 2022; Trujillo et al., 2024). Although multiple studies have identified possible factor scales within the DES, "the scale will reliably only measure the general dissociation factor" (Carlson & Putnam, 1993, p. 21). The color-coded version of the DES-II that circulates and the factor scales (sorting items into depersonalization/derealization, amnesia, and absorption) are somewhat useful for identifying possible features of dissociation; however, the factor scales were not intended for clinical use.

Clinical use of the DES-II has historically been misguided in the Shapiro text, referring to a mean score 'cutoff' of 30 (Shapiro, 2018, p. 96). This error has been parroted by many EMDR trainers and authors. The original DES-II authors recommend the following for its clinical use:

> Most times that a client scores over 20 or 30 on the DES, the clinician will want to know more about the dissociative experiences that contributed to the high score. One approach at further investigation would be

> to use the completed scale to interview the client. For each item with a score of 20 or more, the clinician could ask the client for an example of the dissociative experience. (E.g., Can you give me an example of a time when you found something among your possessions that you didn't remember buying?) With this method, it is possible to find out if a client has understood a question differently than it was intended. … Another approach would be to use one of two available structured clinical interviews for dissociative disorders.
>
> (Carlson & Putnam, 1993, p. 21)

The *Adolescent Dissociative Experiences Scale (A-DES)* was originally developed by Armstrong et al. (1997) and is designed for adolescents (ages 11–19). It has 30 items rated on an 11-point frequency scale (0 = never, 10 = always). Mean scores for clinically relevant dissociation range from 2.6 (Lindfors et al., 2022) to 4 (Armstrong et al., 1997). Lindfors et al. (2022) identified several psychosocial and individual variables associated with higher scores, which may be useful in navigating the complexities of screening and diagnosis in this age group. Similarly to the DES-II, specific symptoms or factors are not reliably measured, with one factor – dissociation – having the most empirical support. An eight-item version has been found to have comparable reliability and validity in measuring the single factor of dissociation (e.g., Martínez-Taboas et al., 2004; Lindfors et al., 2022).

The *Somatoform Dissociation Questionnaire (SDQ-20)* is a 20-item measure that inquires about somatoform experiences of dissociation (e.g., nonorganic body pain, conversion symptoms) in the past year (Nijenhuis et al., 1996). While not significantly different from the DES-II with regard to diagnostic accuracy and high false-positive risk, the SDQ-20 may be helpful when physical/somatic symptoms are identified at intake. A five-item version (SDQ-5) is also available.

The *MID-60* was developed by Mary-Anne Kate et al. (2021) as a screening tool composed of 60 items extracted from the full MID. Items were selected to capture the full range of dissociative symptoms that characterize each of the DSM-5 DDs. An adolescent version for use with ages 16–19 years is available (MID-60-A). The MID-60 offers the advantage of being more robust than the DES-II – by its length and because all items may indicate pathological dissociation (there are no 'normal' items). Cutoff scores are imported from the full MID to guide the practitioner in estimating clinical significance. However, the MID-60 offers no validity scales, and thus is prone to false-negative and false-positive results like other screening tools.

Other Screening Tools

A multitude of screenings have been developed for research and/or clinical purposes. The Multiscale Dissociation Inventory (MDI, Briere, 2002) may objectively be the most robust and well-designed screening tool, but it is only available for purchase through a psychological assessment vendor. The Dissociation Questionnaire (DIS-Q, Vanderlinden et al., 1993) has been used more broadly in some European countries; at 69 items, it is much longer than the DES. It appears to have been developed in English; however, the language and spelling are less approachable for North American populations.

Additional measures identify symptoms and test hypotheses related to dissociation from the perspective of specific theoretical models. For example, the Dissociation-Integration of Self States Scale (D-ISS Scale, Lord et al., 2025) measures between-mode dissociation through the lens of cognitive behavioral theory. Such measures are not intended to be diagnostic, yet may guide treatment for practitioners who are trained in those models.

Diagnostic Tools

In addition to their primary function – diagnosis – we find diagnostic tools valuable to assist in case conceptualization and treatment planning. This section highlights the major diagnostic tools that are publicly available, followed by a discussion of their utility in treatment. Elsewhere, we have written in detail about the conceptual, theoretical, and practical considerations for each of the following instruments (Coy & Madere, 2023).

Dissociative Disorders Interview Schedule (DDIS)

Colin Ross, MD, developed the DDIS to organize a structured interview according to the DSM criteria (Ross et al., 1989; self-report version: Ross & Browning, 2017). The current iteration has been updated for DSM-5 and is available without charge at rossinst.com/ddis. The DDIS is a straightforward clinical interview derived directly from the DSM criteria, and inquires directly about somatic symptoms, trauma, substance abuse, psychosis, and other commonly co-occurring and confounding experiences. The direct questions and Yes/No/Unsure response format of the DDIS is not the best fit for every client-practitioner dyad, as it depends upon the ability of clients to respond accurately to questions about their experience of specific DSM dissociative symptoms. We find the DDIS to be a good fit for practitioners who wish to conduct a valid and reliable diagnostic interview without having to invest in extensive training to do so.

Multidimensional Inventory of Dissociation (MID)

Developed by Paul Dell, PhD (2006), the MID is modeled after the Minnesota Multiphasic Personality Inventory, 2nd Edition (MMPI-2; Butcher et al., 1989) and the DES-II (Carlson & Putnam, 1993). It was developed both to test the subjective-phenomenological model of dissociation and to correct for the all-or-nothing nature of the DSM criteria for dissociative identity disorder that existed through to DSM-IV (American Psychiatric Association, 1994; Dell, 2009a) and persist to some degree in DSM-5-TR (American Psychiatric Association, 2022). We have been stewarding the MID and issuing updates to the *MID Analysis* and *MID Interpretive Manual* since 2017.

The MID questions, scoring document, and interpretive manual are available without charge to students, clinicians, and researchers (mid-assessment.com). What the MID offers that is unparalleled by any other diagnostic or screening tool is a combination of qualitative and quantitative assessment, aided by validity scales and explicit, numeric output. Additionally, we have found that the symptom breakdown is highly compatible with EMDR therapy practice. The MID allows for a broader and deeper assessment of clients' experience that is less reliant on practitioner expertise. A clinician-directed follow-up interview is required to substantiate symptom features and ensure that clients' qualitative experience is congruent with the item(s) endorsed.

Mental Status Examination for Dissociative Disorders (MSE) for Dissociative Disorders

Most mental health professionals are trained in conducting a general mental status exam, or MSE, to assess the client's orientation to time, place, person, etc., at the outset of treatment and to a varying extent at each session. The MSE for DDs was developed by Richard Loewenstein, MD (1991), to aid clinicians in applying these skills, realizing that information relevant to diagnosis often presents intermittently, unfolding over a series of sessions. A two-page summary of this approach is included in Bethany Brand's recent book (2024, pp. 89–90). We find Loewenstein's MSE most suited for guiding what questions to ask – and how to ask them – when gauging clients' readiness to engage in a more comprehensive assessment (i.e., testing how they respond to a few probing questions). It may also augment the follow-up interview subsequent to the administration of another screening or diagnostic instrument.

Semi-Structured Clinical Interview for Dissociative Symptoms and Disorders (SCID-D)

Originally developed in the 1980s by Marlene Steinberg, MD, via her work in psychiatric emergency settings, the SCID-D has long held the position of being the 'gold standard' diagnostic assessment for DDs (Steinberg, 2023; Steinberg et al., 1989-1993). The SCID-D is conceptually independent of DSM and ICD, although findings across five components of dissociation (amnesia, depersonalization, derealization, identity confusion, and identity alteration) can be mapped to their criteria.

Booklets are available for purchase and contain the interview instructions, questions, follow-up questions within each symptom component, and possible intra-interview cues of dissociation. The format is familiar to those trained in conducting psychiatric interviews. As such, the SCID-D relies upon the interviewer's diagnostic skill and knowledge of DDs in order to achieve the 'gold standard' result. In our opinion, it is best suited for forensic or expert evaluation, or as a therapeutic tool within a comprehensive treatment frame.

Trauma and Dissociation Symptoms Interview (TADS-I)

The newest diagnostic tool is the TADS-I, a semi-structured clinical interview developed by Suzette Boon, PhD. Although earlier versions have circulated, the final English version is found in her recently published book (Boon, 2023). In our conversations with Paul Dell, he has described Suzette Boon as "the best diagnostician of this century." Research substantiating the TADS-I as a valid and reliable instrument when used by practitioners other than its originator is forthcoming. The TADS-I offers a European-inflected lens and careful consideration of sleep and post-traumatic symptoms, in addition to ruling in or ruling out a DD. Similarly to the SCID-D, we find it best suited for forensic and expert evaluations.

Self-Report or Clinician Administered: Does It Matter?

A consideration for assessment in general, and the diagnosis of trauma-related disorders specifically, is whether the context in which the assessment is administered, its format and syntax, and the number of questions impact the veracity of a person's self-report. Shinn et al. (2020) discuss this question in their research on voice hearing.

> While semi-structured interviews [i.e, the SCID-D] administered by experienced clinicians are considered the gold standard method of conducting a psychiatric evaluation, a self-administration format [in this

> case, the MID] may allow individuals to disclose about [voice hearing] and other experiences that are considered pathological with potentially less stigma, shame, and judgment. Self-administration forms would thus be expected to increase reporting compared to a clinician administered interview, and this phenomenon has been observed in the PTSD literature [...]. On the other hand, self-reporting could also lead to an effect in the opposite direction.
>
> (pp. 21–22)

The MSE, standard DDIS, and SCID-D are administered via clinical interview, while the MID and the self-report version of the DDIS are self-administered. For example, Brand (2024) lists the MID as a screener – seemingly because the initial administration of the items is via self-report. We think the MID is much more involved than any screening tool discussed above. Research (Lebois et al., 2021) suggests that the MID can reasonably aid the conceptualization of the degrees of (disruptions in) functional connectivity for the average practitioner who does not have access to an fMRI machine. In any case, a follow-up interview is always essential to confirm diagnostic impressions offered by any self-report measure and to inform case conceptualization and treatment planning.

Beyond Diagnostic Labels

Thus far, we have emphasized symptom evaluation and diagnosis. There are indeed other elements to determining preparedness for trauma processing. Adults with complex trauma histories develop many symptoms other than dissociation – for this reason, a transdiagnostic assessment and framework is often recommended (American Psychological Association, 2024; Dominguez, 2023). Balancing the content-heavy focus of screening and assessment tools with process-related observations and inquiry – such as attention to the subjectivity of the practitioner, cultural responsiveness, and other dynamics – enables assessment to be part of a collaborative therapeutic process (Pierorazio et al., 2025). Specific areas of attention will vary according to each practitioner-client dyad and the co-occurring symptoms and concerns presented.

Cultural Factors

Cross-cultural considerations are particularly relevant when exploring dissociation, as it inherently pertains to individuals' internal experience and how they perceive the external world. Diagnostic manuals remind us that if a symptom does not yield distress or impairment, and/or can be explained by cultural factors, it is not to be pathologized. Ways and situations in which social, cultural, and religious phenomena may motivate or be conflated with dissociation are addressed in other sources (e.g., Christensen, 2022; Lewis-Fernández et al., 2007; Madere, 2023; Pierorazio et al., 2023).

Informing Case Conceptualization and Treatment

Without comprehensive foundational knowledge of dissociation, we may view the results of a diagnostic tool, for example, *The MID Report,* without having the capacity to consider much other than the diagnostic impression. This is equivalent to an image from an X-ray, as it simply suggests where or whether a bone is fractured. A deeper understanding of the models of dissociation discussed in Chapter 2 prepares us to view the results with curiosity and to test hypotheses. This combination of 'book knowledge' with our observations of a particular client is where advanced synthesis comes to bear in practice. For example, evidence of child self-states may be suspected in my initial evaluation – does the person endorse those items in the administered scale? What does this endorsement tell me that is new or supports my hypothesis? Alternatively, the results can help me develop alternative hypotheses. Perhaps the client endorsed having a remarkably high incidence of intrusive thoughts (a Schneiderian first-rank symptom listed on *The MID Report*). I might wonder what those are, and what pain the person is and/or was motivated to escape, such that this symptom developed.

The screening and diagnostic tools each lend a particular kind of impression, or image, of the test-taker's symptomatology. Some connect or populate defined elements that are present or absent, and don't move (e.g., the DDIS); others show dots of different colors or sizes that show up in a scattershot according to how the test-taker responds (e.g., the MID). Structured clinical interviews such as the SCID-D and TADS-I map out certain points of the person's landscape that we score and interpret to sketch out the topography of that individual's terrain of experience. For all of them, our clinical brains get to look at them, squint, turn our heads sideways, and conceptualize how the dots connect based on our knowledge of the client, diagnostic criteria, extant literature, and other sources at our disposal.

Types of Amnesia

All amnesia is not equal. Discerning the type and implication of symptoms of amnesia in dissociation is an advanced area of study and skill in itself. It is often essential to accomplish the clinical or follow-up interview associated with diagnostic evaluation. In the DSM, discerning presence and types of amnesia relates to the criteria for DID that refer to "marked [or less than marked, in OSDD] discontinuities in sense of self and agency" and "gaps in the recall…that are inconsistent with ordinary forgetting" (APA, 2022, pp. 330 [347]).

Retrograde amnesia occurs when someone cannot recall memories or information from the past (e.g., before age 10). It can result from numerous physiological causes, which must be ruled out; psychologically, it is associated with posttraumatic experience and DDs. Sidis (1898) refers to *irretraceable* amnesia when the memory material is recoverable and *absolute* amnesia when it is not (see Chapter 2).

Contemporaneous amnesia refers to the present-day, in-the-moment loss of conscious awareness. It may be temporary (minutes or hours) or more enduring (days to years), and either partial or full/total. An example of partial amnesia would be what (Dell, 2009b) calls 'temporary loss of well-rehearsed skills and knowledge,' which someone is aware of *while it is happening*. A person experiencing this may not be able to recall their name, age, or address, but with no idea why. Or they might feel confused when they temporarily 'forget' how to do their job or play a musical instrument they have played for years. Full amnesia means that a self-state has *no* awareness at all for a period of time. Attempts at 'jogging' their memory for the lost information are ineffective (Dell, 2009b). This type of amnesia can be evidence of switching between self-states or the withdrawal of previous knowledge (e.g., of having been abused) from one self-state by another. This has also been referred to as inter-identity amnesia (explored in Beker et al., 2024), a phenomenon thought to be explained by internal avoidance (Dimitrova et al., 2024). Partial and full/total amnesia are both more severe than 'normal' forgetting and are common among people with DDs (Dell, 2009b). Priming or external cueing, or the use of special therapeutic procedures, may elicit recall or retrieval of the dissociated memory material (Sidis's irretraceable amnesia, see Chapter 2).

Absolute amnesia (Sidis, 1898) and *absorptive detachment* may also show up in clients' responses to screening and assessment tools. For Sidis, absolute amnesia is the result of cell death – neurons that once held the material are gone. Absorptive detachment is a severe depersonalization trance state which occurs when the person does not take in the sensory experience to begin with, and thus has no memory for it (Allen et al., 1999); Although Allen et al. (1999) first identified absorptive/dissociative detachment in complex PTSD cases, Laddis et al. (2017) found this extreme detachment to be a significant component of self-reported dissociative experiences in subjects with borderline personality disorder.

These examples and terms are all consonant with Sidis's model for how disruptions in connectivity, due to avoiding a toxin, can result in retraction/avoidance and amnesia – when the amnesia is irretraceable, something or someone else is required to prompt retrieval (Sidis, 1898). Janet similarly observed that "Memories which persist, therefore, are joined together and united around a principal sensation which serves to express and evoke them" (Janet, 2022/1889, p. 91).

For treatment, the presence of contemporaneous amnesia indicates complexity in the self-system, disruptions in functional connectivity, and the need for mapping and careful discernment of the consent for and scope of the treatment plan and interventions. BL-DAS is one of the ways that memory lost to irretraceable amnesia can be suddenly reassociated; absolute amnesia, on the other hand, can manifest in reprocessing as gaps that keep a memory network from resolving – ordinary association and interweaves cannot surmount it. Destabilization may occur when BL-DAS prompts association/connection to and recall for experience that both client and practitioner are wholly unprepared to face, and perhaps before the 'toxin' is removed. Assessing well for amnesia early on can prevent anti-therapeutic outcomes and inform proactive navigation of the internal terrain.

Recognizing Progress and Trajectories in Treatment

Measuring progress and determining whether or how treatment of clients with DDs is progressing has long challenged psychotherapists. Richard Kluft, MD, recognized that clients 'getting better' and 'feeling better' were often disparate experiences, and clinicians tend to become blinded by our own countertransference when assessing therapeutic outcomes. Kluft (Kluft, 1994a, 1994b) developed the *Dimensions of Therapeutic Movement Instrument* (DTMI) in an effort to identify and track features of progress in DD treatment. The DTMI guides the practitioner to rate 12 dimensions of clients' present functioning and engagement in treatment: therapeutic alliance; integration; capacity for adaptive change; management of life stressors; alters' responsibility for self-management; restraint from self-endangerment; quality of interpersonal relationships; need for medication; need for medical care; resolution of transference phenomena; intersession contacts; subjective well-being.

Alongside the development of the DTMI, Kluft observed three styles or trajectories corresponding to how clients were observed to engage in and respond to treatment. These are not synonymous with symptom severity. They reflect the ease and speed at which progress was observed and measured via the DTMI.

- *High trajectory:* Adapt to the therapy easily, build the therapeutic alliance effectively, and gain a sense of efficacy and personal agency early in therapy. Safety and characterological concerns are settled rapidly.

Self-system is swiftly engaged, and the client is committed to and takes ownership of the therapeutic process.

- *Intermediate trajectory:* Progress slowly and gradually, with some ups and downs and/or plateaus. Borderline personality organization, initial denial of DD diagnosis, and difficulty accessing and building communication among self-states are common. While treatment takes longer than for 'high trajectory' clients, hard work yields progress.
- *Low trajectory:* Persistent issues of external locus of control, victim-stance, safety, and/or characterological features. Tend to continually seek the approval of and proximity to the therapist. Self-system is often dominated by child-identifying self-states and/or abdication by the self-state(s) identifying with the client's legal name. Internal repetition of abuse and ongoing or 'enmeshed' contact with reportedly harmful family members is common (summarized from Kluft, 1994b).

We find this framework helpful for estimating the scope and pace of treatment, and when, whether, and how trauma processing via EMDR may be effective. The DTMI has been adapted by two research groups, one from the perspective of the theory of structural dissociation of the personality (Piedfort-Marin et al., 2017) and another for purposes of measuring therapeutic outcomes in the TOP DD study (Schielke et al., 2017). All versions are available in open-access forums.

Reevaluating Diagnosis, Symptoms, and History

EMDR practitioners know that history taking is frequently revisited – at the conclusion of reprocessing a target (single incident or sequence), when feeder or associated memory material arises during reprocessing, etc. This process tends to be iterative when working within a frame that has been ordered to treat complex trauma and dissociation. Existing general therapeutic tools, EMDR therapy, and diagnostic evaluation may be applied to reevaluate symptoms and readiness, and amend the goals and scope of treatment. Thinking deeply about these tools and processes is necessary to ensure personalized care and consent.

Foundational Considerations

Ongoing reevaluation of readiness and confirmation of consent to the current treatment plan is done briefly upon completion of an intervention (resource development, mapping, etc.) to confirm the client's subjective readiness and consent to move forward. The therapeutic alliance evolves over time as the practitioner and the client learn more about each other and encounter their mutual needs and limitations. Treatment goals are clarified, or reoriented to accommodate newly-discovered symptoms, self-states, the abilities (and limitations) of the practitioner, etc. For example, shifts in the client's internal (intrapersonal) experience – i.e., reconfiguration of self-states – may influence changes to dynamics and priorities that impact the therapeutic relationship (interpersonal).

When a treatment plan (e.g., targeting sequence) or goal has been completed or exhausted, reevaluation of the symptoms or reasons associated with that goal/sequence ensures adequate completion and guides next steps. Progress may be quantified via the procedures within standard EMDR therapy, other layers of the treatment frame, and by (re)employing formal screening and assessment measures discussed above. Highlighting changes in symptoms and severity can be ego-strengthening for all parties involved! In longer-term treatment, diagnostic evaluation may be revisited periodically (e.g., once per year) to inform justification or modification of the level of care, area(s) of focus, tailoring models of treatment, referral to other professionals, etc.

Planned termination of treatment – due to reaching goals or other circumstances – is an opportunity to reevaluate the symptoms that led the client to seek therapy. The results can concretize progress, guide next steps, inform self-directed continuance of the healing process, and identify areas that may benefit from future intervention. When clients re-engage in treatment, a thoughtful reevaluation will orient the therapeutic relationship to the present issues, and support the establishment of an updated diagnosis, treatment plan, and focus.

EMDR-Specific Considerations

After proceeding into trauma processing for the first time, we will have the opportunity to reevaluate in a more EMDR-specific manner. If our selection of the target memory material was directly associated with present symptoms, we expect those to be reduced. If not, then our diagnostic assessment, target selection process, thoroughness of reprocessing, or attempted engagement of self-states was somehow off. Reevaluation can include asking questions such as: Did we have consent from the self-system to resolve this symptom? Is there occluded material held on the other side of a functional gap that has been maintained by dissociation (or disaggregation, see Chapter 2)? Is some internal or external 'toxin' still thwarting connectivity necessary for association/generalization? Is there internal re-perpetration?

Including self-system mapping in early phases of treatment (see Chapter 10) will enhance our ability to discern which self-states were involved in which experiences, as well as to (re)evaluate consent in a more informed way. Sometimes 'progress' in one area yields a ripple effect in another. Perhaps the symptoms were not the result of unprocessed memory material or not directly traumagenic. This is one of the ways in which the AIP model may run out of track. When reevaluation leads us to discover a deficit in skills, internal dynamics (related to trauma but not memory material), external dynamics such as homeostasis in a couple or family relationship, or secondary gain (see Shapiro, 2018, p. 93, 186), other layers of our conceptual frame may need to be recruited.

Case Example

Example C, described earlier, reported several 'red flag' indicators for a DD, including: feeling that their current therapist is no longer helping (and "seems to be annoyed with me"), unremitting intrusive images and thoughts, an extensive trauma history, and medically-unexplained sleep problems. Prior EMDR therapy was reported to be unhelpful. Initial administration of the MID yielded the diagnostic impressions of PTSD and Unspecified Dissociative Disorder, passing 8 of 23 symptoms in *Criterion A* and *B* (meaning that no items indicating amnesia were endorsed at a clinically significant level). In the follow-up interview, the practitioner investigated indications of possible underreporting, four *Critical Items* (indicating possible safety concerns), and elevations on the *Child* and *Persecutor* self-state activity scales, and several Schneiderian first-rank symptom scales (especially *Thought Insertion*). No contemporaneous amnesia was identified; nonetheless, many intrusive and jarring experiences were reported and experienced as 'not me' by the client. The treatment trajectory was estimated to be intermediate.

Year One: The "OCD" symptoms the client hoped to address were conceptualized via the MID as self-state intrusions. The client had not previously engaged in ego state therapy, so the initial treatment goal involved mapping and stabilizing relationships among self-states. Many dissociative phobias and psychodynamics were navigated, especially phobias of attachment and attachment loss, and phobias of internal experience. The client struggled to accept the idea of parts/self-states, but gradually recognized self-states representing nearly every emotion and each of the themes of experience identified in the ACES. The practitioner gradually gained insight into the levels of dissociation present around various self-states and the experiences that were held by them, and began to form hypotheses about possible perpetrator-identifying parts that could be repeating patterns of maltreatment internally. This was confirmed, and upon gaining consent to try this 'different way of using EMDR,' one introject was unburdened of their trauma using the *Introject Decathexis* protocol (Chapter 12).

Year Two: The client acclimated to ego state work, and became increasingly adept at 'noticing without judging or reacting' both internally and externally – most of the time. Now less phobic and more curious about experiencing life as a whole person, the client initiated re-administering the MID to measure current/recent symptoms. The diagnostic impression showed PTSD and dissociative diagnosis deferred, with 4 of 23 symptoms passed, and 2 *Critical Items* passed – indicating that dissociative phobias, internal conflict, and safety concerns had greatly reduced. This feedback supported the client's increasing ego strength to allow the establishment of goals to engage in EMDR to directly address two childhood experiences: the death of a parent and sexual abuse by a caregiver.

Year Three: Re-administration of the MID was conducted again. The diagnostic impression indicated PTSD, and the dissociative diagnosis remained deferred, with only 3 of 23 symptoms passed. Only one *Critical Item* was passed. However, now the *Rare Symptoms* had elevated to three, and the *Persecutory Voices* and *Thought Insertion* scales were elevated. Upon inquiry, these elevations were due to internal reorganization around the client's view of the body and sexuality – consequences of realizations following trauma processing – and revealed a constellation of previously undetected self-states, including a(nother) perpetrator introject.

Year Four: The client's functioning increased substantially and reevaluation was focused on the question of "What remains to address before we end treatment?" Re-administration of the MID yielded the diagnostic impression of PTSD, with 2 of 23 symptoms passed: *Flashbacks* and *Persecutory Voices*. Previous areas of note, including *Rare Symptoms, Critical Items*, and *Thought Insertion*, had decreased. These results alongside current relational patterns revealed that both the *Flashbacks* and *Persecutory Voices* were evoked by 'positive' relational experiences such as feeling 'cared for.' We agreed to approach these experiences using the Early Trauma Protocol (Paulsen & O'Shea, 2017) and deep brain reorienting (Corrigan et al., 2025). Gradually, the client became able to perceive and experience interpersonal care without feeling acute internal distress. The cadence of sessions slowed to support continued integration in functioning and tolerance of the idea of eventually concluding treatment.

Conclusion

How we begin treatment matters, and yet the processes common to the start of treatment can also be applied at later stages. Collection of historical information may occur directly, and often the story of the past is told implicitly in the present symptoms, intra-personally and interpersonally. Practitioners' ability to recognize the 'red flags' for dissociation and proceed through the initial sessions of gathering the client's history and establishing the direction of treatment with relative safety requires a great deal of attunement and nuance in many cases. Utilizing established screening and diagnostic tools can strengthen and deepen the initial and ongoing assessment of symptoms and serve as a springboard for case conceptualization, mapping of self-states, and target selection. Deep awareness of individual cultural factors, transdiagnostic overlaps, and treatment trajectories will inform practitioners in determining the scope and focus of treatment. Later chapters will address navigating the standard phases and prongs of EMDR therapy when dissociation is present.

References

Allen, J. G., Console, D. A., & Lewis, L. (1999). Dissociative detachment and memory impairment: Reversible amnesia or encoding failure? *Comprehensive Psychiatry, 40*(2), 160–171. https://doi.org/10.1016/s0010-440x(99)90121-9

American Psychiatric Association. (1994). *DSM-IV – Diagnostic and statistical manual of mental disorders* (4th ed.). American Psychiatric Publishing.

American Psychiatric Association. (2022). *DSM-5-TR – Diagnostic and statistical manual of mental disorders* (5th ed., text revision). American Psychiatric Publishing.

American Psychological Association. (2024). *APA guidelines for working with adults with complex trauma histories.* www.apa.org/practice/guidelines/adults-complex-trauma-histories.pdf

Arbuthnott, A., Bennet, B. J., Hosey, J., & Van Eys, P. (2025). Considerations in screening, assessment, and clinical interviewing. In Gómez, A. M. & Hosey, J. (Eds.) *The handbook of complex trauma and dissociation in children: Theory, research, and clinical applications* (1st ed.) (pp. 206–236). Routledge. https://doi.org/10.4324/9781003350156

Armstrong, J. G., Putnam, F. W., Carlson, E. B., Libero, D. Z., & Smith, S. R. (1997). Development and validation of a measure of adolescent dissociation: The adolescent dissociative experiences scale. *The Journal of Nervous and Mental Disease, 185*(8), 491–497. https://doi.org/10.1097/00005053-199708000-00003

Beker, J. C., Dorahy, M. J., Moir, J., & Cording, J. (2024). Inter-identity amnesia and memory transfer in dissociative identity disorder: A systematic review with a meta-analysis. *Clinical Psychology Review, 114,* 102514. https://doi.org/10.1016/j.cpr.2024.102514

Boon, S. (2023). *Assessing trauma-related dissociation with the trauma and dissociation symptoms interview (TADS-I).* Norton Professional Books.

Brand, B. L. (2024). *The concise guide to the assessment and treatment of trauma-related dissociation.* American Psychological Association. https://doi.org/10.1037/0000386-000

Brand, B. L., Sar, V., Stavropoulos, P., Krüger, C., Korzekwa, M., Martínez-Taboas, A., & Middleton, W. (2016). Separating fact from fiction: An empirical examination of six myths about dissociative identity disorder. *Harvard Review of Psychiatry, 24*(4), 257–270. https://doi.org/10.1097/hrp.0000000000000100

Braun, B. G. (1988a). The BASK model of dissociation. *Dissociation, 1*(1), 4–23. hdl.handle.net/1794/1276

Braun, B. G. (1988b). The BASK model of dissociation: Part II. Treatment. *Dissociation, 1*(2), 16–23. hdl.handle.net/1794/1340

Briere, J. (2002). *Multiscale dissociation inventory (MDI)*. Psychological Assessment Resources.

Butcher, J. N., Dahlstrom, W. G., Graham, J. R., Tellegen, A., & Kaemmer, B. (1989). *MMPI-2: Minnesota multiphasic personality inventory-2*. University of Minnesota Press.

Carlson, E., & Putnam, F. (1993). An update on the dissociative experiences scale. *Dissociation, 6*(1), 16–27. hdl.handle.net/1794/1539

Carlson, E. B., Putnam. F. W., Ross, C. A., Torem, M., Coons. P., Dill, D., Loewenstein, R. J., & Braun, B. C. (1993). Validity of the dissociative experiences scale in screening for multiple personality disorder: A multicenter study. *American Journal of Psychiatry, 150*(7), 1030–1036. https://doi.org/10.1176/ajp.150.7.1030

Carlson, E. B., Waelde, L. C., Palmieri, P. A., Macia, K. S., Smith, S. R., & McDade-Montez, E. (2018). Development and validation of the dissociative symptoms scale. *Assessment, 25*(1), 84–98. https://doi.org/10.1177/1073191116645904

Christensen, E. M. (2022). The online community: DID and plurality. *European Journal of Trauma & Dissociation, 6*(2), Article 100257. https://doi.org/10.1016/j.ejtd.2021.100257

Corrigan, F. M., Young, H., & Christie-Sands, J. (2025). *Deep brain reorienting: Understanding the neuroscience of trauma, attachment wounding, and DBR psychotherapy*. Routledge. https://doi.org/10.4324/9781003431695

Coy, D. M., & Madere, J. A. (2023). Diagnosing the dissociative disorders: conceptual, theoretical, and practical considerations. In M. Dorahy & S. Gold (Eds), *Dissociation and the dissociative disorders: Past, present, future* (pp. 661–672). Routledge. https://doi.org/10.4324/9781003057314

Coy, D. M., Madere, J. A., & Dell, P. F. (2022). *An interpretive manual for the multidimensional inventory of dissociation (MID)* (4th ed.). Unpublished manuscript.

Dalenberg, C., & Carlson, E. (2010, November 3-6). *New versions of the dissociative experiences scale: The DES-R (revised) and the DES-B (brief)* [Conference presentation]. 26th Annual Meeting of the International Society for Traumatic Stress Studies. Montreal, Quebec, Canada.

Dell, P. F. (2006). Multidimensional inventory of dissociation (MID). A comprehensive measure of pathological dissociation. *Journal of Trauma & Dissociation, 7*(2), 77–106. https://doi.org/10.1300/J229v07n02_06sss

Dell, P. F. (2009a). The long struggle to diagnose multiple personality disorder (MPD): MPD. In P. F. Dell & J. A. O'Neil (Eds.), *Dissociation and the dissociative disorders: DSM-V and beyond* (pp. 383–402). Routledge. https://doi.org/10.4324/9780203893920

Dell, P. F. (2009b). The phenomena of pathological dissociation. In P. F. Dell & J. A. O'Neil (Eds.), *Dissociation and the dissociative disorders: DSM-V and beyond* (pp. 225–237). Routledge. https://doi.org/10.4324/9780203893920

Dimitrova, L. I., Lawrence, A. J., Vissia, E. M., Chalavi, S., Kakouris, A. F., Veltman, D. J., & Reinders, A. A. T. S. (2024). Inter-identity amnesia in dissociative identity disorder resolved: A behavioural and neurobiological study. *Journal of Psychiatric Research, 174,* 220–229. https://doi.org/10.1016/j.jpsychires.2024.04.026

Dominguez, S. (2023). EMDR therapy as a transdiagnostic psychotherapy. In D. Farrell, S. J. Schubert, & M. D. Kiernan (Eds.), *The oxford handbook of EMDR* (Online edition). https://doi.org/10.1093/oxfordhb/9780192898357.013.18

Felitti, V. J., Anda, R. F., Nordenberg, D., Williamson, D. F., Spitz, A. M., Edwards, V., & Marks, J. S. (1998). Relationship of childhood abuse and household dysfunction to many of the leading causes of death in adults: The adverse childhood experiences (ACE) study. *American Journal of Preventive Medicine, 14*(4), 245–258. https://doi.org/10.1016/S0749-3797(98)00017-8

Gordon, R. M. (2025, June 21). *The Psychodynamic Diagnostic Manual-3 (PDM-3) and Functional Neurological Disorder* [Webinar]. Center for Christianity and Psychoanalysis. centerforchristianityandpsychoanalysis.org/product/the-psychodynamic-diagnostic-manual-3-pdm-3-and-functional-neurological-disorder/

Howard, H. A. (2017). Promoting safety in hypnosis: A clinical instrument for the assessment of alertness. *American Journal of Clinical Hypnosis, 59*(4), 344–362. https://doi.org/10.1080/00029157.2016.1203281

Janet, P. (1889/2022). *Catalepsy, memory and suggestion in psychological automatism: Total automatism* (1st ed.) (G. Craparo & O. van der Hart, Eds.; A. Crabtree & S. Osei-Bonsu, Trans.). Routledge. (Original work published 1889) https://doi.org/10.4324/9780429287671

Kate, M.-A., Jamieson, G., Dorahy, M. J., & Middleton, W. (2021). Measuring dissociative symptoms and experiences in an Australian college sample using a short version of the multidimensional inventory of dissociation. *Journal of Trauma & Dissociation, 22*(3), 265–287. https://doi.org/10.1080/15299732.2020.1792024

Kluft, R. P. (1994a). Treatment trajectories in multiple personality disorder. *Dissociation, 7*(1), 63–76. hdl.handle.net/1794/1520

Kluft, R. P. (1994b). Clinical observations on the use of the CSDS dimensions of therapeutic movement instrument (DTMI). *Dissociation, 7*(4), 272–283. hdl.handle.net/1794/1558

Laddis, A., Dell, P. F., & Korzekwa, M. (2017). Comparing the symptoms and mechanisms of "dissociation" in dissociative identity disorder and borderline personality disorder. *Journal of Trauma & Dissociation, 18*(2),139–173. https://doi.org/10.1080/15299732.2016.1194358

Lebois, L. A. M., Li., M., Baker, J. T., Wolf, J. D., Wang, D., Lambros, A. M., Grinspoon, E., Winternitz, S., Ren, J., Gonenc, A., Gruber, S. A., Ressler, K. J., Liu, H., & Kaufman, M., L. (2021). Large-scale functional brain network architecture changes associated with trauma-related dissociation. *American Journal of Psychiatry, 178*(2), 165–173. https://doi.org/10.1176/appi.ajp.2020.19060647

Leeds, A. M., Madere, J. A., & Coy, D. M. (2022). Beyond the DES-II: Screening for dissociative disorders in EMDR therapy. *Journal of EMDR Practice and Research, 16*(1), 25–38. https://doi.org/10.1891/EMDR-D-21-00019

Lewis-Fernández, R., Martínez-Taboas, A., Sar, V., Patel, S., & Boatin, A. (2007). The cross-cultural assessment of dissociation. In J. P. Wilson & C. S.-k. Tang (Eds.), *Cross-cultural assessment of psychological trauma and PTSD* (pp. 279–317). Springer Science + Business Media. https://doi.org/10.1007/978-0-387-70990-1_12

Lindfors, K. U. M., Therman, S., Lindgren, M., Kekkonen, V., Tolmunen, T. (2022). Factor structure, measurement invariance, and abbreviated versions of the adolescent dissociative experiences scale (A-DES). *Journal of Trauma Dissociation, 25*(4), 464–479. https://doi.org/10.1080/15299732.2022.2064575

Lingiardi, V., & McWilliams, N. (Eds.). (2017). *Psychodynamic diagnostic manual: PDM-2* (2nd ed.). The Guilford Press.

Loewenstein, R. J. (1991). An office mental status examination for complex chronic dissociative symptoms and multiple personality disorder. *Psychiatric Clinics of North America, 14*(3), 567–604.

Lord, C., Kennedy, F., Smart, K., & Maguire, T. (2025). Developing a scale to measure dissociation between self-states (the Dissociation-Integration of Self States Scale, D-ISS Scale). *The Cognitive Behaviour Therapist, 18*, e18. https://doi.org/10.1017/S1754470X25000042

Macia, K. S., Carlson, E. B., Palmieri, P. A., Smith, S. R., Anglin, D. M., Ghosh Ippen, C., Lieberman, A. F., Wong, E. C., Schell, T. L., & Waelde, L. C. (2023). Development of a brief version of the dissociative symptoms scale and the reliability and validity of DSS-B scores in diverse clinical and community samples. *Assessment, 30*(7), 2058–2073. https://doi.org/10.1177/10731911221133317

Madere, J. A. (2023). A Catholic perspective: dissociative identity disorder or diabolical possession? *Integratus, 1*(2), 130–147. https://doi.org/10.1521/intg.2023.1.2.130

Martínez-Taboas, A., Shrout P. E., Canino, G., Chavez, L. M., Ramírez, R., Bravo, M., Bauermeister, J. J., & Ribera, J. C. (2004). The psychometric properties of a shortened version of the Spanish adolescent dissociative experiences scale. *Journal of Trauma & Dissociation, 5*(4), 33–54. https://doi.org/10.1300/J229v05n04_03

Nester, M. S., Hawkins, S. L., & Brand, B. L. (2022). Barriers to accessing and continuing mental health treatment among individuals with dissociative symptoms. *European Journal of Psychotraumatology, 13*(1), 2031594 https://doi.org/10.1080/20008198.2022.2031594

Nijenhuis, E. R. S., Spinhoven, P., Van Dyck, R., Van Der Hart, O., & Vanderlinden, J. (1996). The development and psychometric characteristics of the Somatoform Dissociation Questionnaire (SDQ-20). *Journal of Nervous and Mental Disease, 184*(11), 688–694. https://doi.org/10.1097/00005053-199611000-00006

Paulsen, S., & O'Shea, K. (2017). *When there are no words: Repairing early trauma and neglect from the attachment period with EMDR therapy*. CreateSpace.

Piedfort-Marin, O., Wisler, D., Spagnoli, D., & Piot, M. (2017). An adapted version of Kluft's dimensions of therapeutic movement instrument (DTMI). *European Journal of Trauma & Dissociation, 1*(4), 263–268. https://doi.org/10.1016/j.ejtd.2017.06.006

Pierorazio, N. A., Nester, M. S., Shandler, G., & Brand, B. L. (2023). "This 'prison' where I cannot heal": Interactions of culture, dissociation, and treatment among individuals who dissociate. *European Journal of Trauma & Dissociation, 7*(2), Article 100325. https://doi.org/10.1016/j.ejtd.2023.100325

Pierorazio, N. A., Brand, B. L., & Goldenson, J. (2025). Dissociation-informed assessment: Process-related guidance. *Psychological Trauma: Theory, Research, Practice, and Policy*. No pagination specified. https://doi.org/10.1037/tra0001997

Ross, C. A. (2015). When to suspect and how to diagnose dissociative identity disorder. *Journal of EMDR Practice and Research, 9*(2), 114–120. https://doi.org/10.1891/1933-3196.9.2.114

Ross, C. A., & Browning, E. (2017). The self-report dissociative disorders interview schedule: A preliminary report. *Journal of Trauma & Dissociation, 18*(1), 31–37. https://doi.org/10.1080/15299732.2016.1172538

Ross, C. A., Heber, S., Norton, G. R., Anderson, D., Anderson, G., & Barchet, P. (1989). The dissociative disorders interview schedule: Structured interview. *Dissociation, 2*(3), 169–189. hdl.handle.net/1794/1505

Salter, M., Brand, B. L., Robinson, M., Loewenstein, R., Silberg, J., & Korzekwa, M. (2025). Self-diagnosed cases of dissociative identity disorder on social media: Conceptualization, assessment, and treatment. *Harvard Review of Psychiatry, 33*(1), 41–48. https://doi.org/10.1097/HRP.0000000000000416

Schielke, H., Brand, B., & Marsic, A. (2017). Assessing therapeutic change in patients with severe dissociative disorders: The progress in treatment questionnaire, therapist and patient measures. *European Journal of Psychotraumatology, 8*(1), 12. https://doi.org/10.1080/20008198.2017.1380471

Shapiro, F. (2018). *Eye movement desensitization and reprocessing (EMDR) therapy: Basic principles, protocols and procedures* (3rd ed.). The Guilford Press.

Shinn, A. K., Wolff, J. D., Hwang, M., Lebois, L., Robinson, M. A., Winternitz, S. R., Öngür, D.,Ressler, K. J., & Kaufman, M. L. (2020). Assessing voice hearing in trauma spectrum disorders: a comparison of two measures and a review of the literature. *Frontiers in Psychiatry, 10*, 1011. https://doi.org/10.3389/fpsyt.2019.01011

Sidis, B. (1898). *The psychology of suggestion: A research into the subconscious nature of man and society*. D. Appleton & Company.

Steinberg, M. (2023). *Semi-structured clinical interview for dissociative symptoms and disorders (SCID-D)*. American Psychiatric Association Publishing.

Steinberg, M., Kluft, R. P., Coons, P. M., Bowman, E. S., Fine, C. G., Fink, D. L., Hall, P. E., Rounsaville, B. J., & Cicchetti, D. V. (1989–1993). *Multi-center field trials of the structured clinical interview for DSM-IV dissociative disorders (SCID-D)*. Yale University School of Medicine.

Trujillo, M., Brown, A., Watson, D., Croft-Caderao, K., & Chmielewski, M. (2024). The Dissociative experiences scale: An empirical evaluation of long-standing concerns. *Psychology of Consciousness: Theory, Research, and Practice. 11*(4), 477–492. https://doi.org/10.1037/cns0000334

Vanderlinden, J., Van Dyck, R., Vandereycken, W., Vertommen, H., & Jan Verkes, R. (1993), The dissociation questionnaire (DIS-Q): Development and characteristics of a new self-report questionnaire. *Clinical Psychology & Psychotherapy, 1*(1), 21–27. https://doi.org/10.1002/cpp.5640010105

Weathers, F. W., Bovin, M. J., Lee, D. J., Sloan, D. M., Schnurr, P. P., Kaloupek, D. G., Keane, T. M., & Marx, B. P. (2018). The clinician-administered PTSD scale for DSM-5 (CAPS-5): Development and initial psychometric evaluation in military veterans. *Psychological Assessment, 30*(3), 383–395. https://doi.org/10.1037/pas0000486

Chapter 7

Modified Preparation and Reprocessing

Jennifer A. Madere

Introduction

The basic protocols and procedures of EMDR therapy can be both too much and not enough for people who experience complex trauma and dissociative disorders (DDs). Nuanced adjustments to the protocols and procedures discussed in the standard Shapiro (2018) text and taught in EMDR therapy basic trainings may be just what is needed, when embedded within a broader treatment framework (see Chapter 3). For clients with dissociative disorders (DDs), more specialized tools and additional approaches described in Part IV may be necessary.

This chapter will guide you toward crafting a balanced approach that aligns with both your competencies and your clients' needs. We will break down *Stage 1: Stabilization* and how EMDR therapy fits within it. To that end, we will first examine *Phase II: Preparation* and its adaptations, encompassing resource development, work on affect tolerance/phobias, identifying and accessing 'adaptive material,' incremental efficacy in containment during and between sessions, and establishing client consent. Then, we will explore fractionating targets and containing processing in *Phase III: Assessment* and *Phases IV–VI: Reprocessing*. This chapter will conclude with examples for measuring progress and determining next steps in treatment.

What's Our Frame?

When it comes to implementing EMDR therapy with DDs, there are a few prominent and polarized perspectives (see Chapter 4). Presumably, all contributors to the discussion are trying to help people in the ways they know best and unilateral application of any approach is unethical practice. Our tools are only as good as our conceptualization – and how well we know each client. In Chapter 3, we proposed a framework for conceptualizing comprehensive treatment in which EMDR therapy is anchored

DOI: 10.4324/9781003410201-10

amongst other theoretical models and practices better suited to treating a wider range of features of complex trauma and dissociation. Others have offered their perspectives on integrating EMDR into the three-stage model (most notably, Gelinas, 2003), ego state therapies, or various theories of dissociation. None have addressed all four layers in the ways that we are conceptualizing them, so we offer this and other chapters that follow to articulate how we see the protocols and procedures of EMDR therapy working when embedded in this way.

Why is this only one chapter, and not two or more? Because *Phase II* is *preparation* for accessing and reprocessing the traumatic memory material. Sometimes the word *Preparation* is used interchangeably with 'resourcing.' While interventions may be similar, the strategy of selection and purpose of the procedures employed are distinct. *Phase II* interventions complement *Stabilization* work, but in an EMDR therapy frame, we are strategically preparing for trauma processing. The treatment goal(s) that we have collaboratively identified with the client, the degree of functional connectivity (or gaps) present among memory networks and self-states, and the expected target memories associated with them will determine the scope of *Preparation.*

When clients have gained *enough* stability and we can collaboratively identify the highest priority symptoms or incidents for *Stage 2: Trauma Processing*, intentional completion of *Phase I: History Taking* is in order. This is our explicit (re)entry into the sub-frame of EMDR. Before this, we (probably) did not have a reason to ask direct questions to gather information about specific timeframes or types of experience in the client's life. Now, we do so to inform the scope of the upcoming reprocessing, and to evaluate readiness and necessary steps to ensure we are adequately prepared to take on this challenge together.

History Taking and *Preparation* are approached with present symptoms and future goals for adaptive and integrated functioning in mind. Two essential questions to keep in focus at this point are:

1. *What do we (practitioner and client) know, and what do we have consent and agreement to work on/toward?*
2. *Why are we doing this? What does the client hope will be different once this bit of processing is complete?*

Having answers to these questions can help us avoid becoming stuck in an aimless infinity loop and instead navigate our way through trauma processing work thoughtfully and intentionally.

Preparation is the bridge by which we move into *Stage 2: Trauma Processing* work when utilizing EMDR therapy as our trauma processing

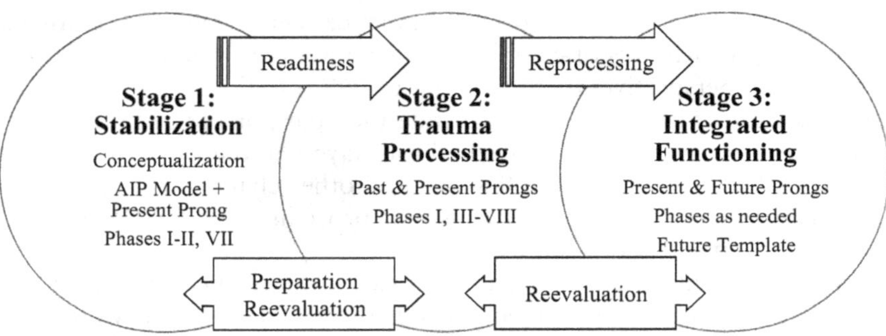

Figure 7.1 Three-Stage Model with Three Prongs and Eight Phases of EMDR Therapy.

approach. Thus, *Preparation* and *Reprocessing* are a recursive process of first determining readiness, consent, and ensuring that we (both the practitioner and the client) are prepared for the journey that we intend to undertake, followed by bits of trauma processing and reevaluation to assess the effect(s) and determine whether we proceed forward, or not (see Figure 7.1). By recursive, I do not mean that we necessarily 'go back' to *Preparation*. Rather, we prepare at each step to access and reprocess the next bit of memory material. This cycle may be repeated multiple times, both per target when fractionating memories for *Reprocessing* and throughout the course of a comprehensive treatment. Eventually, this process will flow into *Present* and *Future* prongs, and *Stage 3: Integrated Functioning*, which is where we hope to see generalization and increased functional connectivity come to bear. Chapter 8 addresses *Present* and *Future* prongs in detail.

Preparation for Trauma Processing: Breaking Down the Components

The scope of the treatment plan is informed by both the diagnostic assessment process and the presenting issues/goals prioritized by the client. In our initial foray into *Stage* 2 with a client, reprocessing may be more circumscribed – with broader goals and a wider scope of treatment allowed after we have evidence of safe, successful processing.

First, containment and *Phase VII*: *Closure* strategies ought to be in place *prior* to intentionally accessing any traumatic memory material – by this I mean both trauma-focused history taking and reprocessing. Francine Shapiro states that the "client must be returned to a state of emotional equilibrium by the end of each session" (Shapiro, 2018, p. 70). In the unmodified application of the standard protocol, this comes at the end of a reprocessing session – however, it is advisable to have these strategies reliably in place and practiced *before* they are needed. The effectiveness of closure strategies also informs the pace of treatment and structure of sessions (see Kluft's 'Rule of Thirds,' Chapter 5). We find that clients with dissociative symptoms often need assistance returning to equilibrium at the close of sessions. Thus, establishing a reliable and effective toolbox of closure methods is essential long before beginning reprocessing.

We may periodically revisit *History Taking* to inform and confirm a plan for *Trauma Processing,* adjusting the focus and depth of questions that we ask by keeping the future in mind. In *Example A* (Chapter 6), the client's most pressing goal is to resolve symptoms related to being in a car as a driver or passenger. These symptoms are interfering with sleep, work, and other aspects of daily life. In this case, we need to know the history of those symptoms, their time of onset, any antecedent events, the experience of being a passenger and/or driver of a vehicle before the antecedent event, and how the client imagines improved functioning will look in the future. Although we are not (yet) setting up a target, we may hear a client reference a possible negative cognition (NC) (e.g., "I'm doomed"). We will also consider the client's sense of self before the antecedent event, and how this relatively recent experience may have (re)ignited previously dormant memory material (e.g., experiences of feeling powerless, self-loathing).

Keeping the future in mind clarifies *why* we are delving into a past traumatic experience. This can be challenging when the person's history includes many traumatic episodes, and the past remains alive in many aspects of their present experience. If a client's stated goal is "to work through my experiences of sexual abuse," we can best honor that goal by identifying how the client hopes the future will be different after working through those experiences and developing the treatment plan accordingly. A related future goal might be "to be able to go to sleep when the room is dark." Specificity will help us to gather the necessary historical information, obtain the appropriate informed consent of self-states involved, take the appropriate preparatory steps, and have something to work *toward* with the client. Thus, the future focus/prong is our long-term objective, and all proximate and intermediate steps can be oriented toward a shared goal.

Gathering specific history also includes identification of available adaptive memory material that will allow the traumatic memory to resolve via association and consolidation in reprocessing. We can explore this by inquiring whether the person has ever experienced the opposite or hoped-for emotional or relational state. For example,

- What might be needed to go to sleep easily when the room is dark?
- Has the client ever been able to go to sleep easily when the room is dark?

- If responses point to the need for a sense of safety, has the client ever felt safe when externally/objectively safe in the present moment?
- When has the client experienced appropriate care, protection, etc.? From whom?

If we identify that the person has *never* experienced any element of the desired future scenario, we may need to search more deeply or cultivate real or imagined resources. Does the client's desired goal represent state change or trait change (see Chapter 3)? We may also identify signs of internal conflict among self-states – for example, one part of the client may desire to go to sleep easily, while another part perceives that it is never safe enough to go to sleep without having the lights on. Internal conflict reminds us to integrate mapping (Chapter 10) and ego state work into EMDR-specific interventions.

When neglect is a prominent theme in someone's history, the development of the ability to tolerate positive/pleasing affect, and in particular shared positive affect (Leeds, 2023), may be necessary. Emotional and psychological neglect make a person vulnerable to further adversity and abuse (Jaffe et al., 2019; Pezzoli et al., 2025; Xaio et al., 2023). Further, emotional neglect has been found to be most highly correlated with dissociative amnesia – more than physical or sexual abuse – according to brain imaging studies (Dimitrova et al., 2021). Thus, the presence of neglect with or without abuse may indicate complexity.

When clients experience DDs, the availability and recall of information about their history may be limited. This applies to both symptomatic experiences (unprocessed or maladaptively processed) and memory networks holding adaptive or positive material. In some cases, a client may lack access to a linear account of their history. This may necessitate extensive ego state work in the service of collecting that history. We do not need to know *everything* going in, but having sufficient information allows us to ascertain what our target is and be reasonably confident in the feasibility of reaching the goal/destination.

Formal Preparation for Trauma Processing

Preparation for the journey into *Trauma Processing* in an EMDR therapy frame may be sorted into three components:

1. Orientation to the procedures of EMDR therapy and client 'jobs';
2. Conditioning via engaging in exercises – using components such as BL-DAS – to build and confirm flexibility and endurance in proportion to the anticipated journey; and

3. Outfitting the train to ensure that the client, practitioner, and the therapeutic relationship are prepared for this journey into the landscape of traumatic memory material.

Clients may understandably want to have a sense of what processing with EMDR will be like before committing to work on a target memory or sequence. Complementarily, it is helpful for practitioners to learn how clients respond to bilateral dual attention stimulation (BL-DAS) and other procedures before confirming the treatment plan. The Calm/Safe Place (CSP) exercise (or an equivalent) may be introduced accordingly:

> There is an orientation exercise that is done before we approach any traumatic memory material in EMDR therapy. I find that it helps people to get a sense of the process while focusing on something that is neutral or positive, and it gives me a chance to learn how some components of EMDR work with you and your brain. This exercise is called Calm, Safe or Peaceful Place. When it goes well, people find it useful for self-regulation at the end of session and between sessions. Even if it's bumpy, we will have a good idea of how to approach other phases of the EMDR process together.

There are many components within the CSP exercise that test a client's readiness and can inform further stabilization, preparation, and/or later reprocessing. I like to think of it as a test of psychological and emotional flexibility, agility, and strength. Orientation to BL-DAS may happen separately from or simultaneously with CSP. While this discussion is oriented to the steps of CSP, it can also be applied to alternatives such as Resource Development and Installation (RDI, discussed later).

If we have already determined a need for a slower pace and a narrower scope of treatment, separating out the components into incremental steps is advisable. The following proposed segments can take place over multiple sessions.

1. Introduce CSP or another positive imagery exercise. This gauges the client's affect tolerance, capacity to hold an experience in their imagination, and their ability to report on it immediately.
2. Introduce BL-DAS and identify at least two options that are tolerable for the client. Preferably, one form of tactile stimulation, one form of eye movement, and perhaps an auditory or another available option. This is simply to observe the client's immediate response to experiencing BL-DAS.
3. Pair CSP imagery or another resource state *with* a chosen form of BL-DAS. This can be accomplished by stepping through the first steps

of the CSP script and pausing after enhancement and a few sets of BL-DAS.

4. Support the client to try self-cueing and self-directed state-shifting (as represented in Shapiro, 2018, p. 118). The pivot from practitioner-guided pairing of CSP imagery and BL-DAS to self-cueing can feel jarring to clients who have experienced profound attachment injury. If the client experienced prior efficacy in self-regulation during *Stage 1* work and has a positive experience from the pairing of CPS imagery with BL-DAS, they may possess the ego strength to try self-cueing with good odds of success.
5. Engage in self-cueing after shifting attention to a recent mildly disturbing/annoying experience (as represented in Shapiro, 2018, p. 118). This is a major feat of emotional agility for some clients – and will be discussed in more detail below.

If someone does not have a positive or successful experience with some component of CSP, that does not *necessarily* mean that EMDR ought to be eliminated from their treatment plan. However, it frequently indicates the need for additional preparation and later modification of reprocessing procedures. With that in mind, let us consider each of the following dissected components carefully.

1. Response to BL-DAS Without Focused Attention on Memory Material

Doing something new with one's body (eyes, hands, feet, ears) can evoke surprising associations on its own. Clients' sensory experience of the BL-DAS may be foreign, overwhelming, or reminiscent of another experience – pleasant or unpleasant. Changing physical proximity between the client and therapist, tactile 'buzzing' or vibrations, hands or lights guiding eye movements can reveal information that was previously unknown in the therapeutic relationship. Some clients who have strong internal defenses perceive the associative process activated by the BL-DAS almost immediately – and may find it to be jarring and otherwise uncomfortable as they feel their 'brain moving.'

2. Identification of Resource Material

When planning to facilitate CSP, I routinely ask clients to identify at least three real or imagined memories or places that represent to them a greater sense of calm, ease, safety, or something else pleasant. There are often immediate associations to disturbing experiences that 'contaminate' the possible resource (e.g., a beloved pet that was also abused by an ex-partner, a baseball field where the client was also bullied, a vacation spot where the client also felt abandoned and alone). Scoping the resource material by zooming in to identify a stable element can be helpful to work within what clients offer. For example, identifying a *specific time* when the beloved pet was a puppy, a *sensory element* such as the smell of a favorite baseball glove, or a *contained place* of adventure, such as a tree fort near the vacation spot.

3. Tolerance of Neutral or Pleasant Emotion and Sensation

The range of affect easily accessed and tolerated by the client (and by self-states) is tested during the CSP exercise. If we did not already work on affect tolerance and mapping of self-states in *Stage 1*, we may be surprised by responses such as grief, shame, or numbness when attempting to access pleasant emotion and sensation. Keeping the scope/range small can help clients to have a successful experience; for example, instructing them to "notice feeling just the tiniest bit of that warmth of the sun… peeking through the trees as you think about the memory."

4. Response to BL-DAS with Resource Material

Because of how we understand BL-DAS operating in moving the proverbial train (see Chapter 2), we expect that the scenery or the client's perception of it will change in some way. I find it helpful to orient the client to their 'jobs' within EMDR therapy:

- ✓ Notice the scenery/memory material, letting it change or stay the same, just observing it without judging it.
- ✓ Notice whatever thoughts, emotions, and/or sensations you are experiencing now as you notice/imagine it.
- ✓ After each set, I will ask you to let it go and take a breath, and tell me what you notice now – I'm asking about anything that stands out to you now, whether it's the same or different from before.
- ✓ If anything happens during a set of BL-DAS that does not feel okay to you, please interrupt the set and use our established stop signal.

For clients who have experienced severe attachment injury, any change in the imagery or their present experience of it can represent a threat of loss. Clients may try to control their experience toward what they think is supposed to happen, be distracted by the BL-DAS, feel further away from the resource experience, or notice an association that evokes distress. All these responses provide an opportunity for practitioners to further orient the client to the process of noticing present experience along with scenery/memory material, and reporting whatever change or associations happen at each set.

5. Agency in Accessing Resource Material

If we get to the self-cueing step, where the client accesses the resource state independently, that's great! Some clients struggle with this change as well, because now they are doing something on their own – without the BL-DAS or being led by the practitioner. People who experience less agency in regulating their own attention and affect may struggle due to many factors, including the simple change in process, feeling a sense of abandonment, or performance anxiety. In such cases, practitioners can offer a reminder of the aspects of the resource or encourage the client to "just notice the experience, however far or close it seems to you right now."

6. State Shifting in and out of (Appropriate) Negative/ Unpleasant Affect

When clients are instructed to think of a recent "minor annoyance" (Shapiro, 2018, p. 118), it is remarkable how, even when given an example of an everyday annoyance, clients immediately identify something of a much higher distress level – such as a recent experience of betrayal. For clients with complex trauma and DDs, perception of distressing experiences and the ability to rank levels of distress are often unpredictable or depersonalized. They may feel numb and 'fine' in response to most things and then experience acute and intrusive distress in response to something that evokes a traumatized self-state. Learning (together) to anticipate and scale distress in a more reliable way, and shift (back) to a positive or neutral state, is an important component of *Preparation* – whether it happens in the context of CSP or otherwise.

7. Ability to Apply Self-Cueing outside of Session

If CSP (or RDI) is successful, practicing self-cueing between sessions is a valuable self-regulation strategy. This objective may already be met via other strategies during *Stabilization.* In the context of *Preparation,* what we need are reliable means for clients to gain agency in self-care and self-regulation outside of sessions, and in response to distress that may arise between sessions.

Reevaluation Within Phase II: Preparation

It is wise to incorporate elements of *Phase VIII: Reevaluation* before we get to *Reprocessing*. This can be done by checking in at the beginning of a session about how the previous session was for the client, listening to any indications that the BL-DAS evoked associations that emerged with a change in symptoms, asking whether self-cueing was used, etc. Overall, what was learned from the prior session and how does that confirm or guide the treatment plan?

Some practitioners suggest that each self-state should have its own CSP. What do you think? If the intention is to establish a resource state that corresponds to the needs of each identified self-state, that could be part of a stabilization-focused treatment plan. However, as a general practice of *Preparation* for trauma processing, I disagree. By the time that CSP and BL-DAS are introduced, formal screening and/or assessment ought to have already been done as well as identification and mapping of known self-states during *Stabilization*. Ego states often emerge and are discovered throughout treatment, so it may not even be possible to identify a CSP for everyone up front. Consent to engage in the treatment plan from as much of the self-system as possible must be gained and maintained, but not all self-states need to participate actively in CSP or in *Reprocessing*. For all these reasons, it seems that developing a CSP for every self-state – if it's possible – might err on the side of delaying *Trauma Processing* unnecessarily.

Anabel González and Dolores Mosquera wrote that "the Safe Place installation could be proposed as a dissociative screening test" (González & Mosquera, 2012, p. 3). While we can certainly learn about our clients throughout the CSP protocol as discussed above, highly dissociative individuals are often skilled at 'going somewhere else' in their mind and may initially 'ace' CSP. For that reason, having a broad view of various indicators of preparedness is important.

Modified and Extended Phase II: Preparation

Utilizing modified and extended *Phase II* procedures is often helpful:

1. To incorporate elements of EMDR therapy into *Stabilization*,
2. To increase access to pleasant or adaptive experience and memory material before entering or returning to *Reprocessing*, and
3. During *Reprocessing*, as an extended interweave when a need for connection to adaptive material is discovered.

Incorporating elements of EMDR therapy into *Stabilization* allows EMDR practitioners to utilize familiar tools and provides clients with opportunities to become increasingly familiar with their 'jobs' in the EMDR layer of the treatment frame. This presumes that clients respond well to BL-DAS, usually meaning that the downregulating response of tactile stimulation is experienced as soothing or grounding, and any associations they experience are within positively valenced networks.

Estimating what adaptive material or connections between/among self-states will be needed for the proposed target memory material to have a good chance to resolve will guide the selection of extended *Preparation* strategies. If such needs are oriented more to self-states than to adaptive material, then consider, what does this client need to facilitate consent along the proposed trauma processing journey? Part IV of this book will address additional ego state approaches. Above, I mentioned that *Example A* client noted a possible NC of 'I'm doomed.' Assessing for adaptive material could include listening for what it would mean for them to no longer feel doomed – and inquire whether they have felt that before. If answers are easily ascertained, and the adaptive counterpart to 'doomed' is identified somewhere within their experience, then it is likely that the necessary adaptive material is present to support full processing of the recent event. If not, extended *Preparation* and/or restricted *Reprocessing* will probably be needed to honor and accomplish the desired treatment goal.

Numerous extended *Preparation* strategies have been presented and published in advanced training workshops, conferences, and literature on EMDR therapy. A few categories and specific strategies are listed here. As with all interventions, the choice to employ them ought to be based on the needs of the client and treatment plan – none are intended to be implemented unilaterally.

Resource Development and Installation (*RDI*; Korn & Leeds, 2002; Leeds, 1998; in Shapiro, 2018, pp. 248–250). One of the first extended *Preparation* strategies, RDI, was developed specifically for clients with complex presentations who needed something more than or instead of the basic implementation of CSP. RDI follows the same procedural steps as CSP, with two additions: identification of the specific resource needed (mastery, relational, symbolic, etc.), and future rehearsal wherein clients are invited to imagine a situation in which the desired response or state is practiced. RDI can be employed as a *Stabilization* strategy (e.g., enhancing a sense of mastery or efficacy), a *Preparation* strategy (e.g., cultivating a sense of connection to an attachment figure), and/or visited as an extended interweave during *Reprocessing* when a need for adaptive material is discovered.

Four Elements (Shapiro, 2009) incorporate three steps of grounding, breathing, and salivary activation *before* identifying and enhancing a positive memory resource (equivalent to CSP). Originally developed for emergency and disaster response situations, it is particularly helpful for clients presenting with anxiety and/or hyperarousal, and who struggle to identify or access positive/pleasant affect. When grounding skills and other self-regulation strategies are part of the *Stabilization* treatment plan, *Four Elements* can be a bridge from those familiar tools to an introduction to EMDR therapy procedures.

Resource figures. For clients with a history of attachment wounding, identification and cultivation of resource figures has been promoted by several authors (e.g., Parnell, 2013; Paulsen, 2009; Schmidt & Hernandez, 2007). These include nurturing figures, protective figures, wise figures, and ideal parents. Within *Stabilization*, this strategy can support clients in fostering self-regulation skills, growing their ability to internalize helpful 'others,' and building their capacity for mentalization. When clients wish to engage in comprehensive treatment of relational trauma, and a survey of their history and self-system yields very little relational and systemic support, development of resource figures is an appropriate *Preparation* strategy to outfit the proverbial train with provisions to address potential stuck points in *Reprocessing*.

Moving Toward Stage 2: Trauma Processing

After we have oriented clients to their role during processing, introduced the basic procedures in CSP, and addressed any glitches, needs, or concerns prompted by those, it is time to revisit consent for proceeding into *Trauma Processing* and confirm treatment goals. Based upon how *Preparation* went, and the anticipated scope of *Reprocessing,* what do we anticipate needing on the proverbial train? For example, I often suggest that the trains departing from my office are quite customizable (note, this is an implicit use of hypnotic imagery to support the EMDR process, as many imaginal and visual interventions within EMDR therapy are). I ask if clients want a window shade that can be raised or lowered to see more of the scenery, what kind of seat they want, and we briefly identify other features or provisions that are needed or lend support for our intended journey. Supplies could include a map of self-states, containment and distancing strategies, grounding skills, established safety in the therapeutic relationship to withstand distress and express needs, and confidence in our mutual abilities to slow down the train and disembark safely at the close of each session.

Trauma Accessing and Reprocessing

How do you know when you are ready to set up a target and begin reprocessing with a client? Often, beginner EMDR therapists struggle to discern the scope and timing of trauma accessing and processing. As a result, they may plow forward into reprocessing, swerve off into another therapeutic modality, or travel around a roundabout of indefinite 'resourcing.' When we have thoughtfully and intentionally reached *Stage 2: Trauma Processing* work, contraindications for EMDR therapy have been addressed in proportion to the treatment plan. A personalized and nuanced approach to *Phase III: Assessment* and *Phases IV–VI: Reprocessing* will include established stabilization and closure strategies. This supports the pacing and safety of trauma processing, confirming consent, and ensuring containment when needed and at the end of each session.

Phase III: Assessment and Activation of the Target Memory

The initial steps of *Assessment* are to establish the scope and reconfirm consent regarding the memory or fragment to be activated and reprocessed. To establish the breadth of the target, we first confirm the treatment planning and target selection strategy that we are utilizing within EMDR therapy. Taking the example of the client who wants "to be able to go to sleep when the room is dark," the following options could be considered.

Broadest

The target is selected by activating and floating back from a recent (*Present* prong) experience of struggling to go to sleep while the room is dark. Using floatback or affect scan, the earliest and related *Past* experiences are identified. If multiple incidents are identified, the client and practitioner choose whether to begin with the earliest/touchstone or the worst/most disturbing memory. Once the target is confirmed, *Assessment* is completed with the intention of going into *Desensitization* immediately. Reprocessing could be restricted at first, with the possibility of allowing associations and generalization once the initial wave of disturbance has diminished.

Narrowest

A target is selected by choosing a *known* single incident that represents the first or worst experience related to darkness in the client's sleeping quarters. Proactive containment is offered, setting aside everything except the target memory. If possible, the timeline of the incident (beginning, middle, end) or BASK elements (behavior, affect, sensation, knowledge) may be identified. One piece of the timeline, sensory element, or fragment of experience is identified as the 'target within the target' or fractionated target. Consent is confirmed to work on this piece/element, containment may again be offered to set aside the other segments of the incident, and the client is invited to ground in the present moment and remember the train metaphor. Then *Assessment* is completed on the fractionated target. Once the elements of the target setup have been identified and the memory network activated, consent is confirmed once more before reminding the client of the train metaphor and stop signal, and then commencing *Desensitization*. Processing is restricted to minimize associations and generalization that would risk breaching the carefully facilitated containment.

The degree of titration of the target memory/fragment may be adjusted to align somewhere in between the examples offered above. Lighting up the memory network begins from the moment we turn our attention to establishing the target. For that reason, proceeding as directly as possible to *Desensitization* capitalizes on the spontaneous movement of the train that begins during *Assessment*, and we need to ensure that the scope of the target and speed of the train honor the consent given by the client and established readiness, etc.

Proactive containment can be utilized at multiple steps along the way to moderate the activation of traumatic material and narrow the scope of the target. This can be done through an established container and other distancing metaphors such as clearing the desk or viewing the memory material on a screen that is held by a remote-controlled drone and can be moved farther or brought closer. Employing grounding strategies and orienting clients to the train *before* engaging in target setup can also reduce anticipatory activation, increase agency in managing the current level of activation, and gain a clear read on the distress particular to the chosen target. If we employ proactive containment and/or fractionation of a target, the implication is that we will also restrict the scope of *Reprocessing*. Within the standard EMDR nomenclature, the most restricted processing is referred to as EMD (eye movement desensitization), and moderately restricted processing is called EMDr (E-M-D-little-r). The process and markers of each will be detailed below.

Establishing clarity and specificity regarding the *scope of the target* is supremely important – this is a juncture where many EMDR treatment plans go awry. It is common for clients to be ready to address an issue of trauma or abuse, and for the memory of it to be amorphous. That is, they don't know exactly when, where, or how many times an experience happened. Knowing is not *necessary*; however, we do need to know *what* our target is to confirm consent, have some confidence that we are activating what we intend to reprocess, and discern when and how to check the target and measure progress in later phases. For instance, if we can ascertain that there were several instances of sexual abuse during summer, and that two different camping experiences have come up in flashbacks, it would be helpful to distinguish the incident when running water could be heard outside the tent from the incident when it was windy outside.

Fractionation of targets refers to separating out aspects of an incident into multiple mini-targets to be processed individually. This can be done chronologically, according to BASK elements (Braun, 1988a, 1988b), by individual or clustered self-states, etc. Examples of chronological fractionation are found in EMDR protocols for recent traumatic events, where the timeline of the experience itself is gathered, then (usually) the 'worst' aspect is desensitized, followed by reevaluation of the timeline or targeting the remaining aspects systematically (see Shapiro, 2018, pp. 222–226). A protocol designed for recent events can be applied to fractionate processing of any incident.

This is not a new idea. Richard Kluft and Catherine Fine developed two styles of this approach, known respectively as the Fractionated Abreaction Technique (Kluft, 1988, 1990, 2013) and the Tactical Integration Model (Fine, 1991, 1999). Fine's model offers a structured, cognitively-based approach to pacing treatment, while Kluft's model is scenario-based and reflects his use of fractionation in hypnosis-facilitated trauma resolution. González et al. (2012, pp. 231–240) drew from these ideas in their development of the Tip of the Finger Strategy, which allows for graduated and progressive trauma processing in an EMDR therapy frame.

Whatever the breadth of the target, *Assessment* serves two primary purposes: Activation of the target memory network and orienting the 'train' in the desired (adaptive) direction. Most of the components intend to accomplish the first purpose; identification of the PC (positive cognition) and measuring the VoC (validity of the PC) aim to accomplish the second. Keeping these in mind, we may accept the client's responses to the standard script so long as those things seem to be happening – this is not the time to get perfectionistic about cognitions, or whether 'upset' is a proper emotion. It may be helpful to encourage clients to voice their first instinctual answer to each question and give themselves permission to set overthinking aside. The PC and VoC serve to orient the train to travel *through* the established target toward adaptive resolution; omission of the PC and VoC steps can implicitly convey that we are only going *into* the target memory. Many clients struggle to identify these when the target memory is becoming activated – that's okay. We can invite clients to choose from a brief menu to identify which domain best represents the belief that they would like to have about themselves in the future – is the desired PC more about being worthy or lovable, it not being my fault, being safe, or about having a sense of control or choice?

Despite our best efforts, sometimes we encounter 'red flags' in *Assessment* indicating that the activation of the memory network is either 'blocked' or has exceeded the client's Window of Tolerance (Siegel, 1999). If concerns such as the following are not easily resolved, this may indicate the need for further *Preparation* or *Stabilization* before proceeding to *Desensitization.*

- Inability to access or respond to questions may indicate hypo-arousal, avoidance, flooding, or other reliving of the incident (hyper-arousal).

Numbing can indicate hypo- and hyper-arousal. All could point to a need for proactive containment or fractionation of the target memory.
- Some mentalization is required to access and verbalize an NC or PC. Incongruent cognitions could indicate hypo-arousal or depersonalization has occurred, or that a self-state is thwarting access to that material. Clients who endorse 'all' of the cognitions on the sample list may be out of their Window of Tolerance.
- If clients cannot distinguish between *then* and *now*, even after being reminded to view the incident from the train, etc., then they may be more activated than either of you realizes.
- Rating the VoC and SUD (subjective unit of distress) numerically requires some metacognitive awareness. This may be challenging if clients are less mentally or emotionally flexible, in which case a visual or external rating scale may be helpful.
- Simple naming of the current emotional experience and the location of where the present distress is identifiable in the body is all that is needed. By this point in *Phase III*, the memory should be activated and heightened emotion evident. Absence of either could indicate inadequate consent by self-states or activation of a dissociative response (numbing, intellectualization, etc.).

If any steps of the basic target setup are missing or intolerable for clients, reevaluation of their readiness and your skills are recommended before proceeding. Gently pausing and containing what was activated will be your next step. When we are intending to titrate or otherwise contain processing, there may be an argument for excluding some elements of *Phase III: Assessment* (e.g., Twombly, 2010); however, I do not think that should be general practice. When *Assessment* is completed and there are no surprises, a quick confirmation of consent is in order before embarking on the *Reprocessing* of the agreed target.

Phases IV–VI: Reprocessing

The scope of the target as defined in *Assessment* is maintained in *Reprocessing* according to how we implement standard procedures once the train is moving. Procedures that influence the restriction vs. generalization of processing include the duration of the sets of BL-DAS, when or how often the practitioner checks the target and/or the SUD, when and how containment is employed, and when the 'stop signal' is utilized. Modification of the standard procedures of *Reprocessing* in the ways depicted in Figure 7.2 has evolved from several sources.

Most Restricted ←	**→ Most Generalized**
• Proactive containment is employed within session to set aside everything except target	• Containment is utilized between sessions according to standard procedure
• Target = fractionated – with multiple targets required to entirely process a memory/incident	• Target = the entire incident or experience (not fractionated)
• Stop signal is utilized when associations occur beyond the target, and at the client's discretion	• Stop signal is utilized at the client's discretion
• Sets of BL-DAS are shorter (5-20 passes)	• Sets of BL-DAS are standard (24 + passes)
• Target and/or SUD are checked frequently – as often as every set	• Target and/or SUD are checked only when processing reaches the end of a channel, or the target needs to be re-activated
• Associations are minimized, and generalization beyond the fragment or target is not expected	• Associations and generalization within and beyond the target memory are expected and welcome
• Appropriate for symptom relief	• Best for comprehensive treatment

Figure 7.2 Adjusting the Scope of Restricted Reprocessing.

Francine Shapiro's original EMD procedure involved checking the target and the SUD after every set of eye movements (see Shapiro, 2018, pp. 220–222). The focus of EMD is desensitization, with reprocessing being a secondary effect. EMD may be employed to restrict processing when the connectivity facilitated by associations and generalization of unrestricted reprocessing is judged to be detrimental to the client, or beyond the scope of the current consent or treatment plan.

We can think of the space between EMD and standard EMDR as a sliding door or zoom setting that can be adjusted across a continuum, as illustrated in Figure 7.3. Elan Shapiro and Bruit Laub (2008) have called this the 'telescopic processing' strategy.

We may continue in the 'zoomed-in' setting of EMD throughout processing of the target, or may 'zoom out' by lengthening sets, etc., if or when the client has settled in and we agree to allow associations and generalization. EMD may continue with successive incidents or fractionated targets until tolerance for accessing traumatic material and the desensitization process has been established.

Both the AIP model and more general research on memory reconsolidation (e.g., Elsey et al., 2018) emphasize how the integration of or associations to contrasting/adaptive information is essential for the memory and related symptoms to resolve (Shapiro, 2018, p. 38). When reprocessing is contained and restricted, fewer associations are allowed – which may prevent linkage to adaptive material. Additionally, when dissociative gaps exist between self-states, the sharing of knowledge and experience between self-states is necessarily reduced. This combination of factors highlights the need for more deliberate introductions or facilitation of connections,

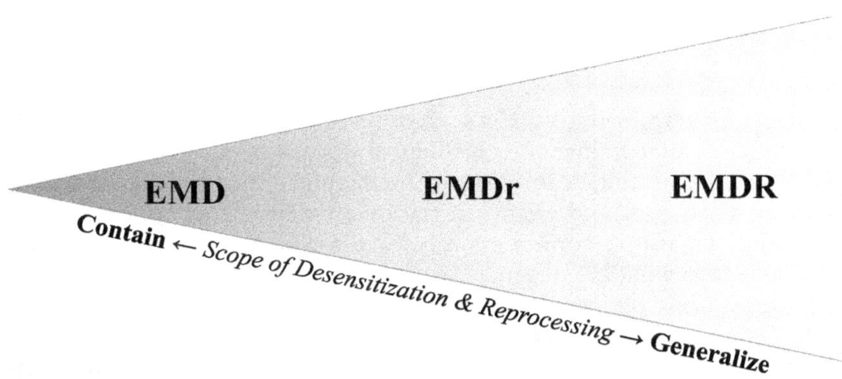

Figure 7.3 Scope of Desensitization and Reprocessing.

Sources: Adapted from E. Shapiro and Laub (2008).

according to when those associations (e.g., to the realization of related BASK material) are both needed and can be tolerated. *Interweaves* are one way to reach the contrasting and adaptive information in *Reprocessing* – when we are ready to intentionally promote functional connectivity.

Interweaves can take a number of forms beyond the standard cognitive and imaginal interweaves introduced in most EMDR basic trainings and Shapiro's textbook (e.g., the therapeutic interweave, Gilson & Caplan, 2000). The therapeutic relationship, the practitioner's presence, the client's internal self-system, previously developed resources, and integrative approaches (somatic, hypnotic, artistic, etc.) can all be sources or avenues of adaptive connections. Many authors and presenters have discussed each of those comprehensively. What we want to highlight here is the importance of knowing the client's own adaptive material and self-system. When working with a person who has significant dissociative symptoms, connection within self and to the present realities is both needed and may be actively thwarted by some self-states. A gentle, attuned, and personalized approach to offering interweaves is essential to ensure that we maintain a 'doing with' stance and avoid sliding into 'doing to.'

Upon reaching *Phases V* and *VI: Installation* and *Body Scan,* we confirm whether and to what degree linkage to adaptive material—that is, generalization—has occurred. In strict EMD, these phases are truncated or omitted; if the incident was fractionated, we may complete *Desensitization* on the entire incident before visiting *Installation* and *Body Scan.* If *Reprocessing* has been restricted, it may not be possible for the VoC to reach seven, or for the *Body Scan* to clear entirely. Nonetheless, we ought to try to reach a full-enough resolution by visiting the standard procedural steps, zooming in or out as necessary, and utilizing interweaves where possible. It is important not to leave a channel unprocessed and the SUD greater than zero or the VOC less than seven without a clear reason. My experience is that tremendous healing can occur between a SUD of two and zero. Facilitating realization of the trauma, functional connectivity between self-states, and easing all the inflammation from the proverbial wound allows it to become a scar – which is usually painless, though still a testament to what happened.

Modifications discussed above in *Desensitization* may apply here as well. Sets of BL-DAS may be shortened in *Installation* and *Body Scan* to limit associations. The brain will naturally move on to other material, and neighboring memory networks, along with associated self-states, may wish to interject if given the opportunity. Being clear about what our current target is (and is not) will help us to discern when an occluded channel has surfaced – and thus needs to be processed – versus when an association to a different memory network (and different target) has occurred (see Figure 7.4). We may need to assist the client to zoom in to see only the current target when measuring the VoC, for instance, and clarify that the felt-trueness is being measured related to this target or fragment *only*.

When multiple self-states were known to be part of the original experience and the reprocessing of this target, it may be helpful or even necessary to elicit the perspectives of each relevant self-state when reevaluating the

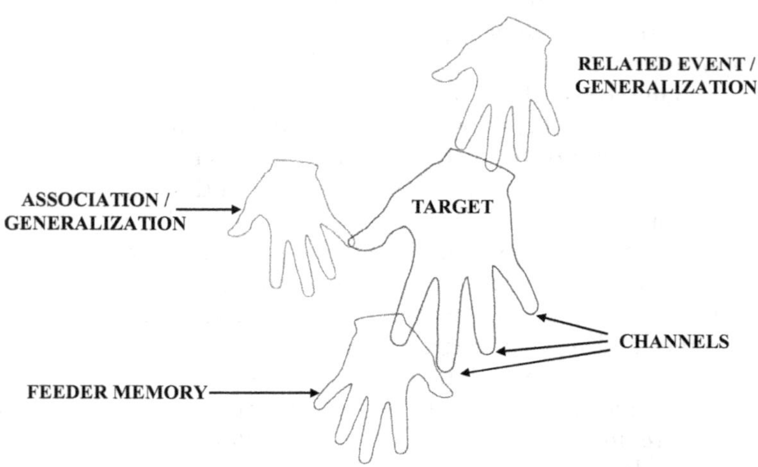

Figure 7.4 Relationships Between Memory Networks.

chosen PC, measuring the VoC, and during the *Body Scan*. Occasionally, self-states may prefer their own PC. Presuming that *Desensitization* was thoroughly complete, this ought to be a brief process and allow some generalization within the self-system.

Internal disagreement about the PC may arise, either in general or specifically about what verbiage feels 'okay' now. A few moments – or a few sessions – may be required to address internal conflict highlighted at this phase. This is important to ensure that functional connectivity is gained and sustained, both in the resolution of the targeted memory network and within the self-system that had previously worked around the unprocessed memory. For instance, a self-state that held the traumatic material related to the NC of 'I'm disgusting' may also maintain the attachment relationship to an unkind and dysregulated parent. It may be internally permissible for the client to feel neutral about the incident (SUD = 0), and it may have been okay to identify a PC in *Assessment*, but the possibility of the PC 'I'm okay as I am' feeling true is still completely unfathomable to this self-state. The self-state may argue that "It's true that I'm disgusting. I'm okay with that. My parent was right." How we proceed will depend upon the scope of processing. If the target was fractionated or reprocessing restricted, we may reach the collaborative decision to close that target and move into another layer of the treatment frame for now. However, if this target is part of a comprehensive treatment plan, taking time to address the internal conflict will be necessary before coming back to and completing full *Reprocessing* of the target.

Common Experiences and Challenges in Reprocessing

Experiences of *Phases IV–VI: Reprocessing* when dissociation is present are infinitely variable and unique. Nonetheless, we have noticed a few recurring themes that show up in our own practice, and the reported experiences of our peers and consultees.

Too Good to be True

Sometimes, *Desensitization* proceeds in an exceptionally linear fashion, with clients reporting on the scenery in exactly the sequence in which the event occurred (also mentioned in Chapter 4). This is often coupled with low emotional and/or somatic activation reported, and the SUD decreases gradually. What seems to happen in these instances is that *Reprocessing* is unintentionally restricted; the person's system or a self-state allows access to limited material – just one or two channels of information. A sense of depersonalization or a 'not me' perspective may also be evident between the self on the train and the self in the target memory. This may occur when the self-state that holds activation related to this memory does not show up for processing.

As a result, there is no generalization, spontaneous or otherwise, and usually little-to-no relief of present symptoms related to the target. Sometimes symptoms do change. For example, new emotional or somatic flashbacks or panic symptoms may emerge. Among other things, this probably means consent was inadequate. Additional mapping (Chapter 10) or a return to *Stabilization* and/or *Preparation* may be necessary before resuming processing of the intended target.

Abreaction, Overwhelm, or Ego State?

EMDR is an abreactive therapy, meaning that the *intentional* release and processing of intense emotion and sensation is welcomed. Abreaction is defined as "reexperiencing of the stimulated memory at a high level of disturbance" (Shapiro, 2018, p. 86). Intense emotion and/or body sensations are not required, necessarily, but are also not avoided. When practitioners do not understand this, struggle to tolerate strong emotion, or cannot discern whether the client's activation is problematic or not, they may brace against strong activation or even see intense emotion or sensation as an unequivocal 'red flag.' Shapiro helpfully outlines how to facilitate an abreaction (2018, p. 165); however, the word 'abreaction' also appears elsewhere in the text in the context of a client abruptly ending a session or discontinuing treatment. Thus, it is reasonable that EMDR trained therapists are confused.

Healing is possible when a strong emotional response is prepared for, accessed intentionally, and facilitated by the practitioner to ensure that the client is not reliving the incident or experiencing other antitherapeutic effects. Discerning between problematic reliving vs. the intentional release of pent-up toxins that will be propulsive (facilitating movement toward healing and integrated functioning) is very important. Some clients with DDs may experience some or all emotions or sensations to be intrusive or otherwise overwhelming – this may be because allowing feeling equates to realization of and connection to what happened at a deeper level.

Sometimes, what appears to be an abreaction may be the unplanned activation of one or more ego states. Ideally, this is an ego state holding very raw, intense emotion or sensation which simply needs to be released – and both the ego state, the person as a whole, and the clinician are ready for this. Other times, a highly motivated self-state may drive the train toward the traumatic memory material to the disregard and peril of others who are also on board, leading to panic or collapse. An ego state that holds material related to the target – and that did not consent to this processing – may pop out. Various ways in which ego states may come forward in *Reprocessing* are quite similar to how complex flashbacks are elaborated in Chapter 11.

Knowing your client, and that client's ability to report on current internal experience is essential. Hopefully, with that knowledge, you can discern and confirm that the high level of disturbance is propulsive in vivo. Indicators such as how clients' experiences and symptoms change following the session, whether the SUD decreases and stays low or neutral, or other indicators of connectivity, healing, and integrative functioning will ultimately provide confirmation.

Interweaves or Hypnotic Suggestion?

Interweaves are often necessary when engaging in *Reprocessing* with clients who have DDs; we do not debate that. However, we notice that some presenters lean on interweaving so heavily that it calls into question whether the treatment effects can be attributed to EMDR (the adaptive information processing (AIP) model and mechanisms related to BL-DAS) or whether what happens is a practitioner-directed process and a series of hypnotic suggestions. Remember, people who develop DDs are often highly hypnotizable and have developed autohypnotic ways of coping with internal and external stimuli (see Part I). When practitioners suggest or direct any action, they are likely riding on or working in the client's trance capacity, whether they realize it or not. Part IV will further address the topics of trance and hypnosis.

SUD Dilemmas – Process to Zero or Not?

Many people have argued or settled for a SUD of greater than zero in *Desensitization*, for vague reasons such as "the client said they cannot imagine it being less than a 2" or "well, it was such a horrible incident, it could never be a 0." Shapiro allows for an 'ecological' SUD (i.e., appropriate to the individual's circumstances; Shapiro, 2018, pp. 68, 151). We can do clients a disservice by not patiently persisting in allowing all the old pain and toxins related to a target memory to be released and reprocessed. Moving on too soon can leave a (psychological) wound only partially cleaned and healed – and prone to reinjury or reinfection. There are many reasons that clients may report a SUD of greater than zero, and it is important to discern why that is to make informed and effective decisions then and at later points in the treatment plan.

The most common reason is that the experience is objectively disturbing – a very terrible thing happened – and clients and/or practitioners think it would be unjust or dismissive to say that the SUD is zero or neutral. The SUD, however, is the measure of *subjective* units of disturbance and is intended to measure the gut punch or 'ouch' factor that the client feels, *now*, when they turn their attention to the target. Shapiro (2018, p. 59) cites Wolpe (1958) when introducing the SUD scale, making it clear that the concept refers to the individual's present level of distress – not whether the target is objectively disturbing. One way to clarify this with a client is to say:

> I understand that this was a very disturbing experience. It will always be a bad thing that happened, and I would be concerned if you told me otherwise! I'm wondering, if it were a physical wound, is it clean and just needs time to heal over, or is there still something that needs to be cleaned out for the wound to heal fully? ... (client response) ... How much does it hurt now – how would you rate that?

A similar metaphor can be applied for the VoC and body scan – a scar often remains after full reprocessing, but the PC ought not to sting when applied to the wound, and by the end of *Phase VI: Body Scan,* we hope to find no more pain in response to a light touch. If pain persists, the wound is not clean and will not remain closed.

If *Reprocessing* was restricted throughout, this may result in the SUD not decreasing to zero and other indicators of incomplete processing. Overlapping memory networks where one channel (part of a finger, in the hand metaphor, see Figure 7.4) overlaps with another incident may result in incomplete reprocessing until or unless the client is ready and consents to work on the other material. Restricted reprocessing also curtails associations and generalizations to adaptive material and present experience, and these combined factors may result in the best outcome being a SUD of more than zero (at least for now).

Self-states may play a role in maintaining gaps in functional connectivity or entirely thwart *Desensitization* and later phases. This may surface in the SUD stalling, etc. Recognizing this as the answer to why the SUD is not reducing to zero is important for many reasons. Appropriate responses can range from a brief acknowledgement that a previously unrecognized self-state is on the train to revisiting *Stabilization* or ego state work until consent and readiness can be (re)confirmed. In all cases, additional consent is needed before re-entering *Reprocessing.*

Realization in Reprocessing

Pathological dissociation is characteristically about gaps in functional connectivity that yield a sense of not knowing, not feeling, not realizing, disconnection from present self and realities, etc. *Trauma Processing* necessarily brings about a greater knowing, feeling, and/or realizing in some way. To the degree that the effects of *Reprocessing* generalize, it ought not be surprising that clients' present view of self, others, and the world will shift. Increased realization of the extent and/or effects of past experiences can evoke a wide range of responses.

A common outcome of *Reprocessing* in DDs is the realization and discovery of a lineage of self-states and associated targets. In the example of difficulty going to sleep in the dark, clients may realize not only the extent of sexual abuse and how it affected them *and* factors such as emotional abuse and neglect that left them vulnerable to this exploitation later in life, including the ways in which they have suffered because of these. Such a realization may be validating or provide an explanation for clients' pain and struggle. It may also feel overwhelming, and clients may need support to appropriately contain and process these realizations – both via EMDR therapy and other layers of the treatment frame.

A deep wave of grief is another common response to growing realization. This grief may be about what happened, existential and concrete losses, loss of time due to years of pain and disconnection from self and others, and loss of the idealized hope that the past could be different. Sometimes this realization also applies to their current life – perhaps discovering a need to make changes that are very difficult. This indicates that we have stepped foot in *Stage 3: Integrated Functioning* work, which will be addressed further in Chapter 8.

Measuring Progress and Moving Forward

Measuring progress occurs in but is not limited to *Phase VIII: Reevaluation*. In earlier chapters, we proposed that *Reevaluation* and the TICES log may be useful at the beginning of and between each session, respectively. This sets a pattern of tracking the effectiveness of *Closure* of the previous session and identifying patterns and changes in triggers and symptoms. A means of recognizing trends of symptoms and functioning is then established and helps to confirm or prompt reevaluation of the treatment plan, scope of *Reprocessing,* etc.

When the implementation of *Reprocessing* was quite narrow and oriented toward addressing one fragment or incident that was highly symptomatic, checking for generalization to the *Present* prong will likely bring us back to *Stage 1: Stabilization*. A return to *Stabilization* will include reassessment and reevaluation of the present symptoms, which involves checking for generalization in the *Present* prong. The treatment plan is reevaluated at that level before possibly revisiting *Preparation* in anticipation of a subsequent foray into *Trauma Processing* work.

Reevaluation will be nuanced toward selecting the remaining memory fragments or determining the appropriate range of *Reprocessing* for the next fragment or target memory, especially when *Reprocessing* has been restricted. When the *Past* prong target or sequence of target memories is reprocessed to the extent possible, it is important to both check and facilitate generalization to the *Present* and *Future* prongs. This will be the topic of Chapter 8. It is easy to forget or disregard those steps, especially when there are many past traumatic experiences clamoring for attention. However, even a tiny thread of generalization to the *Present* and *Future* can be incredibly ego-strengthening for clients – it is an opportunity that ought not be missed!

References

Braun, B. G. (1988a). The BASK model of dissociation. *Dissociation, 1*(1), 4–23. hdl.handle.net/1794/1276

Braun, B. G. (1988b). The BASK model of dissociation: Part II – treatment. *Dissociation, 1*(2), 16–23. hdl.handle.net/1794/1340

Dimitrova, L. I., Dean, Schi L., Schlumpf, Y. R., Vissia, E. M., Nijenhuis, E., Chatzi, V., Jäncke, L., Veltman, D. J., Chalavi, S., & Reinders, A. (2021). A neurostructural biomarker of dissociative amnesia: A hippocampal study in dissociative identity disorder. *Psychological Medicine*, *53*(3), 805–813. https://doi.org/10.1017/S0033291721002154

Elsey, J. W. B., Van Ast, V. A., & Kindt, M. (2018). Human memory reconsolidation: A guiding framework and critical review of the evidence. *Psychological Bulletin, 144*(8), 797–848. https://doi.org/10.1037/bul0000152

Fine, C. G. (1991). Treatment stabilization and crisis prevention: Pacing the therapy of the multiple personality disorder patient. *Psychiatric Clinics of North America, 14*(3), 661–675.

Fine C. G. (1999). The tactical-integration model for the treatment of dissociative identity disorder and allied dissociative disorders. *American Journal of Psychotherapy*, *53*(3), 361–376. https://doi.org/10.1176/appi.psychotherapy.1999.53.3.361

Gelinas, D. J. (2003). Integrating EMDR into phase-oriented treatment for trauma. *Journal of Trauma & Dissociation*, *4*(3), 91–135. https://doi.org/10.1300/J229v04n03_06

Gilson, G., & Kaplan, S. (2000). *The therapeutic interweave in EMDR: Before and beyond: A manual for EMDR trained clinicians.* EMDR Humanitarian Assistance Programs.

González, A., & Mosquera, D. (2012). *EMDR and dissociation: The progressive approach* (First Edition, Revised).

González, A., Mosquera, D. & Fisher, J. (2012). Trauma processing in structural dissociation. In A. González & D. Mosquera (Eds.), *EMDR and dissociation: The progressive approach* (pp. 220–252).

Jaffe, A. E., DiLillo, D., Gratz, K. L., & Messman-Moore, T. L. (2019). Risk for revictimization following interpersonal and noninterpersonal trauma: Clarifying the role of posttraumatic stress symptoms and trauma-related cognitions. *Journal of Traumatic Stress*, *32*(1), 42–55. https://doi.org/10.1002/jts.22372

Kluft, R. P. (1988). On treating the older patient with multiple personality disorder "Race against time" or "make haste slowly." *American Journal of Clinical Hypnosis, 30*(4), 257–266.

Kluft, R. P. (1990). The fractionated abreaction technique. In C. D. Hammond (Ed.), *Handbook of hypnotic suggestions* (pp. 527–528). Norton.

Kluft, R. P. (2013). *Shelter from the storm: Processing the traumatic memories of DID/DDNOS patients with the fractionated abreaction technique.* CreateSpace.

Korn, D. L., & Leeds, A. M. (2002). Preliminary evidence of efficacy for EMDR resource development and installation in the stabilization phase of treatment of complex posttraumatic stress disorder. *Journal of Clinical Psychology, 58,* 1465–1487.

Leeds, A. M. (1998). Lifting the burden of shame: Using EMDR resource installation to resolve a therapeutic impasse. In P. Manfield (Ed.), *Extending EMDR: A case book of innovative applications* (pp. 256–282). Norton.

Leeds, A. M. (2023). Foundations of the positive affect tolerance protocol: The central role of interpersonal positive affect in attachment and self-regulation. *Journal of EMDR Practice and Research, 17*(3), 139–158. https://doi.org/10.1891/EMDR-2023-0006

Parnell, L. (2013). *Attachment-focused EMDR: Healing relational trauma.* W. W. Norton & Co.

Paulsen, S. L. (2009). *Looking through the eyes of trauma and dissociation: An illustrated guide for EMDR clinicians and clients.* Booksurge.

Pezzoli, P., Pingault, J. B., Eley, T. C., McCrory, E. & Viding, E. (2025). Causal and common risk pathways linking childhood maltreatment to later intimate partner violence victimization. *Molecular Psychiatry, 30*, 2027–2037. https://doi.org/10.1038/s41380-024-02813-0

Schmidt, S. J., & Hernandez, A. (2007). The developmental needs meeting strategy: Eight case studies. *Traumatology, 13*(1), 27–48. https://doi.org/10.1177/1534765607299913

Shapiro, E. (2009). *Four elements exercise for stress management.* In M. Luber (Ed.), *Eye movement desensitization and reprocessing (EMDR) scripted protocols: Basics and special situations* (pp. 73–79). Springer.

Shapiro, E., & Laub, B. (2008). Early EMDR intervention (EEI): A summary, a theoretical Model, and the recent traumatic episode protocol (R-TEP). *Journal of EMDR Practice and Research,* 2(2), 79–96. https://doi.org/10.1891/1933-3196.2.2.79

Shapiro, F. (2018). *Eye movement desensitization and reprocessing (EMDR) therapy: Basic principles, protocols and procedures.* (3rd ed.). The Guilford Press.

Siegel, D. J. (1999). *The developing mind: Toward a neurobiology of interpersonal experience.* The Guilford Press.

Twombly, J. (2010). Initial targeting of traumatic material: Steps. In M. Luber (Ed.), *Eye movement desensitization (EMDR) scripted protocols: Special populations* (pp. 297–311). Springer Publishing Company.

Wolpe, J. (1958). *Psychotherapy by reciprocal inhibition.* Stanford University Press.

Xiao, Z., Murat Baldwin, M., Wong, S. C., Obsuth, I., Meinck, F., & Murray, A. L. (2023). The impact of childhood psychological maltreatment on mental health outcomes in adulthood: A systematic review and meta-analysis. *Trauma, Violence & Abuse*, *24*(5), 3049–3064. https://doi.org/10.1177/15248380221122816

Chapter 8

Present and Future Prongs in the Three-Stage Model

Jennifer A. Madere

Introduction

Addressing all three prongs – past, present, and future – can be challenging for EMDR practitioners, especially when working with clients who have histories of complex trauma and current dissociative symptoms. Current crises may dominate the focus of sessions, delaying or preventing entry into *Stage 2: Trauma Processing*. Alternatively, seemingly endless reprocessing of past traumas may lead practitioners to lose sight of the present and future prongs entirely. When treatment plans are abandoned in *Past* prong, and therefore incomplete, wounded memory networks may remain open and leave the client vulnerable to discouragement, (re)traumatization, or both.

These challenges are not unique to working with complex trauma and dissociative disorders (DDs). In Shapiro's (2018) text and in accredited basic training programs, the present and future prongs receive comparatively little emphasis. While accredited training in EMDR therapy must address all three prongs within supervised practice hours, integrating this knowledge into practice is missing for many new learners of EMDR therapy. This may be due to learners struggling to absorb lots of information, and trainers' inadequate attention to the material, among other reasons. We have observed that EMDR practitioners often struggle to effectively conceptualize and complete all three prongs, except in the most straightforward, single-incident treatment plans. EMDR-trained practitioners seem to need additional guidance or advanced consultation to address uncertainties about their skills and gain clarity about the importance of completing all three prongs. Without this clarity, practitioners report being apt to haphazardly shift to new targets or abandon them rather than revise an initial treatment plan as a matter of course. There can be valid reasons to do both of these things, but neither should be the norm.

To address these challenges, two potential solutions within the framework of this book include:

DOI: 10.4324/9781003410201-11

1. Integrating EMDR into an expanded AIP model (Chapter 2) and layered conceptual framework (Chapter 3); and
2. Working in *Present* and *Future* prongs in ways that do not directly flow from the *Past* prong.

Entering the trauma processing layer of our framework – in this case, EMDR therapy – with the *Present* and *Future* prongs in mind fosters a collaborative and effective treatment relationship. It is important that we – both practitioner and client – know *why* we are doing what we're doing, especially when it comes to accessing and (re)processing traumatic experiences.

This chapter will explore how the *Present* and *Future* prongs of EMDR can be incorporated into a broader framework, such as ego state therapy and the three-stage model of treatment for complex trauma and DDs. Sometimes addressing all three prongs sequentially is not indicated – at least not at once. By embedding EMDR therapy within our layered framework, we can draw from its phases and protocols to achieve a variety of therapeutic goals, including and beyond the standard objective of fully resolving a memory network from *Past* prong to *Present* to *Future*.

Past, Present, or Future? What Is Our Starting Point?

It is easy to assume that both the client and the practitioner are starting therapeutic work in the same 'present.' When complex trauma and/or DDs are in the mix, however, that is less likely to be 100% true. Some self-states may not be oriented to present realities but instead feel trapped in a past when their traumatic experience(s) are still happening. Other clients or self-states may be hyper-focused on an anticipated future threat – but is that a clear future-focus, or a flashback from the past clouding their perception of the future? Thus, it is important to assess at what point(s) we are starting.

Establishing a common frame of reference for what 'present' is, and determining which self-states may not share it, is crucial because the present is where the therapeutic alliance is formed, goals are established, and informed consent is obtained (see Chapters 10 and 11). I have noticed that various theories and models of psychotherapy have a bias toward focusing on one temporal domain or another – past, present, or future.

Food for Thought

- What is my natural or professional focus?
- When is it difficult to start in the present?

- Where is the client focused?
- How can we arrive at a collaborative or even a unified focus?

What Did Francine Shapiro Say?

Shapiro (2018) described working in the *Present* prong "when a reevaluation of the past events related to an area of dysfunction indicates that they have been sufficiently resolved" (p. 199). She describes *Present* prong work as serving three basic functions:

a) to identify and log present symptoms and experience to use in float-back or affect scan;
b) to monitor and check for generalization of past prong reprocessing and resolution of dysfunction stemming from past experiences; and
c) to identify areas in which the client may need skill-building and education to cope with present realities (Shapiro, 2018, pp. 199–202).

Shapiro (2018) discusses the *Future* prong in a linear fashion as following immediately after any undue distress in response to present stimuli has been addressed, related to the past prong experiences (pp. 203–207). It is easy to view the *Future* prong and *Future Template* as a simple 'quality control check' to ensure generalization of the reprocessing of *Past* and *Present* prongs. While that is true for standard procedures in a three-prong treatment plan, Francine emphasized the importance of attention to the *Future* prong, especially with issues that are more longstanding, complex, and/or relational.

> This third prong of the EMDR therapy protocol includes adequate education, modeling, and imagining in conjunction with EMDR targeting to allow the client to respond differently in the future. The clinician should help the client assimilate new information and provide her with experiences to help ensure future successes. The third prong of the EMDR standard protocol is a vital aspect of treatment. (Shapiro, 2018, p. 203)

My experience aptly mirrors Shapiro's description. When clients report that they 'did EMDR before' addressing an incident or issue, *and* they report still experiencing discrete symptoms related to it (e.g., flashbacks, nightmares, avoiding reminders), I have often been able to verify that *Present* and/or *Future* prongs were never completed in the prior treatment. Without *Future* prong work, clients' view of self, present experience, relational functioning, and outlook may not change in the ways that they hoped it would after reprocessing of the past traumatic experience(s). Full completion of a standard EMDR treatment plan involves attending to *all three prongs*. Sometimes this involves multiple targets in each prong as

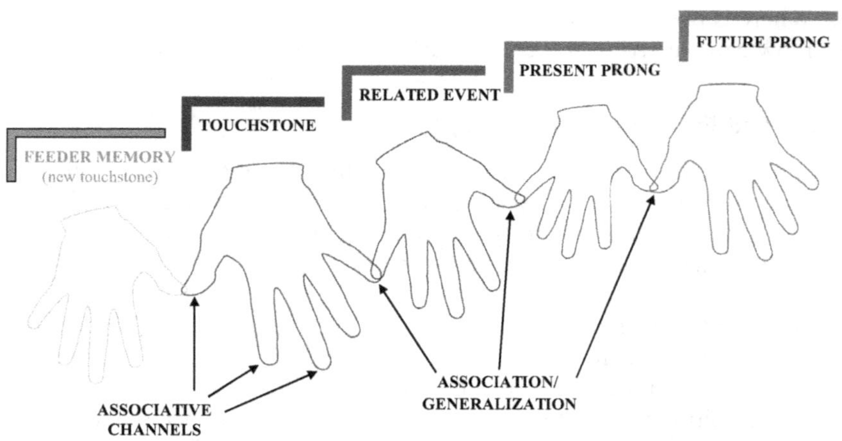

Figure 8.1 Lineage of a Standard Three-Prong Treatment Plan in EMDR Therapy.

depicted in Figure 8.1: The hands represent the entire memory network associated with each target, circles within each represent the node or aspect of the target – whole or fractionated – identified in *Phase III: Assessment.*

While the figure above appears clean and straightforward, we know that in practice it often looks different, especially when complex trauma and DDs are present. Frequently, reprocessing may uncover feeder memories that are earlier than the previously conceived touchstone memory, thus elongating the sequence of the treatment plan. The 'new touchstone' may need to be addressed for comprehensive treatment goals to be attained. Numerous intertwined memory networks could be represented by hands branching off in every direction. When DDs are present, there may be significant amnestic gaps or fissures in the lineage. These examples are why it is helpful – and sometimes necessary – to think beyond the standard EMDR paradigm.

Perspectives from the EMDR Literature

Trainers and consultants have wrestled with how to address *Present* and *Future* prongs more effectively, and how to teach others to do so. A revised worksheet set (published in Luber, 2019) offers a detailed process to check for generalization to the *Future* prong related to significant people/relationships and significant situations. Practitioners may benefit from being guided through the process of completing *Future* prong, despite its strongly cognitive approach.

Several established interventions offer opportunities for creative and nuanced approaches to working in *Present* and *Future* prongs. All assume that clients tolerate bilateral dual attention stimulation (BL-DAS) well. Most of the relevant literature applicable to DDs can be sorted into four buckets: resource development installation, affect tolerance, protocols for recent and critical incidents, and alternate approaches to work in the *Future* prong.

Resource Development

As described in Chapter 7, resource development and installation (RDI; Korn & Leeds, 2002; Leeds, 1998; Shapiro, 2018, pp. 248–250) was developed specifically for the purpose of stabilizing clients with complex presentations. A real or imagined resource may be drawn from the client's past or present experience to support stabilization and/or prepare for reprocessing. The standard script includes future rehearsal of using the resource in an anticipated scenario (Shapiro, 2018, p. 250), which holds promise for application to the context of both *Stage 1: Stabilization* and *Stage 3: Integrated Functioning*. Many creative opportunities may be found even when the aim is not preparation for trauma processing. For instance, in *Stage 1*, RDI can support identification and accessing of resource material to build a sense of hope, efficacy, balance, and ego strength. In *Stage 3*, RDI offers a template to prepare for and rehearse scenarios to bolster clients' growing sense of integrated functioning. The method of constant installation of present orientation and safety (CIPOS), developed by Jim Knipe (2010), leverages clients' subjective experience of being present in the current reality (e.g., the practitioner's office) as a resource, proceeding in a structured fashion to help clients become oriented and gain or sustain dual attention. CIPOS was designed for stabilization in preparation for trauma reprocessing but can be utilized in *Stage 1* as a discrete, present prong intervention.

Affect Tolerance

Affect tolerance protocols focus on clients' present experience of affect, physical sensation, etc., and aim to increase their capacity to tolerate it. This focus is most applicable for *Present* prong and *Stage 1* work. The basic steps for targeting a pleasant or unpleasant feeling state, attributed to the work of Andrew Leeds (2015) and Carol York (2001), are as follows:

1. Identify the emotion/sensation based on a present or recent experience (the internal feeling state is the target).

2. Identify the picture, or discomfort associated with the feeling.
3. Set up the target according to normal *Phase III: Assessment* – instead of 'incident' refer to the target as 'when you feel this way.'
4. Enter *Desensitization* normally, restricting the scope of processing if necessary. The goal is to decrease the SUD (subjective units of distress) level by 2–3 points.
5. Installation may be done (or skipped). If so, proceed normally, for a few sets (VoC may not reach 6–7).
6. Skip body scan, proceed to closure, or resume previous course of treatment.

Other, similar strategies have been presented by Dolores Mosquera (Spain), focusing on the brief processing of an activated defense as the present experience (e.g., Mosquera & González, 2014; Mosquera & Ross, 2016). Leeds has further developed his approach in the direction of helping clients increase their tolerance of shared positive affect in a relational context – such as receiving a compliment (Leeds, 2022).

Protocols for Recent and Critical Incidents

Protocols for recent and ongoing critical incidents are intentionally designed to bypass the *Past* prong in favor of providing psychological first aid – or, in our framework, contained processing in service of stabilization. The fractionation and containment built into these protocols lower the odds of activating past/feeder memory material. This makes them well-suited for use with clients who have a seemingly never-ending series of unfortunate, tragic, and traumatic experiences in their daily life. My personal favorite is the set of protocols developed by Ignacio Jarero, Lucina Artigas (Mexico), and colleagues: protocol for recent critical incidents (PRECI, Jarero et al., 2011), and acute stress syndrome stabilization (ASSYST, Becker et al., 2021). Their recommendation of self-administered tactile BL-DAS, manner of identifying the focus of processing, and attention to present activation in the body are gentle and tend toward fostering clients' ego strength throughout. Moreover, these approaches allow for attending to a present or ongoing situation for a session or two without requiring a commitment to reprocessing an entire target or three-prong treatment plan.

Alternate Approaches to Future Prong

The inverted protocol (Hofmann, 2010) and the flashforward procedure (Logie & de Jongh, 2014) both offer alternative ways to approach the *Future* prong. Arne Hofmann developed the inverted protocol as a structured way to assist clients who meet criteria for complex posttraumatic stress disorder (PTSD) and are currently unstable (requiring psychiatric hospitalization, etc.). The inverted protocol begins with the *Future* prong to address triggering situations and relationships that compromise clients' stability. Then, attention shifts to *Present* prong to address secondary targets that impede functioning or trigger symptoms. Finally, preparation and readiness criteria are proposed for when and how *Past* prong targets may be approached without decompensation. Restricted processing, CIPOS, RDI, and other interventions that have been developed in or adopted into the EMDR literature are utilized throughout the three prongs of the inverted protocol.

The flashforward procedure was developed by Robin Logie and Ad de Jongh to treat anticipatory fears. Originally, it was intended to address fears that remain after a standard three-prong treatment plan has been completed. It guides the reprocessing of the client's mental representation of a future catastrophic event, including any irrational or improbable worst-case scenario. Because it presumes that the *Past* prong has already been completed, and that a high level of distress may be associated with the feared scenario, some modification and/or containment may be required for the flashforward procedure to be employed in other contexts. Nonetheless, it provides a template for processing irrational, future-focused fears that are held by a self-state – when the time is right.

All the above interventions – and many more that are not specifically listed – can be helpful when applied with awareness and knowledge of how dissociation works, and how the specific client experiences dissociation. None of those same interventions ought to be employed without those prerequisites. Remember, all interventions are dangerous when you do not know your client (Kinsler, 2018).

The Three-Stage Model and the Three Prongs

The process of therapy in the three-stage relational model starts in the present, or wherever the client is at. It ultimately aims to accomplish integrated functioning, or internal and external congruence, that is increasingly oriented to present realities, via many mechanisms including psychodynamic processing and gradually increasing realization (Yeates et al., 2024; Van der Hart et al., 1993). I see realization and functional connectivity as complementary, if not synonymous, as each seems to beget the other. Whichever term we use, this process spans all three treatment stages as clients' abilities to recognize experience as 'mine' (or at least the experience of a part of me) increase. This occurs as self-states' knowledge, felt experience, and behaviors become increasingly connected to one another and a shared orientation to and recognition of present reality. According to Van der Hart et al. (1993), "The total process of therapy, moving as it does inexorably towards integration, may, thus also be described in terms of increasing realization" (p. 169).

Present prong usually sits within *Stage 1: Stabilization* and *Future* prong within *Stage 3: Integrated Functioning*; however, the stages are not linear. *Stage 3* is always happening – or ought to be – as increasing realization, connection to one's present experience and realities, and the practitioner's skilled support holds the space for integrative processes. The associative motor of BL-DAS also promotes integration and functional connectivity (see Chapter 2). Throughout every layer of the treatment frame, pacing is important to ensure that we do not try to force realization (which can yield sensitization or re-traumatization) or integration (which may reinforce or prematurely bridge dissociative gaps).

Dissociative Phobias

Pierre Janet (1904) and more recently Steele et al. (2005) and others have identified trauma-related (dissociative) phobias, the presence of which are observed to maintain symptoms and prevent realization, connectivity, and integrated functioning. Awareness of phobias can normalize what is happening in the therapeutic process and help both practitioner and client orient to gradually – and often repeatedly – overcoming them. Steele et al. (2005, p. 28) propose this alignment of the dissociative phobias with the three stages.

Stage 1: Stabilization

- Phobia of attachment and attachment loss with the therapist
- Phobia of mental contents (thoughts, emotions, sensations)
- Phobia of self-states

Stage 2: Trauma Processing

- Phobia of traumatic memories
- Phobias related to insecure attachment to the perpetrator(s)
- Phobia of attachment and attachment loss with the therapist (termination)

Stage 3: Integrated Functioning

- Phobia of normal/present life
- Phobia of healthy risk-taking and change
- Phobia of intimacy

Comprehensive treatment will address all the stages and phobias outlined above, gradually and recursively, as discussed in Chapter 3. In Part IV, Michael will more thoroughly address this work from the perspective of ego state therapies, facilitating internal and external differentiation that is also flexible – knowing and feeling externally or internally what *is* mine, while also gaining separation from what is *not* present and/or what is *not* mine. EMDR therapy interventions and BL-DAS may be employed to soften manifestations of each phobia by applying strategies and interventions such as those outlined previously, customized to fit clients' needs. This focus may enhance 'positive' and pleasant experiences – or increase the client's tolerance of and access to them – to build a fuller and more balanced realization of one's range of experience.

Premature confrontation of dissociative phobias may backfire. Informed by Sidis's perspective (Chapter 2), this may occur if a self-state perceives that the trauma is still happening or the toxin that precipitated the phobia is still within, as with a perpetrator introject (see Chapter 12). When one or more self-states perceive that the trauma is still happening, or deny that it happened, this indicates that there is a gap in synthesis and/or realization. Full realization and movement toward integrated functioning are understood to occur when the person realizes that it happened, it happened to them (personification) and it happened in the past (presentification) (see Van der Hart et al., 2010). In our framework, ego state work helps clarify, navigate, and soften dissociative phobias to assist in moving through all three Stages. EMDR then provides the means to metabolize and release the toxins that contribute(d) to the development of the phobias.

Stabilization and the Three Prongs

We assess clients' need for *Stabilization* by identifying and measuring current symptoms, ability to form a therapeutic alliance, among other factors, all in the present moment. Sometimes this is with an eye toward engaging in *Trauma Processing* of *Past* material, other times it involves the client's view of the future. The trajectory of a client's healing journey is sometimes readily apparent in a readiness to grow in a sense of agency, access to and tolerance of BASK material (Braun, 1988a, 1988b), and demonstration of other signs of ego strength (see treatment trajectories, Chapter 6). Conversely, some clients' sense of agency, tolerance of BASK elements, etc., is so minimal or rigid that there is little room for movement.

For example, I may ask about a client's morning routine as a sample of everyday functioning. Sleep problems are pervasive among people with complex trauma and DDs, so this can be a good example of how clients navigate a challenging time in their day (e.g., Dimitrova et al., 2020).

I listen for awareness and capacity to cultivate a sense of stability in self-care, or sameness to begin the day. Clients may share about how it takes them a while to get started, but after a cup of coffee or tea and some routine activities, they begin to feel okay. In contrast, other clients may perceive that their day is ruined if sleep is disrupted and seem to be 'comfortable' with the apparent homeostasis of chaos or unaware of how they move through each day. This kind of information informs our discernment of the pace and depth of treatment.

Stabilization work in the *Present* prong is commonly appropriate before and after entering *Trauma Processing*. While similar to the standard *Preparation* phase of EMDR, the purpose can be distinct. This entails checking for informed consent amongst the self-system, evaluating what connectivity, generalization, or realization can be tolerated or has occurred, and addressing any destabilization that occurs when the proverbial foundation shifts after *Reprocessing*. Change in homeostasis is often frightening to self-states. When this is the case, focus may remain on *Stage 1* work to the extent that this change involves awareness of 'new' mental contents, emotions, self-states, attachment patterns, etc. For example, the 'fight' response and accompanying rage and anger that had been previously thwarted or inaccessible. Monitoring symptoms and relationships among self-states via the TICES log, mapping, and other strategies will help us keep treatment on track. Affect tolerance and RDI with future rehearsal may help clients tolerate and embrace newfound access to their action systems.

Present prong focus during *Stabilization* may reveal signs of gaps in connectivity and/or intrusions of unprocessed, symptomatic memory material – and the self-states holding this experience. When an episode of stabilization is effective and the proverbial dust of chaos begins to settle, specific triggers or themes become more apparent. Detecting patterns of responses and artful use of the TICES log, mapping, and working with self-states will guide the way toward the (next) foray into *Trauma Processing*. For instance, clients who establish an effective morning routine may discover that their response to certain nightmares can be easily soothed, while other symptoms are not as easily navigated. The latter symptoms and associated self-states and/or BASK elements may highlight where *Stage 2* work – involving any of the three prongs – is needed to sustain stabilization. Specific assessment, history taking, and ego state work will guide subsequent adaptation of the treatment plan.

Stabilization work in the *Present* prong may also flow into *Integrated Functioning* as adaptive connectivity and self-care strategies solidify. Effective stabilization supports clients in building a new relationship with and amongst self-states and learning to plan for today or tomorrow rather than for yesterday. Sometimes clients struggle to allow themselves to have a view of the future at all! Many clients have said that they did not plan to live this long, and thinking of the future may evoke suicidal parts. Working with phobias related to daily life, etc., bridges us into *Stage 3*. In the EMDR layer of our frame, RDI focused on experiences of efficacy and enjoyment, with future rehearsal, may fit here. If catastrophic fears persist, and the associated self-states consent, the flashforward procedure may be useful at this juncture (Logie & de Jongh, 2014). Ego state therapies offer many strategies for updating self-states, revising their job descriptions, etc. For more on this topic, refer to Part IV.

Integrated Functioning and the Three Prongs

Stage 3: Integrated Functioning most directly entails working to increase the degree to which clients are oriented to and functioning in accord with the realities of present life. Learning to tolerate change and risk-taking in ways that are congruent with health and engagement in relationships outside of the psychotherapeutic context are common features of this stage. Remember, though, the three stages are recursive.

'Realization' was depicted in Figure 3.2 as most often corresponding to *Future* prong and *Stage 3*, as a point of arrival or signpost of completion. Realization is a multidimensional factor – a multistage factor, even – defined as "the degree to which individuals become consciously aware of the implications and meaning of their personal experiences" (Steele et al., 2005, p. 23). In persons with DDs, a gap in realization corresponds to amnesia for what other self-states are doing. When functional connectivity increases, more top-down access and control are available. This allows realization to occur; now, what one knows, what one feels, and what one does are (more) congruent.

Occasionally, treatment seems to begin in *Stage 3*. Over the years, I have encountered several clients who placidly endorse a horrific past, and state that they only want to look forward – the past does not matter to them, it's old news. The goal in seeking therapy is often to cope with a career setback and get back on track as soon as possible. However, they chose – or perhaps someone referred them to – a psychotherapist who specializes in working with complex trauma and dissociation. Hmm. Before challenging these clients, I have asked about their current functioning, specifically listening for tolerance of change, attitudes toward risk, and patterns in relationships. Often, the lives of these people have the appearance of stability and success but are quite rigid. The recent setback has exposed a crack in the façade – perhaps revealing a self-state that was 'driving' based upon experiences other than the present situation. Gentle exploration of present or recent experience can yield beginning realizations of this. From there, we may proceed to stabilization, or another direction, depending on what the client is willing to do next.

Across the Three Stages: Relationship with Self

A unifying concept across the three stages and three prongs is the client's relationship with(in) self. Complex, early, and relational trauma tend to disrupt the formation of our sense of self, and our relationship with self and others as we proceed through life. This disruption shows up in the levels of personality organization and mental functioning, such as patterns of idealization and devaluation of self (and others) (see Lingiardi & McWilliams, 2017). Disruption in the person's self-organization may be depicted in the *Criterion B* and *Schneiderian First-Rank Symptom Scales* on the *Multidimensional Inventory of Dissociation* (Dell, 2006), which assess the extent to which the client endorses intrusive experiences, including emotions, sensations, thoughts, and actions.

Relationships within the self-system also influence a person's understanding of how the story of the past is told via internal and external relationship patterns. Self-awareness, a close neighbor to realization, must also grow as clients begin to realize more of how the past affected them, and continues to affect them. Much of *Stabilization* has to do with helping clients to realize their own needs and experiences enough to quell the chaos that emerges from unmet and dismissed needs, especially when the pattern of dismissing needs continues intrapersonally. A tool called the *Self Care Scale* was developed by Anabel González-Vazquez and colleagues (2018) to assess clients' attitudes and practices related to self-care that often get missed. It provides an opportunity to validate and deepen clients' perceptions of self-care, highlighting areas in which psychological needs continue to be unmet.

The idea of having needs at all has been terrifying to many of my clients. A statement that has helped some to overcome this 'phobia of having needs' is: "I need _____ in order to _____." A purpose or reason for the need can make it more tolerable and build toward increasingly integrated functioning. A series of statements may be needed to bridge the gap between the immediate need or self-care strategy to clients' most concrete or generalized goals. For example:

I need to drink water in order for my brain and body to work properly.
I need my brain and body to work properly in order to accomplish my tasks at work.
I need to accomplish my tasks at work in order to keep my job.
I need to keep my job in order to.

Allowing realization of needs often brings a new wave of grief regarding unmet needs in the past. Recollection of times when needs have been acknowledged or met may also be prompted. Both experiences can be approached and incorporated in the EMDR or ego state frame to increase realization, tolerance, and access to the new(ly discovered) knowledge and experience.

A series of sessions focused on realization and stabilization in relationship(s) with(in) self can be enough to quell the symptoms that brought clients to therapy. Some may choose to conclude treatment at this point. If treatment continues, stabilizing the client's internal relationship/s will clarify where trauma processing is needed. When clients have improved stability in their basic daily functioning, and greater awareness of what is 'mine' and truly 'not mine,' any persisting intrusive symptoms more clearly illuminate gaps or interruptions in functional connectivity that require further attention.

Case Example

An adult female client was referred to me upon reaching a 'stuck' point in resolving post-partum mood disturbance. While no explicit trauma or ACES were endorsed, she reported a history of suicide attempts, treatment for major depression with psychotic features, and generalized anxiety. The 'psychotic features' referred to voices that told her to harm or kill herself, and episodes of 'paranoid rage.' The referring practitioner and client reported that she would 'dissociate' whenever they tried to work with experiences of anger or shame.

The client reported being discouraged with therapy, saying "What's the point of therapy when it doesn't help. Can I ever get better?" She reported a tendency to ruminate on the past, and disconnection with others due to this – her spouse and close friends had heard it all before, but her childhood "wasn't that bad" and she felt helpless to be anything other than a burden. We agreed to a treatment plan focused on stabilization and improving her relationship with herself. She mentioned that breathing and grounding strategies had been effective in the past, so we incorporated these into our routine for the closure of sessions, starting at the first meeting.

A diagnostic evaluation using the MID indicated that the client met criteria for an unspecified DD and complex PTSD. During periods of 'rumination' the client would 'space out'; however, no clear indications of full amnesia or full switching in executive control were evident. Due to low ego strength and past treatments that were largely unsuccessful, I suspected that some focus on stabilization and relationship within self may be helpful and illuminate any subsequent steps.

We used her responses to the MID and recent interactions in close relationships to begin to map out her internal and emotional experiences (see Chapter 10). She responded well to seeing 'inside my head' illustrated on a whiteboard in session and agreed to observe her experience throughout the next week to identify what was accurate, inaccurate, or missing. As a result of these observations, I began to wonder out loud whether the experiences of anger and self-loathing might be 'emotional flashbacks' (see Chapter 11). I introduced BL-DAS during one session to see how she responded to it – we found that manual eye movements and the butterfly hug were tolerable, at least initially. I explained that we might use them sometimes and took the opportunity to underscore this preparedness and offer a bit of increased hope to her outlook for therapy.

Significant self-neglect and reluctance to ask for help when she needed it became evident as key areas to address in *Stage 1: Stabilization*. Through careful conversation, we identified that she acknowledged 'eating enough protein' as a legitimate physical need, based on her academic knowledge and personal experience, and was willing to pay extra or make a request in order to meet that need. We enhanced this experience of 'it's okay to need protein' with a brief application of RDI. Finding that resource to be robust, we were able to generalize it to consider what the equivalent of 'protein' might be in her emotional and relational health.

One day, she reached out for an extra session. The neighbor's house had burned down the previous night, and she said, 'I'm not okay.' After a brief moment of grounding, we agreed to process this using a strategy from EMDR therapy, and the butterfly hug (PRECI). I assured her that I thought we could scoop this experience off the top and keep it from adding to her emotional load of past memories. She responded well to PRECI, and I restricted the scope of Reprocessing by keeping sets short and going back to the target often. We completed processing of the event that session. The next session, she mentioned some 'rumination' in response to sirens and fears of what could have happened to her children. I used the flashforward framework to help her process this (still with the butterfly hug, to prevent activation of past memory material).

Over time, she reported taking opportunities for self-care – the emotional equivalent of 'protein' – when she saw the opportunity rather than waiting until she felt desperate. Some future rehearsal built on this sense of knowing, and tending to her needs helped her to prepare for a family reunion and navigate it without undue distress. The self-loathing, or self-hatred, as she has come to call it, likely stems from her early and ongoing interactions with her parents (complex trauma). Her realization of the relational trauma that she experienced is growing and she is increasingly able to see this as validation of her experience rather than proof that she is 'broken.' It is not yet clear whether we will be able to address Past prong memories directly with EMDR, or whether an introject will need to be addressed first (see Chapter 12). I have a sense that the direction will soon become clear.

Conclusions

Present prong focus can apply before or after reprocessing of the *Past* prong to address any destabilization that occurs when the 'foundation' shifts. Incorporating new views of self and others and making intentional and adaptive decisions in life and relationships takes place most clearly in the *Present* prong. This includes the therapeutic relationship, dissociative phobias, and psychodynamics that are central to the comprehensive treatment of complex trauma and DDs.

Working in the *Future* prong may follow completion of other prongs, be visited at the end of resource development, and occur in advance of a challenging situation at the service of *Stabilization* and *Integrated Functioning*. *Future* prong work may be useful even when trauma processing does not occur. *Trauma Processing* is not always necessary to meet a specific client's goals. Other approaches, including ego state therapies and a focus on stabilization and integrated functioning, may be needed instead.

Spontaneous integration of past and present experiences within one's view of self and the future is a normal and expected product of *Trauma Processing* in the EMDR therapy frame. This is adaptive resolution – and enables symptom relief *when* the person is ready for it. In EMDR, adaptive resolution via reprocessing of any prong relies on some generalization and functional connectivity. To the degree that connection between self-states and/or memory networks that hold the activating material can be maintained, we believe that adaptive resolution can occur. However, when the mechanisms that support adaptive resolution are inhibited or thwarted, resolution and generalization are necessarily limited (see Chapter 2), and other layers of our framework are needed.

References

Becker, Y., Estevez, M. E., Perez, M. C., Osorio, A., Jarero, I., & Givaudan, M. (2021). Longitudinal multisite randomized controlled trial on the provision of the acute stress syndrome stabilization remote for groups to general population in lockdown during the COVID-19 pandemic. *Psychology and Behavioral Science International Journal, 16*(2), 555931. https://doi.org/10.19080/PBSIJ.2021.16.555932

Braun, B. G. (1988a). The BASK model of dissociation. *Dissociation, 1*(1), 4–23. hdl.handle.net/1794/1276

Braun, B.G. (1988b). The BASK model of dissociation: Part II – treatment. *Dissociation, 1*(2), 16–23. hdl.handle.net/1794/1340

Dell, P. F. (2006). Multidimensional inventory of dissociation (MID). A comprehensive measure of pathological dissociation. *Journal of Trauma & Dissociation, 7*(2), 77–106. https://doi.org/10.1300/J229v07n02_06

Dimitrova, L., Fernando, V., Vissia, E. M., Nijenhuis, E. R. S., Draijer, N., & Reinders, A. A. T. S. (2020). Sleep, trauma, fantasy and cognition in dissociative identity disorder, post-traumatic stress disorder and healthy controls: A replication and extension study. *European Journal of Psychotraumatology, 11*(1), 1705599. https://doi.org/10.1080/20008198.2019.1705599

González-Vazquez, A. I., Mosquera-Barral, D., Knipe, J., Leeds, A. M., & Santed-German, M. A. (2018). *Self-Care scale* [Database record]. APA PsycTests. https://doi.org/10.1037/t71094-000

Hofmann, A. (2010). The inverted EMDR standard protocol for unstable complex post-traumatic stress disorder. In M. Luber (Ed.), *Eye movement desensitization (EMDR) scripted protocols: Special populations* (pp. 313–328). Springer Publishing Company.

Janet, P. (1904). L'amnésie et la dissociation des souvenirs par l'émotion [Amnesiaand dissociation of memories through emotion]. *Journal de Psychologie, 1,* 417–453. www.persee.fr/doc/psy_0003-5033_1904_num_11_1_4733

Jarero, I., Artigas, L., & Luber, M. (2011). The EMDR protocol for recent critical incidents: Application in a disaster mental health continuum of care context. *Journal of EMDR Practice and Research, 5*(3), 82–94. https://doi.org/10.1891/1933-3196.5.3.82

Kinsler, P. (2018, June 8). Relational aspects of therapy. In *ISSTD Webinar Series VIII*. cfas.isst-d.org/content/relational-aspects-therapy-0

Knipe, J. (2010). The method of constant installation of present orientation and safety (CIPOS). In M. Luber (Ed.), *Eye movement desensitization (EMDR) scripted protocols: Special populations* (pp. 235–241). Springer Publishing Company.

Korn, D. L., & Leeds, A. M. (2002). Preliminary evidence of efficacy for EMDR resource development and installation in the stabilization phase of treatment of complex posttraumatic stress disorder. *Journal of Clinical Psychology, 58*(12), 1465–1487. https://doi.org/10.1002/jclp.10099

Leeds, A. M. (1998). Lifting the burden of shame: Using EMDR resource installation to resolve a therapeutic impasse. In P. Manfield (Ed.), *Extending EMDR: A case book of innovative applications* (pp. 256–282). W. W. Norton & Company.

Leeds, A. M. (2015, August 27-30). *Learning to feel good sharing positive emotion: The positive affect tolerance protocol* [Conference presentation]. EMDRIA Annual Conference, Philadelphia, PA, United States.

Leeds, A. M. (2022). The positive affect tolerance and integration protocol: A novel application of EMDR therapy procedures to help Survivors of early emotional neglect learn to tolerate and assimilate moments of appreciation, praise, and affection. *Journal of EMDR Practice and Research, 16*(4), 202–214. https://doi.org/10.1891/EMDR-2022-0015

Lingiardi, V., & McWilliams, N. (Eds.). (2017). *Psychodynamic diagnostic manual: PDM-2* (2nd ed.). The Guilford Press.

Logie, R., & De Jongh, A. (2014). The "flashforward procedure": Confronting the catastrophe. *Journal of EMDR Practice and Research, 8*(1), 25–32. https://doi.org/10.1891/1933-3196.8.1.25

Luber, M. (2019). Updated worksheets. In M. Luber (Ed.), *EMDR scripted protocols: Treating trauma in somatic and medical-related conditions* (pp. 467–485). Springer Publishing Company.

Mosquera, D., & González, A. (2014). *Borderline personality disorder and EMDR therapy*. D. M. B.

Mosquera, D., & Ross, C. (2016, March 18-19). *EMDR therapy for borderline personality dsorder, dissociation and complex trauma* [Presentation]. Natick, MA, USA.

Shapiro, F. (2018). *Eye movement desensitization and reprocessing (EMDR) therapy: Basic principles, protocols and procedures* (3rd ed). The Guilford Press.

Steele, K., Van der Hart, O., & Nijenhuis, E. R. S. (2005). Phase-oriented treatment of structural dissociation in complex traumatization: Overcoming trauma-related phobias. *Journal of Trauma & Dissociation*, 6(3), 11–53. https://doi.org/10.1300/J229v06n03_02

Van der Hart, O., Steele, K., Boon, S., & Brown, P. (1993). The treatment of traumatic memories: Synthesis, realization and integration. *Dissociation, 6*(2/3), 162–180. hdl.handle.net/1794/1633

Van der Hart, O., Nijenhuis, E. R. S., & Solomon, R. (2010). Dissociation of the personality incomplex trauma-related disorders and EMDR: Theoretical considerations. *Journal of EMDR Practice and Research, 4*(2), 76–92. https://doi.org/10.1891/1933-3196.4.2.76

Yeates, S., Korner, A., & McLean, L. (2024). A systematic review and narrative analysis of the evidence for individual psychodynamically informed psychotherapy in the treatment ofdissociative identity disorder in adults. *Journal of Trauma & Dissociation, 25*(2), 248–278. https://doi.org/10.1080/15299732.2023.2293802

York, C. (2001). *Affect tolerance and management protocol summary*. Unpublished worksheet.

Part IV

Expanding the Realm of Possibility

Chapter 9

Reexamining the Dominant Paradigm for Working with Self-states in EMDR

D. Michael Coy

Introduction

In Part I of this book, we laid a foundation for thinking about dissociation and reexamined bilateral dual attention stimulation (BL-DAS) and the adaptive information processing (AIP) model in that context. We subsequently invited a reconsideration of the standard EMDR conceptualization and treatment frame for working with dissociation, shown below in Figure 9.1. Within that frame, in Part II, we discussed ethical practice and the evolution of the professional self. In Part III, we explored resourcing and memory processing with dissociation across EMDR's three temporal prongs (past–present–future) and eight phases, embedded in the three-stage model and a relational frame. Part IV provides additional material to help strengthen the connections among the frame and every layer embedded within it.

We suggested in Chapter 3 that ego state therapies (embedded within *Models and theories of trauma and dissociation* in Figure 9.1) can help us know enough about a client's self-system to determine readiness and obtain multifaceted consent for any form of resourcing and memory processing. There are several ego state therapies from which to choose. Sandra Paulsen (2009, 2018), a pioneer in the integrative, EMDR therapy-informed treatment of dissociation, has long promoted the use of Ego State Therapy (Watkins & Watkins, 1997) to treat dissociative disorders. Despite her efforts, there has been a near-inescapable gravitational pull in the EMDR therapy field toward Internal Family Systems therapy (IFS; Schwartz, 1995; Schwartz & Sweezy, 2019) and other, IFS-inflected approaches (e.g., Knipe, 2019; González & Mosquera, 2012). IFS, which is usually paired with the Theory of Structural Dissociation of the Personality (TSDP; Van der Hart et al., 2006), has become *the* ego state therapy of choice among EMDR practitioners working with dissociative clients. In this chapter, we will critically examine the basic concepts of the IFS model; discuss the sociopolitics and therapist-specific factors that may lead EMDR practitioners

DOI: 10.4324/9781003410201-13

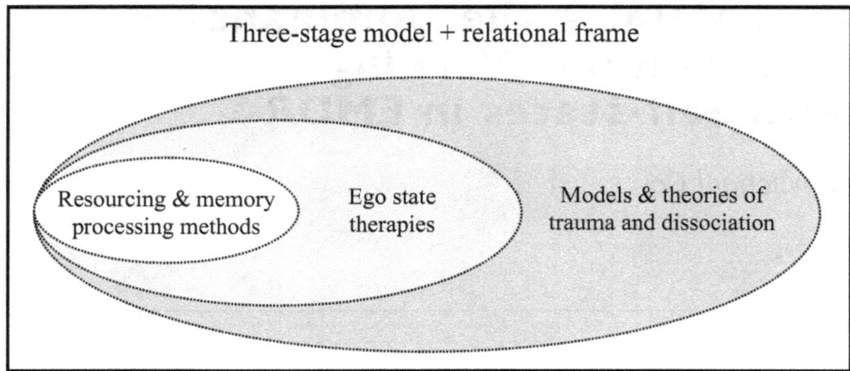

Figure 9.1 Our Conceptualization and Treatment Frame.
Sources: ISSTD (2011); Yeates et al. (2024).

to gravitate to particular practice approaches; and (re)consider Ego State Therapy (Watkins & Watkins, 1997), with its integration of clinical hypnosis and psychodynamic principles, as an approach that offers practitioners greater flexibility in conceptualizing and treating dissociation. A case example will illustrate the expanded palette of treatment possibilities offered by integrating EMDR and Ego State Therapy.

Dissociation Made Simple?

We previously discussed the long-standing controversy surrounding the existence of dissociative disorders, particularly dissociative identity disorder (DID) (see Chapter 1). That controversy arguably hinges on one central feature of DID: The existence within an individual of two or more centers of consciousness with a capacity for executive control and decision-making. Prevailing wisdom dictates that there is and can only be one center of consciousness and volition within a single mind (Hasker, 2010). This belief pervades mental health practitioner education (see Chapter 5) and plants the seeds for implicit biases that may influence what theories and therapies practitioners gravitate toward and how these are used (Gilboa-Schechtman, 2024; Maroda, 2022; Tverskey & Kahneman, 1973; Yager et al., 2021). In fact, the idea of 'one person, one center of consciousness' aligns rather conveniently with the IFS concept of Self and the idea that a (presumed) sole central executive has exclusive rights to it. In more severe forms of dissociation, however, this presumption is an illusion. Richard Kluft (2002) offers that,

> To the clinician who does not understand ego-state phenomena, an encounter with a dissociative patient may prove comforting, because he or she [sic] will not recognize indicators of a dissociative process at work and not be impelled to deal with them; or confusing, if he or she [sic] realizes that the fluctuating and often perplexing presentation of the patient, the dissociative surface [...], is an indication of some process at work which the clinician cannot understand.
>
> (p. 70)

If this is a new idea for you, then take heart: Few of us were knowledgeable, experienced, or observant enough to grasp the complexities of dissociation early on in our journey. Observation suggests that practitioners fall into one or more of the following categories:

1. those who don't know they don't (yet) know, and thus assume they know and understand dissociative phenomena more deeply than they do (i.e., the Dunning-Kruger effect; Kruger-Dunning, 1999);
2. those who believe they know enough about any given client's subjective experience without deeper inquiry;
3. those who recognize there is a lot they don't (yet) know and feel anxious or ashamed about this;
4. those who realize there is a lot they don't (yet) know and feel curious to learn more; and
5. those who either know a little bit about several things, or a lot about a couple of things, and recognize there will always be more to learn.

When I began my learning journey, I was an admixture of categories 1, 3, and 4, depending on the day, whom I was talking to, and how insecure I felt. I certainly thought I knew more than I did ("I know how to use EMDR with dissociation. I've attended a weekend workshop!"). As I learned a bit more, I often felt ashamed of my inexperience and avoided revealing it to other people (bad move). My first major catastrophe using EMDR to treat dissociation, which I only discovered by accident during reprocessing with a client, semi-cured me of my shame about openly acknowledging that I had no idea what I was doing. It also humbled me – kind of. What probably saved me from becoming a danger to my other (covertly dissociative) clients was my insatiable curiosity, desire to develop as a practitioner, and commitment to avoid harming any other clients with EMDR. As a consultant, I have seen echoes of 'back then me' in others. Practitioners with attitudes reflective of categories 1 and 2 above often seem to rely upon a preferred theory, ego state therapy model, personal experience, or a combination of these. Sometimes, the 'preferred' theory or model is the only one they know (so far). Unfortunately, being married to only one way of conceptualizing or practicing can result in a therapist haphazardly deciding on an intervention or treatment trajectory without adequate knowledge, understanding, or experience of working with dissociation. The third practitioner category (not knowing/feeling anxious or ashamed about it) often seems to overlap with the preceding two.

Maslow (1963) suggests that knowledge can serve both "growing forward" and "protective, homeostatic" functions (p. 122). He notes that the former is guided by curiosity, while the latter is driven by the need for a sense of safety. There is nothing simple about dissociation. With that said, if we can't make dissociation less complex, the next best thing might be to adopt conceptual frameworks and practice models that will make dissociation *seem* less complex. The concreteness of conceptualizing and practicing exclusively within a preferred framework may help diminish some practitioners' anxiety about the ambiguities inherent to dissociative disorders. Unfortunately, it can also foster a false sense of certainty. In my opinion, the latter is well-represented in EMDR therapists' widespread adoption of IFS therapy.

Unpacking IFS

In IFS, healing work is ideally conducted via (the) Self, an experiential place from which logic, wisdom, curiosity, resources, etc. are accessible, and in which the client must remain cognitively situated to facilitate work with 'parts.' 'Parts' are described as "discrete, autonomous mental systems, each with their own range of emotion, expression, abilities, desires, and views of the world" (Schwartz & Sweezy, 2019, pp. 30–31), which are characterized as "a population of inner people" (p. 42). The denizens of this inner world are classified according to specific roles. *Managers* are "highly protective, strategic, and interested in controlling the environment;" *exiles* are "the most sensitive members of the system," whom *managers* will "banish [...] for their own protection and the good of the whole system;" and *firefighters* "tr[y] to stifle, anesthetize, or distract from the feelings of exiles, reacting powerfully and automatically, without concern for consequences, to their distress and the overinhibition of managers. [...] [T]hey fight the flames of exiled emotion" (Schwartz & Sweezy, p. 31). The presumed, sole central executive role is described interchangeably as 'the client' and, when unblended from parts, as (the client's) Self (Schwartz & Sweezy, 2019). Self is both an "active inner leader" and an "expansive, boundaryless state of mind" (Schwartz & Sweezy, p. 45), but is not itself a part. It is recommended that, when possible, the work be carried out by the client in Self, who engages with their parts, as opposed to the therapist engaging parts directly. The therapist's direct engagement with the client's parts, through *direct access*, is not considered ideal. Schwartz and Sweezy (2019) offer three reasons for this: (1) working directly with parts is inefficient, (2) the likelihood of violating (unknown) internal rules and unduly activating the client, and (3) engaging parts directly may cultivate their attachment to the therapist rather than to Self (p. 116). However, per Schwartz and Sweezy (2019),

> [W]hen a client's parts have very little trust in the Self, or when the Self is not available, we mostly use direct access, which helps us to help clients manage strong emotions without using grounding practices that can send vulnerable parts the wrong message. At the same time, direct access helps parts trust that unblending [from Self] and letting the client's Self return will be a safe experience with many benefits.
>
> (p. 121)

Elsewhere, they note that direct access "exposes the therapist to the transferred expectations and accusations of extreme parts" (Schwartz & Sweezy, p. 83). Joanne Twombly, author of what is thus far the only book written on the use of IFS to treat complex trauma and dissociation, concedes that "most of the early work with people with Complex PTSD and people with dissociative disorders will need to be done through direct access" (Twombly, 2024, p. 88). She attributes this to trauma-based avoidance and phobias of being in Self. As a 'carrot' to encourage parts to unblend from Self, Schwartz and Sweezy (2019) indicate that the therapist's role is to "offer exiled, distressed parts the attention they crave in return for not overwhelming the Self – an offer they rarely refuse. Asking exiles not to overwhelm the Self is one way of solving the great problem of dysregulated emotion in psychotherapy" (p. 118).

Thinking of my own work with clients, all this provokes several questions. How do you manage the dynamics arising between 'the client' and their 'parts' if you have more than one state that can assume, or previously inhabited, the 'central executive' role? Concomitantly, what if 'parts' are autonomous enough that they can outright refuse to, or simply cannot, cede their 'Self' energy to whichever state fronts in therapy (i.e., unblend)? (Schwartz acknowledges the conceptual issues severe dissociation pose for IFS in his supposition that the parts of clients with DID have their *own* Self and their *own* parts; see Schwartz & Sweezy, 2019.) Additionally, Schwartz and Sweezy seem to suggest it is possible for the therapist to avoid transference simply by not engaging directly with 'parts.' Come again? (This seems highly improbable to me, considering the complexity of transference-countertransference dynamics.) If all parts are 'people,' even if only metaphorically, then why do they not have a right to share access to 'Self' energy? (I suspect this is a conceptual issue, rooted in the assumption that there is only *one* client, synonymous with a presumed, sole central executive.)

Because the discussion of dissociative multiplicity is limited to only a paragraph in the 2019 IFS text, the nuances of operationalizing IFS to treat dissociative clients seem to have been left for others to elaborate. In a way, dissociative disorders 'break' IFS, insofar as they require therapists to bend or break the 'rules' of IFS, both conceptually and practically, to accommodate increasing inner complexity. In Schwartz's (1995) first edition text on IFS, he observes that Freud's shift from "respectful and curious listening to intellectualized interpreting" resulted in "convoluted explanations [for intrapsychic experience] that were removed from people's [lived] experience." (p. 3). He continues that "Freud influenced generations of theorists to trust their theories more than their clients" (p. 3). Arguably, Schwartz may inadvertently have achieved a similar impact as Freud, as many practitioners seem determined to employ *unmodified* IFS to treat persons with dissociative disorders, particularly DID. Although IFS is enriched with many helpful interventions and ways of thinking about the self, its pairing with EMDR therapy compounds a problem that *both approaches* share: Neither was designed, either in theory or practice, to accommodate dissociative complexity.

Ego State Theory and Therapy

Ego, Id, and Superego

An alternative to IFS that *does* take dissociative complexity into account is Ego State Therapy (Watkins & Watkins, 1997). To understand Ego State Therapy, we must first discuss Ego State Theory. This theory has its roots in Freud's tripartite conception of self: The *Id*, the *Ego*, and the *Superego*. The Id is "[t]he unconscious – the source of drives, both pleasurable and unpleasurable, which is "the dark, inaccessible part of our personality" (Freud, 1933, p. 73) and which has "no direct communication with the external world" (Freud, 1940, p. 197). Freud called this 'Das Es,' or 'It', suggesting that it is an object of sorts, which lacks its own sense of 'I'-ness.

The Ego is a "coherent organization of mental processes" to which "consciousness is attached," which mediates the outward expression of impulses and emotion (Freud, 1923, p. 17). Freud clarifies that the Ego is "that part of the Id which has been modified by the direct influence of the external world" through conscious perception (p. 25). Ego is literally 'I' in Latin, and in modern terms, we can think of this as the (sole) central executive that 'owns' the entirety of our lived experience.

The third dimension of Freud's self is the Superego (Freud, 1923) – our 'ideal' self, or 'Über-ich.' This encompasses our values, our conscience, and as self-criticism (Hartmann & Loewenstein, 1962; see also Chapter 12), patterned after early life identifications with caregivers and other influences. The functioning of the id, ego, and superego is shaped by our innate traits and capacities as these interact with what we are exposed to and integrate – or cannot integrate, to a greater or lesser degree – into our emotionally and cognitively developing sense(s) of self.

From Unitary Ego, to Ego States, to Self-States

Paul Federn's (1952) extension of Freud's concept of the singular, unitary Ego – called *ego states* – can be thought of as a collection of individual, semiautonomous states with both shared and differing *but not necessarily conflicting* traits. Federn, who was a student and analysand of Freud, documented his theory of ego states in the early 1950s at the behest of his own student, Eduardo Weiss (Federn, 1952). It was through Weiss that John G. (Jack) Watkins learned of Federn's ideas. Jack Watkins further expanded ego state theory and from that, in collaboration with his second wife, Helen H. Watkins, developed the treatment approach called Ego State Therapy.

Jack Watkins (1977) explains that a group of ego states form a unified 'country' of self that is governed by a central executive ego state. This 'central executive' is consistent with Freud's unitary 'ego,' which, in an ego state framework, we might think of as the 'driver of the bus.' This ego state-central executive configuration also aligns with Sidis's (1898) conceptualization of reproductive (ego state-level) and recognitive (central executive-level) consciousness. It is also consonant with modern, brain-based thinking about vertical (conscious/subconscious) and horizontal/lateral (throughout the subconscious and lower brain structure) integration. (See Chapter 2 for further discussion.) All ego states are hypothesized to possess the capacity for *some* sense of 'I'-ness, regardless of whether they are in executive control. Ego states have variously permeable boundaries and overlap with one another. The more permeability of the individual states' barriers, the more overlap/connection with one another, the more freely energy in the form of somatosensory experience and the meanings made from it circulates among all ego states. The more freely 'I' energy can circulate among ego states, the more coherent and unified one's overall sense of self is.

Expanding Freud's conceptualization of Ego as subject and Id as object, Federn (1952) proposes that "the ego is subject and object simultaneously. As subject, it is referred to as the pronoun 'I,' and as object it is known as 'the Self'" (pp. 8–9). Watkins and Watkins (1997) described *object states* as possessing a 'not-me' quality. This subject–object relationship is evident, for example, when one ego state ('I') observes another ego state that is sufficiently different (or disconnected) from itself ('them/it, over there'). The question of who is 'subject' and who is 'object' depends on an ego state's point of view. This is how it is possible for an ego state to inhabit the roles of subject and object simultaneously. The perception and status of 'object' depends on which ego state(s) possess a higher concentration of ego ('I') energy at a given time.

The Impact of Harm on Ego State Development

Ego state theory suggests that intensely painful experiences may result in ego states with 'thicker,' more rigid boundaries (Watkins & Watkins, 1997). This can result in some ego states being burdened with greater concentrations of bound-up or 'stuck' energy associated with that pain. This 'stuck' energy, and the ego states burdened with holding it, circulate less dynamically. As a result, these more heavily burdened states may be less able to take in new experience that is qualitatively different from what they previously learned – a bit like someone who becomes closed-minded or suspicious. When a person is repeatedly exposed to harm, such as chronic abuse or neglect, ego states' capacity to tolerate and accept adaptive information is further compromised.

Wounded ego states' tendency to gravitate toward or repeat experiences similar to what they already know (i.e., 'like attracts like') (Chu, 1991; Van der Hart et al., 2010). This, paired with a diminished capacity to tolerate or accept new *adaptive* information, may result in their sense of "I"-ness becoming increasingly rigid. Many of these states may lack the observational capacity to discern past from present or even to recognize other states as being part of the same self as they are. Increasingly pervasive absence of connectivity marks the development of more distinct ego states and fuels both intrapsychic and interpersonal conflict (Watkins & Watkins, 1997). Even when states do share (or impose) knowledge, behavior, and somatosensory experience with (or upon) one another, there may be little or no awareness of one another's existence or of the functional connections that make these exchanges possible (Sidis, 1898; Sidis & Goodhart, 1904/1968). Over time, these ego states evolve into highly sophisticated, discrete, self-actualized neural structures: *Self-states*.

Philip Bromberg (2020) describes self-states as "highly individualized modules of being, each configured by its own organization of cognitions, beliefs, dominant affect and mood, access to memory, skills, behaviors, values, actions, and regulatory physiology" (p. 73). Persons with a dissociative disorder experience two or more, simultaneously coexisting senses of self (American Psychiatric Association, 2022). In many cases, self-states' experience of the present is filtered, often distorted, through a painful, seemingly inescapable, as-yet-undigested past that may be the only reality they've ever known. These self-states are thought of as each being in a *trance* – an isolated state of awareness, perception, and experience marked by illogic and paradoxical thinking (Orne, 1959, 1979). Tuck that factoid in your back pocket, because we will need it again shortly.

As we discussed earlier, Ego State Theory evolved from Freud's concepts of ego, id, and superego. Schwartz and Sweezy (2019) suggest that, in contrast to the IFS concept of Self, Freud's *ego* is "a collection of manager parts" (p. 45). This statement seems emblematic of conceptual and practical challenges for employing IFS with clients with multiple self-states, many of which may have a rather highly developed sense of 'I'-ness. If *every* self-state has an ego, then who *isn't* a manager? Ego State Theory allows us to broaden our scope to consider that ego energy is not the sole property of a central executive but instead freely circulates among all ego states. With increasingly complex wounding, that ego energy can become stagnant, bound up by painful experience, and concentrated in distinct self-states that cannot naturally absorb new, contrasting experience (i.e., adaptive information). The gaps in connectivity between self-states are akin to impermeable barriers, or gulfs that are so wide that self-states often perceive themselves to be separate individuals rather than disparate aspects of a single person. Ego State Theory is conceptually compatible with Shapiro's (2018) AIP model, Sidis's thinking (e.g., Sidis, 1898, 1914; Sidis & Goodhart, 1904/1968; see Chapter 2), and the TSDP (Van der Hart et al., 2006).

Ego State Therapy (with a Capital E-S-T)

Ego State Therapy (with a capital E-S-T) integrates and operationalizes Ego State Theory, psychoanalytic and family therapy-informed principles, and clinical hypnosis. Therapeutic change is facilitated by strategically engaging ego and object energies via a variety of hypnotically informed and practical methods (Watkins, 1977; Watkins & Watkins, 1993, 1997).

Cathexis

The process of working with ego and object energies within the self involves the use of *cathexis*. The American Psychological Association (n.d.) defines cathexis as

> the investment of psychic energy in an object of any kind, such as a wish, fantasy, person, goal, idea, social group, or the self. Such objects are said to be **cathected** [sic] when an individual attaches emotional significance (positive or negative affect) to them.

In Ego State Therapy, we can intentionally invest an ego state, a subjective experience, or even a part of the body with emotional energy – that is, *cathecting* it – by bringing attention to that state. The focus of the attention determines whether the ego state is invested, or cathected, with ego ('I') energy or object ('they/them/it') energy. That state is then understood to be *ego cathected. Ego cathexis* is the activation of an ego state – even a part of the body – with first person, 'I' energy. *Object cathexis* occurs when an ego-cathected state's emotional energy or attention is then drawn to something outside them, whether an inanimate object, a person, or another ego state – 'that, over there' – imbuing it with object energy. Working strategically with ego and object energies through *cathexis* can increase permeability and connection between inadequately connected self-states. (For an in-depth discussion of the history and substance of Ego State Theory and Therapy, see Abramowitz & Torem, 2018; Leutner & Piedfort-Marin, 2021; and Watkins & Watkins, 1997).

Hypnosis as a Catalyst for Cathexis and Connection

Although it is not always necessary to employ clinical hypnosis in Ego State Therapy, the intentional use of trance allows the practitioner both to tap into a wide variety of powerful, hypnotic interventions and to more dynamically engage ego and object energies than is often possible *without* hypnosis. Hypnosis is "[a] state of consciousness involving focused attention and reduced peripheral awareness characterized by an enhanced capacity for response to suggestion" (The American Psychological Association, 2014, Definition and description of hypnosis section, para. 1). *Hypnosis* is often used interchangeably with the term *trance*. Trance can be elicited via intentional hypnotic 'induction' by someone else (heterohypnosis); intentional hypnotic induction by oneself (self-hypnosis); and spontaneously, without intentional induction (autohypnosis) (see Coy, 2025). According to Barabasz and Watkins (2005), trance increases a person's capacity to "freely mix perceptions derived from reality with those that stem from [...] imagination" (p. 67).

More importantly, in the context of the present discussion, there is plenty of evidence that trance phenomena co-occur with both posttraumatic stress and dissociative disorders (Bliss, 1983, 1986; Gruenenwald, 1984; Keuroghlian et al., 2010; see also Chapter 1). Although the idea of hypnosis and trance might seem remote and rather esoteric (e.g., something you 'do' to someone), Sándor Ferenczi (1916) discusses trance phenomena as being integral to the therapeutic relationship:

> [...] *[I]t has long been known how greatly sympathy and respect favour the bringing about of a suggestible state;* this fact could not escape the

> competent observers and experimenters in this field. What has not been known, however, and what could only be known through the help of psycho-analysis, is first that *these unconscious affects play the chief part in bringing about the action of suggestion*, and secondly that in the last analysis they are shown to be manifestations of libidinous impulses, which for the most part are *transferred from the ideational complexes bearing on the relation between parent and child to the relation between physician and patient.*
>
> (p. 54; emphasis added)

So, unconscious affects are somehow interwoven with trance phenomena, which in turn may play a role in therapeutic transference (see Chapter 11). In the modern era, Wickramasekera II (2015), Henning (2016), and Baker and Spiegel (2020) have carried through Ferenczi's interest, exploring the intersubjective trance field that develops between therapist and client, and the possible role of mirror neuronal communication (see Chapter 12) in establishing interpersonal resonance.

Trance Logic

Imagine that your client declares, "Whatever's going on inside is not real. *I'm* real, and I wish *they*, and all this pain, would just go away." Let's say you simply buy into your client's point of view. Based on what you learned in a typical, accredited EMDR basic training, you may opt for a symptom-focused EMDR therapy treatment-as-usual.

Wait a minute, though. Your client just said that whatever is going on inside – that *they* (i.e., wounded ego states – aren't real. It's almost as if your client perceives these 'others' as somehow 'not me,' rather than as dissociated facets of who they are as a whole person. At the same time, if those ego states are not real, that means they don't exist. *How can something that does not exist go away?* This paradoxical thinking is an example of *trance logic* (Orne, 1959, 1979). The hallmark of trance logic is a "characteristic tolerance of logical inconsistencies," which is "closely related to the concrete thinking or primary process that characterizes […] dissociative reactions […] and children" (Barabasz and Watkins, 2005, p. 67).

It is possible that you could be drawn *unwittingly* into your client's trance. What if you are highly susceptible to that sort of thing, and just kind of *drift* into trance because of how emotionally attuned you are to your client? (For a discussion of practitioners' experiences, both positive and negative, of being drawn into therapeutic trance with clients, see Meyerson et al., 2025.) If you are trance-prone, it is important to be aware of that. Knowing how *you* experience trance can help you avoid being drawn *unwittingly* into a client's trance-laden way of perceiving and thinking. Otherwise, there is a heightened risk of being hypnotically lulled into seeing and working only with your client's dissociative surface presentation. This might look like you picking up the "there's nothing to see here" end of the rope, allying with your client's avoidant fronting state in an invisible tug of war about what inside them is and is not real. And who or what within your client is tugging on the other end of that rope? Maybe something that has different thoughts, feelings, perspectives, and priorities than the one up front. It is from this "there's nothing to see here" perspective that you might just proceed with EMDR treatment-as-usual – but without enduring that you have consent from your client's whole self to move forward with reprocessing.

Ego States, Cathexis, and EMDR Therapy

Let us consider a therapist preparing to reprocess a traumatic memory with their client by setting up the target memory in *Phase III: Assessment.* Leading into *Phase IV: Desensitization*, the therapist speaks directly to the client (the assumptive central executive, in this case; let's call them 'George') and asks George to bring to mind the image that represents the 'worst part' of the memory. George, cathected with ego ('I') energy, then cathects the worst part of the memory with object ('it') energy.

Let's say that, during *Phase IV: Desensitization*, processing begins to 'loop' on a persistent, unpleasant sensation in the stomach. The therapist first attempts to resolve this 'block,' unsuccessfully, via 'mechanical' interventions (i.e., changes in BL-DAS). The therapist then redirects George's attention to a new channel of information (e.g., emotion, cognition). When this does not, the 'block' posed by the sensation in the stomach, the therapist returns to the target memory in hopes of identifying new information that can help move processing forward. The therapist is seeking a 'detour' around the 'block' posed by the disturbance in the stomach. The therapist then resorts to employing a cognitive interweave. Even that doesn't help. The looping, stuck on that sensation in the stomach, persists. Despite all these interventions, neither the therapist nor George, at the level of conscious recognition of his own experience, has access to what is needed to resolve the block and allow processing to move forward.

This might be the time to attempt an *ego state* interweave (Bergmann, 2008; Gilson & Kaplan, 2000). The therapist wonders about what George's stomach (and, implicitly, any ego state associated with it) might know about the looping. They have two options for inquiring: *Talking through* and *talking past.*

- *Talking through* (Kluft, 1982) involves working through the current 'central executive' by cathecting them with ego energy. A real-life analogy for *talking through* would be (1) calling someone on the phone, then asking them to (2) share what you've said with a second person who is in the room with them, and (3) relay that second person's response back to you.

- *Talking past*, which Kluft (1982) refers to as *talking over*, means bypassing whoever inhabits the central executive role and cathecting another ego state, part of the body, symptom, etc., with ego energy by speaking directly to them/it. (I call it *talking past* because *talking over* sounds like interrupting someone.) Returning to that real-life phone call, *talking past* might look like being on *speakerphone* with that same person, but instead of speaking to them, you speak directly to that second person in the room. Doing this doesn't prevent the first person from hearing or participating in the conversation –unless, of course, they step out of the room and are out of earshot. For clients with DID, stepping out of the room might mean a full dissociative switch. In that case, a typically fronting self-state's memory for the discussion may be obscured by inter-identity amnesia.

Now, back to reprocessing and that 'block' in the stomach. If the therapist opts to *talk through*, they would ego cathect George by addressing him directly. Then, then therapist would ask George to cathect the stomach with object energy by asking it what is happening. *Example: George, just listen inside and notice what you become aware of…If your stomach could speak to you right now, I wonder what words you might hear?*. Let's say, though, that George gets nothing at all in response. In that case, the therapist may, with permission, *talk past* George, cathecting the stomach with ego ('I') energy by asking it directly. George may also be explicitly cathected with object energy. *Example: This is a message for the stomach [ego cathected], so I wonder if you can listen in. This is the therapist speaking. George [the client, object cathected] tells me that you may be hurting. If you had words right now, and it felt safe enough to use them, I wonder what you might tell George about the hurt?*

Talking through is the 'default mode' for engaging ego states in IFS. *Talking past* (i.e., direct access) is used only when it is unavoidable. Although in both IFS and EST, the focus is upon increasing permeability (i.e., connectivity) among states, it is only in EST that *talking through* and *talking past* are considered equally valid options for achieving that. In treating dissociative clients, the line delineating these two methods can be thin, and to some degree may disappear, especially as the work with different states deepens. (For an excellent example of a seamless shift in ego cathexis between a 'central executive' and a part of the body, see *Chapter 22* in Watkins, 1978.) However, *talking past* is only one step removed from intentionally calling forth self-states into executive control, a technique which is much more clearly associated with Ego State Therapy and dissociative disorders treatment. For some therapists, the idea of calling forth self-states intentionally sets the stage for an anxiety-provoking dilemma about whether to stick with IFS or expand their horizons to explore EST. That anxiety may be less rooted in concerns about theory than in concerns about practice – specifically, *malpractice*.

The Risk of Iatrogenesis

For several EMDR therapists I've spoken with, the idea of intentionally engaging with non-fronting self-states in an Ego State Therapy frame (or even via IFS 'direct access') stokes fears of *iatrogenesis*. Iatrogenesis is "harm brought forth by a healer or any unintended adverse patient outcome because of a health care intervention, not considered the natural course of the illness or injury" (Hartford Institute for Geriatric Nursing, 2025). Brand et al. (2012) found no empirical evidence that working directly with nonexecutive self-states exacerbates DID. They do, however, direct attention to Kluft (1989) regarding the potential, deleterious effects of "inappropriate interventions" (Brand et al., 2012, p. 492).

Kluft (1989) discusses the risk of iatrogenically creating new self-states while treating dissociative clients in some depth. His is a thoughtful and measured discussion rooted in extensive experience, which acknowledges that inept treatment can heighten this risk. Other thinkers, who dismiss the existence of DID, assert that iatrogenesis arises not from *uninformed* treatment but instead from the therapist's suggestion that different self-states exist at all (e.g., Merckelbach et al., 2002). Lilienfeld et al. (1999) advocated this viewpoint, citing a specific example from the dissociative disorders literature:

> Ross (1997) [...] recommended giving names to alters and stated that "giving an alter a name may 'crystallize' it and make it more distinct" (Ross, 1997, p. 311). According to Ross, this technique is used primarily among patients with possible DID as a means of clarifying the individual's personality system.
>
> (p. 513)

Expert consensus in the dissociative disorders field indicates it is not advisable for a practitioner to name a client's self-states (ISSTD, 2005/2011). So, fair point. However, Lilienfeld et al.'s reading of Ross (1997) decontextualizes what Colin Ross wrote. I would like to indulge in a bit of myth deconstruction by re-contextualizing Ross's words. Discussing the treatment of persons with dissociative states, Ross (1997) observed that,

> In some patients, especially those on the border between DDNOS [OSDD] and DID, *the personality system is not distinct or structured, or there may be structured and amorphous regions*. Sometimes neither patient nor therapist is sure who is out [fronting], or who was just out. If nobody can tell, it may not matter much as long as there is coconsciousness [shared awareness]. The only way to deal with this kind of fuzziness in a system is to ask for clarification and work with the parts that are clearest. Things may become clearer over time. *Another observation of Janet (Binet, 1896, p. 147) may be helpful: Giving an alter a name may 'crystallize' it and make it more distinct. This may be a therapeutic form of iatrogenic modification of the phenomenology if used sparingly.*
>
> (p. 311; emphasis added)

Lilienfeld et al. (1999) were bothered by Ross allegedly advocating for naming self-states, in essence making alleged figments of imagination into something 'real' (that's *reification*) by iatrogenically reinforcing the existence of different self-states, thus 'creating' DID. Scott Lilienfeld was a major proponent of the sociocognitive model of dissociation. He and his colleagues clearly have an axe to grind in this paper, but it is unclear whether the point they are making is based on an unintentional or intentional misreading of Ross (1997). In either case, Lilienfeld et al. (1999) seem not to have finished their homework.

Ross described a situation in which self-states seem *less distinct from one another*, rather than being more clearly delineated. What did he mean by *iatrogenic modification*? This process involves intentionally applying an intervention that would typically be considered an iatrogenic treatment effect in service of long-term healing. (Think *short-term pain equals long-term gain.*) Examples of iatrogenic modification in the medical and dental fields include re-breaking a bone as a precursor to properly setting a fracture and drilling a cavity to fill a tooth, respectively. In EMDR therapy practice, we might consider the act of accessing and reprocessing traumatic memory material, which can be temporarily painful and destabilizing for a client, to be a form of iatrogenic modification. Ross is thus describing a technique (naming or labeling an indistinct state) that could feed iatrogenesis (increasing separation, thus distinctiveness, between states), but is instead employed to set the stage for healing (*reducing* separation between states). What is Ross's precedent for advocating this approach?

Lilienfeld et al. (1999) quote Ross (1997), who cites Binet (1896), who recounts Pierre Janet's (1889/2022) discovery of a second self-state within a person named 'Lucie'. This discovery arose through Janet's investigation of hypnotic phenomena related to Lucie's dissociative experiences.

This second state wrote their responses to Janet's spoken questions while 'executive' Lucie was otherwise occupied in conversation with another person in the room. Janet does indeed ask whether the one who can hear him might be given a name. However, in his own defense, Janet (1889/2022) reflects that,

> No doubt it was I who suggested that she name this personage and thus gave her a sort of individuality, *but one can see how far she had already developed in that direction spontaneously*. These namings of the subconscious personage greatly facilitate experiments. Moreover, *automatic writing almost always takes a name of this kind, without anyone having suggested anything*, as I have seen in automatic letters spontaneously written by Léonie [another subject of study].
>
> (p. 64; emphases added)

Janet himself did not actually name a state; instead, he invited someone to name a state of their own, in the context of an experiment, at a time when very few were formally studying dissociative phenomena. Lilienfeld et al. (1999) thus illustrate not the risk of reification but of taking out of context an author's words to make a point.

A better example of the potential for mishap in working with self-states may be found in a paper written by Walter F. Prince in the *Journal of Abnormal Psychology*. Prince (1916) studied the dissociation experienced by a woman called Doris, whom he characterized as a 'quintuple personality.' He described his contact with what appeared to him to be a more rudimentary or fragmentary self-state, which only appears while 'waking' Doris was asleep. Despite his recognition that this state possessed memories that belonged only to her, suggesting that this was indeed a separate consciousness, Prince (1916) found himself feeling cautious in his engagements with her:

> There is no doubt whatever that by experimenting with different types of stimuli [sleeping Doris] could have been educated into self-consciousness and sundry forms and degrees of mental functioning. Indeed, she showed such a disposition to respond to the few tentative essays which were made in this direction that I took alarm and wholly abstained from any unnecessary repetition.
>
> (p. 89)

The risk, then, seems *not* to be one of making something imaginary real, but rather of engaging indiscriminately (and unwittingly) with different self-states without a clear treatment-related intent. Even then, W. F. Prince (1916) did not *create* Doris's distinct states. They already existed.

Richard Kluft (1989, pp. 86–87) highlighted therapist-dependent factors that *can* legitimately contribute to the iatrogenic creation of new/more fully developed self-states within a client who *already has* dissociative states:

1. fascination with or reinforcement of specific self-states (i.e., preferential treatment of certain states);
2. poor therapist object constancy in relation to different self-states, due to unchecked countertransference reactions;
3. a lack of (ongoing) engagement with literature or participation in training;
4. limited or no experience with long-term treatment and psychodynamic practice;
5. imposing unrealistic or overwhelming demands and re-enacting past traumas;
6. unwitting or irresponsible accessing/use of the client's hypnotic capacities;
7. inexperience with or difficulty pacing and/or managing memory work, including inadequate preparation or lack of recognition that the client is overwhelmed;
8. conflating states that never intentionally influence or assume executive control and those states that can and do (i.e., true 'alters'), and which are invested in their separateness from other states (see Chapter 10); and
9. imposition of one's theory and/or beliefs (e.g., overreliance on internal self-helpers, identification of 'demonic' alters, etc.).

Kluft (1989) notes that "[m]any of the events that occur in the course of treatment of [DID] may be considered as iatrogenic, in that they emerge from the impact of the clinician's interventions, yet they are not necessarily an indication that something is amiss" (p. 86). That said, elsewhere, Kluft (2002, p. 75) observes that there are compelling *client-centered* reasons to work only with a predominant front(ing) self-state:

1. the risk of negatively impacting an active legal case,
2. the risk of destabilization if self-states are already overwhelmed or universally trauma-bound,
3. the necessity of focusing on concrete stabilization in the here-and-now rather than exploring the there-and-then,
4. the risk of (further) destabilizing a person who has inadequate ego strength to tolerate deeper work with other self-states or the trauma itself, and

5. the therapy is supportive rather than depth-oriented, in which case direct work with other states is only undertaken if it seems unavoidable.

Perhaps unsurprisingly, these reasons are similar to Shapiro's (2018) potential contraindications for employing BL-DAS in treatment. Whether in the context of EMDR therapy or any other approach that involves memory work – and employing an ego state therapy most definitely counts as memory work – ensuring both treatment efficacy and safety may be less about the approach itself than it is about the qualifications, training, knowledge, and experience of the person employing it (see Chapters 4 and 5). Furthermore, we must do what we can to ensure we are emotionally mature and self-aware enough to avoid (further) harming our clients (Maroda, 2022).

Case Example

Let's say you feel reasonably confident and are undaunted by the idea of both *talking through* and *talking past*, working dynamically with ego and object energies in an Ego State Therapy frame, and even calling forth other states into executive control. What might all this look like in practice?

'Ash' is a White, middle-aged, gay, cisgender male who was referred to individual therapy by his couple's therapist due to ongoing conflict with his partner and, secondarily, concerns that he may have early-onset dementia. The ongoing conflict is most evident in Ash's ambivalence about his relationship (feelings that he cannot explain) and arguments that have arisen between him and his partner due to Ash's 'blank spells.' Ash's partner experiences him as being 'like a different person' during these episodes: Erratic, argumentative, and at times confusing or nonsensical – and 'younger' than Ash typically seems. Ash endorses using alcohol leading up to what he experiences as 'blackouts,' but says his use has been rather modest – even if his use *during* the blackouts has been heightened, per Ash's partner. Because the alcohol use seemed to be heightened during the blank spells rather than preceding them, it did not make sense to Ash or his therapist that they were alcohol-induced. Prior to the therapy referral, Ash had already sought out a neurological evaluation, including undergoing an MRI, to rule out organic brain deterioration/damage as an explanation for the memory problems. This was eventually ruled out in consultation between the neurologist and Ash's new therapist.

Ash has an extensive history of 'shock' trauma, emotional neglect, and attachment trauma spanning back to infancy. Ash was given benzodiazepines by his mother in childhood as a substitute for parental soothing. He has struggled with periods of acute alcohol and other substance misuse in adolescence and earlier adulthood. (At the time of the intervention described below, Ash still contended with isolated, situational overuse of alcohol.) Ash experiences amnesia for significant aspects of his history, including both his general autobiography and traumatic events/periods in his life. He also experiences amnesia for day-to-day experiences, particularly those that are more stressful, some of which have involved alcohol misuse. As noted above, however, his present-day substance use does not appear acute enough to cause this. Formal diagnostic evaluation of Ash's dissociative symptoms strongly indicated a diagnosis of DID. This was soon confirmed by spontaneous dissociative switches in early therapy sessions, with different self-states assuming executive control.

The primary, fronting self-state – the one who most often presents in therapy – is referred to by the rest of the self-system as the 'adultest one.' This 'adultest' Ash had no idea what was happening inside for him when he first came to therapy. The adultest Ash is rarely alone when he fronts, as a handful of other self-states are usually (undetectably) copresent to help navigate daily life. Self-states, including adultest Ash, have responded well to learning different hypnotic resourcing and containment techniques to enhance daily coping.

Adultest Ash historically has not been explicitly aware of these other self-states. In therapy, he has developed a greater capacity for awareness of confusing emotions, impulses, etc., as being attributable to other self-states functioning in the background. Over a period of two to three years, with extensive negotiation and trauma-focused work with specific self-states, adultest Ash has gradually developed a capacity for shared (if limited) awareness with some other states. Adultest Ash has also been able to recognize and accept that his periods of amnesia are attributable to the activity of other self-states, who sometimes assume full executive control – even though he does not like this.

During Ash's isolated episodes of alcohol misuse, which we have come to learn are precipitated in part by a cluster of self-states that identify as 24–27 years old, Ash 'loses time' and later 'comes to' (waking up into executive control again), finding that he has said or done something that he doesn't remember. Adultest Ash does not yet have explicit awareness or a capacity to communicate with the self-states associated with these actions. Because of this lack of communication, and due to the 'trouble' they cause in his relationship with his partner, adultest Ash has decided that he doesn't like these 'drinking parts.'

In today's session, adultest Ash reports that they received 'bad news' about a potentially serious health issue in the past week. He shares that he became quite intoxicated (alcohol) and sustained an injury, leaving a hole in the wall at home. Ash expresses upset that he 'lost his mind' after hearing the bad news. His expression appears increasingly dysphoric as he drifts into ruminating on "all of the people I've lost to cancer." Ash expresses worry that he would not be able to take care of his own needs if he were left alone. This calls back to Ash's early life abandonment by his parents. Ash then shifts from his rumination back to the present-day story, describing what led up to his intoxication and a blackout. Ash said he did recall falling, noting that it was the fall that "woke me up."

Ash vaguely recalls trying to 'talk himself out of' falling apart. He was later told (by his partner) that he had called his partner, tearful and scared. Ash doesn't recall this. As Ash recounts this event, I find myself repeatedly yawning. Ash knows what this usually means: Something is 'up' below the surface level, outside his conscious awareness, and I'm somehow resonating with it.

Adultest Ash: You're yawning. What are you picking up on?

Michael: *I'm not sure, but I think there might be some value in looking below the surface to see if there are any answers. Would that be ok?*

Adultest Ash: [Somewhat reluctantly, because he realizes he may 'switch.'] Yeah.

Michael: *[Talking past adultest Ash] This is a message for the whole self, so please listen in. I'd like to speak directly to whoever may know something about the drinking that happened after getting the upsetting news. If there's no one who knows something, that's fine. If you're there but don't want to talk right now, just say 'No.'*

Another self-state assumes full executive control via a dissociative switch. I confirm with other self-states whether Adultest Ash is now unaware of what's happening. He is not present, as is typical when he switches. This self-state, which identified as 26 years old, is in distress and crying immediately upon arriving 'up front.' This state has a different tone of voice and mannerisms, which seem pronouncedly 'younger' than those of adultest Ash.

26 y.o. Self-state: I don't want to be seen crying. It's weak.

Michael: *You're in pain. Can you help me understand what happened?*

26: They found cancer in my prostate...."Cancer" is a dirty word. It's caused us so much pain and grief.

I sat with Ash's grief and wondered aloud whether it would be helpful for this to be shared with adultest Ash, even though this connection has not existed, and has even been actively prevented by other self-states, up to now. The 26 y.o. self-state and others agreed to allow it.

Michael: *Everyone, listen in if you can. I'd like to convene the 'meeting place' and invite the 'adultest' Ash [who, up to this point in the conversation, was entirely unaware of the exchange] to join this 26-year-old there.*

The 26-year-old self-state confirmed the arrival of adultest Ash in the previously established meeting place, depersonalized from their typical executive, 'up front' state, while also still consciously aware. Talking past the 26-year-old self-state to adultest Ash in the meeting place, I facilitated an introduction, as this was the first time these two aspects of Ash had 'met.' I asked both of them about the possibility of employing an EMDR-influenced intervention, in the form of tactile BL-DAS, to help soften the pain and foster a connection. Consent was granted to allow this, both from these two self-states and others within the self-system.

At this point, I invited the 26-year-old and adultest Ash to imagine sitting across from one another in the meeting place, knee-to-knee, and begin tapping each other's knees in short 'sets' of 10–15 taps. (Each of these states was already familiar with EMDR from previous work.) Ash's self-tapping of his actual knees accompanies the mutual, imaginal tapping in the meeting place. What follows is an account of this processing, following the first set of 10-15 taps.

Michael: *OK, just take a pause from tapping for a moment: What are you noticing now? [I say this each time, but the language will not be repeated from here in the transcript.]*

26: We're too old for this [drinking]. It hurts us.

Michael: *Just notice that and tap.* [Again, I say something like this to resume processing, but will only note it once for your information; 10-15 taps]

26: Sometimes it's better to talk about things instead of trying to do it myself. [10-15 taps]

26: Sometimes it's better to talk about things instead of trying to do it myself. [10-15 taps]

26: I don't want to hurt us again. [10-15 taps; a spontaneous, discernible shift in executive control and presence occurred during this set. Adultest Ash returned to executive control.]

Adultest Ash: I don't think [the 26 y.o.] wants to hurt. I just think they're scared. There's a very strong fear of dying. I don't understand why.

Further processing was paused there. The 26-year-old self-state is one that holds memories of many of their friends dying of AIDS. Before anyone knew what it was, AIDS was referred to, colloquially, as 'gay cancer.' Since those days, Ash has also lost good friends to cancers of different kinds, intensifying the impact of the previous losses. The 26-year-old self-state has been particularly impacted by these present-day losses.

Following this brief intervention, any lingering trauma material was set aside in a container, the 'meeting place' was closed, and all active self-states were invited to return to their respective end-of-session states. Because Ash tends to be quite responsive to hypnotic work, even without a formal trance elicitation, I checked to ensure that he felt fully re-alerted, oriented, and present in the moment and in himself.

In the following week's session, Ash reflected on how 'extraordinary' it was to see – and feel – a glimpse of a part of his past in such an immediate, visceral way without feeling overwhelmed by it. Further trauma work would be necessary to address the sources of activation for the 26-year-old self-state, but ongoing internal conflict – the result of competing ways of coping with pain – lessened considerably. Episodes of alcohol use driven by the 26-year-old self-state diminished in frequency and intensity, in part because of his effort to refrain from using alcohol to soothe himself during crises.

With less internal conflict and greater, largely implicit connectivity established between the adultest Ash and the 26-year-old self-state, adultest Ash reported that he was finding it increasingly easy to see positives in his life. He observed that his capacity to cope with stress seemed to be improving. We have since learned that, with increased connection to the 26-year-old self-state, adultest Ash also gained more conscious access to his previously dissociated history.

Communication Problems?

Dissociation maintains functional separateness between the explicitly known and the not-yet-known, in all dimensions of experience (e.g., behavior, affect, sensation, and knowledge; Braun 1988a, 1988b; ISSTD, 2011). Anything, or anyone, that seeks to reduce that separateness may be met with both reflexive and conscious, intentional avoidance, in a variety of forms (van der Hart et al., 2006). The dissociation was seemingly necessary to ensure psychological, emotional, and physical survival. Clients who have chronic, ongoing experiences of boundary violation – psychological, emotional, physical, sexual – may have a presenting self-state in therapy who has little to no intentional access to/awareness of what's going on inside. And our own characteristics as the therapist and our practice frame matter, too: How we present to the world, the language we use, the setting (whether virtual or in-person) in which we practice, how emotionally mature we are, and more. We have no idea how we are being experienced, and even the "fronting" self-state may not be (fully) aware of whether/how outside reality is perceived by other aspects of their system (see Chapter 10). These and other factors could impact whether self-states are able or willing to engage. This is not an issue exclusive to IFS, Ego State Therapy, or any other "parts" therapy approach. It's about attachment.

Some people – or certain self-states – may have become averse to the sense of anyone "trying to get in" to their mind because they were/are never allowed to develop and maintain self-defined boundaries with other power figures in their life. As such, it can be helpful – and more empathically attuned – to consider a lack of explicit communication as a covert assertion of boundaries rather than as 'resistance.' In a way, even an implicit expression of 'No, you cannot come in' is very positive and encouraging, because it may be a sign that you, as the therapist, are perceived, at least by some part(s), as a safe enough person. You may be the first person with whom they can assert their boundaries free of harm. Even a seeming negative can be reframed as a positive, then explored in that context.

I always keep in mind that people may have several self-states but only have one set of ears. Kluft (2017) highlighted that there are likely different 'cognitive apparati' monitoring what's going on out in the world. He recommends both closely observing the client's dissociative surface (presentation) for subtle indicators of copresence and passive influence, and assuming that all self-states are always listening – even if this isn't strictly true – with the understanding that everything that is said and done in therapy has an impact. (See also: Franklin, 1988.) Words are not the only way that self-states may 'talk' to you – some may not have access to language or speech – so look out for indicators of (and be prepared with ways to engage) self-states' nonverbal communication (Kluft, 1985; see also Chapter 11). Alison Miller (2012) offers important considerations, as described by one of her client's self-states, that can help deeper work feel safer, regardless of a client's inner complexity:

1. strong boundaries, especially at the start, when [self-states are testing the therapist's boundaries];
2. showing compassion and respect for each insider;
3. making it clear that the client does not have to answer your questions;
4. asking minimally intrusive questions early in therapy; deeper ones should be asked only when trust has been established with most of the system;

5. trying to get the [self-states] to work together as a democratic team, turning what was a hierarchy gradually into a representative democracy, "knights of the round table," a "football team," or a healthy family. (p. 132).

Alison Miller specializes in treating survivors of ritualistic, extreme, and organized abuse, which relies heavily upon behavioral conditioning. We are all conditioned by our relational experience, and individual therapy, by its very nature, is very much a relational 'two-way street' (see Casement, 1991; Maroda, 1999).

Conclusion

The 'self' develops organically as an integration of the lived experience of *all* ego states – except when chronic exposure to inescapable pain makes that integration impossible. The experience of different self-states deserves recognition and thoughtful, maybe even direct, engagement in a way that honors each in service of supporting integrative functioning on the *whole* client's terms. The considerations we have discussed in this chapter, including the assumption of a sole, central executive implied by the language we use, carry significant weight in clinical practice. The theoretical and practical differences between IFS and Ego State Therapy matter less, perhaps, when a therapist is treating a non-dissociative individual. Those differences can become more problematic when a person has distinct self-states and, thus, more than one center of consciousness from which decisions are made and actions taken. The self-state that occupies the central executive position is not necessarily 'special' or superior to other ego states, even if states are *qualitatively* different from one another. In this chapter, we explored several considerations that may influence how far EMDR therapists might be willing to extend themselves to work more dynamically with clients' entire self-system. These are not theoretical considerations, as they arise rather frequently when IFS-trained therapists 'run out' of track in practical application of the approach in working with dissociative clients. With that in mind, consider what I've shared as both an introduction to Part IV and an invitation to be curious about new possibilities for treatment in an expanded frame.

References

Abramowitz, E. G., & Torem, M. S. (2018). The roots and evolution of ego-state theory and therapy. *International Journal of Clinical and Experimental Hypnosis, 66*(4), 353–370. https://doi.org/10.1080/00207144.2018.1494435

American Psychological Association. (2014). *About the society of psychological hypnosis*. www.apadivisions.org/division-30/about

American Psychiatric Association. (2022). *DSM-5-TR – Diagnostic and statistical manual of mental disorders* (5th ed., text revision). American Psychiatric Association Publishing.

American Psychological Association. (n.d.). Cathexis. In *APA dictionary of psychology*. Retrieved May 4, 2025, from dictionary.apa.org/cathexis

Baker, E. L., & Spiegel, E. B. (2020). Dancing in the in-between: Hypnosis, transitional space, and therapeutic action. *American Journal of Clinical Hypnosis, 62*(1-2), 31–59. https://doi.org/10.1080/00029157.2019.1585328

Barabasz, A., & Watkins, J. G. (2005). *Hypnotherapeutic techniques* (2nd ed.). Brunner-Routledge.

Bergmann, U. (2008). Hidden selves: Treating dissociation in the spectrum of personality disorders. In C. Forgash & M. Copeley (Eds.). *Healing the heart of trauma and dissociation with EMDR and ego state therapy* (pp. 227–265). Springer Publishing Company.

Binet, A. (1896). *Alterations of personality* (H. G. Baldwin, Trans.). D. Appleton and Company.

Bliss, E. L. (1983). Multiple personalities, related disorders, and hypnosis. *American Journal of Clinical Hypnosis, 26*(2), 114–123. https://doi.org/10.1080/00029157.1983.10404151

Bliss, E. L. (1986). Multiple personality, allied disorders and hypnosis. Oxford University Press.

Brand, B. L., Myrick, A. C., Loewenstein, R. J., Classen, C. C., Lanius, R., McNary, S. W., Pain, C., & Putnam, F. W. (2012). A survey of practices and recommended treatment interventions among expert therapists treating patients with dissociative identity disorder and dissociative disorder not otherwise specified. *Psychological Trauma: Theory, Research, Practice, and Policy, 4*(5), 490–500. https://doi.org/10.1037/a0026487

Braun, B. G. (1988a). The BASK model of dissociation. *Dissociation, 1*(1), 4–23. hdl.handle.net/1794/1276

Braun, B. G. (1988b). The BASK model of dissociation: Part II. Treatment. *Dissociation, 1*(2), 16–23. hdl.handle.net/1794/1340

Bromberg, P. M. (2020). *The shadow of the tsunami: And the growth of the relational mind*. Routledge.

Casement, P. J. (1991). *Learning from the patient*. The Guilford Press.

Chu, J. A. (1991). The repetition compulsion revisited: Reliving dissociated trauma. *Psychotherapy: Theory, Research, Practice, Training, 28*(2), 327–332. https://doi.org/10.1037/0033-3204.28.2.327

Coy, D. M. (2025). The autohypnotic model of dissociation. In A. M. Gomez & J. Hosey (Eds.), *The handbook of complex trauma and dissociation in children: Theory, research and clinical applications* (pp. 89–106). W. W. Norton & Company. https://doi.org/10.4324/9781003350156

Federn, P. (1952). *Ego psychology and the psychoses*. (E. Weiss, Ed.). Basic Books.

Ferenczi, S. (1916). *Contributions to psycho-analysis*. Richard G. Badger.

Franklin, J. (1988). Diagnosis of covert and subtle forms of multiple personality disorder. *Dissociation, 1*(2), 27–33. hdl.handle.net/1794/1342

Freud, S. (1923). The ego and the id. In J. Strachey et al. (Trans.), *The standard edition of the complete psychological works of Sigmund Freud.* (Vol. XIX). Hogarth Press.

Freud S. (1933). *New introductory lectures on psycho-analysis, standard edition.* (Vol. XXII). Hogarth Press.

Freud S. (1940). *An outline of psycho-analysis, standard edition.* (Vol. XXIII). Hogarth Press.

Gilboa-Schechtman E. (2024). Case conceptualization in clinical practice and training. *Clinical psychology in Europe*, *6*(Spec Issue), e12103. https://doi.org/10.32872/cpe.12103

Gilson, G., & Kaplan, S. (2000). *The therapeutic interweave in EMDR: Before and beyond – a manual for EMDR trained clinicians.* EMDR Humanitarian Assistance Programs.

González, A., & Mosquera, D. (2012). *EMDR and dissociation: The progressive approach* (First Edition, Revised).

Gruenewald, D. (1984). On the nature of multiple personality: Comparisons with hypnosis. *International Journal of Clinical and Experimental Hypnosis, 32*(2), 170–190. https://doi.org/10.1080/00207148408416008

Hartford Institute for Geriatric Nursing. (2025). *Protocols.* Retrieved June 9, 2025, from hign.org/consultgeri/resources/protocols/iatrogenesis#:~:text=From%20the%20Greek%20word%20iatros,of%20the%20illness%20or%20injury

Hartmann, H., & Loewenstein, R. M. (1962). Notes on the superego. *The Psychoanalytic Study of the Child, 17*, 42–81. https://doi.org/10.1080/00797308.1962.11822838

Hasker, W. (2010). Persons and the unity of consciousness. In R. C. Koons & G. Bealer (Eds.), *The waning of materialism* (pp. 175–190). Oxford University Press. https://doi.org/10.1093/acprof:oso/9780199556182.001.0001

Henning, J. A. (2016). An intersubjective view of empathy and hypnotic trance: Response to wickramasekera II. *American Journal of Clinical Hypnosis, 58*(3), 256–273. https://doi.org/10.1080/00029157.2015.1102701

International Society for Study of Dissociation. (2005). Guidelines for treating dissociative identity disorder in adults (2005). *Journal of Trauma & Dissociation, 6*(4), 69–149. https://doi.org/10.1300/j229v06n04_05

International Society for the Study of Trauma and Dissociation. (2011). Guidelines for treating dissociative identity disorder in adults, third revision. *Journal of Trauma & Dissociation, 12*(2), 115–187. https://doi.org/10.1080/15299732.2011.537248

Janet, P. (2022). *Subconscious acts, anesthesias, and psychological disaggregation in psychological automatism: Partial automatism.* (G. Craparo & O. van der Hart, Eds.). Routledge. (Original work published 1889) https://doi.org/10.4324/9781003198727

Keuroghlian, A. S., Butler, L. D., Neri, E., & Spiegel, D. (2010). Hypnotizability, posttraumatic stress, and depressive symptoms in metastatic breast cancer. *International Journal of Clinical and Experimental Hypnosis*, *58*(1), 39–52. https://doi.org/10.1080/00207140903310790

Kluft, R. P. (1982). Varieties of hypnotic interventions in the treatment of multiple personality. *American Journal of Clinical Hypnosis, 24*(4), 230–240. https://doi.org/10.1080/00029157.1982.10403310

Kluft, R. P. (1985). Using hypnotic inquiry protocols to monitor treatment progress and stability in multiple personality disorder. *American Journal of Clinical Hypnosis, 28*(2), 63–75. https://doi.org/10.1080/00029157.1985.10402636

Kluft, R. P. (1989). Iatrogenic creation of new alter personalities. *Dissociation, 2*(2), 83–91. hdl.handle.net/1794/1428

Kluft, R. P. (2002). The inevitability of ego state therapy in the treatment of dissociative identity disorder and allied states. In B. Peter, W. Bongartz, D. Revenstorf, & W. Butollo (Eds.), *Munich 2000: The 15th international congress of hypnosis* (pp. 69–77). MEG-Stiftung. www.meg-stiftung.de/index.php/de/publikationen/3-hypnosis-international-monographs/21-munich-2000-the-15th-international-congress-of-hypnosis

Kluft, R. P. (2017). Trying to keep it real: My experience in developing clinical approaches to the treatment of DID. *Frontiers in the Psychotherapy of Trauma and Dissociation, 1*(1), 18–44. https://doi.org/10.46716/ftpd.2017.0002

Knipe, J. (2019). *EMDR toolbox: Theory and treatment of complex PTSD and dissociation* (2nd ed.). Springer Publishing.

Kruger, J., & Dunning, D. (1999). Unskilled and unaware of it: How difficulties in recognizing one's own incompetence lead to inflated self-assessments. *Journal of Personality and Social Psychology, 77*(6), 1121–1134. https://doi.org/10.1037/0022-3514.77.6.1121

Leutner, S., & Piedfort-Marin, O. (2021). The concept of ego state: From historical background to future perspectives. *European Journal of Trauma & Dissociation, 5*(4), Article 100184. https://doi.org/10.1016/j.ejtd.2020.100184

Lilienfeld, S. O., Kirsch, I., Sarbin, T. R., Lynn, S. J., Chaves, J. F., Ganaway, G. K., & Powell, R. A. (1999). Dissociative identity disorder and the sociocognitive model: Recalling lessons of the past. *Psychological Bulletin, 125*, 507–523. https://doi.org/10.1037/0033-2909.125.5.507

Maroda, K. J. (1999). *Seduction, surrender, and transformation: Emotional engagement in the analytic process.* Analytic Press.

Maroda, K. J. (2022). *The analyst's vulnerability: Impact on theory and practice.* Routledge.

Maslow, A. H. (1963). The need to know and the fear of knowing. *Journal of General Psychology, 68*(1), 111–125. https://doi.org/10.1080/00221309.1963.9920516

Merckelbach, H., Devilly, G. J., & Rassin, E. (2002). Alters in dissociative identity disorder. Metaphors or genuine entities? *Clinical Psychology Review, 22*(4), 481–497. https://doi.org/10.1016/s0272-7358(01)00115-5

Meyerson, J., Edry, N., & Feldman, B. (2025). Exploring hypnotist trance: The experiences of skilled practitioners. *The American Journal of Clinical Hypnosis, 67*(2), 129–141. https://doi.org/10.1080/00029157.2024.2398431

Miller, A. (2012). *Healing the unimaginable: Treating ritual abuse and mind control.* Karnac.

Orne, M. (1959). The nature of hypnosis: Artifact and essence. *Journal of Abnormal and Social Psychology, 58*(3), 277–299. https://doi.org/10.1037/h0046128

Orne, M. (1979). On the simulating subject as a quasi-control group in hypnosis research: What, why, and how. In E. Fromm & R. E. Shor (Eds.), *Hypnosis: Developments in research and new perspectives* (2nd ed.)(pp. 519–566). Routledge.

Paulsen, S. L. (2009). *Looking through the eyes of trauma and dissociation: An illustrated guide for EMDR clinicians and clients*. Booksurge.

Paulsen, S. L. (2018). Neuroaffective embodied self therapy (NEST): An integrative approach to case formulation and EMDR treatment planning for complex cases. *Frontiers in the Psychotherapy of Trauma and Dissociation, 1*(2), 125–148. https://doi.org/10.46716/ftpd.2017.0009

Prince, W. F. (1916). The Doris case of quintuple personality. *Journal of Abnormal Psychology, 11*(2), 73–122. https://doi.org/10.1037/h0072650

Ross, C. A. (1997). *Dissociative identity disorder: Diagnosis, clinical features, and treatment of multiple personality* (2nd ed.). Wiley.

Schwartz, R. (1995). *Internal family systems therapy*. The Guilford Press.

Schwartz, R., & Sweezy, M. (2019). *Internal family systems therapy* (2nd ed.). The Guilford Press.

Shapiro, F. (2018). *Eye Movement Desensitization and Reprocessing (EMDR) therapy: Basic principles, protocols and procedures* (3rd ed.). The Guilford Press.

Sidis, B. (1898). *The psychology of suggestion: A research into the subconscious nature of man and society*. D. Appleton and Company.

Sidis, B. (1914). *The foundations of normal and abnormal psychology*. Richard G. Badger.

Sidis, B., & Goodhart, S. P. (1968). *Multiple personality: An experimental investigation into the nature of human individuality*. Greenwood Press. (Original work published 1904)

Tversky, A., & Kahneman, D. (1973). Availability: A heuristic for judging frequency and probability. *Cognitive Psychology, 5*(2), 207–232. https://doi.org/10.1016/0010-0285(73)90033-9

Twombly, J. (2024). *Trauma and dissociation informed internal family systems: How to successfully treat C-PTSD and dissociative disorders* (2nd ed). Self-published.

Van der Hart, O., Nijenhuis, E. R. S., & Solomon, R. (2010). Dissociation of the personality in complex trauma-related disorders and EMDR: Theoretical considerations. *Journal of EMDR Practice and Research, 4*(2), 76–92. https://doi.org/10.1891/1933-3196.4.2.76

Van der Hart, O., Nijenhuis, E. R. S., and Steele, K. (2006). *The haunted self: Structural dissociation and the treatment of chronic traumatization*. W. W. Norton & Company.

Watkins, J. G. (1977). The psychodynamic manipulation of ego states in hypnotherapy. In F. Antonelli (Ed.), *Therapy in psychosomatic medicine* (Vol. 2, pp. 398–403). Symposia.

Watkins, J. G. (1978). *The therapeutic self: Developing resonance – key to effective relationships*. Human Sciences Press.

Watkins, H. H., & Watkins, J. G. (1993). Ego-state therapy in the treatment of dissociative disorders. In R. P. Kluft & C. G. Fine (Eds.), *Clinical perspectives on dissociative identity disorder* (pp. 277–299). American Psychiatric Press.

Watkins, H. H., & Watkins, J. G. (1997). *Ego states: Theory and therapy.* W. W. Norton & Co.

Wickramasekera II, I. E. (2015). Mysteries of hypnosis and the self are revealed by the psychology and neuroscience of empathy. *American Journal of Clinical Hypnosis, 57*(3), 330–348. https://doi.org/10.1080/00029157.2014.978495

Yager, J., Kay, J., & Kelsay, K. (2021). Clinicians' cognitive and affective biases and the practice of psychotherapy. *American Journal of Psychotherapy*, *74*(3), 119–126. https://doi.org/10.1176/appi.psychotherapy.20200025

Chapter 10

Mapping a Self-System

D. Michael Coy

Introduction

Memory mapping is a process familiar to EMDR therapists as a means for identifying dysfunctionally stored memories linked by common elements. These include components of five-sense perception, emotion, inner body sensation, negatively valenced beliefs (e.g., negative cognitions), and even time, if we consider that these components may link past, present, and anticipated future experiences. The purpose of and approach to mapping may vary according to the degree of dissociation/disaggregation and the current stage or phase of treatment. In the face of dissociative symptoms and disorders, mapping must account for memories whose elements may be distributed in a fragmented fashion among different self-states (see Van der Hart et al., 1993).

These self-states may (or may not) have recognizable linkages to other states spanning multiple time periods and possess varying degrees of developmental sophistication. It is not only about memory, however. States' connections are also relational and may be either distant or enmeshed, collaborative and nurturing, adversarial, or even persecutory. Their relationships may exist only within the inner world or extend into the outer world, either partially, through 'intrusions' into a fronting state's executive functioning, or entirely, when another state fully assumes executive control. Sometimes, experiences sourced from subconscious states seep into, commingle with, and distort a central executive's perception, resulting in what Kluft (1999) called the 'third reality.' These and other factors, both encompassing and transcending the mapping of the memories themselves, must be considered.

In this chapter, we will discuss the context for mapping with increasingly complex trauma in EMDR therapy. We will then define and touch upon the history of the practice of mapping as it relates to dissociation and EMDR therapy. This will open the door to clarify basic directions

DOI: 10.4324/9781003410201-14

for mapping and discuss additional approaches to accommodate different practitioner styles and client capacities. We will then discuss several dimensions of and routes of inquiry within the mapping process itself. The chapter will conclude with an illustrated case example, which will begin with indicators of potentially high-risk self-state activity noted in a client's diagnostic results, progress to initial mapping, and illustrate a process of inquiry to identify the more deeply embedded sources of that risk.

Mapping Traumatic Memory: Simple, Complex, Multiplex

An expanded adaptive information processing model can help us consider how chronic exposure to inescapable, toxic experience, possibly beginning in an early developmental period, precipitated disaggregation (or non-aggregation) within and among neural networks (see Chapter 2).

Mapping can be a relatively straightforward process when a client's traumatic experience is less complicated or more discrete in nature. In this case, the person's sense of self is relatively well developed and remains largely unified and coherent following the trauma. In other words, there may be some wounded ego state(s) whose overwhelming pain has become fused with context-specific maladaptive beliefs (e.g., 'I should have known better,' 'It's all my fault'). This level of memory disaggregation may manifest as 'simpler' posttraumatic stress disorder (PTSD), phobias, depression, anxieties, and so on. Relational aspects of the trauma(s) may feature more prominently in the 'now' as sequela rather than as a central feature of the source wounding. Even when they *are* connected to the past, however, such as with moral injuries, the experiences may still be more identifiable, discrete, and concretely addressed. Here, we are mapping memories. In EMDR therapy, 'standard' memory mapping involves creating a standard target sequence across the three temporal prongs by (1) identifying present-day difficulties, (2) tracing back to sources of these difficulties rooted in the past, and (3) creating new templates for resilient functioning in the future, based on enduring past and present scenarios. EMDR employs BL-DAS in structured, planful ways to facilitate adaptive resolution of these dysfunctionally stored memories and a return to health by both metabolizing painful experience and (re)establishing connections between previously disaggregated neural networks (Shapiro, 2018; Sidis, 1898; see also Chapter 2).

For clients whose 'country of self' (Watkins, 1977) has been repeatedly invaded and colonized by painful experience, there may be heightened and ongoing intra- and interpersonal conflicts and pervasive shame rooted in earlier developmental periods. Their sense of self is likely less cohesive overall owing to less functional connectivity, and thus more isolation, among ego states. Depending on the nature of the harm (i.e., type, age of onset, intensity, duration), the wounding experiences may be both discrete and diffuse, and possibly less recognizable at times as the result of old wounding. 'Present triggers' may be mistaken for the first occurrence of an issue rather than as inflammation of an existing wound with a potentially long lineage. This is the terrain of complex trauma, broadly speaking, including Complex PTSD (World Health Organization, 2022). Finer-grained mapping may include identifying current challenges, existing and potential new resiliencies, and sources of complex and long-standing difficulties, for both individual ego states and the person overall. Straightforward target identification or sequencing may be challenging or, at times, impossible, at least initially. Ego state exploration may be helpful and, for some clients, unavoidable. A staged, integrative, and relationally oriented approach is often necessary and advisable (e.g., Herman, 1992; Ford & Courtois, 2020). EMDR may take an alternately leading and supporting role in the treatment.

In dissociative disorders, disaggregation and fragmentation rule, to a greater or lesser degree, and centralized leadership from a consistently central executive ego state may at times (or all times) be entirely absent. Unlike in standard EMDR therapy, in practice with non-dissociative clients, it may be neither possible nor advisable to tunnel down into the depths of a dissociative client's trauma history at the start of treatment. On one hand, a client may either not recall large swathes of their past, or else their memory for the past – especially their younger years – may be spotty (i.e., retrograde amnesia). On the other hand, asking a client to dig down more deeply into their history prematurely may exacerbate their symptoms. As such, collecting a trauma history may take place over time. (Refer to Chapter 6 for further discussion of history taking.) However, a client's ability to produce a relatively continuous timeline of their history does not obviate the need to screen/assess for structural dissociation, particularly if affect is missing from their narrative (see Braun, 1986a). Mapping here is considered by many to be critical for effective treatment, due to the absence of or breakdown in both infrastructure and communication throughout the self-system (e.g., Braun, 1986a; Fine, 1991, 1993, 1999; Kluft, 2013; Ross, 1989, 1997). Sequencing and processing of discrete 'memories' in an unmodified EMDR frame can pose risks and, in some instances, may be impossible owing to the severity of internal fragmentation. EMDR takes a decidedly supportive/adjunctive role in this treatment, which is psychodynamic and relational in nature (see Chapter 3).

Self-System Mapping: Origins, Uses, and Role in EMDR

Just as creating a basic EMDR therapy targeting sequence supports our conceptualization of the wounding memories that are the focus of the healing work, self-system mapping can provide us a "map, diagram, or schema" of self-states' "best understanding of how they fit together or their sense of their inner world" (Putnam, 1989, p. 210). This is somewhat like developing a genogram for an external family system (Jolly et al., 1980; Kitchur, 2005), but at the individual/intrapsychic level. Just as a genogram can depict the transgenerational story of a family's members and inner workings, a self-system map can similarly offer a visual representation of the self-states, their relational dynamics, and the source of symptoms within a dissociative self. The earliest discussions of self-system mapping, though not by name, appeared in the *Journal of Abnormal Psychology* and associated literature (A., 1908, 1909; Prince & Peterson, 1908; Prince, 1916). In more contemporary literature, Braun (1986a), Dawson (1990), Fine (1991, 1993), Fraser (1991, 2003), Kluft (1999, 2013, 2018), Miller (2012b), Putnam (1989), and Ross (1989, 1997) have discussed mapping as part of the overall treatment of dissociation. According to Braun (1986a), mapping allows for a "more complex organization" of information gathered during treatment, serves as a visual means for client and therapist alike to track treatment progress, provides ideas for the direction of therapy, and helps guide "how, among whom, and when" to facilitate greater integrative functioning amongst different self-states (p. 14).

Mapping as History Taking

Initial diagnostic evaluation and history taking can both be thought of as early-stage layers of mapping (Kluft, 2018). Kluft (1993, p. 155) notes that he works early on to identify and engage any state(s) who (1) can openly communicate and serve as a "resource or guide" in navigating the self-system; (2) have concerns about him or the work itself; and (3) "want to die, commit suicide, or inflict injury to the body." Focusing first on these states can mitigate the risk of retaliation for communicating (via internal perpetration) and/or decompensation resulting from prematurely accessing traumatic memory material or states associated with it. A client's available history may be overlaid with a mapping of self-states associated with or generating specific issues and symptoms to develop a more dimensional conceptualization. Notably, the multidimensional inventory of dissociation (MID; Dell, 2006) can be very helpful for cross-referencing these, owing to how *The MID Report* organizes information about clients' self-reported symptoms. (The case example later in this chapter will illustrate such an application of the MID.)

Catherine Fine's (1991) basic, two-step 'recipe' for working with a client to create an initial self-system map involves:

1. using a large sheet of paper, whiteboard, etc., whether physical or online, the client places their preferred name at the center, after which
2. the 'fronting' self-state and/or other states fill in any accompanying names, roles, ages, etc., arranged in a way that reflects "how similar or dissimilar they feel toward or about one another" (p. 670).

Depending on the number of self-states and the degree of shared awareness (Prince, 1916), as well as which states are invited (Kluft, 2018) or opt to participate, the map can range in detail from "a blank page" to a "scattergram" (Fine, 1991, p. 671). Any states that wish to remain anonymous, or who have no sort of 'designation' (name, age, or other signifier), can be invited to indicate their existence with a dash (Kluft, 2009), an X, etc. Although we as practitioners may be tempted to create a sophisticated spreadsheet that exhaustively catalogs every self-state, this is not recommended. Doing so poses the risk of bogging down the therapy with a glut of information without any immediate way to make sense of it and, in some instances, may only feed an inexperienced therapist's personal (i.e., voyeuristic) interest in a client's self-states (Ross, 1997). Additional options for establishing the composition and organization of a client's self-system include making a list (rather than a visual map) of self-states (Kluft, 2018; Putnam, 1989), employing sand tray (Gómez, 2012, 2025; Sachs, 1993), and engaging artistic expression (Cohen & Cox, 1995; Spring, 1993).

As mapping can involve engagement of traumatic memory material, contraindications for the scope and pace of mapping are essentially the same as those for proceeding with ego state work or trauma processing (see Chapter 9). However, these 'externalized' approaches for mapping can be very useful to create a bit of distance (in case of a tendency toward intense activation or avoidance) and accommodate the needs of persons who experience aphantasia (an inability to visualize in one's mind). For readers who are trained in clinical hypnosis, Kluft (2018) describes his use of glove anesthesia as a means for distancing the conscious, central executive from the activity. This can help reduce a 'fronting' self-state's capacity to recall what has been written down, if remembering might pose problems for the self-system in the short-term. (For more on why this might matter for a typically amnesic 'fronting' state, see Marano et al., 2025; Richardson & Lacroix, 2024.)

EMDR, Dissociation, and Mapping

Most of the dissociation-focused EMDR therapy literature features some variation on George Fraser's (1991, 2003) *Dissociative Table* technique as the vehicle for mapping states in EMDR therapy. This technique is a very adaptable, powerful, hypno-projective method (i.e., using hypnotically facilitated imagery) for identifying and working with ego/self-states. It can be used to facilitate resourcing and preparation for memory processing, to organize the processing itself, and to address new treatment challenges as they surface. In the dissociation-focused use of EMDR therapy, consult the writings of Bergmann (2008), Mosquera (2019), Gonzalez and Mosquera (2012), Knipe (2019), Martin (2012), Paulsen (2009), and Shebini (2019) for information on mapping – though not all these authors frame the process as mapping *per se*.

Although the recommendation to use the *Dissociative Table* technique is helpful, it often seems to be infused, at least in the EMDR therapy literature, with a bias toward the point-of-view of a 'fronting' state. Citing Paulsen (1995), Bergmann states that, "The detailed features of the [conference] room supplant the need for either switching or formal hypnosis and therefore save time and enhance co-consciousness" (p. 241). I disagree with this stance for two reasons. First, in some instances, switching and working directly with other self-states is both unavoidable and necessary to move the work forward (Kluft, 2006). Second, the absence of formal hypnosis does not equate to the absence of either hypnotic/trance phenomena or the need for the therapist to be aware of and conversant with clinical hypnosis. The hypnotic capacity is in the client – not the therapist – thus, it is best to know what one is getting oneself into (Coy, 2025; MacHovec, 1986; see also Chapter 9). This is one of many reasons that I recommend EMDR therapy practitioners, especially those who treat dissociation, seriously consider training in clinical hypnosis. I took to heart what one trainer in my initial clinical hypnosis course said: "Everything you say in therapy is a hypnotic suggestion," formal trance elicitation or no. Besides, asking someone to give focused attention to their inner experience via the *Dissociative Table*, which is essentially a hypnotic intervention, demands that we take greater care.

So, even if you are not trained in hypnosis, I recommend using the *Howard Alertness Scale* (HAS; Howard, 2017) if you are going to use the *Dissociative Table* technique. The *HAS* is a pre- and post-intervention tool for helping ensure that clients are fully alert, aware, and present in their self and in the room, at least to the degree they were at the start of a session (i.e., their baseline), following therapeutic work during which the client experienced trance. This is achieved by engaging the client in orienting their concrete senses to the present moment and environment and gauging their alertness on a 1-to-10 scale. If your client has not returned to their baseline level of alertness, then more time will be needed to ensure they have prior to concluding the session. Although you might assume Knipe's (2019) *Back-of-the-Head Scale* (BHS) is a fine substitute for the HAS, please keep in mind that the BHS was developed to assess *depersonalization* rather than environmental *alertness*. (Refer to Howard, 2017 for the *HAS* instructions and Kluft, 2012 for further information about addressing challenges in re-alerting clients.)

Considerations for Mapping a Client's Self-System

The following considerations for mapping a client's self-system were derived from a variety of sources, including Braun (1986a), Fine (1991, 1993, 1999), Kluft (1983, 2006), Miller (2012a, 2012b, 2012c), Prince (1916), Paulsen (2009), Paulsen & Golston (2014), Putnam (1989), Ross (1997), Sidis (1898), Van der Hart et al. (1993), and Vogt (2012), as well as my own experience. Keep in mind that this is not necessarily exhaustive.

Your Intention and Experience

- Are you seeking information about a specific issue or about the self-system more generally?
- What will you do with that information once you obtain it?
- Depending on your client's diagnostic profile, how prepared to do feel to work with whatever may surface in this process?

Your Client's Relationship to Their Subjective Experience

- *How does your client respond to the idea of 'parts,' 'aspects,' 'states of mind,' etc.?*
  If they seem phobic/avoidant, then it is critical to understand whether this is a natural component of their experience (i.e., dissociative phobias; Van der Hart et al., 2004; Van der Hart et al., 2006; Gonzalez & Mosquera, 2012) or whether they have been intentionally conditioned to avoid their inner experience (e.g., Miller, 2012a,b). If they experience heightened fear of what's within, then this depth of inquiry for the sake of mapping may be premature. (Refer to Miller, 2012c, for helpful considerations regarding pacing this aspect of the work, regardless of internal complexity.) If you are unaccustomed to working with dissociative clients, then seek training (e.g., through ISSTD; https://www.isst-d.org) and consultation before proceeding.

Who (or What) is Revealed and Not Revealed

- *Names or ages?*
  Not all states will have names, and it is advisable for the therapist to avoid assigning one (see Chapter 9). States may identify with no age, one age (e.g., 5 years old), or a range of ages (e.g., 7–9 years old). Additionally, states may not present as recognizably human, but instead as a member of some other species. They may appear to be noncorporeal or nonhuman (e.g., a spirit, shadow, a cloud, a four-legged mammal), in which case the form they take may be culturally influenced, the result of systematic/organized/extreme abuse (Miller, 2012b). Sometimes self-states' presentations, characteristics, and, if applicable, names, may be rooted in fantasy, metaphor, or take the form of 'fictives' literalized from media sources (Christensen, 2022).
- *How many of each of them, and in what ways do they connect?*
  There may be more than one state of the same age associated with a single experience – though each may hold different and/or overlapping BASK elements (Braun, 1988a,b) or they may each contain multiple BASK elements encapsulated within a discrete period of time, rather like a 'bucket brigade' in which, for example, one state holds five minutes of an experience, then another state holds the material for the next five minutes, and so on. (Refer to Van der Hart et al., 1993 for a discussion of memory fragmentation.) There may also be multiple states of the same age associated with different experiences during that same time period. States may also be associated with other, less visible/accessible states patterned after the characteristics and behaviors of an abuser (i.e., perpetrator introjects; see Chapters 11 and 12) or older, self-identifying states who have in some way aligned with and mimic the behavior of an abuser ('perpetrator-imitating' states; Van der Hart et al., 2010).
- *Do different states have distinguishing psychophysiological traits?*
  Self-states may exhibit physiological traits (visual acuity, eye color, voice, paralysis, headaches, physical capacities, etc.) that distinguish them from other states (e.g., Coons, 1988).
- *How do different states affect one another's presentation?*
  In other words, how do the traits of one self-state influence the presentational traits of another state that follows them when they assume executive control (i.e., 'order effect'; Kluft, 1988, citing personal communication with Frank Putnam)?
- *Do any states speak different languages, or present as nonverbal?*
  Regarding states' differing language use and comprehension, some states may be nonverbal or preverbal. In that case, ideomotor signaling (e.g., Kluft, 1985), head nods, etc., may be necessary to facilitate

communication. There are differences among being (1) incapable of verbalizing, (2) unwilling to verbalize, and (3) unable to verbalize due to fear of punishment. In the third case, identifying the source of this fear would be important. Some state(s) may use or understand a different language than the state that typically presents in therapy. For example, (1) the language your client typically uses in session may not be their native tongue (e.g., Ateş-Barlas, 2022), (2) states may have learned languages during the period(s) they inhabited executive control (e.g., Schimmenti, 2017), (3) the spoken language of a perpetrator was internalized along with other traits of that individual, and so on.

- *When did they come into existence, and what has their story been since then?*
  Some states may have an answer to this question. Others may offer that they have been around 'for as long as they can remember,' which in some instances may point to their having come into existence very early in life – making them potentially both old(er) and young(er) at the same time. The answer to the second question may also help clarify whether they are a fully formed or fragmentary state (see below).
- *What do they do?*
  This refers to the state's role, function, or purpose within the self-system. In other words, how do they fit into both the 'local' and overall functioning of the self-system? It is possible that some states will not know how to answer a question like, 'What is your job?,' so asking what they do may be more helpful.
- *To(ward) whom, how, and when do they do it? How do they influence or align with observable/reported signs and symptoms?*
  By 'to(ward)', we are interested in whether there is an object for whatever it is they do. The object(s) of their behavior(s) may be within the self (other states), outside the self, or both. 'How' helps us understand how they achieve the 'what' (see above) – for example, "I keep the little ones quiet" – "How do you do that?" – "I [yell at/scare/punish] them." Knowing this can help us correlate internal activity with symptom features (e.g., voices, crying, intrusive emotions/thoughts/impulses) reported by a "fronting," central executive state. This could mean intrusive symptoms or partial switches (where they retain some awareness of what is happening, even if they feel they have no control over it), or full switches (accompanied by amnesia). Finding out which self-states are capable of assuming executive control by coming fully 'up front' and what it looks/feels like when they do can be helpful for reducing (the therapist's) confusion. 'When' here means 'in what time period' – what year(s) do they perceive/believe it to be? 'Back then', or the actual now? This can help us determine whether time orientation work could be helpful (i.e., presentification; Van der Hart et al., 2010).

- *What activates ('triggers') the self-state connected to symptoms, behaviors, etc., and what does that look like?*
  Think of this as akin to tracing symptoms associated with a present trigger back to their source (past) memory material. In this case, however, the source is a self-state or states.
- *How do they feel about what they do?*
  This may sound like an odd question, but it is especially relevant for self-states whose role involves keeping other self-states contained. Sometimes, even if orienting a state to the present moment is not possible, they may be open to change if they do not like their job (see Chapter 12).
- *Do any self-states also have self-states of their own?*
  It is possible. These are described in some online sources as 'subsystems,' or 'sub-parts' (Miller, 2012a). However, the former term can also be used to describe split-off clusters/groupings of related states within a self-system (e.g., Gruenewald, 1984).
- *If you were seeking information about a symptom, did anyone/anything associated with that symptom make itself known or not?*
  If not, it may be that either (a) no state is specifically associated with the symptom, or (b) the state(s) that are connected to that symptom did not hear you, were not invited in a way that they identified with, or (c) state(s) are evading detection in service of self-preservation, or (d) some other reason.
- *If you convened an internal 'meeting place,' did any state show up disguised as another state?*
  This possibility was a new one for me when I encountered it only a couple of weeks before writing this. The intended focus of mapping with a client was "all self-states of a certain age" patterned after the client's brother. Two of these self-states were previously known, but three showed up in the meeting place in response to the invitation. The third 'brother' state's story did not make sense, owing to their chronology and alleged experience not matching up. The 'fronting' state, which was a witness to and participant in this discussion, suddenly declared that this state was not a 'brother' but instead a 'grandmother.' The newly 'unmasked' grandmother state's explanation for the disguise was that she needed to 'keep an eye on' one of the two brother self-states to "make sure he doesn't say something he's not supposed to." This revelation resolved the confusion. (The disguised 'grandmother' state *was* already known as being connected to the 'brother' state, as part of a larger cluster.)
- *Who/what seems 'missing' from the puzzle?*
  Expect that there may be plenty missing, particularly introjects. Self-states will likely reveal themselves during treatment, in context-specific

ways, rather than all at once. However, this is not the same as just waiting for self-states to show up (see Kluft, 2006).

- *Are the states fully formed, or are they fragmentary?*
Answering this last question likely will require that the practitioner interact more directly with the relevant self-state(s). Because the organization of a client's self-system represents the fragmentation of memory material, the nature of the fragmentation unavoidably will influence the context for consent and the content of treatment planning, resourcing, and trauma processing (e.g., Van der Hart et al., 1993). Helpfully, Bennett Braun describes differences he observed between fully formed self-states (i.e., 'personalities') and fragmentary states.

Fully Formed Self-States

Fully formed self-states have reached a level of sophistication beyond Sidis's (1898) secondary level of synthesis (reproductive consciousness, i.e., ego states) to achieve some degree of central executive-level recognitive capacity (see Chapter 2) in line with what we might expect in a more fully realized individual. According to Braun (1986b, p. xii), these self-states:

1. Exhibit consistent response patterns for given stimuli (i.e., whatever the behavior, it probably will be repeated under the same circumstances at another time),
2. Have experienced/can report a relatively continuous history (i.e., a significant life history of chained (associated) memories), and
3. Have both a range of emotions (rage, fear, sadness, joy, etc.) and a range of affective expression for these emotions (e.g., from mild anxiety to full-on terror)

Fragmentary Self-States

Braun (1986b, pp. xii–xiii) highlights that fragmentary self-states tend to possess consistent response patterns for given stimuli, as well as either a relatively continuous history or a range of emotions/affect, but not both. He also describes two specific types of fragmentary states. The first of these is *special-purpose fragments*, which, Braun notes, are "less than a fragment" with a "limited set of response patterns to stimuli and minimal life history and range of emotion/affect" (p. xiii), which may serve a specific function or deal with specific scenarios (e.g., enacting an isolated, trauma-related behavior). The second of these is *memory trace fragments*, which Braun suggests have "only a minimal set of response patterns to stimuli, life history, and range of emotion/affect but has knowledge for a short period of time" (p. xiii). Refer to Braun (1986b) for a fuller discussion of these classifications.

How Do Self-States Influence One Another and Connect with the Inner and Outer Worlds?

- *How are self-states more generally connected (or not connected) to one another, and what is the function of any connections?*
  It seems reasonable to consider that form follows function, even when we are referring to how self-states become organized (i.e., like attracts like). Here, it can be helpful to conceptualize in terms of the elements of EMDR *Phase III: Assessment.* Are different states connected by behavior, affect, sensation, knowledge (BASK elements; Braun, 1988a,b), a shared belief, etc.? Where are the 'gaps' in connection, and what accounts for those gaps: Is there simply an absence of information, or are there self-states hidden or obscured that fill in the gaps? What purpose do the connections and gaps serve?
- *To what degree and in what ways are self-states aware of and have insight into the experience and behaviors of other self-states (including whoever may predominantly 'front' in executive control)? To what degree and in what ways are self-states aware of internal (subconscious) and external (conscious) realities? How do these realities interact, overlap, etc. (Kluft's 'third reality')?*
  This refers both to coconsciousness – which can mean either that self-states are concurrently conscious regardless of degree of awareness (Taylor & Martin, 1944) or aware of one another's presence and activity (Greaves, 1989) and intraconsciousness, meaning that one self-state is aware of both the existence and thoughts of another self-state (Taylor & Martin, 1944). These awarenesses – and the amnesias that mark their absence – can be uni-, bi-, or multidirectional, partial or complete.
- *Are any self-states at risk of harm from other states? Do any self-states pose outward-facing risks?*
  It is critical to address risks of harm to the self or others. Self-directed harm could mean ideation or actions of a non-suicidal, suicidal, or implicitly homicidal nature. The latter would take the form of one state wishing to kill another state. It could also take the form of self-states acting upon one another intrapsychically in an emotional, physical, or sexual way – even absent any obvious external indicators that harm is occurring. There may also be self-states focused on harming other people, either non-homicidally or homicidally. (See, for example, Bliss, 1980; Goodman & Peters, 1995; Şar & Öztürk, 2009.)

- *Are there any trauma bonds between/amongst self-states?*
One example of this would be a child-identifying self-state who idealizes an abusive, persecutory state that it perceives to be 'mother.' The 'child' state may prevent the therapist from engaging their 'mother' in any kind of transformative work, as a means of maintaining the relationship's status quo (see Chapter 12).
- *How do self-states' perceptions, etc., influence how an executive state engages with you?*
Is therapy, and the therapist, safe or not-safe? How accurate (or distorted) are self-states' perceptions and experience of the therapist's presentation? This would include the therapist's actual identity, as well as their gender; voice register, volume, and tone; working style, etc. How might different states' transferences toward the therapist impact treatment (Wilbur, 1988)? Transference is a critical consideration in treatment (see Chapter 11) and may be quite complex, particularly when a client has a history of being harmed in therapy or has been subject to abuse that in some way mimics therapy dynamics (Loewenstein, 2018; Miller, 2012a,b)
- *What kinds of hierarchies exist within (a) clusters of self-states and (b) the self-system overall?*
The internal composition may replicate, to a greater or lesser degree, the 'pecking order' of relational dynamics in, for example, an abusive family system (Frankel & O'Hearn, 1996; Paulsen, 2009; Paulsen & Golston, 2014). For example, for one of my clients, mapping revealed an introjected family composed of a self-identifying child state (a younger version of the adult client), an older brother introject, a mother introject, a father introject, and even grandparent introjects. All of these states were bound together in a time-specific abuse dynamic. When considering hierarchies, we also want to consider whether they developed organically, due to spontaneous chaotic experience, or created intentionally via systematic/organized/extreme abuse (Miller, 2012a,,cb)?
- *What is left unanswered regarding internal dynamics and symptoms?*
Employing Karpman's (1968) *Drama Triangle* can be helpful in instances where there are lingering questions about why something might be happening inside when clear explanations have not been forthcoming (see Chapters 11 and 12).

It would be impossible to collect *all* the information reflected in the preceding questions in an initial mapping, but I decided to describe all these dimensions simply to highlight that they exist. One's initial case conceptualization and treatment approach will be unavoidably impacted by what is either unknown to or unimaginable to us as therapists and our client.

Case Example

Presenting Problem

TaMar (pronounced tuh-MAR; he/him), a Black, transgender man in his 20s, presented for treatment complaining of difficulty sleeping. He reported frequently (though not exclusively) at night feeling as though he wanted to die – without having any idea why this might be. He described feeling both 'depressed' and internally agitated much of the time. After several sessions getting to know TaMar and his available history, the therapist (Michael, a clinical social worker) could not identify much, pointing to DSM Criterion A traumas. TaMar was vague about the dynamics in his family of origin. He did, however, report lifelong difficulties connecting emotionally with others, with limited exception. TaMar shared that he felt very close with his partner, whom he has been with for five years, and at the same time often feeling emotionally 'stirred up' by the relationship. TaMar reported feeling safe with his partner's immediate family, who have been extremely supportive of them as a couple.

Michael conducted an initial screen for dissociation and found more questions than answers. He discussed this with TaMar, noting the value of moving forward with a more extensive, diagnostic evaluation, in this case, the MID (Dell, 2006), to identify less overt symptoms. TaMar expressed openness to this because he wanted to understand what was happening for him, too. The MID results were inconclusive for a dissociative disorder, but they did indicate a handful of notable dissociative symptoms. These included general posttraumatic dissociative symptoms such as retrograde amnesia (which might help contextualize the vagueness in some of TaMar's self-report during initial history taking) and flashbacks (including nightmares). Additionally, the results indicated the possible presence of active self-states, as evidenced by a remarkable frequency of partially dissociated intrusive experiences, including internal voices/struggle, persecutory voices, and identity confusion. There was no clinically significant evidence of contemporaneous (day-to-day) amnesia, which would point either to dissociative identity disorder (DID) or to a form of Other Specified Dissociative Disorder. However, TaMar *did* endorse isolated amnesic experiences in the past, coinciding with higher stress while they lived at home. It was clear that *something* was happening for TaMar.

A closer examination of TaMar's MID results drew Michael's attention to the "Critical Items" scale, which represents dissociative experiences that can be dangerous and potentially life-threatening. What most stood out were TaMar's endorsement of experiences that indicate internalized perpetrator activity and 'dangerously toxic' PTSD-type flashbacks:

Functionality and impairment scales *(refer to clinical summary graph for comparative norms)*			
Critical Items			**Raw mean Score**
Dangerous persecutory voices			
3	84.	**(2)**	Hearing a voice in your head that wants you to hurt yourself.
2	159.	**(2)**	Hearing a voice in your head that wants you to die.
Dangerously Toxic PTSD			
2	105.	**(1)**	Having traumatic flashbacks that make you want to inflict pain on yourself.
2	137.	**(1)**	Having traumatic flashbacks that make you want to die.

Figure 10.1 TaMar's MID Critical Items Scale (Detail).

Sources: Excerpted from MID Analysis v6.0 (Coy, Dell, & Schmidt, 2022).

These symptom features indicated several potential points of entry to better understand what might be happening. Michael explored these experiences with TaMar, who reported that he did not feel at risk of harming himself in any way. TaMar shared that the feelings of wanting to hurt himself or die didn't feel like "his." Rather, he described these feelings as being inside him, but it was as if they belonged to someone else. What next?

Identifying Contraindications for Deeper Exploration

Michael considered whether possible ego state work was appropriate this early in treatment (Stage 1). He recognized that the purpose was to reduce internal struggle to increase stabilization and thus reduce the risk of harm for TaMar in his daily life. Michael discussed with TaMar the possibility of exploring more deeply the presenting issue of 'wanting to die,' with those MID Critical Items in mind. Michael revisited a previous discussion with TaMar, when they covered what ego states are, as well as how an imaginal 'meeting place' (i.e., the *Dissociative Table* technique) can be a helpful way to engage ego states. Michael did say he wasn't sure whether they would end up doing any ego state work in this session. He suggested, instead, that creating an initial mapping of the ego states TaMar was aware of might be a good starting place. TaMar expressed openness to this, especially because he did not want to hurt himself or die. He found the internal messages and intrusive feelings to be really upsetting. Michael consulted his mental checklist for potential risks of engaging the client in deeper work.

- ☑ Client and therapist seem to have established an adequate, initial rapport.
- ☑ Client has no obvious phobias of either outwardly depicting or imaginally exploring their inner experience.
- ☑ Client has no pending or anticipated legal proceedings.
- ☑ Client appears to be stable in daily life and does not appear to be at heightened risk for suicide/non-suicidal self-injury or aggression toward others.

- ☑ Client's ego strength and emotional resources appear to be reasonably intact, comorbid mental health issues appear to be managed, and there are no risks related to substance use.
- ☑ Client has demonstrated in past sessions that they feel comfortable asking the therapist to pause so they can re-regulate when needed.
- ☑ Client has no treatment-complicating medical illnesses, etc.
- ☑ It is not solely a supportive psychotherapy; the client's overall interest in understanding what is happening for them is evident; the client seems accepting of the reality that this is a paced process, despite their desire to feel relief.
- ☑ Therapist has training and experience working with persons with dissociative disorders – including an attachment-based, psychodynamic/relational foundation; clinical hypnosis; Ego State Therapy; EMDR; Deep Brain Reorienting (Corrigan et al., 2025), etc. – and has both consultants and experienced peers to rely upon for ongoing support.
- ☑ Neither the client nor the therapist has any plans for an upcoming break in therapy (e.g., vacation or health leave).
- ☑ Client has granted initial consent to proceed.

With initial history taking and diagnostic evaluation completed (if inconclusive), no obvious contraindications for exploring TaMar's inner experience, and TaMar having a general idea of the proposed approach, the two decided to move forward. Even though they had no plan to engage in deeper work in this session, Michael still opted to use the *HAS* (see above) to establish TaMar's baseline alertness before beginning. In initial mapping, TaMar drew this:

Most recognizable to TaMar were the self-identifying states:

- TaMar at his current age of 22 (the one creating the map)
- States that identify with and correspond to TaMar's lived experience from ages 4–6; 8–12; 13 (lots of anger energy there); and 17–19

TaMar was familiar with the painful experience held by these states. More confusing to TaMar was the 'sun' that showed up in the meeting place, along with three 'primary color' states (red, yellow, blue) of indeterminate origin. Inquiry with all the states indicated on the initial map revealed no obvious correlations with the Critical Items symptoms. Subsequently, Michael discussed with TaMar the possibility of proceeding with a more symptom-focused exploration, using the 'meeting place,' with the intention of clarifying whether any states were connected with the 'wanting to die' feelings. TaMar wasn't sure what might show up, but he wanted to know. It was agreed to return to this in the next session. In

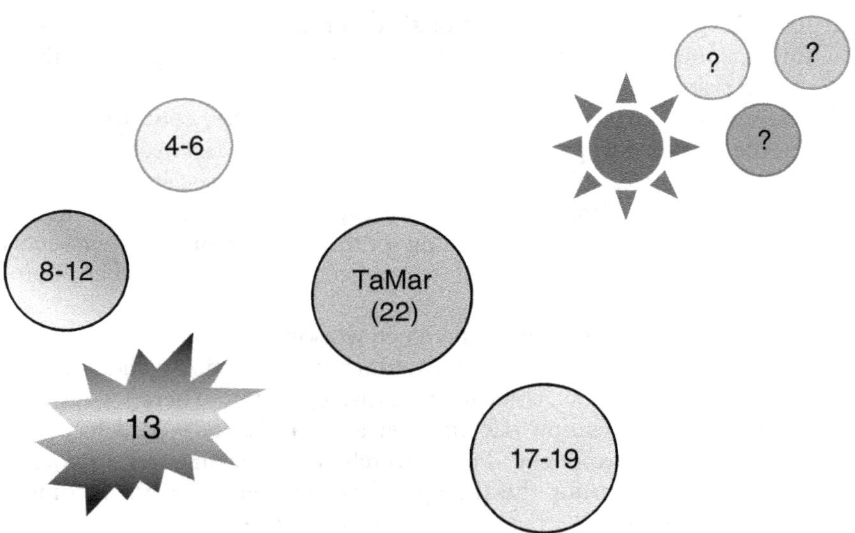

Figure 10.2 TaMar's Initial Self-System Mapping.

Phase VII: Closure, TaMar used the standard 'container' he had developed early on in treatment to set mental contents aside. On the 1-to-10 *HAS*, TaMar was able to endorse feeling like a '10' – fully alert, aware, and oriented to himself and the present moment. It was agreed to schedule a double (90-minute) session, with an adjusted fee to accommodate TaMar's financial limitations, which would provide the space to explore his self-system more deeply for the first time.

At the beginning of the next session, Michael and TaMar checked in about how TaMar felt immediately following and since the last session. TaMar said the symptoms were still there, but that they hadn't worsened. He said he couldn't think of anything else to report. Michael also checked back in about moving forward with exploring symptoms via the 'meeting place.' Michael discussed with TaMar that, in ego state exploration, it can be helpful to use formal hypnotic elicitation/induction as a way of increasing a client's access to what is happening at the subconscious level. However, Michael noted he was not going to suggest that quite yet, in part to understand how responsive TaMar might be to the approach without a formal elicitation (see Bliss, 1986). Michael did make TaMar aware that it was possible he may still experience an alteration in consciousness, simply by giving focused attention inside. TaMar expressed being ok with this possibility, since he knew Michael would make sure things were contained and that he was alert before ending the session. Michael turned to the *HAS* to check how alert, aware, and present/oriented TaMar felt pre-intervention. Michael then invited TaMar to turn his attention inward, visualize his meeting place, imagine taking a seat at the table if that felt ok to them, and listen inside.

Michael: *This is a message for the whole self, so please listen in: I'm reaching out to anyone or anything within reach of my voice, whether you're near or far, awake or asleep, inside or outside, alive or dead. I'd like to invite into the meeting place anyone or anything that wants to die, tells them they should die, or makes them feel like dying. If there's no one or nothing doing those things, that's all right. And if you're there but don't want to come in right now, then just say, 'No'. Let me know when you notice anything at all – even if you notice nothing.*

TaMar: Um, I felt like something said, "No," but I'm not sure. [Michael takes note of this for later.] Two things showed up. One looks like a dark grey cloud. [Now, TaMar looks confused.] The other one looks like...my brother Mal? When he was like 12 or 13 years old? (We can see this illustrated in Figure 10.3.)

Michael: *Thanks, TaMar. Now, just listen in and let me know what you become aware of as we check in with these two directly. Let's begin with Mal [ego cathecting the 'Mal' state]: Thanks for being here. I'm Michael the Social Worker. We're visiting to learn about what's happening for you. Can you tell me what you do?*

'Mal': [speaking through 'fronting' TaMar, who is both a participant and an observer right now]: I pick on her. I can't stand her, and I want her to go away. I wish she'd just die so Mom and Dad

Figure 10.3 TaMar's Dissociative Table, First Pass.

would pay attention to me. [Michael thinks back to the MID results: "Hearing a voice in your head that wants you to die."]

Michael: *Mal, can you tell me whom 'she' is?*

'Mal': My sister, Tammy. [TaMar (named TaMara at birth, nicknamed Tammy) did not yet openly identify as trans-]

Michael: *I see. Where is Tammy right now?*

'Mal': She's watching TV in the other room. I'm babysitting her. [This 'Mal' state has not been adequately connected with other, present-oriented states up to now. It's as if he is frozen in time.]

Michael: *Mal, could you tell me how old Tammy is?*

'Mal': She's seven. I hate her.

Michael: *I see. Are your parents around, or no?*

'Mal': They're not here. They're gone for a minute.

Michael: *Ah, ok. I wonder...if they decided they wanted to listen in right now to what we were talking about, do you think they'd be able to do that? [Michael is checking for internalized parent states that may be part of this 'cluster,' along with 'Mal' and 7yo TaMar, to ensure he has adequately accounted for any hierarchy.]*

'Mal': I told you, they're out. They're not here. I don't know where they are.

Michael: *Thanks for helping me understand that better, Mal. Is there anything else you'd like to share right now?*

'Mal': No.

Michael: *OK. Do you think you'd be open to talking again some time?*

'Mal': Yeah, whatever.

Michael: *Very good. [Shifting ego cathexis back to TaMar] So, TaMar, how was that for you?*

TaMar: It was super weird hearing myself say my 'dead' [pre-transition] name. I know it's me talking, but when I was saying all those words, I felt Mal's anger and I also felt afraid of him, like I did when I was a kid. The fear didn't really feel like 'mine,' though. It felt young. It's like it was coming from somewhere else. [This comment led Michael to wonder whether the 'no' may have come from the child state in the other room watching TV, though there could be other sources of 'no,' as well.]

Michael: *I can see how that would seem weird. Even though you felt afraid, would it be ok if we shifted our attention to the grey cloud now, or would you prefer to pause here?*

TaMar: I think I want to keep with this. I'm kind of wondering what it's is about.

[NOTE: Had TaMar expressed reticence about engaging with the 'cloud,' then Michael would have considered the possibility that a dissociative phobia, whether in the form of anger, fear, shame, etc., contributed to TaMar's avoidance, and asked about exploring that first.]

Michael: *[Shifting ego cathexis to the 'cloud'] This is a message for the 'cloud.' I'm Michael the Social Worker. Are we getting it right that you're a dark grey cloud?*

'Cloud': No, I'm not a cloud. I'm smoke.

Michael: *Thanks for letting me know. Would you be open to telling me what it is that you do?*

Smoke: I keep her hidden. Invisible.

[Michael notices a change in TaMar's expression at having spoken 'her' rather than 'him.' This discrepancy suggested to Michael that this 'smoke' state's development predated TaMar's adoption of he/him pronouns.]

Michael: *Ah, I see. Maybe you can tell me the reason you want her to be invisible.*

'Smoke': Because. If she's invisible, she won't be scared. [Michael silently observes that this resembles child-like logic, akin to 'If I cover my eyes, then no one can see me.']

TaMar: Michael, I think there's something inside the smoke. Like, hiding inside? It might be more than one. I'm not sure. And why does it keep calling me 'she'?

Michael: *TaMar, thanks for letting me know. Let's keep that in mind. As far as the pronouns go, I wonder if this may call back to a time before you identified as TaMar?*

TaMar: That seems really weird and it feels strange saying it, but…in a way, I guess it makes sense.

Michael: *Would it be ok to pay more attention to what this 'Smoke' can tell us, or would you rather pause?*

TaMar: Yeah, it's ok to keep going.

Michael: *All right, then. [Redirecting attention to 'Smoke' now.] 'Smoke,' can you tell us what makes her scared?*

'Smoke': Her parents' fighting.

Michael: *And where are her parents right now?*

'Smoke': In the kitchen. Can't you hear them screaming at each other? It's really loud.

Michael: *I'm afraid I can't hear them from where I am. Can they hear* us *talking?*

'Smoke': Maybe. [This response seemed a bit cagey, but it was unclear why that might be. Rather than follow up on this in the moment, it seemed of value to learn more about the vulnerable state(s) 'Smoke' is protecting.]

Michael: *'Smoke,' can you tell us how old the one is that you're keeping hidden?*

'Smoke': Young. But it's more than one. Don't tell.

Michael: *I see. So, if they're invisible, then they won't be afraid of their parents' screaming? Have I got that right or wrong?*

'Smoke': That's right.

Michael: *So, I wonder…if the parents can hear us talking, then could they talk to me if they decided they want to?*

'Smoke': Yes…but they *don't* want to talk to you. [Michael surmised that 'Smoke' may know quite a bit about more about what is happening than they are letting on.]

Michael: *I imagine there must be important reasons they don't want to talk to me. I appreciate that. I'd really like to hear their concerns, whenever they feel ready to talk about them.*

'Smoke': They want to know why.

Michael: *Because what happens for them matters.*

'Smoke': Why?

Michael: *Well, it seems like they might be hurting. [TaMar's eyes suddenly well up with tears.]*

TaMar: Ok, this is weird. Why am I crying? And I just heard, "We are" in my head. Is this normal?

Michael: *Well, I don't know what 'normal' means, because this is different for each client I've worked with. What you're describing does sound like the kinds of experiences some other clients have when we do 'parts' work, though. The tears might make sense, since it sounds like these parts may be holding some hurt. Does it seem like it would be ok to check in with whatever said, "We are"?*

TaMar: Yeah. It's….my mom and dad? It's vague, but it kind of feels like they're not in the meeting place, but kind of just outside, almost like they're hidden behind something. (See Figure 10.4.)

Michael: *That's good to know. So, parents, this is Michael the Social Worker. Is this mom and dad? [From here, M(other)/F(ather)]*

M/F: We don't trust social workers. What do you want?

[A discussion with the Mother and Father states to explain Michael's role and purpose followed. Once they understood that Michael was not a child protection worker and was not interested in taking away their 'kids,' they were a bit more open to engaging.]

Michael: *Thanks for letting us know that you're hurting. I wonder if it might be possible for you to feel better.*

M/F: We don't believe you.

Figure 10.4 TaMar's Dissociative Table, Second Pass.

Michael: *That's all right. I wonder if we could still talk about what's happening for you – if not now, then maybe another time.*
M/F: Maybe.
Michael: *I appreciate you talking with me today.*
M/F: Right. Sure you do.

During Closure, Michael guided TaMar through clearing and closing up the 'meeting place,' ensuring that all states were able to (1) contain any painful memory material they were responsible for holding and (2) make their way to somewhere within the self, whether nearby or far away, that they could either rest or watch over things. TaMar was able to endorse feeling like a '10' on the *HAS* – fully alert, aware, and oriented to himself and the present moment.

Discussion

Further exploration with these 'Mother' and 'Father' states in subsequent sessions helped reveal the connections between TaMar's problems with sleep and what had been happening inside: The grey smoke was protecting younger states from the parents' rage more generally, but TaMar was still left with bedtime fears, because this is when his parents' fighting would intensify.

The brother 'Mal' self-state was a separate matter. It turned out that TaMar's flashbacks were generated by both continued, internal bullying by Mal toward a younger self-state – the one watching TV in the other room – and by 'cries for help,' via visual images shared by other states inside seeking rescue from the suffering caused by Mal and the Mother and Father states. (See Chapter 11 for more on this topic.) Just knowing this was happening helped TaMar cope more ably, as he felt less 'in the dark' about his experiences. Although it was tempting to introduce EMDR therapy methods at this stage, Michael was uncertain that he had enough information based on this initial 'sampling' to propose anything specific. However, what he and TaMar learned during subsequent, deeper ego state exploration aided the development of both short-term soothing strategies and a plan for resolving these longstanding issues.

There are several possibilities for integrating EMDR therapy methods into this work. For example, Michael could use BL-DAS to help metabolize the younger, more vulnerable states' fear of (or other phobic/ambivalent feelings toward) the Mother, Father, and Brother Mal introjects. Michael could help TaMar reduce his ambivalence toward (thus increase his capacity for empathy for) the younger states that identify as a different gender than TaMar does. Michael could also engage the perpetrator-identifying states directly. This might look like helping soften the Mother and Father introjects' ambivalence toward engaging in the therapy process. Additionally, Michael could help increase the Mother, Father, and Brother Mal introjects' orientation to present reality. Or he might work with the Mother, Father, and Brother Mal introjects to process the anger they are bound up in.

Conclusion

In this chapter, we discussed a context for mapping increasing complexity, first of experience in the form of memories and, subsequently, of self-states associated with those memories. We established a basic frame for the process of mapping, with additional enhancements to accommodate different styles and capacities. Then, we discussed in some depth what the mapping process can reveal about a client's self-system functioning and symptoms. An extended case example illustrated some nuances of gathering information through both an initial mapping and, when this proved to be less enlightening, a deeper inquiry in service of addressing critical, safety-related questions. Possibilities for employing EMDR therapy were touched upon at the close of this chapter. We will discuss in further depth different approaches to address fraught internal dynamics, including an integrative EMDR therapy protocol for unburdening perpetrator introjects of rage, in Chapter 12.

References

A., B. C. (1908). My life as a dissociated personality. *Journal of Abnormal Psychology, 3*(4), 240–260. https://doi.org/10.1037/h0070353

A., B. C. (1909). *My life as a dissociated personality*. The Gorham Press.

Ateş-Barlas, A. (2022). EMDR therapy for bilinguals: Utilizing linguistic diversity for improved therapeutic success. *Journal of EMDR Practice and Research, 16*(1), 39–46. https://doi.org/10.1891/EMDR-2021-0022

Bergmann, U. (2008). Hidden selves: Treating dissociation in the spectrum of personality disorders. In C. Forgash & M. Copeley (Eds.). *Healing the heart of trauma and dissociation with EMDR and ego state therapy* (pp. 227–265). Springer Publishing Company.

Bliss, E. L. (1980). Multiple personalities. A report of 14 cases with implications for schizophrenia and hysteria. *Archives of General Psychiatry, 37*(12), 1388–1397. https://doi.org/10.1001/archpsyc.1980.01780250074009

Bliss, E. L. (1986). *Multiple personality, allied disorders, and hypnosis*. Oxford University Press.

Braun, B. G. (1986a). Issues in the psychotherapy of multiple personality disorder. In B. G. Braun (Ed.), *Treatment of multiple personality disorder* (pp. 3–28). American Psychiatric Press.

Braun, B. G. (1986b). Introduction. In B. G. Braun (Ed.), *Treatment of multiple personality disorder* (pp. xi–xxi). American Psychiatric Press.

Braun, B. G. (1988a). The BASK model of dissociation. *Dissociation, 1*(1), 4–23. hdl.handle.net/1794/1276

Braun, B. G. (1988b). The BASK model of dissociation: Part II – treatment. *Dissociation, 1*(2), 16–23. hdl.handle.net/1794/1340

Christensen, E. M. (2022). The online community: DID and plurality. *European Journal of Trauma & Dissociation, 6*(2), Article 100257. https://doi.org/10.1016/j.ejtd.2021.100257

Cohen, B. M., & Cox, C. T. (1995). *Telling without talking: Art as a window into the world of multiple personality*. W. W. Norton & Company.

Coons, P. M. (1988). Psychophysiologic aspects of multiple personality disorder: A review. *Dissociation: Progress in the Dissociative Disorders, 1*(1), 47–53. hdl.handle.net/1794/1330

Corrigan, F. M., Young, H., & Christie-Sands, J. (2025). *Deep brain reorienting: Understanding the neuroscience of trauma, attachment wounding, and DBR psychotherapy*. Routledge. https://doi.org/10.4324/9781003431695

Coy, D. M. (2025). The autohypnotic model of dissociation. In A. M. Gomez & J. Hosey (Eds.), *The handbook of complex trauma and dissociation in children: Theory, research and clinical applications* (pp. 89–106). W. W. Norton & Company. https://doi.org/10.4324/9781003350156

Coy, D. M., Dell, P. F., & Schmidt, J. (2022, December 30). *MID Analysis v6.0. MS Excel-based program to generate diagnostic impressions via The MID Report, The MID Extended Report, and MID Line and Bar Graphs.*

Dawson, P. L. (1990). Understanding and cooperation among alter and host personalities. *American Journal of Occupational Therapy, 44*(11), 994–997. https://doi.org/10.5014/ajot.44.11.994

Dell, P. F. (2006). The multidimensional inventory of dissociation (MID): A comprehensive measure of pathological dissociation. *Journal of Trauma & Dissociation, 7*(2), 77–106. https://doi.org/10.1300/J229v07n02_06

Fine, C. G. (1991). Treatment stabilization and crisis prevention: Pacing the therapy of the multiple personality disorder patient. *Psychiatric Clinics of North America, 14*(3), 661–676. https://doi.org/10.1016/S0193-953X(18)30294-6

Fine, C. G. (1993). A tactical integrationist perspective on the treatment of multiple personality disorder. In R. P. Kluft & C. G. Fine (Eds.), *Clinical perspectives on multiple personality disorder* (pp. 135–154). American Psychiatric Press.

Fine, C. G. (1999). The tactical-integration model for the treatment of Dissociative Identity Disorder and allied dissociative disorders. *American Journal of Psychotherapy, 53*(1), 361–376. https://doi.org/10.1176/appi.psychotherapy.1999.53.3.361

Ford, J. D., & Courtois, C. A. (Eds.). (2020). *Treating complex traumatic stress disorders in adults* (2nd ed.). The Guilford Press.

Frankel, A. S., & O'Hearn, T. C. (1996). Similarities in responses to extreme and unremitting stress: Cultures of communities under siege. *Psychotherapy Theory Research & Practice, 33*(3), 485–502. https://doi.org/10.1037/0033-3204.33.3.485

Fraser, G. A. (1991). The dissociative table technique: A strategy for working with ego states in dissociative disorders and ego-state therapy. *Dissociation, 4*(4), 205–213. hdl.handle.net/1794/1467

Fraser, G. A. (2003). Fraser's "dissociative table technique" revisited, revised: A strategy for working with ego states in dissociative disorders and ego-state therapy. *Journal of Trauma and Dissociation, 4*(4), 5–28. https://doi.org/10.1300/j229v04n04_02

Gómez, A. (2012). *EMDR therapy and adjunct approaches with children: Complex trauma, attachment, and dissociation.* Springer Publishing Company.

Gómez, A. (2025). *EMDR-sandtray-based therapy: Healing complex trauma and dissociation across the lifespan.* W. W. Norton & Company.

Gonzalez, A., & Mosquera, D. (2012). *EMDR and dissociation: The progressive approach.* Amazon Imprint.

Goodman, L., & Peters, J. (1995). Persecutory alters and ego states: Protectors, friends, and allies. *Dissociation, 8*(2), 91–99. hdl.handle.net/1794/1601

Greaves, G. B. (1989). Precursors of integration in the treatment of multiple personality disorder: Clinical reflections. *Dissociation, 2*(4), 224–230. hdl.handle.net/1794/1489

Gruenewald, D. (1984). On the nature of multiple personality: Comparisons with hypnosis. *International Journal of Clinical and Experimental Hypnosis, 32*(2), 170–190. https://doi.org/10.1080/00207148408416008

Herman, J. (1992). *Trauma and Recovery: The aftermath of violence – from domestic abuse to political terror.* BasicBooks.

Howard, H. (2017). Promoting safety in hypnosis: A clinical instrument for the measurement of alertness. *American Journal of Clinical Hypnosis, 59*(4), 344–362. https://doi.org/10.1080/00029157.2016.1203281

Jolly, W., Froom, J., & Rosen, M. G. (1980). The genogram. *The Journal of Family Practice, 10*(2), 251–255. cdn.mdedge.com/files/s3fs-public/jfp-archived-issues/1980-volume_10-11/JFP_1980-02_v10_i2_the-genogram.pdf

Karpman, S. B. (1968). Fairy tales and script drama analysis. *Transactional Analysis Bulletin, 7*(26), 39–43. www.karpmandramatriangle.com/pdf/DramaTriangle.pdf

Kitchur, M. (2005). The strategic developmental model for EMDR. In R. Shapiro, (Ed.), *EMDR solutions: Pathways to healing* (pp. 8–56). W. W. Norton & Company.

Kluft, R. P. (1983). Hypnotherapeutic crisis intervention with multiple personality. *American Journal of Clinical Hypnosis, 26*(2), 73–83. https://doi.org/10.1080/00029157.1983.10404147

Kluft, R. P. (1985). Using hypnotic inquiry protocols to monitor treatment progress and stability in multiple personality disorder. *American Journal of Clinical Hypnosis, 28*(2), 63–75. https://doi.org/10.1080/00029157.1985.10402636

Kluft, R. P. (1988). The phenomenology and treatment of extremely complex multiple personality disorder. *Dissociation, 1*(4), 47–58. hdl.handle.net/1794/1396

Kluft, R. P. (1993). The initial stages of psychotherapy in the treatment of multiple personality disorder patients. *Dissociation, 6*(2-3), 145–161. hdl.handle.net/1794/1632

Kluft, R. P. (1999). Current issues in dissociative identity disorder. *Journal of Psychiatric Practice, 5*(1), 3–19. https://doi.org/10.1097/00131746-199901000-00001

Kluft, R. P. (2006). Dealing with alters: A pragmatic clinical perspective. *Psychiatric Clinics of North America, 29*(1), 281–304. https://doi.org/10.1016/j.psc.2005.10.010

Kluft, R. P. (2009). A clinician's understanding of dissociation: Fragments of an acquaintance. In P. F. Dell & J. A. O'Neil (Eds.), *Dissociation and the dissociative disorders: DSM-V and beyond* (pp. 599–623). Routledge. https://doi.org/10.4324/9780203893920

Kluft, R. P. (2012). Approaches to difficulties in realerting subjects from hypnosis. *American Journal of Clinical Hypnosis, 55*(2), 140–159. https://https://doi.org/10.1080/00029157.2012.660891

Kluft, R. P. (2013). *Shelter from the storm: Processing the traumatic memories of DID/DDNOS patients with the fractionated abreaction technique.* CreateSpace.

Kluft, R. P. (2018, March 15-18). The *treatment of pathological dissociation and dissociative identity disorder* [Presentation]. 60th Annual Conference of the American Society of Clinical Hypnosis. Kissimmee, Florida, United States.

Knipe, J. (2019). *EMDR toolbox: Theory and treatment of complex PTSD and dissociation* (2nd ed.). Springer Publishing Company.

Loewenstein, R. J. (2018, October 15). Negative *therapeutic reaction and stuck cases: Mind control transference in the treatment of dissociative identity disorder* [Webinar]. ISSTD webinar series VIII. cfas.isst-d.org/content/negative-therapeutic-reaction-and-stuck-cases-mind-control-transference-treatment – group-tabs-node-course-default1

MacHovec, F. J. (1986). *Hypnosis complications: Prevention and risk management.* Charles C. Thomas.

Marano, G., Kotzalidis, G. D., Lisci, F. M., Anesini, M. B., Rossi, S., Barbonetti, S., Cangini, A., Ronsisvalle, A., Artuso, L., Falsini, C., Caso, R., Mandracchia, G., Brisi, C., Traversi, G., Mazza, O., Pola, R., Sani, G., Mercuri, E. M., Gaetani, E., & Mazza, M. (2025). The neuroscience behind writing: Handwriting vs. typing – who wins the battle? *Life (Basel, Switzerland), 15*(3), 345. https://doi.org/10.3390/life15030345

Martin, K. M. (2012). How to use Fraser's dissociative table technique to access and work with emotional parts of the personality. *Journal of EMDR Practice and Research, 6*(4), 179–186. https://doi.org/10.1891/1933-3196.6.4.179

Miller, A. (2012a). *Becoming yourself: Overcoming mind control and ritual abuse.* Routledge.

Miller, A. (2012b). *Healing the unimaginable: Treating ritual abuse and mind control.* Karnac.

Miller, A. (2012c). *Dialogue with the higher-ups.* In R. Vogt (Ed.), *Perpetrator introjects: Psychotherapeutic diagnostics and treatment models* (pp. 111–132). Asanger Verlag GmbH Kröning.

Mosquera, D. (2019). *Working with voices and dissociative parts: A trauma-informed approach.* INTRA-TP.

Paulsen, S. L. (1995). Eye movement desensitization and reprocessing: Its cautious use in dissociative disorders. *Dissociation, 8*(1), 32–44. hdl.handle.net/1794/1592

Paulsen, S. L. (2009). Looking *through the eyes of trauma and dissociation: An illustrated guide for EMDR clinicians and clients.* Booksurge.

Paulsen, S. L., & Golston, J. (2014). Stabilizing the relationship among self-states. In U. F. Lanius, S. L. Paulsen, & F. M.Corrigan, (Eds.), *Neurobiology and treatment of traumatic dissociation: Towards an embodied self* (pp. 321–340). Springer Publishing Company.

Prince, M., & Peterson, F. (1908). Experiments to determine co-conscious (subconscious) ideation. *Journal of Abnormal Psychology, 3*(2), 114–131. https://doi.org/10.1037/h0073923

Prince, W. F. (1916). The doris case of quintuple personality. *Journal of Abnormal Psychology, 11*(2), 73–122. https://doi.org/10.1037/h0072650

Putnam, F. (1989). *Diagnosis and treatment of multiple personality disorder.* The Guilford Press.

Richardson, L., & Lacroix, G. (2024). Which modality results in superior recall for students: Handwriting, typing, or drawing? *Journal of Writing Research, 15*(3), 519–540. https://doi.org/10.17239/jowr-2024.15.03.04

Ross, C. A. (1989). *Multiple personality disorder: Diagnosis, clinical features, and treatment.* Wiley.

Ross, C. A. (1997). *Dissociative identity disorder: Diagnosis, clinical features, and treatment of multiple personality* (2nd ed.). Wiley.

Sachs, R. G. (1993). Use of sand trays in the beginning treatment of a patient with dissociative disorder. In R. P. Kluft & C. G. Fine (Eds.), *Clinical perspectives on multiple personality disorder* (pp. 301–310). American Psychiatric Press.

Şar, V., & Öztürk, E. (2009). Psychotic presentations of dissociative identity disorder. In P. F. Dell & J. A. O'Neil (Eds.), *Dissociation and the dissociative disorders: DSM-V and beyond* (pp. 535–545). Routledge. https://doi.org/10.4324/9780203893920

Schimmenti, A. (2017). Elena: A case of dissociative identity disorder from the 1920s. *Bulletin of the Menninger Clinic, 81*(3), 281–298. https://doi.org/10.1521/bumc_2017_81_08

Shapiro, F. (2018). *Eye movement desensitization and reprocessing (EMDR) therapy: Basic principles, protocols and procedures* (3rd ed.). The Guilford Press.

Shebini, N. (2019). EMDR for safe desensitization of memories and fusion of parts in DID. Conference room technique, trauma mapping, and management of unplanned abreactions. *Frontiers in the Psychotherapy of Trauma & Dissociation, 3*(2), 136–150. https://doi.org/10.46716/ftpd.2019.0030

Sidis, B. (1898). *The psychology of suggestion: A research into the subconscious nature of man and society.* D. Appleton and Company.

Spring, D. (1993). Artistic symbolic language and the treatment of multiple personality disorder. In E. S. Kluft (Ed.), *Expressive and functional therapies in the treatment of multiple personality disorder* (pp. 85–99). Charles C. Thomas.

Taylor, W. S., & Martin, M. F. (1944). Multiple personality. *The Journal of Abnormal and Social Psychology, 39*(3), 281–300. https://doi.org/10.1037/h0063634

Van der Hart, O., Nijenhuis, E., Steele, K., & Brown, D. (2004). Trauma-related dissociation: Conceptual clarity lost and found. *The Australian and New Zealand Journal of Psychiatry, 38*(11-12), 906–914. https://doi.org/10.1080/j.1440-1614.2004.01480.x

Van der Hart, O., Nijenhuis, E. R. S., & Solomon, R. (2010). Dissociation of the personality in complex trauma-related disorders and EMDR: Theoretical considerations. *Journal of EMDR Practice and Research, 4*(2), 76–92. https://doi.org/10.1891/1933-3196.4.2.76

Van der Hart, O., Nijenhuis, E. R. S., & Steele, K. (2006). *The haunted self: Structural dissociation and the treatment of chronic traumatization.* W. W. Norton & Company.

Van der Hart, O., Steele, K., Boon, S., & Brown, P. (1993). The treatment of traumatic memories: Synthesis, realization, and integration. *Dissociation, 6*(2-3), 162–180. hdl.handle.net/1794/1633

Vogt, R. (2012). *Perpetrator introjects: Psychotherapeutic diagnostics and treatment models.* Asanger Verlag GmbH Kröning.

Watkins, J. G. (1977). The psychodynamic manipulation of ego states in hypnotherapy. In F. Antonelli (Ed.), *Therapy in psychosomatic medicine* (Vol. 2, pp. 398–403). Symposia.

Wilbur, C. B. (1988). Multiple personality disorder and transference. *Dissociation, 1*(1), 73–76. hdl.handle.net/1794/1334

World Health Organization. (2022). *ICD-11: International classification of diseases. 11th Revision.* https://icd.who.int/

Chapter 11

Not All Flashbacks Are Created Equal

D. Michael Coy

Introduction

EMDR, in its standard protocol form, has been shown to be effective in treating the sequelae of posttraumatic stress, including flashbacks and nightmares, without the need to integrate other approaches. The original Adaptive Information Processing (AIP) model and standard EMDR therapy practice seem to assume that treatment will occur, at least within reason, under the typical, posttraumatic conditions. However, when discrete self-states are present, as is the case in dissociative disorders (DDs), there are added dimensions of flashbacks that may, at the surface, resemble a 'typical' PTSD-type presentation but confound the use of EMDR treatment-as-usual. This chapter will name and elaborate four ways that more complex flashbacks may manifest, using a deductive reasoning tool to contextualize each, as well as discuss the implications for EMDR therapy conceptualization and treatment of each 'kind' of flashback.

'Classic' Flashbacks and EMDR Therapy

According to DSM-5-TR (American Psychiatric Association, 2022), a flashback is an intrusive, dissociative symptom associated with a traumatic event. Flashbacks may manifest in the following ways:

1. Recurrent, involuntary, and intrusive distressing memories of the traumatic event(s),
2. Recurrent distressing dreams in which the content and/or affect of the dream are related to the traumatic event(s), and
3. Dissociative reactions (e.g., flashbacks) in which the individual feels or acts as if the traumatic event(s) were recurring, up to and including full reexperiencing and loss of present awareness (APA, pp. 301–302).

DOI: 10.4324/9781003410201-15

Although the DSM criteria suggest the first two of these are distinct from the third – all are intrusive symptoms, but only the third is considered a flashback – the PTSD *Diagnostic Features* section seems to contradict this characterization:

> The individual may experience dissociative states that typically last a few seconds and rarely are of a longer duration, during which components of the event are relived and the individual behaves as if the event were occurring at that moment (Criterion B3). Such events occur on a continuum, *ranging from brief visual or other sensory intrusions about part of the traumatic event without loss of reality orientation* to a partial loss of awareness of present surroundings to a complete loss of awareness. *These episodes, often referred to as "flashbacks," are typically brief but can be associated with prolonged distress and heightened arousal.*
>
> (emphasis added; APA, p. 306)

Dell (2006) characterizes flashbacks as encompassing all these features, in line with the passage quoted above. In any case, the DSM's framing of flashbacks implies certain conditions, namely that,

1. The experiencer is 'flashing back' to (in a waking state) or experiencing dreams about a past event that they recognize as actually having occurred,
2. The flashback experience is entirely involuntary and spontaneous, and
3. The experience is indeed a memory and thus 'inert,' at least insofar as it is seen as a phenomenon that does not, itself, possess a point of view, motivation, or intention – it's just a "thing," a simple, ancillary symptom like a cough or a sore knee.

Research has demonstrated that EMDR, in its standard form, is effective for treating the sequelae of 'classic' posttraumatic stress, including waking flashbacks and nightmares, without the need to integrate other approaches (Shapiro, 2018; Shapiro & Solomon, 2017). The implied conditions noted above seem 'baked into' the AIP model, as well as how EMDR therapy is practiced and taught, owing to the exclusive focus upon memory processing. Newer EMDR research advocates for increasing the taxation of working memory to achieve more robust memory consolidation (e.g., Littel et al., 2017; Matthijssen et al., 2021), even with more complex trauma. This conflicts with years of evidence that using bilateral dual-attention stimulus (BL-DAS) for memory processing without first evaluating indicators of severe dissociation is both inadvisable and potentially dangerous, for the client, the therapist, and the therapy relationship (ISSTD, 2011; Shapiro, 2018; also, refer to Chapter 4). Kluft (2017) has rightly pointed out that things are not always what they seem at the (dissociative) surface. It is for this reason that EMDR therapists need a more nuanced conceptualization of flashbacks.

Flashbacks as Dissociative Phenomena

Although the DSM-5-TR (APA, 2022) refers to flashbacks as dissociative in nature, that descriptor seems casual and, as such, easily overlooked. What's more, PTSD and DDs often co-occur, though the symptoms of the former – particularly flashbacks as defined in the DSM – may be either absent or less recognizable, at least initially. I have observed that, for some clients, explicit (i.e., 'classic') flashbacks only become evident later in treatment, as we connect with deeper layers of trauma and the self-states associated with them. This being the case, what should we consider when looking for evidence of flashbacks? Drawing from the DSM as well as Blank (1985), Bliss (1986), Loewenstein (1993), and Putnam (1989), I would like to recommend that EMDR therapists consider a more all-encompassing range of flashback-related symptoms:

With consistent, explicit recall that the traumatic experience occurred

- Intrusive recall with or without a total loss of contact with the present moment (i.e., full reexperiencing),
- Vivid dreams and nightmares that recede/subside after waking,
- Vivid dreams and nightmares that extend into waking experience, causing reality confusion/disorientation.

Without consistent, explicit recall that the traumatic experience occurred

- Vivid dreams or nightmares in which the experience(s) take shape in "cryptic or disguised forms" (Bliss, 1986, p. 108),
- "Chance contemporary encounters containing elements associated with the original event [i.e., present triggers] [...] [that] provoke a flashback, a *sudden trance*, when the memory is relived only to be forgotten once again" (Bliss, p. 109; see below),
- Present-day enactments involving behavior, emotions, sensations, thought patterns, etc., for which there is limited/no awareness of the connection between the present-moment symptom(s) and past trauma (e.g., 'body memories'),
- "Auditory pseudo-hallucinations, such as having the sensory experience of hearing one's thoughts spoken in one or more different voices" (American Psychiatric Association, 2022, p. 309).

It is possible to conceptualize the first three of these manifestations, which do not involve pervasive amnesia, solely in terms of 'classic' PTSD. The source material is often more accessible without special procedures such as hypnosis. We can therefore treat them in a relatively straightforward fashion, using EMDR therapy methods, even when there is a reflexive phobia of approaching the traumatic material (e.g., Knipe, 2019; Manfield et al., 2017; Wong, 2021). (However, in the case of full reexperiencing, a person would have amnesia for the period during which they are out of contact with the present moment. This suggests a more complex diagnostic picture than PTSD alone can encompass.) The last four of these manifestations involve amnesia to a greater or lesser degree. This may include either a lack of explicit awareness of the event, or an absence of awareness between the traumatic event and its associated posttraumatic symptoms, or both. Sidis (1898) would characterize these as forms of irretraceable memory (see Chapters 2 and 6). All seven of these flashback symptoms can result from covert interactions among self-states. Notably, the last of these – so-called auditory 'pseudo-hallucinations' that may be voice-like (i.e., voice-hearing) – seems not unlike a near-universal symptom of DDs associated with self-state activity. (This symptom is tucked away in the *Associated Features* for PTSD.)

In Chapter 9, we discussed the development of self-states in a psychodynamically informed, Ego State Theory/Therapy (Watkins & Watkins, 1997) frame. (If you have not read that, I suggest you pause here and do so. I'll wait for you.) Recall Bromberg's (2020) description of self-states as "highly individualized modules of being, each configured by its own organization of cognitions, beliefs, dominant affect and mood, access to memory, skills, behaviors, values, actions, and regulatory physiology" (p. 73). This lack of adequate interconnectivity (Sidis, 1898) may be reinforced, as suggested by Bliss (1986), by subsequent situations during which the traumatic material is re-enlivened, accompanied by a moment of shock – and a trance state. Trance is an altered state of awareness, perception, and experience marked by illogic and paradox in which the present is filtered, perhaps distorted, through a painful, seemingly inescapable, and as-yet-undigested past that may be the only reality that some self-states have ever known.

Owing to the presence of these states and a distinct absence of connectivity among them, some kinds of flashbacks and voices may be deeply embedded in more severe dissociation, rather than being a mere symptom to be extinguished with a few waves of a hand. As such, these can prove challenging to address without greater context – and no 'adult self' oriented state(s) may have insight into these intrusive experiences, at least initially, owing to a lack of ready access to what other states know, feel, etc. (Kluft, 2006; Van der Hart et al., 1993). Injudicious use of BL-DAS, regardless of the protocol or technique in which it is used, can prematurely create too much connectivity between self-states, each of which is entangled in its own, trance-enveloped experience. This, among other factors, makes it necessary for us to understand both the impact of BL-DAS, which both helps metabolize toxic experience and facilitates new connectivity, and the complexities of dissociative and trance phenomena (which help reduce painful connectivity) that can complicate its use (ISSTD, 2011; Lipke, 2000; Shapiro, 2018). This seems like an invitation to lay down more conceptual 'track' than is available to us by working exclusively within the traditional AIP frame (Shapiro, 2018), which conceptualizes pathology only in terms of memory (see Chapter 2).

Conceptualizing Flashbacks in a Relational Frame

Sometimes, we run out of conceptual track while trying to sort out what's happening for a client. In that case, we need an interweave of our own – some novel way of thinking about what's happening within the client or between the client and us. In the face of more severe dissociation, the 'track' we need should help us think critically about the psychodynamics of complex flashbacks involving different self-states in relation to one another…and to the therapist. Understanding the psychodynamics allows for more tailored interventions and, hopefully, as a result, less 'splatter' of traumatic material and adverse impacts upon a client's self-system. For this purpose, we can look to a model drawn from Transactional Analysis (Berne, 1957a, 1957b, 1958): Karpman's (1968, 2014, 2019) *Triangle* (aka Karpman's *Drama Triangle*). The three roles that represent the unfolding dynamic in the *Drama Triangle* are Persecutor, Victim, and Rescuer:

In Figure 11.1, the solid arrows indicate the directionality of 'action' (i.e., coming from/directed at one or both roles) among the Persecutor, Victim, and Rescuer roles in the present day. The double-lined arrows represent the same dynamic in the past, potentially involving only one of the present-day participants who serves as the common linkage between past and present. The dotted arrows indicate the 'seepage' of a past dynamic into the present. Karpman (1968) explains that "there is no drama unless there is a switch in the roles" (p. 40). In other words, the unwitting participants pivot around the *Drama Triangle* in relation to one another, at least until they recognize they are caught up in a drama and extricate themselves from it. Those role pivots are indicated by the curved arrows in Figure 11.1.

Karpman also mentions the role of the audience in this dynamic, also known as the Bystander, who exists outside the *Drama Triangle*. Clarkson (1987) notes that the Bystander(s) observe the drama but make no effort

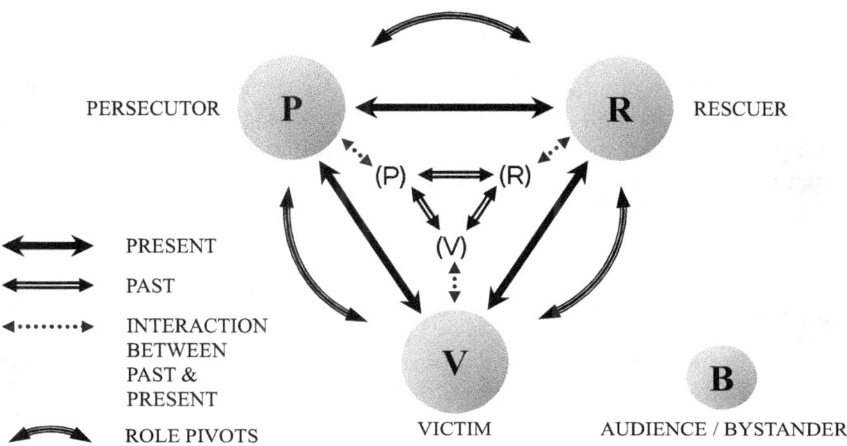

Figure 11.1 Karpman's Drama Triangle.

Source: Adapted from Karpman (1968).

to intervene in it, such as a parent who is aware their child is being perpetrated against but is either unable or unwilling to protect them. Danylchuk and Connors (2024) offer a different take on the Bystander role, suggesting that the therapist may serve as an objective observer who sees drama unfolding and, without falling into the Rescuer role, helps the client recognize and disrupt the dynamic. Both ways of understanding the Bystander role are helpful. Let us now turn our attention to how the *Drama Triangle* can be used as a deductive reasoning tool to make sense of flashbacks.

Flashbacks and the Dissociative Self

As I noted above, a client may not always be aware of traumatic flashbacks, due to amnesia for the trauma itself or for the self-states connected to their symptoms. These flashbacks may manifest in one or more of the following ways:

1. An externalized relational enactment of past trauma,
2. A form of help-seeking between self-states,
3. A preemptive strike or retaliatory warning by a self-state,
4. An enactment of past trauma between self-states.

We will discuss each of these in turn, employing Karpman's *Drama Triangle* to help us bring into the light what may at first be shrouded in a dissociative fog.

An Externalized Relational Enactment of Past Trauma

Past relational wounding can show up in the present-day relationship between therapist and client. These past-as-present 'enactments' are a metaphorical (and sometimes painfully literal) way for an underlying, often unrecognized, story of wounding to be told. These dynamics can be understood through the lens of transference and countertransference.

The Psychodynamics of Enactments: Transference and Countertransference

Broadly speaking, transference is a phenomenon wherein one's past experience, including relational templates, is brought to bear in, or 'transferred' into (or onto), a present-day (therapeutic) relationship, from outside explicit awareness. In a therapeutic context, the client generates 'transference' (Breuer & Freud, 1895/1956, p. 302), while the therapist generates 'countertransference' (Freud, 1910/1957) – the latter encompassing *all* the therapist's responses and reactions to their client. The resulting dynamics sometimes are more obvious and at other times are covert and less easily recognized, but nonetheless crucial to understand. We will touch on four forms of transference: (1) projection, (2) projective identification, (3) introjection, and (4) introjective identification.

Projection

Projection (Freud, 1895/1966, p. 208) is a relational phenomenon through which thoughts, motivations, wants, needs, and emotions that cannot be accepted as one's own are unconsciously resolved by being attributed to someone else, as if they were projecting them onto a screen. The communication is not necessarily targeted at the therapist. It's more like 'sending up a flare,' like an SOS. However, any SOS call is only effective if there is a receptive audience. In treatment, that audience is the attuned, cognizant therapist.

For example, a client might angrily accuse their therapist: "I think you want to fire me as a client. I think you hate meeting with me week after week." Maybe they *want* to be fired. This may be underpinned by the client's ambivalence about being in therapy, but it may not be possible for them to say so. Even more, what if they are not aware that they want to flee, owing to how deep-seated the urge is – especially if, for example, only one 'part' of them wants this. If this were so, the 'fronting' state may not realize that another state's desire to end therapy is being communicated (projected on) to their therapist. Revisiting Karpman's (1968) *Drama Triangle*, it could be very easy for a therapist to feel hurt (Victim) by their client's accusation (Persecutor). However, one of the client's self-states might only be preemptively protecting (Rescuer) other, vulnerable states (Victim) against an anticipated rejection by the therapist (Persecutor).

Projective Identification

Through *projective identification* (Klein, 1946; Segal, 1964), aspects of oneself are unconsciously split off and projected *into* (rather than merely onto) another person, who then "becomes possessed by[,] controlled [by,] and identified with" (Scharff, 1992, p. 21) those projected aspects. Lest this sound like some sort of assaultive behavior, I will clarify the psychoanalytic context for this phenomenon. An infant, who has not yet developed an ego (i.e., a 'self'), must somehow be able to communicate its feelings to the mother in an embodied way to compel her to meet the infant's needs (see Eekhoff, 2016; Schore, 2003).

In therapy, an instance of projective identification might look like this: A client is recounting a story of profound betrayal with a totally flat affect. The therapist feels increasingly angry, though. When the therapist asks their client whether *they* feel angry, the client replies, "I feel nothing at all. This happened in the past, and what good would anger do me now, anyway?" We could imagine the possibility that a self-state is unemotionally reporting the play-by-play, while other Victimized states that hold the felt experience of the betrayal – as well as any state(s) patterned after the Persecutor – are dissociated from awareness. Imagine the therapist struggles to tolerate feeling the implicit message they have received from an angry state that needs desperately to be acknowledged. The therapist and client may enter the *Drama Triangle* at the point when the therapist unconsciously identifies with, then feels overwhelmed and 'taken over' by, the state(s) holding client's dissociated anger. The therapist who feels 'Victimized' by this identification with the client's angry state(s) could react overtly. This angry reactivity may situate the therapist in the Persecutor role by overtly reacting negatively toward their client, replicating the Victimized client's original betrayal dynamic. This could lead to all kinds of internal activation for client's states who are reactive toward displays of anger. Or, the therapist could assume the Rescuer role by employing a poorly timed intervention focused on client's disavowed emotion or even by changing the subject as a means of reducing their own distress. Or, the therapist may freeze in place, rendered a helpless, hopeless Bystander with no idea how to handle the situation. The client could pivot into the Rescuer role by attempting to help their therapist feel better. Or the client might become angry themselves, thus taking on a more obvious Persecutor role (at least, in the eyes of the therapist). Or they might simply submit to their therapist's dominance to make the problem disappear. This dynamic could perpetuate if the therapist cannot recognize these pivots on the *Drama Triangle* and disrupt the dynamic. The therapist would be well-advised to consider that the pivots on the *Drama Triangle* may be influenced by covert self-state activity.

Introjection

The process of *introjection* (Ferenczi, 1912/1994a; Klein, 1946; Scharff, 1992) involves aspects of another person (attitudes, behaviors, emotions, etc.), whether positive or negative, being unconsciously taken into oneself. These aspects of another may be either implicitly accepted (identified with) or rejected (but not discarded) as aspects of oneself.

For example, a client may speak very poorly of themselves, saying, "My dad (Persecutor) always told us kids (Victim) how horrible we were. I tend to agree with him. I still feel that way." From the vantage point of a resourceful Bystander, their therapist may wonder whether their client (Victim) somehow introjected their Persecutor father's negative assessment. And, perhaps to maintain their connection with their father, the client came to identify with that assessment (and, by extension, their father) – now, in essence, embodying both the Persecutor and Victim. I think of this as the "if you can't beat 'em, join 'em" school of maintaining attachment security, and maybe an indicator of a maladaptively harsh superego (see Howell, 1997). Imagine that this therapist has their own, similar history of dealing with a Persecutory father, and have developed a tendency to overidentify with their clients' experiences of Victimization. In the context of therapy, this overidentification might manifest for the therapist in feeling de-skilled, incompetent, inadequate, and ashamed. Perhaps the therapist will resolve this by trying to Rescue the client (or themselves) by siding with the client against their father. Suddenly, from the client's vantage point, the therapist has become the Persecutor, the client's father is the Victim, and the client becomes their father's Rescuer. Instead, maybe the therapist, drowning in shame (Victim), begins to feel that this client is too much for them and suggests that another therapist may be a better fit for the client's needs. The therapist is now the abandoning Persecutor who Victimizes their client to distance from the intensity of their emotions. Although it may appear at the surface that this is simply a 'relational issue,' it is important to look below the surface to understand any internal dynamics (for both the client and the therapist) that may be fueling the drama.

Introjective Identification

Judy Eekhoff (2016) describes *introjective identification* as "the capacity of the [therapist] to be at-one-with the evolving experience of the moment with the patient. The identification involves psychically fusing and merging with the patient, both via reception of their projective identifications and introjecting them" (p. 355). In essence, this is the 'receiving end' of projective identification. The preceding scenario would be an example of this, as the therapist did indeed seem to 'be at one' with the client's shame. Unfortunately, it also seems they felt entirely taken over by it, losing their observational capacity and potentially their client's trust.

A common way that this phenomenon shows up in therapy is through the client's 'identification with the aggressor' (Ferenczi, 1955/1994b). This could be a very literal identification, in an instance when a particular self-state takes on the viewpoint or traits of their perpetrator. It could also look like compliance with the actual or perceived wishes of the perpetrator, for example, to remain silent about the abuse. When this identification shows up in therapy, it might take the form of the client's and therapist's mutual compliance with avoiding an unpleasant topic or situation, with neither party even aware that they're avoiding anything (e.g., Frankel, 2002). The client may avoid the topic because it was *always* off limits, and the therapist may do the same because something *feels* off limits. The client is the Victim of an unseen Persecutor from the past and an anticipated Persecutor in the present, courtesy of the therapist whom they fear could shut them down. At the same time, the therapist may pivot between the roles of Victim (having identified with their client and as such feeling equally reticent to broach a tough subject) and the helpless, hopeless Bystander who has no idea what to do. As these dynamics unfold, our role as therapists is to recognize and to make sense of them (including whose story is being told), and only then determine whether and how to employ EMDR therapy methods.

How we conceptualize the pivoting of roles on the *Drama Triangle* depends upon the point of view from which we are seeing the drama unfold. The purpose of elaborating these dynamics is not to suggest that they should be avoided by trying in vain to be a Bystander. In fact, finding oneself drawn in a transferential dynamic (i.e., an enactment) with a client may be the client's best, perhaps the only, way to recognize and metabolize the pain of any old, unhealed relational wound (e.g., Bromberg, 1998; Casement, 1991; Chefetz, 1997, 2015; Maroda, 2004; Orange, 1995).

Baker (1997) points out that transference can manifest both interpersonally *and* intrapsychically. In the latter case, the mind's splitting of the 'good' (attachment-enhancing) and 'bad' (attachment-threatening) aspects of, for example, a neglectful and/or abusive caregiver is achieved through the development of new states that serve to compartmentalize the toxic experience. Thus, when a therapist perceives unconscious communication from a client with discrete self-states (e.g., Hoppenwasser, 2008;

Lyons-Ruth, 1999), it is helpful to keep in mind that the transference may be emanating from more than one source within the client *as well as from within therapist.* An additional layer is that there can be more than one dynamic at play concurrently, as each state may have its own unique perceptions, experiences, and ways of relating to others.

A Form of Help-Seeking Between Self-states

Self-states that feel very vulnerable, those that feel very young, those that are in great pain – may either become activated involuntarily ('triggered') or take the initiative to communicate to another self-state the only way(s) they can, in a plea for help. This communication may manifest for another self-state, including the 'fronting' one, as images or other sensory material, may lack any meaningful context to explain its origin, and may fuel a phobic reaction as the brain reflexively attempts to distance itself from the painful, traumatic material activated within. The lack of context arises from the central executive's amnesia for the original, source material that put this 'triggering' dynamic in motion (Blank, 1985; Bliss, 1986). In Figure 11.2, let us imagine that a client became emotionally activated by a discussion in session and began to experience their therapist as a Persecutor:

At this point, there is no identified Rescuer. It would not take much for the therapist to assume that role, though. Who wants to feel 'stuck' in

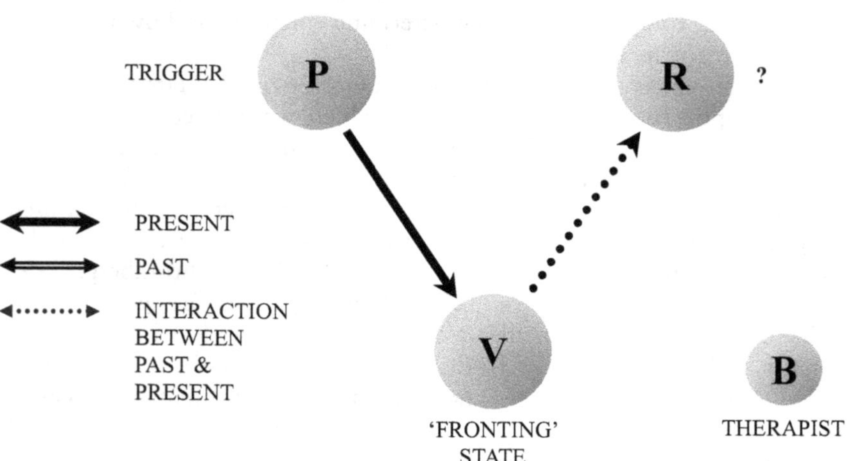

Figure 11.2 Help-seeking Drama Triangle, Take 1.

Source: Adapted from Karpman (1968).

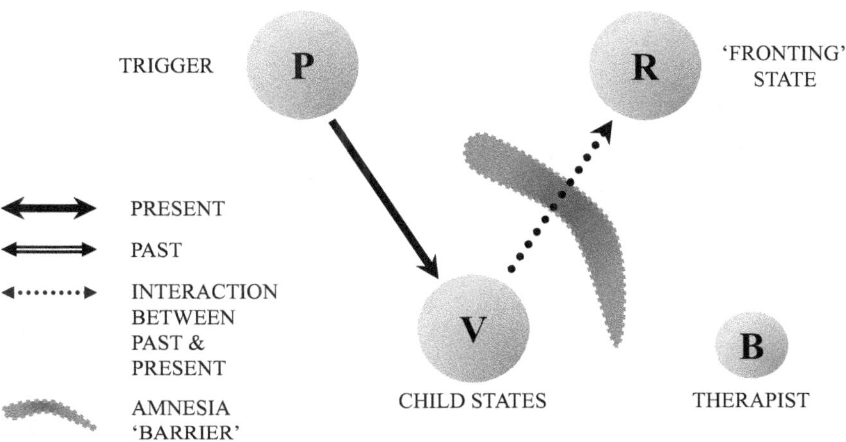

Figure 11.3 Help-seeking Drama Triangle, Take 2.

Source: Adapted from Karpman (1968).

the role of the Bystander who witnesses this triggering and does nothing, especially when we could simply target and resolve the 'trigger' and/or the phobia(s) it fuels using EMDR (Knipe, 2019; Shapiro, 2018)? In this case, we might conceptualize the 'trigger' as Persecutor to the client's Victim. However, further investigation would reveal that the *actual* Victim appears to be one or more child states hidden from the 'fronting' state's conscious awareness, as shown in Figure 11.3.

In Figure 11.3, we see that the child states are activated and, although the 'fronting' state is unaware of their presence, executive functioning can still be flooded by the images, emotions, body sensations, etc., that the child states hold. The child states appear to be sending out an SOS via the only resources they have at their disposal: The unmetabolized trauma, which here manifests as crying and noise in the "fronting" state's mind, along with feelings of terror. From the perspective of the child states, the 'fronting' state is the Rescuer. Let us imagine that the therapist opts to proceed with reprocessing without first investigating what is happening below the conscious level. It is here that the switch in roles can happen that sets the *Drama Triangle* in motion, as reflected in Figure 11.4.

There is a lot happening here! The 'fronting' state, as Victim, looked to their therapist to Rescue them from what is happening inside. Their therapist obliged, and the BL-DAS they employed to reduce the intensity of their client's distress created too much connectivity too quickly. This led to a lifting away of the amnesia 'barrier.' Now, the child and 'fronting' states, at least temporarily merged and all experiencing themselves as Victims,

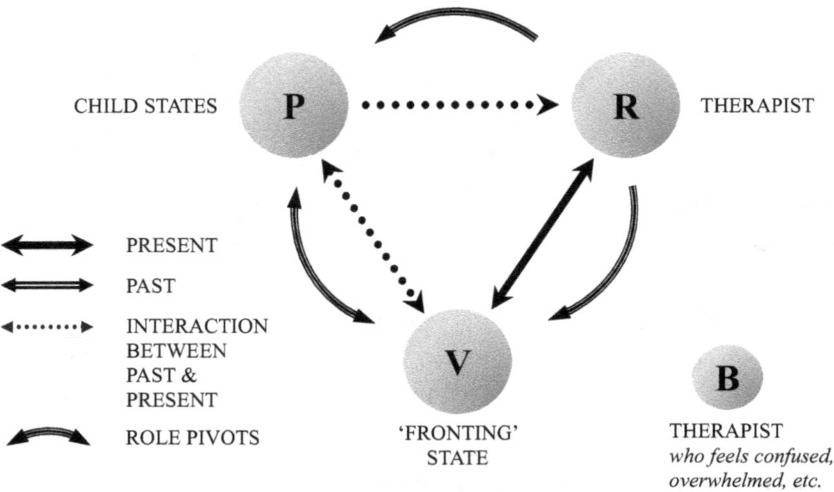

Figure 11.4 Help-seeking Drama Triangle, Take 3.
Source: Adapted from Karpman (1968).

seek Rescue from the therapist. (The child states may not even be aware that the 'fronting' state exists. If this were so, or if the 'fronting' state has in the past been unwittingly dismissive or avoidant of the child state's cries for help, it could help explain their desire for 'outside' assistance. Additionally, the child states have no awareness of whom the therapist is in the present. They may simply be seeking help from someone – anyone – who can rescue them.)

At the same time, the flooding leads the 'fronting' state to experience both the child states and the therapist as Persecutors. The 'fronting' state wants the child states, which are the source of the flooding, to go away. (Remember, the 'fronting' state is only newly aware that these child states exist – or, at least, that there is crying, noise, and terror coming from somewhere inside.) Concurrently, the 'fronting' state feels harmed by their therapist, who was just doing what they thought might help. The therapist, in turn, feels like a Victim of both the child and 'fronting' states. The therapist feels Victimized by the newly emergent child states' acute need for Rescue and Persecuted by their client, who is now suffering even more than before the intervention and feels very angry about it. The therapist is at a loss for what to do, essentially 'freezing,' inhabiting the confused, overwhelmed Bystander role.

This dynamic, taken as a whole, may replicate the client's experience growing up if, for example, they were forced to seek Rescue from a caregiver who was also either their Persecutor or a Bystander who did not protect them. For the therapist, if Rescuer is a role to which they are accustomed (maybe they learned it in their own family), then becoming the perceived Persecutor and Victim in turn may lead them to react in ways that further harm their client. If, however, the therapist avoids slipping into the Rescuer role, they instead can serve as the objective, yet still empathic, observer. As such, they could work with their client to stabilize/ground, identify and make sense of what just happened, clarify any underlying dynamics feeding the client's reaction, and only then determine how best to address the underlying issue(s). Is this process always straightforward and easy? Absolutely not. Is it necessary? Very much so, if we want to avoid causing (more) harm.

A Preemptive Strike or Retaliatory Warning by a Self-state

Whether in therapy or in daily life, some self-states may be responsible for maintaining safety in ways that are not obvious to other self-states. Warnings of impending harm, or else punishment for allowing potential harm, may 'intrude' into executive control/functioning in the form of sudden pain, hyper- or hypo-arousal, intrusive sensory information (images, sensations, odors, etc.), or other jarring experiences. For example, let us imagine a client is in session with their therapist reprocessing a memory of their father's past, abusive behavior. Suddenly, and seemingly out of nowhere, the client's 'fronting' state experiences a sharp, headache-like pain:

In Figure 11.5, the headache appears to be the Persecutor, with the 'fronting' state the perceived Victim. No one has been invited to or assumed the Rescuer role at this point. The therapist is merely a witness to the client's experience as they facilitate reprocessing. Under 'typical' circumstances, we might just assume the symptom will diminish or resolve through continued reprocessing. This is the fork in the road for the therapist. They can either assume the Rescuer role or remain in the Bystander/Audience role. In this case, the therapist opts to avoid becoming the Rescuer and instead suggests ego state exploration, keeping Karpman's *Drama Triangle* in mind, in hopes of revealing the full(er) context for the headache.

In Figure 11.6, we can see an unidentified Persecutor focused on the Victim child's states. The Victim child states have reached out to an adolescent protector state to Rescue them, and the adolescent state has obliged by sending a signal to the 'fronting' state, which is reprocessing experience(s) of their father's abuse. The adolescent state, in turn, acts as a Persecutor (of sorts) in its use of the headache (Ross, 1989) to compel the Victim 'fronting' state to stop giving attention to the father's abuse. We

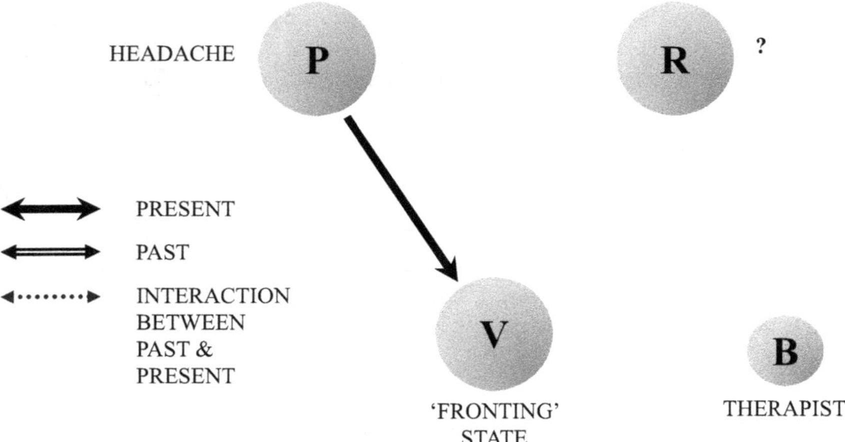

Figure 11.5 Retaliatory Warning Drama Triangle, Take 1.

Source: Adapted from Karpman (1968).

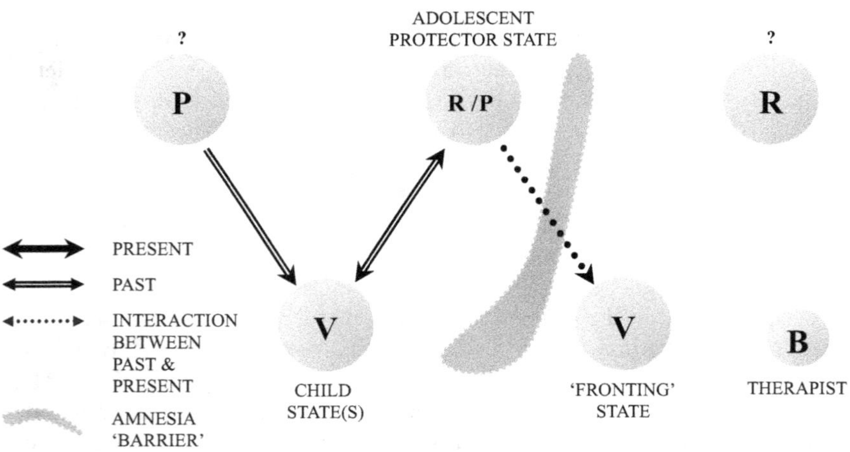

Figure 11.6 Retaliatory Warning Drama Triangle, Take 2.

Source: Adapted from Karpman (1968).

might imagine that 'someone will get in trouble' if the 'fronting' state does not stop thinking about it (i.e., reprocessing), though at this point we do not know the source of the threat that motivated the adolescent state to act. Due to amnesia, the 'fronting' state registers the headache, but has no awareness of its source. In this case, taking a step back from further reprocessing would be the wisest choice – at least until the internal dynamics can be further elaborated, which may help clarify what role EMDR therapy methods can play to help resolve them.

An Enactment of Past Trauma Between Self-states

One self-state may persecute another in a way that replicates past harm, with those self-states involved in the drama 'frozen in time,' repeating an episode either on a 'loop' or when an internal or external stimulus – even something like the time of day (e.g., bedtime) activates them (Blizard, 1997, 2001; Kluft, 2006; Loewenstein, 1993; Putnam, 1989). A solid, informed conceptualization is key if the therapist intends to avoid intervening in a way that either prematurely dismantles a defense or leads to more deeply entrenched internal struggle. The possible existence of an as-yet-unrevealed Persecutor state focused on Victimizing the child state(s) invites closer attention. Zooming in on a segment of the previous example's dynamic, the *Drama Triangle* depicting an enactment of past trauma between self-states might look like this:

A similar dynamic unfolded in my work with a client some years ago. I was employing O'Shea and Paulsen's Early Trauma Approach (Paulsen, 2017) with a client who did not meet criteria for DID, but who did have a handful of rather distinct self-states beyond the sole 'fronting' state.

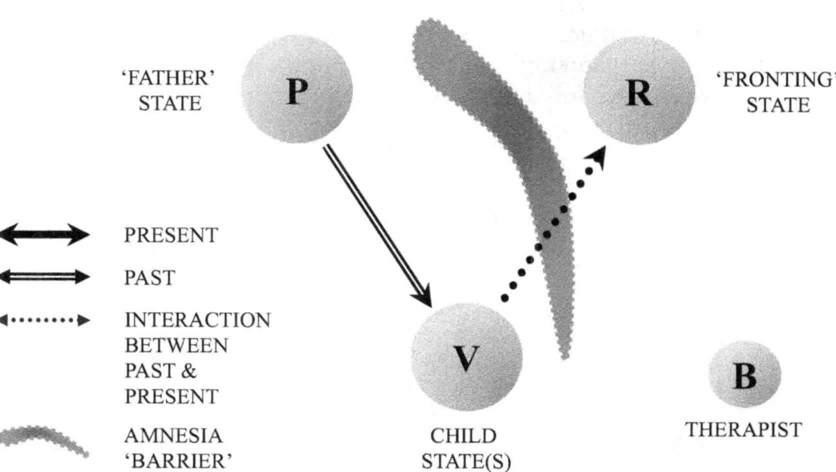

Figure 11.7 Enactment Between Self-states Drama Triangle.

Source: Adapted from Karpman (1968).

With a focus on "baby's story," the client and I were processing their pre-verbal experience. Unconsciously, I assumed a soothing tone of voice. Suddenly, the client leapt out of his chair, knocking aside the footrest – and me, who was tapping his ankles – and angrily yelled, "Get the fuck away from them!" I had no idea what had just happened. I quickly learned that I should not be processing trauma with 'the children' without permission from this protector state, whom I came to learn had the name 'Joan.' 'Joan' served dual roles, as both a Rescuer of child states and a Persecutor of another state called 'Crystal Meth Dave,' whom she perceived to be a Persecutor who Victimized the rest of the self, including the child states, through his (past) substance misuse. As a result of my lack of awareness, and my failure to obtain appropriate consent, the internal drama seeped into the therapeutic relationship. (We will revisit my work with this client in further depth in the next chapter.)

Conclusion

I have found Karpman's *Drama Triangle*, filtered through a psychodynamic lens, to be invaluable for making sense of understanding both intrapsychic and interpersonal dynamics, including those that manifest, often in disguised ways, in flashbacks. When there are self-states associated with flashback-type phenomena, then a standard, AIP-informed case conceptualization may fail us as we attempt to figure out how best to address what is happening – even when we (think we) have the appropriate methods at our disposal. My focus in this chapter has been contextualizing flashback-type dynamics rather than offering guidance on how to resolve them. In the next chapter, we will look at a novel way of dismantling the persecutor-victim dynamics that can manifest within the self-system.

References

American Psychiatric Association. (2022). *DSM-5-TR – Diagnostic and statistical manual of mental disorders* (5th ed., text revision). American Psychiatric Association Publishing.

Baker, S. (1997). Dancing the dance with dissociatives: Some thoughts on countertransference, projective identification and enactments in the treatment of dissociative disorders. *Dissociation, 10*(4), 214–222. hdl.handle.net/1794/1800

Berne, E. (1957a). Intuition v. the ego image. *The Psychiatric Quarterly, 31*(1), 611–627. https://doi.org/10.1007/BF01568754

Berne, E. (1957b). Ego states in psychotherapy. *American Journal of Psychotherapy, 11*(2), 293–309. https://doi.org/10.1176/appi.psychotherapy.1957.11.2.293

Berne, E. (1958). Transactional analysis: A new and effective method of group therapy. *American Journal of Psychotherapy*, *12*(4), 735–743. https://doi.org/10.1176/appi.psychotherapy.1958.12.4.735

Blank, A. S. (1985). The unconscious flashback to the war in Viet Nam veterans: Clinical mystery, legal defense, and community problem. In: S. M. Sonnenberg, A. S. Blank, & J. Talbott (Eds.), *The trauma of war: Stress and recovery in viet nam veterans* (pp. 293–308). American Psychiatric Press.

Bliss, E. L. (1986). *Multiple personality, allied disorders, and hypnosis.* Oxford University Press.

Blizard, R. A. (1997). Therapeutic alliance with abuser alters in DID: The paradox of attachment to the abuser. *Dissociation, 10*(4), 246–254. hdl.handle.net/1794/1812

Blizard, R. A. (2001). Masochistic and sadistic ego states: Dissociative solutions to the dilemma of attachment to an abusive caretaker. *Journal of Trauma & Dissociation,* 2(4), 37–58. https://doi.org/10.1300/J229v02n04_03

Breuer, J., & Freud, S. (1956). Studies on hysteria. In J. Strachey & A. Strachey (Eds.), *The standard edition of the complete psychological works of sigmund freud* (Vol. II). The Hogarth Press. (Original work published 1895)

Bromberg, P. M. (1998). *Standing in the spaces: Essays on clinical process, trauma, and dissociation.* Psychology Press.

Bromberg, P. M. (2020). *The shadow of the tsunami: And the growth of the relational mind.* Routledge.

Casement, P. J. (1991). *Learning from the patient.* The Guilford Press.

Chefetz, R. A. (1997). Special case transferences and counter-transferences in the treatment of dissociative disorders. *Dissociation, 10*(4), 255–265. hdl.handle.net/1794/1814

Chefetz, R. A. (2015). *Intensive psychotherapy for persistent dissociative processes: The fear of feeling real.* W. W. Norton & Company.

Clarkson, P. (1987). The bystander role. *Transactional Analysis Journal, 17*(3), 82–87. https://doi.org/10.1177/036215378701700305

Danylchuk, L. S., & Connors, K. J. (2024). *Treating complex trauma and dissociation: A practical guide to navigating therapeutic challenges* (2nd ed.). Routledge.

Dell, P. F. (2006). The multidimensional inventory of dissociation (MID): A comprehensive measure of pathological dissociation. *Journal of Trauma & Dissociation,* 7(2), 77–106. https://doi.org/10.1300/J229v07n02_06

Eekhoff, J. K. (2016). Introjective identification: The analytic work of evocation. *American Journal of Psychoanalysis, 76*(4), 354–361. https://doi.org/10.1057/s11231-016-9048-3

Ferenczi, S. (1994a). On the definition of introjection. In M. Balint (Ed.), *Final contributions to the problems and methods of psycho-analysis* (pp. 316–318) (E. Mosbacher, Trans.). Routledge. (Original work published 1912)

Ferenczi, S. (1994b). Confusion of tongues between adults and the child. In M. Balint (Ed.), *Final contributions to the problems and methods of psycho-analysis* (pp. 156–167) (E. Mosbacher, Trans.). Routledge. (Original work published 1955)

Frankel, J. (2002). Exploring Ferenczi's concept of identification with the aggressor: Its role in trauma, everyday life, and the therapeutic relationship. *Psychoanalytic Dialogues, 12*(1), 101–139. https://doi.org/10.1080/10481881209348657

Freud, S. (1957). The future prospects of psycho-analytic therapy. In J. Strachey et al. (Trans.), *The standard edition of the complete psychological works of sigmund freud* (Vol. XIV, pp. 139–152). The Hogarth Press. (Original work published 1910)

Freud, S. (1966). Extracts from the Fliess papers. In J. Strachey & A. Strachey (Eds.), *The standard edition of the complete psychological works of sigmund freud*(Vol. I). The Hogarth Press. (Original work published 1895)

Hoppenwasser, K. (2008). Being in rhythm: Dissociative attunement in therapeutic process. *Journal of Trauma & Dissociation, 9*(3), 349–367. https://doi.org/10.1080/15299730802139212

Howell, E. F. (1997). Desperately seeking attachment: A psychoanalytic reframing of the harsh superego. *Dissociation, 10*(4), 230–239. hdl.handle.net/1794/1806

International Society for the Study of Trauma and Dissociation (2011). Guidelines for treating dissociative identity disorder in adults, third revision. *Journal of Trauma & Dissociation, 12*(2), 115–187. https://doi.org/10.1080/15299732.2011.537247

Karpman, S. B. (1968). Fairy tales and script drama analysis. *Transactional Analysis Bulletin, 7*(26), 39–43. www.karpmandramatriangle.com/pdf/DramaTriangle.pdf

Karpman, S. B. (2014). *A game free life: The definitive book on the drama triangle and compassion triangle by the originator and author*. Drama Triangle Publications.

Karpman, S. B. (2019). Script drama analysis II. *International Journal of Transactional Analysis Research & Practice, 10*(1), 21–39. https://doi.org/10.29044/V10I1P21

Klein, M. (1946). Notes on some schizoid mechanisms. *International Journal of Psychoanalysis, 27*(3-4), 99–110. https://doi.org/10.1080/21674086.1949.11925749

Kluft, R. P. (2006). Dealing with alters: A pragmatic clinical perspective. *Psychiatric Clinics of North America, 29*(1), 281–304. https://doi.org/10.1016/j.psc.2005.10.010

Kluft, R.P. (2017). Trying to keep it real: My experience in developing clinical approaches to the treatment of DID. *Frontiers in the Psychotherapy of Trauma & Dissociation, 1*(1), 18–44. https://doi.org/10.46716/ftpd.2017.0002

Knipe, J. (2019). *EMDR toolbox: Theory and treatment of complex PTSD and dissociation*. Springer Publishing.

Lipke, H. (2000). *EMDR and psychotherapy integration: Theoretical and clinical suggestions with focus on traumatic stress*. CRC Press.

Littel, M., Remijn, M., Tinga, A. M., Engelhard, I. M., & van den Hout, M. A. (2017). Stress enhances the memory-degrading effects of eye movements on emotionally neutral memories. *Clinical Psychological Science, 5*(2), 316–324. https://doi.org/10.1177/2167702616687292

Loewenstein, R. J. (1993). Posttraumatic and dissociative aspects of transference and countertransference in the treatment of multiple personality disorder. In R. P. Kluft & C. G. Fine (Eds.), *Clinical perspectives on multiple personality disorder* (pp. 51–85). American Psychiatric Press.

Lyons-Ruth, K. (1999). The two-person unconscious: Intersubjective dialogue, enactive relational representation, and the emergence of new forms of relational organization. *Psychoanalytic Inquiry, 19*(4), 576–617. https://doi.org/10.1080/07351699909534267

Manfield, P., Lovett, J., Engel, L., & Manfield, D. (2017). Use of the flash technique in EMDR therapy: Four case examples. *Journal of EMDR Practice and Research, 11*(4), 195–205. https://doi.org/10.1891/1933-3196.11.4.195

Maroda, K. J. (2004). *The power of counter-transference: Innovations in analytic technique*. The Analytic Press.

Matthijssen, S. J. M. A., Brouwers, T., van Roozendaal, C., Vuister, T., & de Jongh, A. (2021). The effect of EMDR versus EMDR 2.0 on emotionality and vividness of aversive memories in a non-clinical sample. *European Journal of Psychotraumatology, 12*(1), 1956793. https://doi.org/10.1080/20008198.2021.1956793

Orange, D. M. (1995). *Emotional understanding: Studies in psychoanalytic epistemology*. The Guilford Press.

Paulsen, S. L. (2017). *When there are no words: Repairing early trauma and neglect from the attachment period with EMDR therapy*. Bainbridge Institute for Integrative Psychology.

Putnam, F. (1989). *Diagnosis and treatment of multiple personality disorder*. The Guilford Press.

Ross, C. A. (1989). *Multiple personality disorder: Diagnosis, clinical features, and treatment*. Wiley.

Scharff, J. S. (1992). *Projective and introjective identification and the use of the therapist's self*. Jason Aronson.

Schore, A. N. (2003). *Affect regulation and the repair of the self*. W. W. Norton & Company.

Segal, H. (1964). *Introduction to the work of Melanie Klein*. Heinemann.

Shapiro, F. (2018). *Eye movement desensitization and reprocessing (EMDR) therapy: Basic principles, protocols and procedures* (3rd ed.). The Guilford Press.

Shapiro, F., & Solomon, R. (2017). Eye movement desensitization and reprocessing (EMDR) therapy. In S. N. Gold, J. M. Cook, & C. J. Dalenberg (Eds.), *Handbook of trauma psychology: Vol. 2. Trauma practice* (pp. 193–212). American Psychological Association.

Sidis, B. (1898). *The psychology of suggestion: A research into the subconscious nature of man and society*. D. Appleton and Company.

Van der Hart, O., Steele, K., Boon, S., & Brown, P. (1993). The treatment of traumatic memories: Synthesis, realization, and integration. *Dissociation, 6*(2-3), 162–180. hdl.handle.net/1794/1633

Watkins, H. H., & Watkins, J. G. (1997). *Ego states: Theory and therapy*. W. W. Norton & Company.

Wong, S.-L. (2021). A model for the flash technique based on working memory and neuroscience research. *Journal of EMDR Practice and Research, 15*(3), 174–184. https://doi.org/10.1891/emdr-d-21-00048

Chapter 12

The Introject Decathexis (Id) Protocol

D. Michael Coy

Introduction

In the preceding chapter, I highlighted Kluft's (1993) tendency, early in treatment, to try to mitigate risk to the client by identifying and engaging with any state(s) preoccupied with dying or inflicting injury upon/killing the body. In line with this, Frankel & O'Hearn (1996), Paulsen (2009), and Paulsen and Golston (2014) have discussed the importance of identifying and working with persecutory self-states modeled after external perpetrators (i.e., perpetrator introjects). The EMDR therapy and dissociative disorder (DD) literatures have established that ego state interventions can be both helpful and frequently necessary to achieve stabilization/containment, adaptive resolution of traumatic experience, and integration of treatment gains. Work with persecutory ego states, such as those patterned after perpetrators, tends to focus on (1) orienting them to present realities, (2) persuading them to 'stand down' or reconsidering/realigning how they protect, and (3) helping other states feel less afraid of them. However, many of these interventions also present conceptual and/or practical issues that can make it difficult to achieve or maintain treatment gains with clients who present with more complex trauma and dissociative disorders.

This chapter will begin with a discussion of the development of perpetrator introjects, as well as their function within and impacts upon a self-system. Existing approaches to working with perpetrator introjects and similar states will be examined. The focus will then pivot to elaborate the *Id Protocol*, a novel, yet effective, integrative EMDR therapy approach I developed, which permanently 'unbinds' perpetrator introjects from the traumatic material in which they are seemingly, inexorably bound. The protocol will be illustrated through a case example, which will provide further context for the treatment frame and necessary preparatory tasks and precautions for its safe use.

DOI: 10.4324/9781003410201-16

The Development and Paradoxical Functioning of Perpetrator Introjects

What is a Perpetrator Introject?

We established in Chapter 11 that introjection (Ferenczi, 1912/1994a; Klein, 1946; Scharff, 1992) is a relational process in which aspects of another person (attitudes, behaviors, emotions, etc.), whether positive or negative, are unconsciously taken into oneself. Introjection is thought to occur through implicit identification (Watkins, 1977) with an important other, sourced from interpersonal contact, media representations, imagination, etc. (e.g., self-objects; Kohut, 1985). The development of a more sophisticated internal representation may be possible through the activity of mirror neurons, which Gallese (2009) describes as "premotor neurons that fire both when an action is executed and when it is observed being performed by someone else" (p. 520). The earliest 'someone else(s)' that we encounter are our caregivers. Lyons-Ruth (1999) highlights that if a caregiver responds to a child's highly charged emotions (e.g., anger, fear) with hostility, shaming, or withdrawal, then the child's emotion may be 'excluded' from subsequent communication and thus not integrated into the greater context of the child's emotional development. Notably, in some instances, such an 'exclusion' of emotion may lead a person to believe they are either unfeeling or autistic (M. Korzekwa, personal communication, August 3, 2025). Lyons-Ruth correlates this breakdown in communication between child and caregiver with the development of disorganized attachment patterns and the "collapse of intersubjective space so that only one party's subjective reality is acknowledged" (p. 593). This may, in turn, contribute to the development of DDs (Barach, 1991; Liotti, 1992, 2006).

In concert with this conceptualization, Howell (1997) has suggested that mirror neuronal activity and the self-other identification it facilitates could contribute to the development of perpetrator introjects. Through the process of introjection, a person subject to inescapable harm by others may not only internalize negative messages/perceptions about themselves (i.e., 'the inner critic'; Jung, 1970) but also absorb such intense destructive energy from the perpetrator of harm that a self-state becomes a 'facsimile' that possesses the perpetrator's harmful qualities. Although perpetrator introjects may begin their existence as a form of ally within the self-system, at some point the balance shifts from absorbing toward meting out harm, though there is no definitive explanation for why (Goodman & Peters, 1995). This type of state can be strongly cathected (i.e., emotionally energized) with an outside perpetrator's perceived behavior, affect, words, and perceptions, resulting in a perpetrator introject (Goodman & Peters, 1995;

Ross, 1989; Watkins & Watkins, 1988). The perpetrator introject's unique nature combines qualities of Freud's id, ego, and superego (see Chapter 9). These states can develop at any stage in a person's life.

We can think of a perpetrator introject as a combat veteran of sorts: Highly valued and efficient on the field of battle as a buffer against atrocity, but upon returning from war, their valued battlefield assets become problematic liabilities. Trapped in trauma time, they do not know that the original war ended, and they cannot recognize that they are not the outside perpetrator. Sometimes they revisit old aggressions, enacting harm toward other self-states or outside people in the mold of the original perpetrator. At other times, they may influence the self to gravitate toward more harm in the name of being redeployed (i.e., once again useful) to maintain attachment, thus survival, at any cost. Other self-states may perceive the perpetrator introject as monstrous (Paulsen, 2009), something to be avoided or destroyed. All these states are frozen in time together, trapped in an unending cycle of perpetration and victimization both intrapsychically and interpersonally (see Chapter 11). Perpetrator introjects are often challenging to identify and engage, and they may be unresponsive to efforts at facilitating lasting change, even when they seem to want things to be different. Owing to the intensity of the traumatic material in which they are bound, perpetrator introjects are not easily *de*cathected of their emotional energy. Thus, special procedures are often needed to help them transform in a way that allows them the choice to exist as a 'typical' ego state like any other.

The Paradox of Perpetrator Introjects

Perpetrator introjects' strategies for coping with intense and potentially unremitting pain initially are helpful, but they may become problematic if (when) they become divorced from their original context. Blizard (1997a, 2001) suggests that persecutory states such as introjects come to serve four core purposes within the self-system: (1) To help maintain dissociative compartmentalization; (2) to protect against (further) interpersonal harm; (3) to help contain intolerable rage and aggression; and (4) to avoid the experience of victimhood and triumph over pain.

Maintaining the Dissociation

The perpetrator introject may prevent traumatic memory material (i.e., BASK elements; Braun, 1988a, 1988b) from being accessible by both 'fronting' self-states with no memory of past harm and self-states holding the dissociated aspects of memory. They may also actively prevent self-states from disclosing secrets to the outside world. Additionally, the external perpetrator may have been 'split' into separate or multiple introjects representing the 'good caregiver' and the 'bad perpetrator.' Such a split may spare a victim – or at least some victimized self-states – from recognizing the harm befalling them, effectively allowing them to remain attached to a toxic caregiver (see Fairbairn, 1952; Freud, 1894/1964). Other self-states may have relationships with either or both introjects represented in the 'good/bad' split (Blizard, 1997b; Putnam, 1989; Ross, 1989; Sinason, 2017; Watkins & Watkins, 1988).

Problematically, neither the introject nor other self-states can recognize that the introject is not the outside perpetrator, owing to both the intensity of the energy contained by the introject and the self-contained, trance-laden internal dynamics. The introject also perceives other self-states to be their child, spouse, sibling, partner, etc. Emotional activation, whether originating from within or outside the self, stokes perpetual conflict amongst self-states, via intra-psychic and interpersonal enactments of past and present abuse and neglect (Blizard, 1997a, 1997b, 2001; Young, 1992).

Protecting Against (Further) Interpersonal Harm

The perpetrator introject may create suspicion that harm could happen again (thus keeping distance from anyone who is perceived as a potential threat) or punish other self-states to control behavior that has brought on harm in the past – and could again. The introject may also serve as an internal, if paradoxical, buffer to prevent abandonment in present-day relationships, by keeping unmet needs and boundary-setting urges contained/silenced (Goodman & Peters, 1995; Ross, 1989; Watkins & Watkins, 1988).

Owing to perceptual and cognitive distortions arising from traumatic experience, other people's motivations and behaviors may be misperceived or misunderstood. For example, either a genuinely harmful person may be experienced as a viable source of needs-meeting/survival in the mold of the original abuser-victim relationship, or a non-harming or genuinely safe person is perceived as a potential/actual threat, resulting in interpersonal turmoil, aggression, or relational difficulties (Howell, 1996; Sinason, 2017; Watkins & Watkins, 1988). This phenomenon may be related to 'negatively valenced SEEKING' (Corrigan et al., 2025; Panksepp & Biven, 2012), meaning that the child's natural tendency to seek care, etc., becomes interwoven with maladaptive, attachment-wounding informed ways of obtaining it (e.g., fight, flee, please/appease).

Containing Intolerable Rage and Aggression

The perpetrator introject may inflict verbal, emotional, physical, or sexual harm upon the body, other self-states connected to the body, and other, outside people, as well as project intrusive thoughts, sensations, images, etc., into conscious awareness as a means for managing both the rage internalized from the external perpetrator(s) as well as thwarted fight responses originating from self-identifying states (Putnam, 1989; Ross, 1989; Watkins & Barabasz, 2008; Watkins & Watkins, 1988). Paired with the perpetrator introject are the victim state(s) that defer to the perpetrator's dominance or anticipated harm. This is one manifestation of the phenomenon called *identification with the aggressor* (Ferenczi, 1955/1994b; Frankel, 2002).

The perpetrator introject may repeat an episode either on a 'loop' or when an internal or external stimulus – even something like the time of day (e.g., bedtime) activates them. Although perhaps serving as a warning against outside harm – or to buffer against the impact of ongoing harm resulting from continued attachment to an outside perpetrator – abuse by introjects can manifest toward other self-states inside/on the body exactly as if it were inflicted by the original perpetrator (Blizard, 1997a, 2001; Bloch, 1991; Kluft, 2006; Loewenstein, 1993; Putnam, 1989; Ross, 1989).

Avoiding the Experience of Victimhood and Triumphing over Pain

By (involuntarily) identifying with the external perpetrator(s), perpetrator introjects may engage in abusive behavior as a means of distancing from the 'victim' role. This can serve both to contain the pain and shame associated with that role and to create a sense of control in the face of helplessness (Howell, 1996, 1997; Lahav et al., 2019; Watkins & Watkins, 1988). A person may be subconsciously driven to engage in repetitions of their prior traumatic experience in new situations, with the underlying need to 'master' and thus put a definitive end to the trauma (Ferenczi 1955/1994b; Howell, 1997, 2014). These actions may also serve to demonstrate the story of harm in the absence of explicit recall of or a capacity to articulate it (see Chapter 11).

Perpetrator Introjects' Impact on Treatment

Treatment – or any kind of intervention – may be perceived by perpetrator introjects as a potential, life-endangering threat to the self (or specific self-states), and thus must be stalled, discouraged, or abandoned. Alternatively, the states that are beholden to introjects may seek boundary-free forms of care and comfort from the therapist and, when it is denied, struggle to accept this. There may be no clear, conscious awareness of the source of these treatment difficulties/barriers, which could culminate in a client's violent outbursts or the "sudden" motivation to drop out of therapy. Additionally, the inexperienced therapist may oblige themselves to meet a client's needs and damage or destroy the therapy frame (Blizard, 2001; Goodman & Peters, 1995; Kluft, 1994; Sachs, 2013; Watkins & Watkins, 1984; Wilbur, 1988).

Working with Perpetrator Introjects

Overview

All approaches that aid in the unburdening of self-states of traumatic experience, both within and outside EMDR therapy practice, appear to include two central elements. These are (1) a 'parts' therapy, used to engage with and relate to ego/self-states and (2) an integration-facilitating mechanism that can reduce or transform the intensity of 'stuck' elements of traumatic experience. The three most prominent ego state therapies integrated into EMDR therapy are Internal Family Systems (Schwartz & Sweezy, 2019), Ego State Therapy (Watkins & Watkins, 1997), and the Developmental Needs-Meeting Strategy (Schmidt, 2009). (See Chapter 9 for a discussion of the first two of these.) Integration facilitating mechanisms include:

- hypnotically facilitated (i.e., abreactive) synthesis (e.g., Fine, 1993; Kluft, 1990; Phillips & Frederick, 1995; Steele, 1989; Van der Hart et al., 1993);
- cognitive/suggestive interventions (e.g., Fine, 1991, 2012; Kluft, 2012a, 2017; Paulsen, 2009; Phillips & Frederick, 1995; Schmidt, 2009; Shapiro, 2016);
- EMDR therapy (e.g., Gelinas, 2003; Knipe, 2019; Gonzalez & Mosquera, 2012; Shebini, 2019; Paulsen, 2009, 2018; Twombly, 2000; Van der Hart et al., 2010); and
- Deep Brain Reorienting (Corrigan et al., 2025).

The EMDR-inflected approaches engage persecutory states, including perpetrator introjects, both indirectly and directly. In an indirect approach, the therapist engages persecutory states, typically in an Internal Family Systems-informed/aligned frame, by 'talking through' and processing with an identified, executive adult state (e.g., Forgash & Knipe, 2008; Gonzalez, 2020; Gonzalez & Mosquera, 2012; Knipe, 2019; Mosquera, 2019; Shapiro, 2016). In a direct approach, the therapist works with persecutory states either by inviting them into executive control or by 'talking past' a fronting state in executive control. This does not exclude working through an identified adult, but it does not exclude working directly with other states. This more emblematic of Ego State Therapy practice. (For further comparison of IFS and Ego State Therapy, see Chapter 9.) In the EMDR therapy world, the direct approach has been most apparent in the work of Sandra Paulsen (2008, 2009, 2018; see also Lanius & Paulsen, 2009, and Paulsen's contributions in Lanius, Paulsen, & Corrigan, 2014).

Regardless of the approach, the focus of the work is reducing/eliminating cognitive distortions, including maladaptive loyalty to the external perpetrator (e.g., Paulsen, 2009; Paulsen & Golston, 2014), dissociative phobias, and ultimately, the harm that arises from all of these. Methods are typically cognitive/suggestive and include appealing to the persecutory state's logic/reason to counter paradoxical thinking, offering appreciation for the sacrifices they made in service of survival, and helping them orient to time, place, person, situation, and other aspects of present reality (i.e., presentification; Van der Hart et al., 2010). Additionally, quasi-hypnotic language may be employed to reveal the child or other, non-perpetrating state underneath the internalized perpetrator's 'costume' or 'mask' (e.g., Paulsen, 2009; Schmidt, 2009; R. Shapiro, 2016; Twombly, 2012). In the indirect approach, there is an emphasis upon reducing adult and other, more vulnerable states' phobic avoidance of or anger toward a perceived internal perpetrator (e.g., Gonzalez, 2020; Knipe, 2008; Gonzalez & Mosquera, 2012; Veerbeek, 2021). Bilateral dual attention stimulation (BL-DAS) may or may not be employed in conjunction with these methods. Whether cognitive/suggestive interventions are employed on their own or with BL-DAS, intentional hypnotic engagement is rarely (if ever) a component of the work (see Chapter 9). For further discussion of perpetrator introjects beyond the previous citations, refer to Vogt (2012).

Potential Challenges in Existing Approaches

Problematically, perpetrator introjects – as opposed to persecutory states more generally – seem neither fully conceptualized nor addressed in their own right in the approaches that work primarily/exclusively through a 'fronting' state. With limited exception, none of the published EMDR therapy-inflected literature seem to adequately acknowledge the profound chaos and actual, physical harm that perpetrator introjects can cause in their efforts to achieve what they may perceive as safety. Furthermore, dissociative identity disorder (DID) and other specified dissociative disorder (OSDD) are *not* analogous to complex trauma/complex posttraumatic stress disorder (C-PTSD). Despite this, the EMDR therapy-inflected interventions focused on persecutory states, with limited exception, frame the work in ways that does not make clear that they are very different phenomena and cannot be treated uniformly.

Additionally, with limited exception, BL-DAS seems to be an optional component in these approaches. Unfortunately, cognitive/suggestive interventions, absent any kind of facilitated synthesis (e.g., hypnosis, BL-DAS), can have limitations, as they may not yield full, energetic transformation and long-term symptom reduction for the self-system overall. In fact, they may only provide temporary respite (e.g., Schmidt, 2009) or, in the case of orienting to present-day realities, may simply not 'sink in' despite repeated efforts (Paulsen & Golston, 2014).

Outside the dissociation-informed EMDR therapy literature, both Watkins and Watkins (1988) and Watkins and Barabasz (2008) discuss using hypnotically facilitated synthesis and hypnoanalysis to relieve persecutory states holding intense rage. However, these require advanced knowledge of Ego State Therapy and clinical hypnosis as well as, potentially, repeated abreactive episodes to achieve full resolution of the encapsulated disturbance. Although the *Id Protocol* does not employ hypnotically facilitated synthesis, it does employ hypnotic techniques, and in some instances formal trance elicitation, largely in service of ensuring that the perpetrator introject may be worked with directly.

Directly Engaging Perpetrator Introjects

Two questions have often arisen since I first presented the *Id Protocol* in 2020: First, why must we work with the introject directly? Second, why is it necessary to know/use clinical hypnosis? In response to the first question, I will offer that there is plenty of evidence in the EMDR therapy literature that affect, even if contacted only fleetingly, is a critical ingredient in reprocessing wounding experience (e.g., Manfield et al., 2017). Baddeley & Hitch (1974) propose an empirically supported, tripartite view of memory, with a 'Central Executive' who controls a working memory split into language/verbal and visuo-spatial domains (see also Hitch et al., 2025). This lends hypothetical support for the importance of ensuring that the introject is fully cathected and is primarily in control of working memory, rather than the introject being an object in the working memory of another self-state in executive control, to achieve adaptive resolution. In the context of working with ego states, Emmerson (2013, p. 237) asserts that it is "impossible" to process another state's wounding second-hand simply by a 'fronting' state being aware, absent any direct, felt experience of it. It must be available to be experienced, first-hand, at the executive level of functioning. (In the EMDR therapy literature,

Jim Knipe (2008) seems implicitly to acknowledge this in his *Loving Eyes* intervention.) Laing (1969) points out that, if we feel someone else's anger directed at us, we naturally will react with defensive fear. My observations have suggested that the intense emotions instilled in many states – including a 'fronting' adult – by a self-state perceived/experienced as a past perpetrator of harm is formidable. Without the introject being more executive, the unavoidable focus can only be other states' feelings toward the introject.

The matter of how to facilitate a perpetrator introject assuming executive control leads us directly to the question about the necessity of clinical hypnosis. According to Barabasz and Watkins (2005), the only way they had been able to achieve full ego cathexis with an internal, not-typically executive object, in this case an introject, under 'in-treatment' conditions, is through hypnotic elicitation. Trance allows a sole, central executive (in a client with who does not/cannot switch) to 'let go of the steering wheel' enough to allow another state to come fully into executive control. This may also apply for persons with OSDD and DID who cannot readily/easily 'switch' under the contrived conditions that exist in therapy, regardless of the setting. Using clinical hypnosis in this case offers an added benefit for EMDR therapy: Some evidence suggests a hypnotic state itself taxes working memory (see Khodaverdi-Khani, 2017; Khodaverdi-Khani & Laurence, 2016), which is complementary with taxation of working memory as one hypothesized mechanism of action in EMDR therapy (Maxfield et al., 2008).

Regarding the use of clinical hypnosis in the *Id Protocol*, not all clients will require a formal trance elicitation, especially if they are hypnotically 'gifted' and responsive (i.e., unguarded and open to the process). That reality notwithstanding, I invite you to consider your own clinical knowledge and skillset: Have you ever *intentionally* engaged your client in trance work via a formal hypnotic elicitation and re-alerting? If not, I recommend deferring your use of the *Id Protocol* until you (1) have at least obtained basic training in clinical hypnosis; (2) know your client more fully, including their hypnotic capacities, traits, and potential treatment complications and remedial interventions (e.g., Kluft, 1982, 1983; MacHovec, 1986); and (3) have a solid understanding of dissociative phenomena. Additionally, consider whether your client has ever been hypnotically manipulated by their perpetrator(s). If you know or suspect this is the case, then *hold off on using this protocol and seek consultation*, especially if this topic is new for you. Separately, for the sake of client safety, it is recommended that a 'baseline' measure of your client's alertness be taken prior to eliciting a hypnotic trance and as part of re-alerting. (See Chapter 11 and *Phase VII: Closure*.)

For those curious to dig deeper, there is a limited, English language, peer-reviewed literature on integrating clinical hypnosis with EMDR therapy (e.g., Corsetti et al., 2020; Harford; 2010; see also the special issue of the *American Journal of Clinical Hypnosis* on EMDR [2001; Vol. 43, Iss. 3–4]). For discussion of similarities/contrasts between EMDR therapy and hypnosis in English language publications, refer to Gilligan (2002), Nicosia (1995), and Pagani et al., (2012).

Phase-by-Phase: The Introject Decathexis (Id) Protocol

There are rarely new ideas under the sun. As I noted above, Watkins and Watkins (1988) employed hypnotically facilitated synthesis with perpetrator introjects to relieve them of their burdens. I did not know that at the time I created the *Id Protocol*. I was familiar with and had used Knipe's (2008, 2019) techniques, including *Loving Eyes* and the *Level of Urge to Avoid*. I was at a loss for how to resolve the pain of more intense perpetrator introjects, though, because rage is not an easy affect to work with. There was no roadmap, at the time, for directly engaging and processing rage with a perpetrator introject using EMDR therapy, and I was not inclined (or, frankly, knowledgeable enough) to process trauma using hypnotic techniques. So, on-the-fly, I put together what I knew: Clinical hypnosis, Ego State Therapy, and EMDR therapy. It felt a bit like "leftovers from the 'fridge' " – but I had guests over, so to speak, which put me in a pinch.

Watkins and Watkins (1988) describe the impact of processing a state's rage, noting that, "The resulting change is not fusing but integration, a process in which the previous [self-states] retain their unconscious sense of self." "[...] [T]hey move down the differentiation-dissociation continuum and become covert, cooperative ego states – like those we find in [non-dissociative] individuals." (p. 71). Arguably, the degree of post-intervention differentiation will depend on a client's individual circumstances and preferences. Regardless, greater (choiceful) cooperation is what the *Id Protocol* achieves, and the effect appears to be permanent. Within the EMDR therapy field, this protocol's existence owes a debt to the work of Sandra Paulsen, Jim Knipe, A. J. Popky, and, of course, Francine Shapiro. The *Id Protocol* has evolved since I first used it in 2016 and later systematized and presented it publicly (Coy, 2020). What I will describe below differs from what I have presented at conferences to date, as I have now fully aligned it with the standard EMDR protocol. Although I make no assumption that the client with whom you use the *Id Protocol* meets criteria for a dissociative disorder – I've used it with plenty of clients who didn't – having an adequate understanding of dissociative and hypnotic phenomena, including how self-states (may) interact with one another, and Ego State Therapy, are necessary for its use. The *Id Protocol* may be used in any of the three stages of complex trauma treatment, as it can be employed for the purpose of stabilization, to address internal conflicts that inhibit trauma processing, as well as during *Stage 3*, when needed. All the same cautions apply here that would for any kind of memory work, whether in the form of ego state exploration, clinical hypnosis, or the use of BL-DAS. In the next section, I will provide a phase-by-phase walk-through of the *Id Protocol* and, subsequently, a case example to illustrate its application and results.

Phase I: History Taking

In Chapter 10, we touched upon the importance of accounting for internal hierarchies and the associations among different self-states through the process of self-system mapping. We can weave in the model for conceptualizing a Standard Protocol targeting sequence, described in Chapter 8, to help us understand why this matters for processing with perpetrator introjects:

In Figure 12.1, we see the 'fronting' state living in the present day, but beholden to the possible 'intrusion' of earlier states' traumatic material into its daily functioning and sense of self via the connections ('association/generalization') shown above. These intrusions are often precipitated by

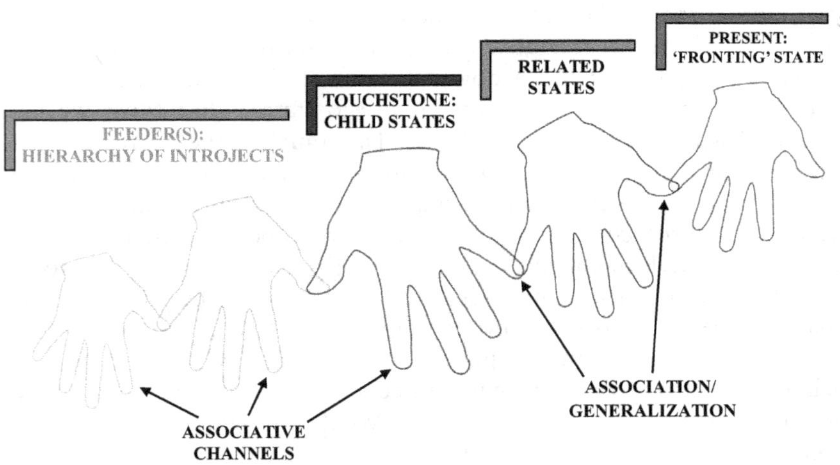

Figure 12.1 Targeting Sequence with Introject Hierarchy.

present 'triggers' that activate states hidden from a 'fronting' state's awareness, though sometimes ego state work quickly reveals the source(s) of activation. However, what is revealed may not represent the full picture. Instead, the most accessible states may be embedded in a dyad, triad, or cluster of related states. Contained within these clusters may be states patterned after a person's perpetrator(s), though these states may not be obvious, depending on how deeply embedded they are. Sometimes, not only were singular perpetrators introjected, but, if they were couched in a hierarchy or system (such as a family), one or more elements of that hierarchy may also have been internalized. And there can be multiple internal representations of a perpetrator hailing either from a single moment in time (i.e., fragmented) or across time, each with its own 'descendants.' Additionally, there may be 'related states' that help buffer more vulnerable states from their associated perpetrator introject(s). An example of this might be an older, anger-energized, self-identifying state (e.g., an adolescent version of the client) who bullies a child state to keep them quiet to avoid activating a perpetrator introject. Van der Hart et al. (2010) refer to these as 'perpetrator-imitating' states.

These clusters of states may function *internally* as the outside hierarchy did. I described in Chapter 10 an introjected family system consisting of a self-identifying child state representing that client at a younger age, an older brother introject, a mother introject, a father introject, and even grandparent introjects. It is entirely possible that an introject may direct its rage at another, more vulnerable state, and at the same time feel afraid of another introject more powerful than itself. For example, everyone in the cluster I just described was afraid of 'grandmother,' but 'father' was not afraid of 'mother' (his spouse), as she was less powerful/intense and thus lower in the hierarchy.

Conceptually, the most powerful introject in a cluster of associated states is analogous to Shapiro's (2018) 'earliest' or 'worst' target memory. In EMDR therapy, it is ideal, when possible, to process touchstone memories first. We might assume that touchstone memories are held by child (or at least younger) states. However, this assumption may prevent us from considering the possibility of internal perpetration. I am not suggesting that *all* self-states' traumas are associated/linked with an introject. I just try to avoid assuming the *absence* of introjects (see Chapters 10 and 11).

Adding to the conceptual complexity is the fact that, even though I mostly see discussion of persecutory introjects patterned after adult caregivers (e.g., parents), they can develop at any point in someone's life. An example would be a persecutory state patterned after a client's abusive partner from twenty years ago. This introject was 'trapped' in a dyad with a client's self-identifying, younger adult state, which he continued to stalk and abuse internally. Hypothetically, the reason that the client was so adept at remaining in that abusive relationship hinged upon child states, of which the sole, central executive adult had no awareness. These child states each held different, distinct dimensions of the same experience. One child state was accustomed to idealizing an abusive parent in whom they only saw the good. A second child state knew very well how to tolerate abuse in service of getting their attachment needs met. A third child state held rage that could never be safely expressed. Each of these child states was associated with the same perpetrator introject, and each also participated in the relationship with the abusive ex-partner, whose behavior mirrored that of the client's abusive parent.

There are several ways we could visualize this dynamic. To simplify things, let us first conceptualize as if the client were still in a relationship with the abusive partner:

In Figure 12.2, the 'fronting' adult state and abusive partner represent the present – *at the time when the client was in the relationship*. To clarify the source of the distress experienced by the 'fronting' state, we must look below the conscious level. Because there appears to be limited, direct connectivity with this level of experience, it may be of value to employ clinical hypnosis to increase access to engage with the child states. At this point, however, we might wonder whether there is anything more than three child states, each of which appears to have a relationship with the abusive partner. Child 1 is idealizing, Child 2 is absorbing the abuse, and Child 3

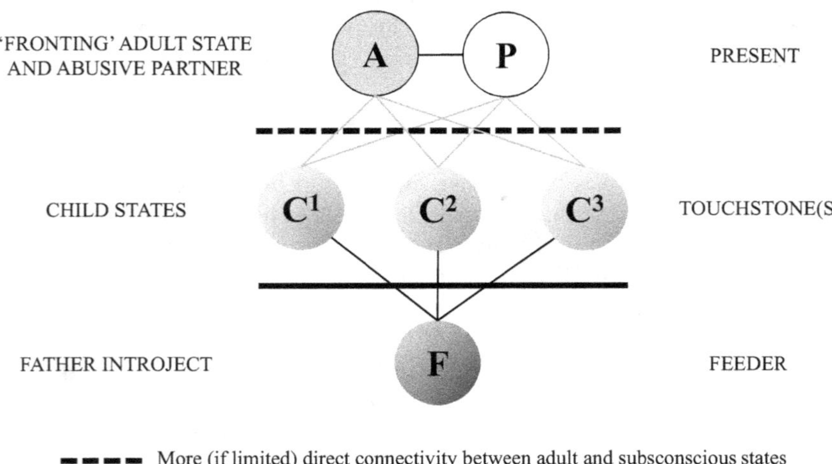

Figure 12.2 Mapping with Targeting Sequence Overlay, Single Introject.

is containing unexpressed rage, but are they only relating to the abusive partner? This is an instance in which Karpman's (1968) *Drama Triangle* (see Chapter 11) may be useful as a deductive reasoning tool. If, in the present day, the abusive partner is the Persecutor and the 'fronting' adult is the Victim, then who (if anyone) was the identified Persecutor of the child Victims in the past? This might be a cue to investigate whether there may be a 'feeder' in the form of an internalized perpetrator. (The case example in Chapter 10 illustrates this.)

I conceptualize perpetrator introjects as being akin to 'feeder' memories because they most frequently seem to be modeled after or align with the qualities of a person's earliest attachment figures. Even with introjects that develop in adulthood, there is often 'root' material with which they become associated, either more directly or distantly. For example, in the scenario I describe above, a younger adult 'version' of the client was in a dyad with an introject of her abusive ex-partner. Child states appear to have driven a conflicted attachment to the ex-partner. Those child states were related to a 'root' or 'feeder' state modeled after their father. Taking that into account, the *actual* present-day cluster of self-states might look like this:

In Figure 12.3, the 'fronting' adult who is in therapy may have access to the younger adult state, stuck in time twenty years ago, but she does not appear to have any direct connection to the introject of her abusive

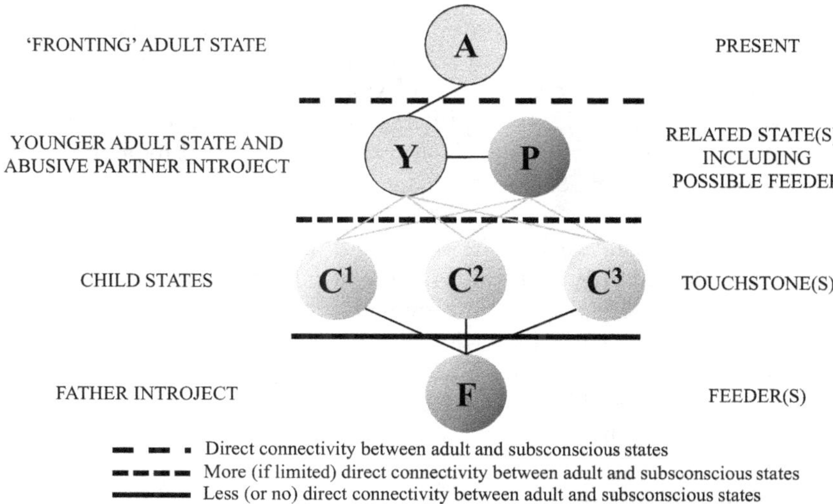

Figure 12.3 Mapping with Targeting Sequence Overlay, Two Introjects.

ex-partner. As a result, she may only register pervasive and/or periodically 'triggered' fear associated with that subconscious dynamic. The therapist could try to process the trauma from twenty years ago, but without knowledge of the abusive partner introject, that might not get very far. The therapist would need to better understand and determine how best to work with that 'feeder' of ongoing internal abuse. Additionally, the younger adult state and the abusive partner introject have ties to child states (touchstones), which in turn appear to have a relationship with a father introject. It is likely that further mapping will be necessary prior to working out with the 'fronting' adult state how best to proceed. One thing seems certain, though: The introjects will likely not cease their abusive behavior without some kind of direct engagement. Let us imagine that this therapist and client dyad laid all the necessary history taking and any additional mapping with different states. Now, imagine this therapist is you, and that you are considering using the *Id Protocol* with one of the two identified introjects. What next?

Phase II: Preparation

A. Elicit a Trance and Convene a Meeting Place

First, elicit a trance with your client. I feel compelled to reiterate that *if you are not trained in the intentional use of clinical hypnosis, then you should not proceed with any form of hypnotic elicitation. Period.* Although I often employ a simple eye fixation elicitation with clients, I make certain before this point that the form of elicitation I use aligns with my client's preferences and hypnotic responsiveness. It is important to be aware that some clients may not be (as) responsive to hypnotic elicitation by a therapist (e.g., Di Filippo & Perri, 2024; Miller, 2012). This is an important issue to be worked through with the client prior to engaging in hypnotic work (e.g., Bliss, 1986; Steele & Van der Hart, 2019).

Next, convene a previously established 'meeting place' using Fraser's (1991, 2003) *Dissociative Table* technique (see Chapter 10). Finally, ensure that all states relevant to the issue you and your client have decided to address have arrived in the meeting place. Otherwise, you will need to figure out who is missing, why they may not have shown up, and any states' initial concerns (see Chapter 11). Use this opportunity to (re) evaluate more vulnerable states (i.e., those that are targeted by an introject) for evidence of intense phobias of or trauma bonds with the introject.

Terrified States

Vulnerable states' phobic avoidance of the introject may be so intense that engaging with the introject may be impossible until the terror itself is reduced. If this occurs, you may need to focus first upon reducing the felt intensity of the phobia/terror from the hated object's point-of-view using BL-DAS or cognitive-suggestive techniques (e.g., Knipe, 2019; Gonzalez & Mosquera, 2012; Paulsen, 2009). However, this alone will not directly, or permanently, impact the energy held by the introject. Knowing all the states associated with the introject will help ensure you have not missed possible sources of terror.

Trauma-bonded States

Trauma-bonded self-states (e.g., a child state that idealizes an abusive, parental introject) may act to protect their 'parent' – and their attachment to it – by preventing the introject from engaging in the process. We can conceptualize this as a form of dysfunctional positive affect (Level of Positive Affect; Knipe, 2005, 2019) held by the child state toward the perpetrator introject. If this instance, you may first need to target and process with BL-DAS the felt intensity of the trauma-bonded state's idealization of the introject.

Despite your best attempts to identify phobias and trauma bonds upfront, these may not become obvious until you invite the introject into executive control (see *Step F* below), so be thoughtful and careful about moving too quickly. Also, be certain you know how to help different self-states ground and orient if dysregulation occurs.

B. Determine the Introject's and Associated States' Openness to Change

Although an introject achieving full, enduring orientation to present reality is ideal, it is often not possible. Repeated attempts to orient, even over a series of sessions, may not 'sink in' (Paulsen & Golston, 2014). This is not unusual, owing to recurring amnesia after each session, but necessitates reminding the introject repeatedly of the year, their nature as an internalization of an external perpetrator, etc. Some introjects don't mind being informed of this, but others do not like being faced with external reality, no matter how gently I've attempted it. (I once made what I thought was a misstep, when I became perturbed and asked a particularly fact-averse mother introject, "Have you looked in the mirror lately?" They disappeared and refused to speak with me for weeks. There was, however, a silver lining. The following week, a self-state spontaneously assumed executive control to inform me that, "We all heard you last week, and we decided to look in the mirror. We had no idea we got old!")

In assessing the introject(s)' interest in change, the 'million-dollar' question is: *Do they want to do their job any longer?* I typically ask an introject how they feel about their role (i.e., do they like their job?) and follow with the question of whether they want to do it any longer. Often, introjects do not like their job, but feel they have no choice, owing to their critical role in ensuring survival by maintaining attachment to an outside source of harm, over many years, etc. However, for this same reason, some introjects are reticent to consider any kind of transformation. If an introject loves its job, then it may be worth considering whether and how you might address their dysfunctional positive affect.

Sometimes, introjects voice that they are concerned about being rendered powerless. I have pointed out in some instances that they already *are* powerless: They have no connection to the rest of the self except through bullying or other harm. They are trapped in trauma time. They are stuck holding a burden forced upon them by suffering through inescapable and potentially annihilating pain. Taking a cue from Motivational Interviewing (Miller & Rollnick, 2023), I cannot overstate the value of asking the introject, "How is this working for you?"

C. Orient the Self-system to the Procedure and Its Potential Impact(s)

Once the introject has agreed that it does not want to do its job any longer, it is possible to discuss processing and potential impact(s). Ideally, the day you and your client decide to process using the *Id Protocol* is not the first time that states have been provided an opportunity to discuss it. Here are the aspects of the *Id Protocol* I recommend covering with your client:

- Explain the basic procedure (all these phases), then clarify whether they prefer gradual change over a series of sessions (i.e., titration) or complete transformation in "one go." Since it is sometimes not possible to process an introject's entire experience in a single session – processing may unfold over a series of sessions.
- Complete transformation, whether in a single session or gradual, may result in seepage of trauma material from other, associated states, though that material tends to process relatively quickly. Ask whether any states have concerns about being able to tolerate that.
- There can be ripple effects to other, associated clusters/sub-systems of states, and these effects may not be predictable – just as in standard EMDR therapy. That said, the results have generally been positive, when all (associated) self-states have been made aware of the process and given the opportunity to ask questions, express concerns, and consent.
- 'Positive' tends to mean increased calm, at least 'locally' in the cluster of states and possibly beyond that cluster, since the introject will likely be unable to do its job (i.e., employ harm in service of protection)

in the same way – or at all. Make clear that the processing has been observed to facilitate permanent change, and that the effects appear to be irreversible.

Ask whether there are any concerns about proceeding, based on the discussion of the procedure and its possible effects. Ensure, as best as possible, that all questions have been asked and answered.

D. Obtain Consent to Proceed

If there are no additional concerns, and all questions have been addressed, then ask the client/self-system for permission to proceed. Just remember, *no means no* – even when it is not verbalized. Look for any non-verbal indicators of reticence. Some clients may struggle to object and instead will do what they believe you want them to do. (I have yet to encounter an introject who behaved this way, but the introject is not the only one who is a party to this process.)

E. Buffer the Object(s) of Hatred from the Introject

Looking upon the object(s) of hate is more concrete, visceral, and emotionally activating than using the abstraction of asking the introject to 'think about' the object 'in the next room.' Buffering vulnerable states from the introject targeting them is akin to, though functionally different than, Shapiro's (2018, p. 125) practice of creating a 'safe place.' In this case, we are establishing safety for the vulnerable state(s) that can last for the duration of the processing to follow. Employing imagery that allows visual and auditory "partitioning" is especially valuable for ensuring that vulnerable, terrified self-states remain protected from a particularly rageful and potentially harmful introject. Consider the following options for buffering the hated object(s):

OPTION 1: The hated object(s) occupy the same space/"room" in the meeting place, but are stationed behind a protector state who does not harm them.

OPTION 2: The hated object(s) are sequestered in a separate space but directly visible to the introject. In this case, the rooms are connected by a one-way (aka two-way) mirror (e.g., Paulsen, 2009), so that the introject can see them but they are spared from seeing the introject.

OPTION 3: The hated object(s) can only be seen via a monitor installed in the main meeting place. They may either be on a 'live feed' or seen as a picture shown on the screen.

Be careful about how self-states are 'seen' by the introject during this process, particularly if your client's trauma history included their thoughts and/or activity being actively watched, controlled, or recorded, regardless of whether this was/is actual or perceived. (This would include their thoughts or activity being 'known' by an omniscient/omnipotent, corporeal being or even a deity.) Additionally, it may take time, negotiation, and multiple attempts to ensure that the hated object(s) are adequately buffered from the introject targeting them. You may not know whether the level of 'protection' you have established is adequate until the introject has been brought into executive control (see immediately below) or when their hatred toward the object(s) is evaluated in *Phase III: Assessment*.

F. Invite the Introject to Assume Executive Control

I have employed language such as 'come forward,' 'step forward,' and 'come all the way to the front.' Be mindful of the language you use to achieve this, particularly if your client has experienced other people in their life calling upon self-states, such as in organized abuse. (If it's happened, it most likely hasn't been under positive circumstances.) The amount of cathexis needed to harness the introject's rage is both client- and state-dependent. A good indicator of adequate cathexis is either that a) the introject speaks to you in the first person ('I') from up front and/or b) the client endorses 'first-person' embodiment of the introject's felt experience without any phobic reaction toward it. You may notice a shift in the client's tone of voice, style of speaking, physical position (e.g., slight turning or drooping of the head, hunching or tension in the shoulders, increased body rigidity), eye position (left/right/up/down) or closure, affect, etc., when the introject arrives up front. If you encounter challenges when you invite the introject to assume executive control, it's best to be curious about why this may be rather than to try to push for them to come up front.

Phase III: Assessment

Once *Preparation* is complete, the introject's experience can be assessed for processing. In the EMDR standard protocol, we ask for seven elements during *Phase III: Assessment*. For the *Id Protocol*, we collect only a subset of these elements: (1) The 'worst part,' which in this case is represented by the object(s) of the introject's hatred/harm; (2) any emotions elicited in the introject when they look upon the object(s) of their hatred/harm; (3) The introject's subjective units of disturbance (SUD) toward the object(s) of hatred/harm on a modified scale; and (4) the location of that disturbance in the body. Assessment of negative and positive cognitions and the VoC are entirely excluded. Why?

Gómez (2013) discusses at some length the importance of helping children mediate intense emotions through the development of language to describe their experience prior to processing trauma. She specifically cites Siegel (2010), who notes that, "We can use the left language centers to calm the excessively firing right emotional areas" (p. 116). Under typical circumstances, processing with a client whom we are concerned may quickly move beyond their Window of Tolerance (Siegel, 1999), we may exclude *Assessment* items that could hasten such an 'excursion' (i.e., titration; see Kluft, 1988; Paulsen, 2009; Twombly, 2010). In the *Id Protocol*, we want to heighten the intensity rather than dampen it, so we exclude the more cortical aspects of *Assessment*, including explicitly linking cognition to emotion and sensation. It is for this same reason that we do not employ a sequential, number-based scale to assess the SUD (see Knipe, 2009, p. 88), which we instead measure based on the 'size' of the hatred. It is not that cognitive distortions are absent for perpetrator introjects – in fact, quite the opposite is true. However, their 'baked in' cognitive and perceptual distortions have been seen to evolve – and resolve – in real-time during processing.

Intensity of Affect

Littel et al. (2017) offer evidence suggesting that the greater the stress experienced by a client upon activating the memory, the more responsive memory material is to the effects of BL-DAS. Although Flash technique research suggests this may not (always) be the case (e.g., Manfield et al., 2017; Wong, 2021), the question of which state has executive control and, by extension, is in charge of working memory, is not addressed. The introject must assume executive control so that what resides in *their* working memory is front-and-center as the focus of processing (i.e., the hated object(s) and the introject's anger toward them). The affective intensity should be as much as the introject can tolerate. My experience suggests that it is unlikely that the introject will phobically avoid feeling their own anger/rage, as this type of state seems to possess a significant capacity for tolerating the affects it is 'tasked' with containing. That notwithstanding, it is still wise to know how to titrate the affect/sensation when needed (e.g., strategies described in Kluft (1990, 2012a) or Fine and Berkowitz's (2001) EMDR-centered wreathing protocol). As I mentioned earlier, it is important that other states, who may have little to no tolerance for an introject's rage, are adequately buffered from it. Otherwise, feelings of terror from vulnerable states may override the rage, making a focus on the introject impossible. Below is sample language for an introject-focused *Phase III: Assessment*:

1. *When you turn toward/look at [the object of the introject's hatred/harm, i.e., the 'worst part'], what emotions do you feel?*
2. *Are those emotions really big, medium size, pretty small, or nothing at all?*
3. *Where do you feel that in your body?*

From here, we reconfirm that we have consent to proceed, then, just as in Standard Protocol, move forward into *Phase IV: Desensitization.*

Phase IV: Desensitization

To begin processing, we invite the introject to look upon the hated object(s) (i.e., the 'worst part'), the emotions/sensations that they feel, and where they feel them in the body. Then, we introduce successive sets of bilateral dual-attention stimulus (BL-DAS) to process the disturbance.

BL-DAS: Form, Speed, and Set Length

The *Id Protocol* specifically employs tactile BL-DAS. Eye movements may expel the introject from executive functioning prematurely (i.e., spontaneous switching; see Paulsen, 1995). Although auditory tones have not been tested, there is compelling evidence for favoring tactile BL-DAS, which aligns with research indicating the efficacy of 'modality specific interference' – that is, using tactile DAS for somatic disturbance, eye movements for visual disturbance, etc. (Matthijssen, et al., 2019). Although combining forms of BL-DAS (e.g., tactile + visual) may be more effective in some cases (Matthijssen, et al., 2021; Paulsen & Serin, 2018), here tactile BL-DAS alone is adequate, and, most importantly, allows for more precise titration of the processing.

We can deliver tactile BL-DAS in a variety of formats. In person, the therapist can tap the sides of the client's knees (where the ball joint is, as there are fewer nerve endings thus less sensitivity) or tap on the backs of client's hands when they are resting palm-down on their own knees. Both in-person and via tele-health, electronic tappers may be used. Or, the client can employ self-tapping, either on the legs or via the *Butterfly Hug* (Artigas & Jarero, 2013). I have become quite partial to and now prefer self-tapping, owing to the level of control the client exerts in processing. More rapid BL-DAS is preferable, just as in typical reprocessing. If you prefer using electronic tappers, and the client has a history of exposure to electric shock (whether accidental or intentional), then ensure that they can tolerate the vibration of the tappers. If they cannot, then default to self-tapping.

Shorter sets of BL-DAS (8–15 seconds of tapping versus the standard 20–25) help titrate the processing. As opposed to longer sets, the shorter sets reduce the time of exposure to the toxic affect, increase the client's sense of control over the process, and create more space for the introject and self-system to adjust slowly and gradually to the shifting of realities. Longer sets will facilitate more associations and more rapid change, which is not necessarily desirable in this case. I typically will not exceed 20 seconds of BL-DAS.

Checking in Between Sets of BL-DAS

After each set, 'return to target' by inviting the introject's attention back to the object(s) of their hated. Then, ask what the introject notices, in one of two ways.

1. To maintain restricted processing (i.e., EMD), ask the introject, "*When you look at [the object] now, is the feeling bigger, smaller, or the same as it was?*" This is similar to checking in between sets when using the *Blind to Therapist Protocol* (Blore & Holmshaw, 2009).
2. To allow for *less* restricted processing, as in EMDr (E. Shapiro & Laub, 2008) or standard EMDR, ask, "*When you look at [the object] now, what do you notice?*" or "*What do you notice now?*" With less restricted processing, check the SUD (really big, medium-size, etc.) either when associations remain unchanged for two successive sets or when there is a discernible, enduring shift in the introject's view of the object of their hatred (e.g., Knipe, 2019, p. 80).

Reducing the SUD to 'nothing at all' (i.e., '0') will spontaneously reveal underlying trauma material, if it is there – very much in line with the findings of Knipe (1995, 2005, 2019) in his conceptualization of targeting defenses, particularly avoidance defenses (i.e., Level of Urge to Avoid, or LoUA). As is the case when using EMDR therapy methods to treat addiction, reducing the disturbance over a series of sessions will allow for closer monitoring of effects and a gentler, more slowly paced transformation (Popky, 2005). If you (1) know your client well, (2) have enough time in session to deal with any traumatic material that might surface (Kluft, 1991) once the rage has diminished, and (3) the introject and the self-system in general are responding well, then less restricted processing is probably 'ok.' Otherwise, it is advisable to process in a more restricted manner.

Progression and Completion of Processing

The course of processing will depend on the complexity and intensity of the material held by the introject, the composition of the hierarchy, how many states were bound up in the dynamic(s) with the introject, and other, client-specific traits, etc.

Processing has been observed to follow a predictable if not always identical thematic progression: Diffusion of intense affect → Identity or related confusion → Recognition of the object of hate as vulnerable, young, a victim, etc. → RESPONSIBILITY: Guilt/shame for harming the object of their hatred (see Ferenczi, 1955/1994b) → SAFETY: Fear or concern about connecting with the hated object → CONTROL/CHOICES: 'I don't like feeling this way'/'I don't want to feel this way'/'I don't want to do this anymore' → the introject's grief → Positive feelings toward the (previously) hated object (e.g., admiration, compassion, or love) → Spontaneous shift in ego cathexis to another (usually, but not always adult) state, often accompanied by sudden re-alerting from trance → Adult's recognition of introject as 'just a child' or 'just me' → Adult's grief → Calm/peace and/or 'pops the cap' off the hated object's trauma material. Introjects appear to process rather consistently through Shapiro's (2018) three domains of experience, though, as with any client, the progression will not always look the same. Processing appears to be complete when one or more of the following conditions has been met:

1. The introject's level of disturbance is 'nothing at all' (SUD=0) when it looks at the object it was focused upon; and/or
2. the introject has transformed and is no longer experienced as the outside (or any kind of) perpetrator. Introjects formed in early life have typically transformed into a child ego state. Those that formed in adulthood seem to organically assume a new role within the self; and/or
3. If there was underlying trauma material 'capped' by the introject's activity, then the intervention is complete once the state holding it has processed it. The hated object's trauma material is typically fragmentary – usually Behavior, Affect, and/or Sensation (Braun, 1988a, 1988b) – requiring fewer sets of BL-DAS to discharge, at which point calm/peace (i.e., SUD=0) is achieved.

Processing Effects

Introjects have been observed to transform either into a self-identifying state, a more subdued and engaged form of what they previously were, or into something else, such as a benign or caring/supportive state. Examples of positive change have included reduction in/elimination of physical pain, terror, spontaneous bruising, flashbacks, etc., when the introject's abuse ceases; the cessation of compulsive behavior associated with an introjected abuser; a significant reduction in emotional dysregulation (anger in particular) and, in one instance, perfectionism (imposed upon child states by a mother-identifying state); noticeably increased self-confidence and assertiveness; and, in one instance, recovery of a lost skill/capacity.

A cisgender female client learned from an early age to fear her grandmother, whom she referred to as a 'strong woman.' The client's assertiveness was closely guarded/hindered by a grandmother introject; it also fueled the client's phobia of strong, assertive women in her adult life. Another client found that she regained her capacity for managing her finances once an intimidating, insulting father introject had transformed. More recently, a client shared that for years they felt a terrible foreboding, which was always 'triggered' by a specific stimulus that they encountered on a weekly basis (watching the clock, waiting for the time they had to go home). This, we learned, was caused by a perpetrator introject patterned after their abusive ex-partner and directed at a perpetually terrified, self-identifying state representing the client at the age when this dynamic began. Processing the introject's rage and hatred eliminated the enduring terror.

Stalled Processing (aka 'Looping')

Stalled processing using the *Id Protocol* is indicated when the level of disturbance does not diminish and/or there is no thematic progression as indicated above. Owing to Francine Shapiro's recommendation to 'stay out of the way' of processing, even in the face of 'looping', I made a conscious choice to avoid using cognitive interweaves in the *Id Protocol.* Notably, the only time I have encountered 'looping' using this protocol is when I have unwittingly begun a course of processing with a 'middle manager' – my term for an introject or other protective state that is lower in the 'pecking order' in a cluster of states with a hierarchy of introjects (e.g., grandmother, mother, father, and sibling).

Early on in my development of this protocol, this 'looping' occurred with two different clients – oddly, in the same week. In both cases, it came to light during processing that a previously unknown mother introject was more powerful than the father introject that was the focus of the intervention. The process moved along smoothly in both instances until the point when ego energy naturally and spontaneously would have shifted back to the adult (in effect, 'dissolving' the trance and resolving the accompanying distortions that prevented the adult from seeing another state as a part of themselves rather than as an introject). Instead, each client's father introject became 'stuck' in the ambivalence between releasing their ego energy (and sense of 'self,' thus being unable to fully discharge the animosity they held toward a vulnerable child state) and continuing to protect via fear/

hatred/harm. In both cases, without full decathexis, these introjects continued to possess a fully egotized sense of self.

In one case, I only discovered why this was so as we transitioned into *Phase VII: Closure*. I asked a father introject if they would be open to 'laying off' creating anxiety for other states over the next week, just to see what that might be like. Their cryptic response was, *"I'm used to doing what I'm told."* Then, mostly re-alerted, the client (adult, 'fronting' state) said, "All I'm getting from the father part is this: 'You haven't even talked to my wife yet…'." This was a tip-off that this may not be the most powerful introject in this hierarchy: There was a 'feeder,' in the form of a mother-identifying state, that precipitated the looping. In the other case, I asked when the 'looping' became obvious, inquiring of the father introject, *"There isn't by chance a mother part that's more powerful than you, is there? I'm not sure."* There were indeed both mother and previously unknown (maternal) grandmother introjects that appeared to be 'higher ranking' than the father-identifying state that was the focus of the intervention. These occasions illustrate why I have become such a strong advocate for careful mapping!

Phase V: Installation

This phase is excluded from the *Id Protocol*. Since (1) we do not collect information about cognitions in *Phase III: Assessment* and (2) the introject transforms and is no longer egotized as it was prior to the intervention, thus reinforcing the introject's sense of 'I'-ness via the introduction of a self-referencing positive cognition in *Phase V: Installation* does not make sense. That said, evidence suggests that the client's perception does naturally (and satisfactorily) shift from a negative to a positive emotional valence during processing.

Phase VI: Body Scan

Because the protocol is based most closely upon EMD (Shapiro, 1989, 2018), which does not include *Phase VI: Body Scan*, I opted to exclude it from the *Id Protocol*, as well. In line with the rationale for avoiding the *Body Scan* in EMD, it is preferable to fractionate the processing by focusing only upon the immediate cluster or hierarchy states associated with an introject. This minimizes the risk of flooding that can come from inviting attention to additional, body-based associative channels.

Phase VII: Closure

Although standard *Phase VII: Closure* approaches are sometimes adequate, often they are not, particularly in the context of active trance. Since we have worked hypnotically, it is critical to help the client ground, contain trauma material, *and* re-alert. Re-alerting is the process of ensuring that the 'central executive' self-state you started the session with (assuming you did!) has returned to executive control, all trauma-holding states have set aside their traumatic material, and non-executive states have made their way to a place of rest, protection, or observation from a distance (Kluft, 2012a; Paulsen, 2009).

Accepting the client's insistence that "I'm fine" as a definitive sign that they *are* fine or taking at face value their appearance of being 'awake' is rarely sufficient, particularly with naturally trance-prone clients. Even the client may be unaware of their altered state of consciousness (Kluft, 2012b, 2012c). Appearances can be deceiving, so revisiting the *Howard Alertness Scale* (HAS; Howard, 2017; see Chapter 10) is ideal for confirming full alertness. Ensure that your client feels totally alert, aware, and oriented – or at least as at the same place on the HAS 1-to-10 scale as they were at the start of the session – prior to wrapping up.

Remind the client that processing may continue after the session, and to take note of anything that seems new, unusual, or different (i.e., TICES; Shapiro, 2018). Also, ensure that your client has adequate means for coping with any new, disturbing material that arises, and that you have a plan in place for checking in between sessions if it is necessary.

Phase VIII: Reevaluation

Typical *Reevaluation* tasks include checking in with the client about how they felt following their last session, reviewing TICES, and checking the previous session's work. This does not differ for the *Id Protocol.* However, checking our work requires reconvening the meeting place, discussing the impact of the processing, and determining how to proceed. If there is no more processing to be done with the introject due to a full transformation, then you may decide to continue working through the introject hierarchy (if there was one). Or, if applicable, you may decide to work through trauma material held by vulnerable states 'left behind' following the transformation of their associated introject. Or, you may shift attention to another symptom and its associated cluster of states. Or, maybe you will decide to take a break from further processing to further digest the change the client has experienced.

Case Example

'Joan' Revisited

In Chapter 11, I described a client – here, let's call him 'David' – within whom I encountered a state called 'Joan.' What I did not realize at that initial, jarring introduction was that David already knew of this state. However, it seemed 'Joan' had been spoken of in previous therapies more as a metaphorical representation of David's intense feelings of anger than as an introject. David, a cisgender, White gay man, had an extensive attachment trauma and substance use history, many pockets of which had already been processed, both with me and with a previous therapist, through an integrative EMDR therapy-based approach.

Although we met for weekly therapy for over two years, the context for our work at the time the *Id Protocol* came into being was a revisitation of early trauma clearing in a multi-day, brief intensive treatment format. Our original attempt at this work, a few years prior, led to the first emergence of 'Joan.' David had long-term struggles with anger – being both fearful of it and at times outwardly reactive toward others in his life. During our weekly work, intense anger had emerged for David in the therapy relationship, directed at me, particularly when I expressed empathy for him. In all fairness, I also made plenty of therapeutic missteps. Despite the challenges, David and I had been able to maintain a strong therapeutic alliance.

Subsequent exploration via hypnotically facilitated Ego State Therapy revealed a somewhat complex self-system, with ego energy particularly bound up in two states: 'Crystal Meth Dave' and 'Joan.' Although David had been in recovery and sober for years, 'Crystal Meth Dave' was a self-identifying state associated with his history of using substances, methamphetamine in particular, as a means for connecting with others via sexual contact. 'Joan' was a protector patterned after her namesake in 'Mommie Dearest' melded with David's mother's rage. These two states had a highly charged adversarial relationship, with each experiencing the other as persecutory. Repeated attempts at using standard cognitive/suggestive approaches had not been successful at helping 'Joan,' despite a desire for change. At this point in early trauma processing, therapeutic work had again ground to a halt due to entrenched internal conflict.

At this point, I would like to take a few steps back to provide more context for the intervention that will follow. I will begin with a snippet of mapping as it pertains to my dynamic with David, 'Joan,' and associated states.

Phase I: History Taking

Here, I illustrate a progressive mapping that reflects how I came to learn of 'Joan' and a few other states. Figure 12.4 reflects how I initially experienced David's expression of anger, illustrated through Karpman's (1968) *Drama Triangle*:

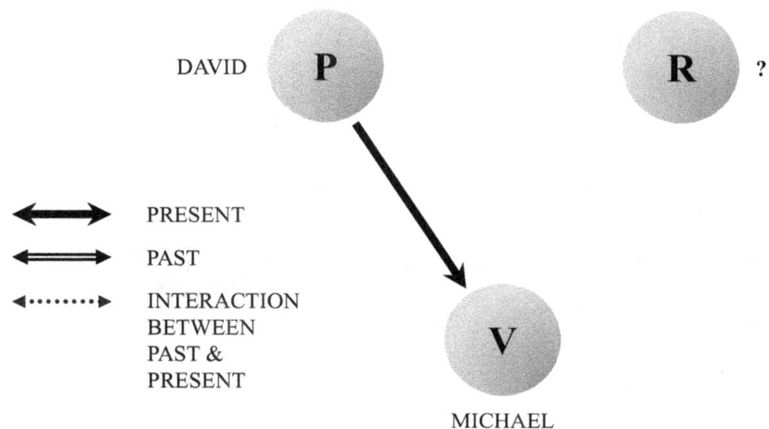

Figure 12.4 Initial Mapping of Interaction with David.

Source: Adapted from Karpman (1968).

The positions on the *Triangle* are (P)ersecutor, (V)ictim, and (R)escuer. In that first interaction, David felt to me like a Persecutor to me as a Victim. There was no apparent Rescuer. Below, in Figure 12.5, we see what I later discovered:

Here, I am perceived by 'Joan' to be a Persecutor who is Victimizing the child states. 'Joan' must Rescue the child states by lashing out at me. Thus, I pivot into the Victim role as 'Joan' becomes my Persecutor. At the same time, 'Joan' and 'Crystal Meth Dave' are also in a *Triangle*, pivoting between being each other's Victim and Persecutor. The child states, which are not reflected in the second *Triangle*, also seemed to inhabit the Victim role in the dynamic with 'Crystal Meth Dave,' – from his point of view, he may well have felt like the Victim, beholden to the child states' unmet early attachment needs. Regardless of which configuration of the drama we consider, it does appear that 'Joan' is the fulcrum of the internal dynamics.

In line with the previous targeting sequence examples earlier in this chapter, here is one for this situation:

In Figure 12.6, we can see the 'fronting' adult David in the present. Below the conscious surface we find the 'Crystal Meth Dave' state, who is related to and chronologically descended from unspecified child states, who represent touchstone experiences from early life. Undergirding all of these, in this cluster of states, is the quasi-mother introject 'Joan.' Take note that there appears to be a 'mystery' child state that is more strongly connected to both 'Joan' and 'Crystal Meth Dave.' The (true) nature of these three states will become clearer as processing unfolds.

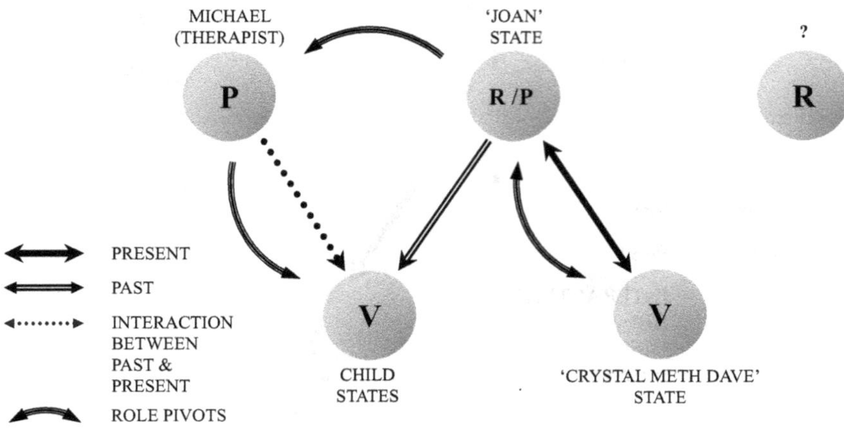

Figure 12.5 Second Mapping of Interaction with David.

Source: Adapted from Karpman (1968).

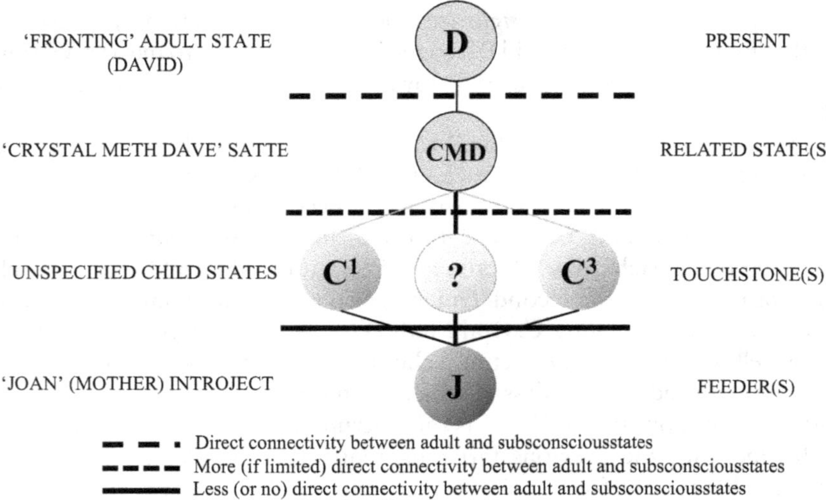

Figure 12.6 Mapping with Target Sequencing Overlay with David.

Phase II: Preparation

Shifting the focus away from further early trauma processing, I suggest that ego state work, specifically in the context of trance, might be helpful to get a clearer sense of what was happening. The client consented and he readily responded to a trance elicitation via eye fixation, which we deepened with a slow count down from 20.

I first convened a meeting place: "This is a message for the whole self, so please listen in: I'd like to invite into the meeting place 'Joan,' 'Crystal Meth Dave,' and anyone or anything that has concerns related to them. Whenever you're ready, just say, 'here.' " David verbally signals the arrival of three states: 'Joan,' 'Crystal Meth Dave,' and 'Flannel Shirt Guy,' the latter known to be a 'helper' to some other states. I welcome them, thank them for participating, and re-assess present orientation:

Michael: *Welcome, all. Hello, 'Joan' part-of-self. We've met before, but I'll remind you that I'm Michael. We're at my office, working with younger ones. Joan part-of-self, do you* remember us *talking before about you being a part of David, what year it is, etc.?*

Joan: It's hard to remember things like that.

Michael: *It does seem that way. It's been a bit of time since we last spoke, and I wonder how things are for you?*

Joan: Well, I have to protect everyone. It's exhausting, but I don't have a choice.

Michael: *I can sense your tiredness. Can you remind me: You're protecting them against what or whom?*

Joan: The one who uses drugs and has sex – "Crystal Meth Dave."

A discussion about David's long-term sobriety ensued. I invited 'Joan' to consider ongoing outbursts of anger at times, as well as the grind of being constantly vigilant. 'Joan' admitted that it might be nice to have more choices, and expressed an openness to change, even though she believed that nothing would, or could, improve after all this time. It was agreed to employ tactile dual-attention stimulus in an EMDR therapy frame to facilitate change. Other states also agreed.

Michael: *Speaking directly to the 'Joan' part-of-self, I'd like to invite you to step forward to the front. Just let me know when you're here.*

I pick up on subtle shifts in the body, and 'something different' about the energy moving between David and me, which, based on experience doing this work with him, indicated a change in ego cathexis. 'Joan' reports that she is up front, and I notice a slightly different tone of voice. I then asked 'Flannel Shirt Guy' to stand in front of 'Crystal Meth Dave' to offset the experience of rage coming from 'Joan' toward 'Crystal Meth Dave.'

Phase III: Assessment

Michael: *Joan, what do you notice when you look at 'Crystal Meth Dave'?*
Joan: [Disdainfully] He's a mess. He's trouble. He's going to bring us all down.
Michael: *When you look at 'Crystal Meth Dave' and think about him bringing you all down, what emotions do you notice?*
Joan: Angry, and kind of afraid.

When 'Joan' was asked to look at 'Crystal Meth Dave' and notice the felt intensity of those emotions, she reported it as 'high.' (Owing to this client's extensive experience with EMDR, they reflexively reported a SUD of 8/10.) The location of the disturbance was in the jaw and chest. At this point, I asked for and was granted consent to proceed with tactile BL-DAS. I reminded David that we could pause at any point. He had previously demonstrated that he had no qualms about telling me to stop if it felt necessary.

Phase IV: Desensitization

Michael: *Can you look at Crystal Meth Dave and notice how that feels? Just notice. [BL-DAS; 15-20 seconds.] And what are you noticing now?*
Joan: Tension between protecting others and protecting Crystal Meth Dave.
Michael: *Just notice that. [BL-DAS] And what are you noticing now?*
Joan: (Sobbing.) I feel so badly for how I've treated him.
Michael: *Just notice that. [BL-DAS] And what are you noticing now?*
Joan: (Sobbing.) It feels like everything is connected.
Michael: *Just notice that. [BL-DAS] And what are you noticing now?*
Joan: (Sobbing.) Feels like 'Crystal Meth Dave' is just a child.
Michael: *Just notice that. [BL-DAS] And what are you noticing now?*
Joan: (Sobbing) 'Crystal Meth Dave' is a child I've been abusing.
Michael: *Just notice that. [BL-DAS] And what are you noticing now?*
Joan: (Tears subsiding) I'm just a child, too.
Michael: *Just notice that. [BL-DAS] And what are you noticing now?*
Joan: I was really afraid.
Michael: *Just notice that. [BL-DAS; David spontaneously and quite discernibly re-alerted from the trance and re-assumed executive control during this set of taps.] And what are you noticing now?*
David: 'Joan' was just created out of fear. [David offered the same response after the next set of BL-DAS, as well, and added, "… and she's just a child, too."]

Michael: *[Returning to the original Target with David ego cathected] And when you look at 'Crystal Meth Dave' now, what do you notice?*
David: I just feel compassion.
Michael: *David, what does the idea of sex without "Joan" or 'Crystal Meth Dave' running the show feel like? Just notice. [I asked this question based on the historical relationships among David, Joan, and Crystal Meth Dave related to physical intimacy. It was not employed with the intention of using an interweave; BL-DAS] And what are you noticing now?*
David: I just feel solid.
Michael: *Just notice that. [BL-DAS] And what are you noticing now?*
David: I just feel solid and centered.
This marked the end of processing.

Phase VII: Closure

I invited David and all states in the meeting place to set aside any remaining memory material, and then for those in the meeting place and anyone else listening to make their way to places of rest, protection, or observation. Then, the meeting place was closed. I ensured that David felt fully alert, aware, and oriented prior to a scheduled lunch break.

Phase VIII: Reevaluation

Reconvening after an hour-long lunch break, I invited David to reevaluate the effects of processing and asked him how he experienced the Joan' state now. He responded in a neutral way: " 'Joan' is a child." I then asked David about 'Crystal Meth Dave.' He said: "He was a child who was forced to 'freeze' for 20 to 30 years." Both states appeared to have decathected to the point of appearing as child states when David looked inside.

Discussion

Following this piece of work, David discovered an increased ability and openness to engage in early trauma processing. Post-intensive, David reported less agitation and a sense that 'Joan' had transformed and was accepted as a part of the self. The next time I saw David, about six months later, he reported that this work with 'Joan' and 'Crystal Meth Dave' had been 'transformative.' He reported much less anger, more top-down impulse control, and more ease around attachment and intimacy with his partner. To be sure, 'Joan' was not the stereotypical introject, as she was a imaginal merger of a terrifying 'mother' character from a film and David's own mother's rage. Nevertheless, there was clear, and lasting, change.

Conclusion

This protocol is by no means a cure-all; however, I have seen it repeatedly resolve a previously intractable problem in a relatively brief amount of time. The most highly energized perpetrator introject I have worked with, a Mother-identifying state who fueled a client's lifelong perfectionism, became fully decathected of this energy after three successive 45-minute weekly sessions. The Mother state became integrated into client's overall functioning, and the perfectionism was no longer a central feature of the client's difficulties. Subsequent experience with other clients whose self-systems were not composed of intentionally created states (i.e., those not subject to a history of systematic/organized/extreme abuse), including introjects that were physically abusive, has yielded very similar results (e.g., increased internal harmony and less overall inhibition) I make no guarantees regarding the course/results of this protocol with your clients, as each person's self-system is unique. That said, reports from other therapists who have used it with their clients have consistently, to date, supported the results I have seen in my own work. Continued use and study of this protocol, including anecdotal reports from other practitioners, suggested that the phases laid out in this chapter are necessary to ensure full adaptive resolution.

References

Artigas, L. & Jarero, I. (2013). The butterfly hug. In M. Luber (Ed.), *Implementing EMDR early mental health interventions for man-made and natural disasters: Models, scripted protocols, and summary sheets* (pp. 127–130). SpringerPublishing Company.

Baddeley, A., & Hitch, G. J. (1974). Working memory. In G. A. Bower (Ed.), *Recent advances in learning and motivation* (Vol. 8, pp. 47–89). Academic Press.

Barach, P. M. (1991). Multiple personality disorder as an attachment disorder. *Dissociation, 4*(3), 117–123. hdl.handle.net/1794/1448

Barabasz, A., & Watkins, J. G. (2005). *Hypnotherapeutic techniques* (2nd ed.). Brunner-Routledge.

Bliss, E. L. (1986). *Multiple personality, allied disorders, and hypnosis*. Oxford University Press.

Blizard, R. A. (1997a). Therapeutic alliance with abuser alters in DID: The paradox of attachment to the abuser. *Dissociation, 10*(4), 246–254. hdl.handle.net/1794/1812

Blizard, R. A. (1997b). The origins of dissociative identity disorder from an object relations and attachment theory perspective. *Dissociation, 10*(4), 223–229. hdl.handle.net/1794/1803

Blizard, R. A. (2001). Masochistic and sadistic ego states: Dissociative solutions to the dilemma of attachment to an abusive caretaker. *Journal of Trauma & Dissociation, 2*(4), 37–58. https://doi.org/10.1300/J229v02n04_03

Bloch, J. P. (1991). *Assessment and treatment of multiple personality and dissociative disorders*. Professional Resource Press.

Blore D. C., & Holmshaw M. (2009). EMDR "blind to therapist protocol." In M. Luber (Ed.), *Eye movement desensitization and reprocessing: EMDR scripted protocols basic and special situations* (pp. 233–240). Springer Publishing Company.

Braun, B. G. (1988a). The BASK model of dissociation. *Dissociation, 1*(1), 4–23. hdl.handle.net/1794/1276

Braun, B. G. (1988b). The BASK model of dissociation: Part II – treatment. *Dissociation, 1*(2), 16–23. hdl.handle.net/1794/1340

Corrigan, F. M., Young, H., & Christie-Sands, J. (2025). *Deep brain reorienting: Understanding the neuroscience of trauma, attachment wounding, and DBR psychotherapy*. Routledge. https://doi.org/10.4324/9781003431695

Corsetti, M. T., Rossi, E., Bonvino, S., & Randazzo, P. (2020). Psychological distress and quality of life are improved in autoimmune patients through tandem-psychotherapy, combining individual hypnosis and eye movement desensitization and reprocessing (EMDR) treatment for trauma, followed by supportive-expressive group therapy. *Clinical Rheumatology, 39*(4), 1331–1339. https://doi.org/10.1007/s10067-019-04862-1

Coy, D. M. (2020, May 15-17). *The introject decathexis protocol: An integrative EMDR therapy approach to unbind perpetrator parts* [Conference Presentation]. International Society for the Study of Trauma and Dissociation 2020 Virtual Congress. cfas.isst-d.org/content/emdr-introject-decathexis-protocol-integrative-approach-unbind-perpetrator-parts

Di Filippo, G., & Perri, R. L. (2024). Intimate relationships and hypnosis: Insecure adult attachment affects emotions and absorption during hypnosis. *Frontiers in Psychology, 15*, 1326170. https://doi.org/10.3389/fpsyg.2024.1326170

Emmerson, G. (2013). The vaded ego state and the invisible bridging induction. *International Journal of Clinical and Experimental Hypnosis, 61*(2), 232–250. https://doi.org/10.1080/00207144.2013.753835

Fairbairn, W. R. D. (1952). *Psychoanalytic studies of the personality*. Tavistock Publications.

Ferenczi, S. (1994a). On the definition of introjection. In M. Balint (Ed.), *Final contributions to the problems and methods of psycho-analysis* (pp. 316–318) (E. Mosbacher, Trans.). Routledge. (Original work published 1912)

Ferenczi, S. (1994b). Confusion of tongues between adults and the child. In M. Balint (Ed.), *Final contributions to the problems and methods of psycho-analysis* (pp. 156–167) (E. Mosbacher, Trans.). Routledge. (Original work published 1955)

Fine, C. G. (1991). Treatment stabilization and crisis prevention: Pacing the therapy of the multiple personality disorder patient. *Psychiatric Clinics of North America, 14*(3), 661–676. https://doi.org/10.1016/S0193-953X(18)30294-6

Fine, C. G. (1993). A tactical integrationist perspective on the treatment of multiple personality disorder. In R. P. Kluft & C. G. Fine (Eds.), *Clinical perspectives on multiple personality disorder* (pp. 135–154). American Psychiatric Press.

Fine, C. G. (2012). Cognitive behavioral hypnotherapy for dissociative disorders. *American Journal of Clinical Hypnosis, 54*(4), 331–352. https://doi.org/10.1080/00029157.2012.656856

Fine, C. G., & Berkowitz, A. S. (2001). The wreathing protocol: The imbrication of hypnosis and EMDR in the treatment of dissociative identity disorder and other maladaptive dissociative responses. *American Journal of Clinical Hypnosis, 43*(3-4), 275–290. https://doi.org/10.1080/00029157.2001.10404282

Forgash, C., & Knipe, J. (2008). Integrating EMDR and ego state treatment for clients with trauma disorders. In C. Forgash & M. Copeley (Eds.), *Healing the heart of trauma and dissociation with EMDR and ego state therapy* (pp. 1–59). Springer Publishing Company.

Frankel, J. (2002). Exploring Ferenczi's concept of identification with the aggressor: Its role in trauma, everyday life, and the therapeutic relationship. *Psychoanalytic Dialogues, 12*(1), 101–139. https://doi.org/10.1080/10481881209348657

Frankel, A. S., & O'Hearn, T. C. (1996). Similarities in responses to extreme and unremitting stress: Cultures of communities under siege. *Psychotherapy Theory Research & Practice, 33*(3), 485–502. https://doi.org/10.1037/0033-3204.33.3.485

Fraser, G. A. (1991). The dissociative table technique: A strategy for working with ego states in dissociative disorders and ego-state therapy. *Dissociation, 4*(4), 205–213.

Fraser, G. A. (2003). Fraser's "dissociative table technique" revisited, revised: A strategy for working with ego states in dissociative disorders and ego-state therapy. *Journal of Trauma and Dissociation, 4*(4), 5–28. https://doi.org/10.1300/j229v04n04_02

Freud S. (1964). *The neuro-psychoses of defence.* In J. Strachey (Ed.), *The standard edition of the complete psychological works of sigmund freud*(vol. III, pp. 41–61). Hogarth Press. (Original work published in 1894)

Gallese, V. (2009). Mirror neurons, embodied simulation, and the neural basis of social identification. *Psychoanalytic Dialogues, 19*(5), 519–536. https://doi.org/10.1080/10481880903231910

Gelinas, D. J. (2003). Integrating EMDR into phase-oriented treatment for trauma. *Journal of Trauma and Dissociation, 4*(3), 91–135. https://doi.org/10.1300/J229v04n03_06

Gilligan, S. (2002). EMDR and hypnosis. In F. Shapiro (Ed.), *EMDR as an integrative psychotherapy approach: Experts of diverse orientations explore the paradigm prism* (pp. 225–238). American Psychological Association. https://doi.org/10.1037/10512-009

Goodman, L., & Peters, J. (1995). Persecutory alters and ego states: Protectors, friends, and allies. *Dissociation, 8*(2), 91–99. hdl.handle.net/1794/1601

Gómez, A. M. (2013). *EMDR therapy and adjunct approaches with children: Complex trauma, attachment, and dissociation.* Springer Publishing Company.

Gonzalez, A. (2020). Working through the adult self. *Frontiers in the Psychotherapy of Trauma and Dissociation, 4*(1), 4–16. https://doi.org/10.46716/ftpd.2020.0032

Gonzalez, A., & Mosquera, D. (2012). *EMDR and dissociation: The progressive approach*. Amazon Imprint.

Harford, P. M. (2010). The integrative use of EMDR and clinical hypnosis in the treatment of adults abused as children. *Journal of EMDR Practice and Research, 4*(2), 60–75. https://doi.org/10.1891/1933-3196.4.2.60

Hitch, G. J., Allen, R. J., & Baddeley, A. D. (2025). The multicomponent model of working memory fifty years on. *Quarterly Journal of Experimental Psychology, 78*(2), 222–239. https://doi.org/10.1177/17470218241290909

Howard, H. (2017). Promoting safety in hypnosis: A clinical instrument for the measurement of alertness. *American Journal of Clinical Hypnosis, 59*(4), 344–362. https://doi.org/10.1080/00029157.2016.1203281

Howell, E. F. (1996). Dissociation in masochism and psychopathic sadism. *Contemporary Psychoanalysis, 32*(3), 427–453. https://doi.org/10.1080/00107530.1996.10746961

Howell, E. F. (1997). Desperately seeking attachment: A psychoanalytic reframing of the harsh superego. *Dissociation, 10*(4), 230–239. hdl.handle.net/1794/1806

Howell, E. F. (2014). Ferenczi's concept of identification with the aggressor: Understanding dissociative structure with interacting victim and abuser self-states. *American Journal of Psychoanalysis, 74*(1), 48–59. https://doi.org/10.1057/ajp.2013.40

Jung, C. G. (1970). The transcendent function. In G. Adler & R. F. C. Hull (Eds.), *The collected works of C. G. Jung, vol. 8: Structure and dynamics of the psyche* (pp. 67–97). De Gruyter Brill.

Karpman, S. B. (1968). Fairy tales and script drama analysis. *Transactional Analysis Bulletin, 7*(26), 39–43. www.karpmandramatriangle.com/pdf/DramaTriangle.pdf

Khodaverdi-Khani, M. (2017). *The relationship between hypnotisability, working memory, and the process of automatization* [PhD thesis]. Concordia University: Montréal, Quebec, Canada. spectrum.library.concordia.ca/id/eprint/982195/1/Khodaverdi-Khani_PhD_S2017.pdf

Khodaverdi-Khani, M., & Laurence, J. R. (2016). Working memory and hypnotisability. *Psychology ofConsciousness: Theory, Research, and Practice, 3*(1), 80–92. https://doi.org/10.1037/cns0000058

Klein, M. (1946). Notes on some schizoid mechanisms. *International Journal of Psychoanalysis,* 27(3–4), 99–110. https://doi.org/10.1080/21674086.1949.11925749

Kluft, R. P. (1982). Varieties of hypnotic interventions in the treatment of multiple personality. *American Journal of Clinical Hypnosis, 24*(4), 230–240. https://doi.org/10.1080/00029157.1982.1040331

Kluft, R. P. (1983). Hypnotherapeutic crisis intervention with multiple personality. *American Journal of Clinical Hypnosis, 26(*2), 73–83. https://doi.org/10.1080/00029157.1983.10404147

Kluft, R. P. (1988). On treating the older patient with multiple personality disorder: Race against time or make haste slowly? *American Journal of Clinical Hypnosis, 30*(4), 257–266. https://doi.org/10.1080/00029157.1988.10402748

Kluft, R. P. (1990). The fractionated abreaction technique. In D.C. Hammond (Ed.), *Handbook of hypnotic suggestions and metaphors* (pp. 527–528). W. W. Norton & Company.

Kluft, R. P. (1991). Multiple personality disorder. In A. Tasman & S. M. Goldfinger (Eds.), *The American psychiatric press annual review of psychiatry, vol. 10* (pp. 161–188). American Psychiatric Press.

Kluft, R. P. (1993). The initial stages of psychotherapy in the treatment of multiple personality disorder patients. *Dissociation, 6*(2–3), 145–161. hdl.handle.net/1794/1632

Kluft, R. P. (1994). Treatment trajectories in multiple personality disorder. *Dissociation, 7*(1), 63–76. hdl.handle.net/1794/1520

Kluft, R. P. (2006). Dealing with alters: A pragmatic clinical perspective. *Psychiatric Clinics of North America, 29*(1), 281–304. https://doi.org/10.1016/j.psc.2005.10.010

Kluft, R. P. (2012a). Hypnosis in the treatment of dissociative identity disorder and allied states: An overview and case study. *South African Journal of Psychology, 42*(2): 146–155. https://doi.org/10.1177/008124631204200202

Kluft, R. P. (2012b). Issues in the detection of those suffering adverse effects in hypnosis training workshops. *American Journal of Clinical Hypnosis, 54*(3), 213–223. https://doi.org/10.1080/00029157.2011.631228

Kluft, R. P. (2012c). Approaches to difficulties in realerting subjects from hypnosis. *American Journal of Clinical Hypnosis, 55*(2), 140–159. https://doi.org/10.1080/00029157.2012.660891

Kluft, R. P. (2017). Trying to keep it real: My experience in developing clinical approaches to the treatment of DID. *Frontiers in the Psychotherapy of Trauma and Dissociation, 1*(1), 18–44. https://doi.org/10.46716/ftpd.2017.0002

Knipe, J. (1995). Targeting avoidance and dissociative numbing. *EMDR Network Newsletter, 5*(3), 4–5.

Knipe, J. (2005). Targeting positive affect to clear the pain of unrequited love, codependence, avoidance, and procrastination. In R. Shapiro (Ed.), *EMDR solutions: Pathways to healing* (pp. 189–211). W. W. Norton & Company.

Knipe, J. (2008). Loving eyes: Procedures to therapeutically reverse dissociative processes while preserving emotional safety. In C. Forgash & M. Copeley (Eds.), *Healing the heart of trauma and dissociation with EMDR and ego state therapy* (pp. 181–225). Springer Publishing Company.

Knipe, J. (2009). "Shame is my safe place": Adaptive information processing methods of resolving chronic shame-based depression. In R. Shapiro (Ed.), *EMDR Solutions II: For depression, eating disorders, performance, and more* (pp. 49–89). W. W. Norton & Company.

Knipe, J. (2019). *EMDR toolbox: Theory and treatment of complex PTSD and dissociation* (2nd ed.). Springer Publishing Company.

Kohut, H. (1985). *Self psychology and the humanities: Reflections on a new psychoanalytic approach.* (C. B. Strozier, Ed.). W. W. Norton & Company.

Lahav, Y., Talmon, A., Ginzburg, K., & Spiegel, D. (2019). Reenacting past abuse – identification with the aggressor and sexual revictimization. *Journal of Trauma & Dissociation, 20*(4), 378–391. https://doi.org/10.1080/15299732.2019.1572046

Laing, R. D. (1969). *The divided self.* Penguin Books.

Lanius, U. F, Paulsen, S. L., & F. M. Corrigan (Eds.) (2014). *Neurobiology and treatment of traumatic dissociation: Towards an embodied self.* Springer Publishing Company.

Liotti, G. (1992). Disorganized/disoriented attachment in the etiology of the dissociative disorders. *Dissociation, 5*(4), 196–204. hdl.handle.net/1794/1722

Liotti G. (2006). A model of dissociation based on attachment theory and research. *Journal of Trauma & Dissociation, 7*(4), 55–73. https://doi.org/10.1300/J229v07n04_04

Littel, M., Remijn, M., Tinga, A. M., Engelhard, I. M., & van den Hout, M. A. (2017). Stress enhances the memory-degrading effects of eye movements on emotionally neutral memories. *Clinical Psychological Science, 5*(2), 316–324. https://doi.org/10.1177/2167702616687292

Loewenstein, R. J. (1993). Posttraumatic and dissociative aspects of transference and countertransference in the treatment of multiple personality disorder. In R. P. Kluft & C. G. Fine (Eds.), *Clinical perspectives on multiple personality disorder* (pp. 51–85). American Psychiatric Press.

Lyons-Ruth, K. (1999). The two-person unconscious: Intersubjective dialogue, enactive relational representation, and the emergence of new forms of relational organization. *Psychoanalytic Inquiry, 19*(4), 576–617. https://doi.org/10.1080/07351699909534267

MacHovec, F. J. (1986). *Hypnosis complications: Prevention and risk management.* Charles C. Thomas.

Manfield, P., Lovett, J., Engel, L., & Manfield, D. (2017). Use of the flash technique in EMDR therapy: Four case examples. *Journal of EMDR Practice and Research, 11*(4), 195–205. https://doi.org/10.1891/1933-3196.11.4.195

Matthijssen, S. J. M. A., Brouwers, T., van Roozendaal, C., Vuister, T., & de Jongh, A. (2021). The effect of EMDR versus EMDR 2.0 on emotionality and vividness of aversive memories in a non-clinical sample. *European Journal of Psychotraumatology, 12*(1), 1956793. https://doi.org/10.1080/20008198.2021.1956793

Matthijssen, S. J. M. A., van Schie, K., & van den Hout, M.A. (2019). The effect of modality specific interference on working memory in recalling aversive auditory and visual memories. *Cognition and Emotion, 33*(6), 1169–1180. https://doi.org/10.1080/02699931.2018.1547271

Maxfield, L., Melnyk, W. T., & Hayman, C. A. G. (2008). A working memory explanation for the effects of eye movements in EMDR. *Journal of EMDR Practice and Research, 2*(4), 247–261. https://doi.org/10.1891/1933-3196.2.4.247

Miller, A. (2012). *Healing the unimaginable: Treating ritual abuse and mind control.* Karnac Books.

Miller, W. R., & Rollnick, S. (2023). *Motivational interviewing: Helping people change and grow* (4th ed.). The Guilford Press.

Mosquera, D. (2019). *Working with voices and dissociative parts: A trauma-informed approach.* INTRA-TP.

Nicosia, G. J. (1995). Eye movement desensitization and reprocessing is not hypnosis. *Dissociation, 8*(1), 69. hdl.handle.net/1794/1596

Pagani, M., Di Lorenzo, G., Verardo, A. R., Nicolais, G., Monaco, L., Lauretti, G., Russo, R., Niolu, C., Ammaniti, M., Fernandez, I., & Siracusano, A. (2012).

Neurobiological correlates of EMDR monitoring – an EEG study. *PloS One, 7*(9), e45753. https://doi.org/10.1371/journal.pone.0045753

Panksepp, J., & Biven, L. (2012). *The archaeology of mind: Neuroevolutionary origins of human emotions.* W. W. Norton & Company.

Paulsen, S. L. (1995). Eye movement desensitization and reprocessing: Its cautious use in dissociative disorders. *Dissociation, 8*(1), 32–44. hdl.handle.net/1794/1592

Paulsen, S.L. (2008). Treating dissociative identity disorder with EMDR, ego state therapy, and adjunct approaches. In C. Forgash & M. Copeley (Eds.), *Healing the heart of trauma and dissociation with EMDR and ego state therapy* (pp. 141–179). Springer Publishing Company.

Paulsen, S. L. (2009). *Looking through the eyes of trauma and dissociation: An illustrated guide for EMDR clinicians and clients.* Booksurge.

Paulsen, S. L. (2018). Neuroaffective embodied self therapy (NEST): An integrative approach to case formulation and EMDR treatment planning for complex cases. *Frontiers in the Psychotherapy of Trauma and Dissociation, 1*(2), 125–148. https://doi.org/10.46716/ftpd.2017.0009

Paulsen, S. L., & Golston, J. (2014). Stabilizing the relationship among self-states. In U. F. Lanius, U., S. L. Paulsen, & F. M. Corrigan (Eds.), *Neurobiology and treatment of traumatic dissociation: Towards an embodied self.* Springer Publishing Company.

Paulsen, S. L., & Serin, A. (2018, October 4-7). *Seven tips from neuroscience for EMDR practice: Because all BLS isn't* equal [Conference presentation]. 23rd Annual Conference of the EMDR International Association. Atlanta, Georgia, USA.

Phillips, M., & Frederick, C. (1995). *Healing the divided self: Clinical and Ericksonian hypnotherapy for dissociative conditions.* W. W. Norton & Company.

Popky, A. J. (2005). DeTUR, an urge reduction protocol for addictions and dysfunctional behaviors. In R. Shapiro (Ed.), *EMDR solutions: Pathways to healing* (pp. 167–188). W. W. Norton & Company.

Putnam, F. (1989). *Diagnosis and treatment of multiple personality disorder.* The Guilford Press.

Ross, C. A. (1989). *Multiple personality disorder: Diagnosis, clinical features, and treatment.* Wiley.

Sachs, A. (2013). Boundary modifications in the treatment of people with dissociative disorders: A pilot study. *Journal of Trauma & Dissociation, 14*(2), 159–169. https://doi.org/10.1080/15299732.2012.714677

Scharff, J. S. (1992). *Projective and introjective identification and the use of the therapist's self.* Jason Aronson.

Schmidt, S. J. (2009). *The developmental needs meeting strategy: An ego state therapy for healing adults with trauma and attachment wounds.* DNMS Institute.

Schwartz, R., & Sweezy, M. (2019). *Internal family systems therapy* (2nd ed.). The Guilford Press.

Shapiro, E., & Laub, B. (2008). Early EMDR intervention (EEI): A summary, a theoretical model, and the recent traumatic episode protocol (R-TEP).

Journal of EMDR Practice and Research, 2(2), 79–96. https://doi.org/10.1891/1933-3196.2.2.79

Shapiro, F. (1989). Efficacy of the eye movement desensitization procedure in the treatment of traumatic memories. *Journal of Traumatic Stress, 2*(2), 199–223. https://doi.org/10.1002/jts.2490020207

Shapiro, F. (2018). *Eye movement desensitization and reprocessing (EMDR) therapy: Basic principles, protocols and procedures* (3rd ed.). The Guilford Press.

Shapiro, R. (2016). *Easy ego state interventions: Strategies for working with parts.* W. W. Norton & Company.

Shebini, N. (2019). EMDR for safe desensitization of memories and fusion of parts in DID. Conference room technique, trauma mapping, and management of unplanned abreactions. *Frontiers in the Psychotherapy of Trauma & Dissociation, 3*(2), 136–150. https://doi.org/10.46716/ftpd.2019.0030

Siegel, D. J. (1999). *The developing mind: Toward a neurobiology of interpersonal experience.* The Guilford Press.

Siegel, D. J. (2010). *Mindsight: The new science of personal transformation.* Bantam Books.

Sinason, V. (2017). Dying for love: An attachment problem with some perpetrator introjects. *Journal of Trauma & Dissociation, 18*(3), 344–355. https://doi.org/10.1080/15299732.2017.1295407

Steele, K. (1989). A model for abreaction with MPD and other dissociative disorders. *Dissociation, 2*(3), 151–159. hdl.handle.net/1794/1503

Steele, K., & Van der Hart, O. (2019). The hypnotherapeutic relationship with traumatized Patients. In G. Craparo, F. Ortu, & O. van der Hart (Eds.), *Rediscovering Pierre Janet: Trauma, dissociation, and a new context for psychoanalysis.* Routledge. https://doi.org/10.4324/9780429201875-12

Twombly, J. H. (2000). Incorporating EMDR and EMDR adaptations into the treatment of clients with dissociative identity disorder. *Journal of Trauma and Dissociation, 1*(2), 61–81. https://doi.org/10.1300/J229v01n02_05

Twombly, J. (2010). Initial targeting of traumatic material: Steps. In M. Luber (Ed.), *Eye movement desensitization (EMDR) scripted protocols: Special populations* (pp. 297–311). Springer Publishing Company.

Twombly, J. H. (2012). Overt and covert perpetrator ego states in dissociative disordered patients. In R. Vogt (Ed.), *Perpetrator introjects: Psychotherapeutic diagnostics and treatment models* (pp. 133–147). Asanger Verlag GmbH Kröning.

Van der Hart, O., Nijenhuis, E. R. S., & Solomon, R. (2010). Dissociation of the personality in complex trauma-related disorders and EMDR: Theoretical considerations. *Journal of EMDR Practice and Research, 4*(2), 76–92. https://doi.org/10.1891/1933-3196.4.2.76

Van der Hart, O., Steele, K., Boon, S., & Brown, P. (1993). The treatment of traumatic memories: Synthesis, realization, and integration. *Dissociation, 6*(2–3), 162–180. hdl.handle.net/1794/1633

Veerbeek, H. (2021, July 7). *Treating anger, resentment and revenge from a trauma perspective: A new anger protocol* [Webinar]. Envision Workshops.

Vogt, R. (2012). *Perpetrator introjects: Psychotherapeutic diagnostics and treatment models.* Asanger Verlag GmbH Kröning.

Watkins, J. G. (1977). The psychodynamic manipulation of ego states in hypnotherapy. In F. Antonelli (Ed.), *Therapy in psychosomatic medicine* (Vol. 2, pp. 398–403). Symposia.

Watkins, J. G. & Barabasz, A. (2008). *Advanced hypnotherapy: Hypnodynamic techniques*. Routledge.

Watkins, J. G., & Watkins, H. H. (1984). Hazards to the therapist in the treatment of multiple personalities. *Psychiatric Clinics of North America, 7*(1), 111–119. https://doi.org/10.1016/S0193-953X(18)30784-6

Watkins, J. G., & Watkins, H. H. (1988). The management of malevolent ego states in multiple personality disorder. *Dissociation, 1*(1), 67–72. hdl.handle.net/1794/1333

Watkins, H. H., & Watkins, J. G. (1997). *Ego states: Theory and therapy*. W. W. Norton & Company.

Wilbur, C. B. (1988). Multiple personality disorder and transference. *Dissociation, 1*(1), 73–76. hdl.handle.net/1794/1334

Wong, S.-L. (2021). A model for the flash technique based on working memory and neuroscience research. *Journal of EMDR Practice and Research, 15*(3), 174–184. https://doi.org/10.1891/emdr-d-21-00048

Young, L. (1992). Sexual abuse and the problem of embodiment. *Child Abuse & Neglect, 16*(1), 89–100. https://doi.org/10.1016/0145-2134(92)90010-O

Afterword

Jennifer A. Madere and D. Michael Coy

This book is the net result of a decade of collaboration. Many steps in our respective and shared journeys helped to build our understanding, including massive amounts of reading; conversations with peers, mentors, and consultees; and the process of synthesizing ideas through numerous presentations at local, national, and international conferences. Although books are generally not considered a 'peer reviewed' source for citation purposes, we received comprehensive feedback from multiple reviewers, some of whom are experienced authors and editors in their own right. We are immensely grateful for the feedback, which helped us correct, clarify, and further bridge gaps evident in the working drafts of the book. Some of these reviewers generously provided the endorsements that are found on the front pages and back cover of this text.

EMDR therapy is by no means the end-all, be-all of trauma processing methods. We both utilize other approaches in our practices and find them useful. Despite the risks, EMDR therapy ironically may be more controllable and modular, and in some ways better suited for treating dissociation than other more body-based approaches – especially when practitioners employ EMDR with thoughtfulness, skill, and nuance. We hope that you feel more equipped to do just that after reading this book.

A handful of years ago, we presented for both EMDRIA and ISSTD on the topic of EMDR and dissociation – past, present, and future. The 'future' segment of these presentations was a call to action for the EMDR and dissociative disorders fields to close the gaps that had long separated them. It was only as we concluded the writing of this book that we realized we had, over the course of 12 chapters, heeded our own call. If we could boil the book down to its essence, this is what we would say.

Dig Deeply into the Literature

Having only a cursory understanding of *any* subject is going to impose limitations at some point. Dabbling in dissociation – whether in terms of the literature or training – simply won't do. Digging deeply into the literature informing the components of your practice frame definitely pays off. This is one reason we made the conscious decision to draw upon a deep well of literature spanning over a hundred years of collective wisdom. Our priority was enriching the conceptualization and treatment of severe dissociation in an expanded EMDR therapy frame. Contemporary theory and science are critical for progress. However, this does not mean we should ignore what came before. What enriches our conceptualization might be *old* – like the work of Boris Sidis, into whose work we delved more deeply. We have intentionally not provided a universal recommended reading list. Rather, the citations that we have provided in each chapter serve as a bridge to finding what makes sense for *you* to read next.

Avoid Assuming We Know Something – Or Everything – When We Don't (Yet) Know

Approaching situations with humility, curiosity, and a sense of responsibility helps us to realize we don't know as much as we thought we did. Learning about dissociation, through self-study, formal training, and ongoing consultation, opens a door to another world – a world that is different for every client. We come to see our clients as the whole diamond rather than as a single facet. Once that happens, there's no going back.

Implement Best Practices

Trainers and consultants must be students of the literature and teach current best practices. *EMDR Therapy According to Me* might be good for one's ego and pocketbook, but treatment driven by either or both of these has caused harm to clients and exploited naive clinicians who are apt to "take someone else's word for it." If there is one thing that we learned and have been reminded of repeatedly in writing this book, it is that so much was known before 1920 – or 1995, in the case of EMDR – and then forgotten or disregarded due to conflicting personalities, fraught politics, and our human fascination with novel stimulus.

Clinicians must be informed consumers of training and literature. Basic, 'boring' tasks like reading and thinking critically about research, learning multiple theories and practice frameworks, and developing a solid case conceptualization can take us a long, long way. Understanding the value of recognizing and examining transference and countertransference in supervision and consultation will help us listen more carefully to the aspects of clients' stories (and our own) for which there are no words, all in service of deep healing.

Contextualize EMDR Therapy Within a Comprehensive Treatment Frame

Laliotis et al. (2021) proposed that EMDR is a psychotherapy, as opposed to an intervention, when the therapeutic relationship is emphasized in the treatment of complex trauma. We agree, except for ending at complex trauma: This also applies to treating dissociative disorders.

As Chefetz (2017) pointed out, clinicians' affect intolerance (of shame, rage, etc.) can contribute to impasses in the therapy when the path to healing requires that we encounter them. All psychotherapists were first 'trained' by their caregivers. Our relational skills, wounds, and tendencies continue to live on in our work with clients. Because of this, we cannot overemphasize how important it is for practitioners to acknowledge and attend to the relational/psychodynamic realities of treating clients with complex trauma. This includes the necessity for therapists to participate in their own psychotherapy. If working with complex trauma is new for you, we hope that the attention we have given to transference dynamics throughout this book inspires you to invest in continued learning – about your clients and yourself. The rewards of doing both are innumerable.

Where Do We Go from Here?

Our hope is that this book contributes something to both further diminish the dissociative phobias that have kept the EMDR therapy, clinical hypnosis, and dissociative disorders fields apart all these years and increase meaningful connections among them. These connections, in our eyes, would translate to an increase in curiosity and collaboration without a loss of integrity for ANY of these. So, the 'beyond' in the book's title refers in part to where we all go from here. Here is our 'wish list':

- Researchers – and those who fund research – conducting valid and reliable diagnostic evaluations when studying the intersection of EMDR and dissociation;
- More recognition of and training in the breadth and depth of dissociative phenomena, and increased attention to these in treatment;
- Acknowledgement amongst EMDR practitioners of (auto)hypnotic phenomena in trauma, and training in the safe use of hypnosis;
- Increased focus on both conceptualization for more complex forms of dissociation, and understanding the context for our interventions; and
- Cross-pollination among the fields of hypnosis, EMDR, and dissociation, particularly in researching mechanisms of action and overlaps in functional connectivity in the brain.

We hope you will accept our invitation to join us on this journey. Thank you for reading.

References

Chefetz, R. A. (2017). Issues in consultation for treatments with distressed activated abuser/protector self-states in dissociative identity disorder. *Journal of Trauma & Dissociation, 18*(3), 465–475. https://doi.org/10.1080/15299732.2017.1295428

Laliotis, D., Luber, M., Oren, U., Shapiro, E., Ichii, M., Hase, M., La Rosa, L., Alter-Reid, K., St. Jammes, J. T. (2021). What is EMDR therapy? Past, present, and future directions. *Journal of EMDR Practice and Research, 15*(4), 186–201. https://doi.org/10.1891/EMDR-D-21-00029

Index

Note: Endnotes are indicated by the page number followed by "n" and the note number e.g., 111n5 refers to note 5 on page 111.

For Product Safety Concerns and Information please contact our EU representative GPSR@taylorandfrancis.com
Taylor & Francis Verlag GmbH, Kaufingerstraße 24, 80331 München, Germany

www.ingramcontent.com/pod-product-compliance
Lightning Source LLC
Chambersburg PA
CBHW050331270326
41926CB00016B/3406
* 9 7 8 1 0 3 2 7 1 2 3 5 2 *